Hana-Kimi

For You in Full Blossom

1

story and art by
HISAYA NAKAJO

HANA-KIMI
For You In Full Blossom
VOLUME 1

STORY & ART BY HISAYA NAKAJO

Translation/David Ury
English Adaptation/Gerard Jones
Touch-Up Art & Lettering/Gabe Crate
Design/Izumi Evers
Editor/Jason Thompson

Managing Editor/Megan Bates
Editorial Director/Elizabeth Kawasaki
Editor in Chief/Alvin Lu
Sr. Director of Acquisitions/Rika Inouye
Sr. VP of Marketing/Liza Coppola
Exec. VP of Sales & Marketing/John Easum
Publisher/Hyoe Narita

Published by VIZ Media, LLC, P.O. Box 77010, San Francisco, CA
94107

Shôjo Edition
10 9 8 7 6 5 4

First printing, March 2004
Fourth printing, June 2006

www.viz.com
store.viz.com

CONTENTS

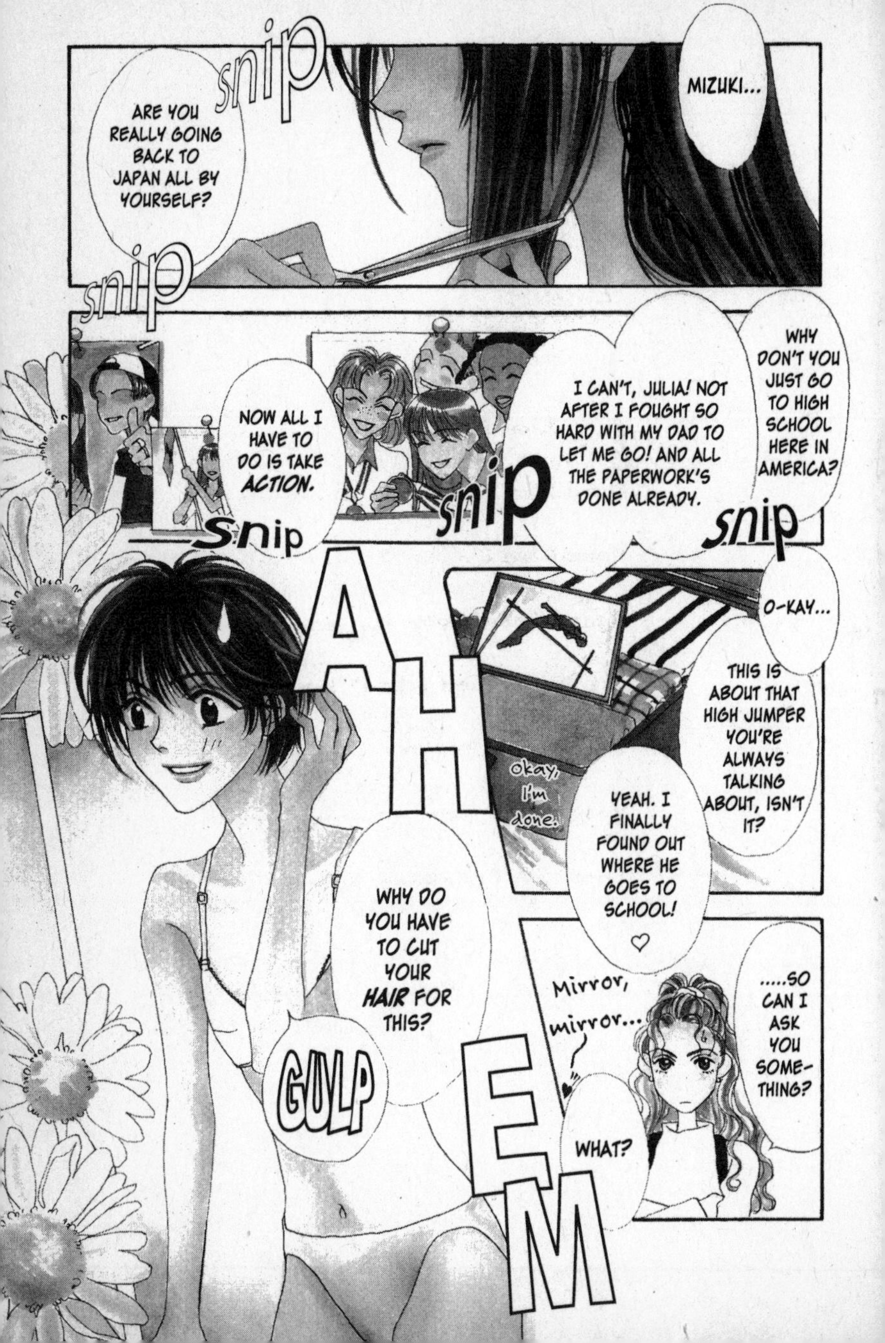
MIZUKI...
snip
ARE YOU REALLY GOING BACK TO JAPAN ALL BY YOURSELF?
snip
WHY DON'T YOU JUST GO TO HIGH SCHOOL HERE IN AMERICA?
I CAN'T, JULIA! NOT AFTER I FOUGHT SO HARD WITH MY DAD TO LET ME GO! AND ALL THE PAPERWORK'S DONE ALREADY.
snip
snip
NOW ALL I HAVE TO DO IS TAKE ACTION.
snip
O-KAY...
THIS IS ABOUT THAT HIGH JUMPER YOU'RE ALWAYS TALKING ABOUT, ISN'T IT?
YEAH. I FINALLY FOUND OUT WHERE HE GOES TO SCHOOL! ♡
okay, I'm done.
.....SO CAN I ASK YOU SOMETHING?
WHAT?
Mirror, mirror...
WHY DO YOU HAVE TO CUT YOUR HAIR FOR THIS?
GULP
AHEM

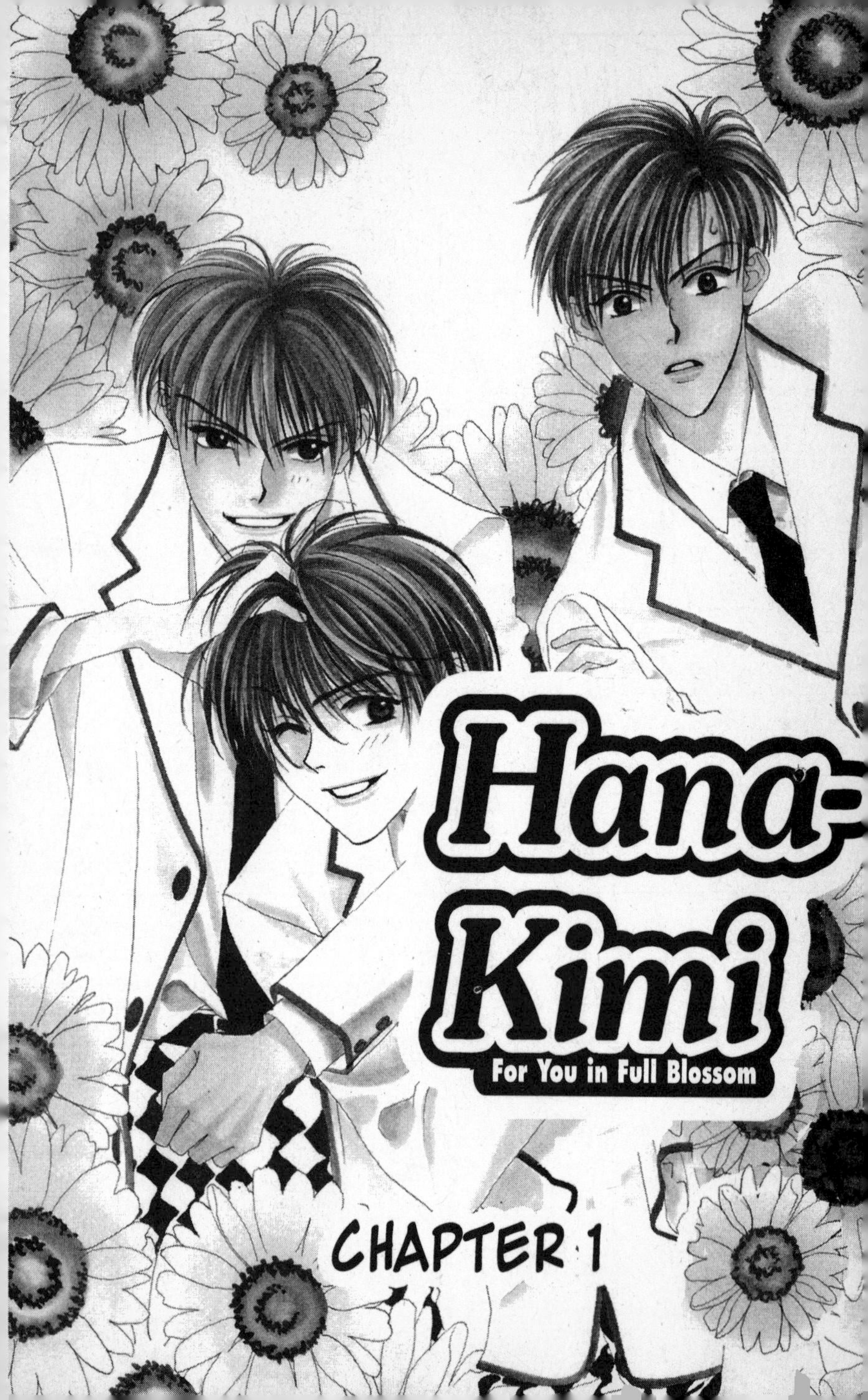
Hana-Kimi
For You in Full Blossom
CHAPTER 1

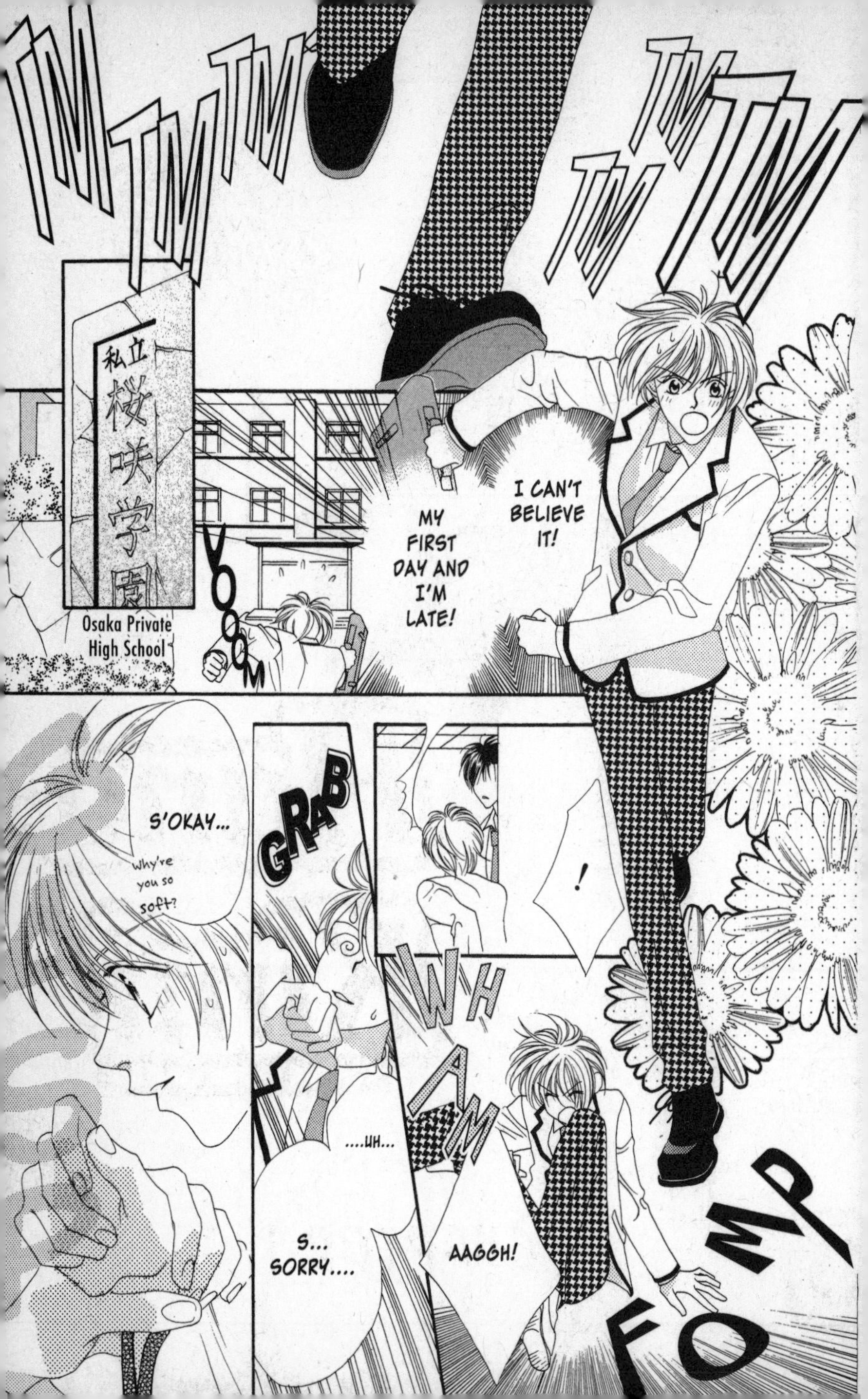
TMP TMP TMP
TMP TMP TMP
I CAN'T BELIEVE IT!
MY FIRST DAY AND I'M LATE!
VOOOOM
私立
桜咲学
Osaka Private High School
!
WHAM
AAGGH!
FOMP
GRAB
....UH...
S... SORRY....
S'OKAY...
why're you so soft?

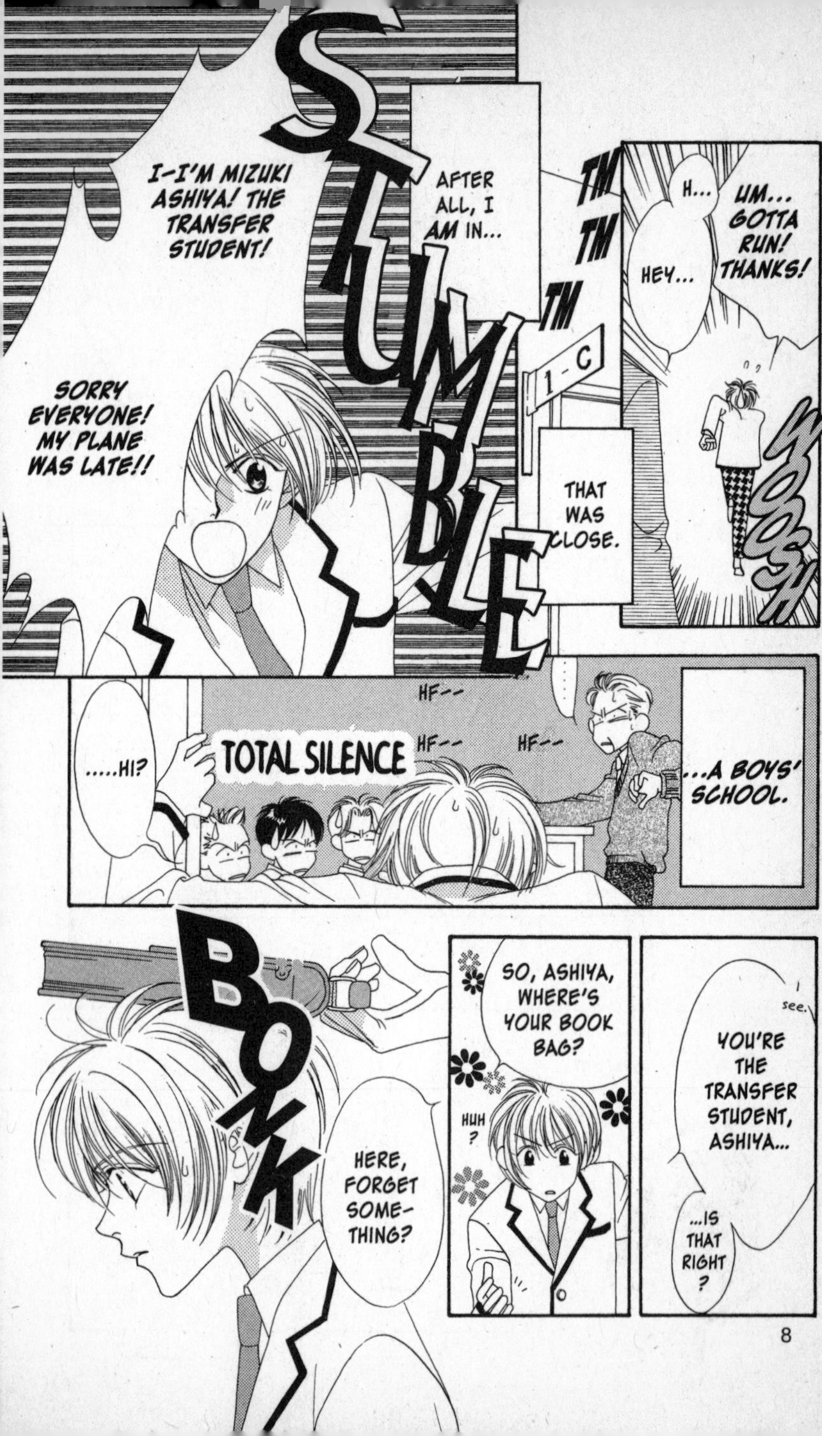
H... HEY...
UM... GOTTA RUN! THANKS!
WHOOSH
TM TM TM TM
AFTER ALL, I AM IN...
1-C
THAT WAS CLOSE.
I-I'M MIZUKI ASHIYA! THE TRANSFER STUDENT!
SORRY EVERYONE! MY PLANE WAS LATE!!
STUMBLE
...A BOYS' SCHOOL.
.....
HF-- HF-- HF--
TOTAL SILENCE
.....HI?
I see.
YOU'RE THE TRANSFER STUDENT, ASHIYA...
...IS THAT RIGHT?
SO, ASHIYA, WHERE'S YOUR BOOK BAG?
HUH?
HERE, FORGET SOMETHING?
BONK

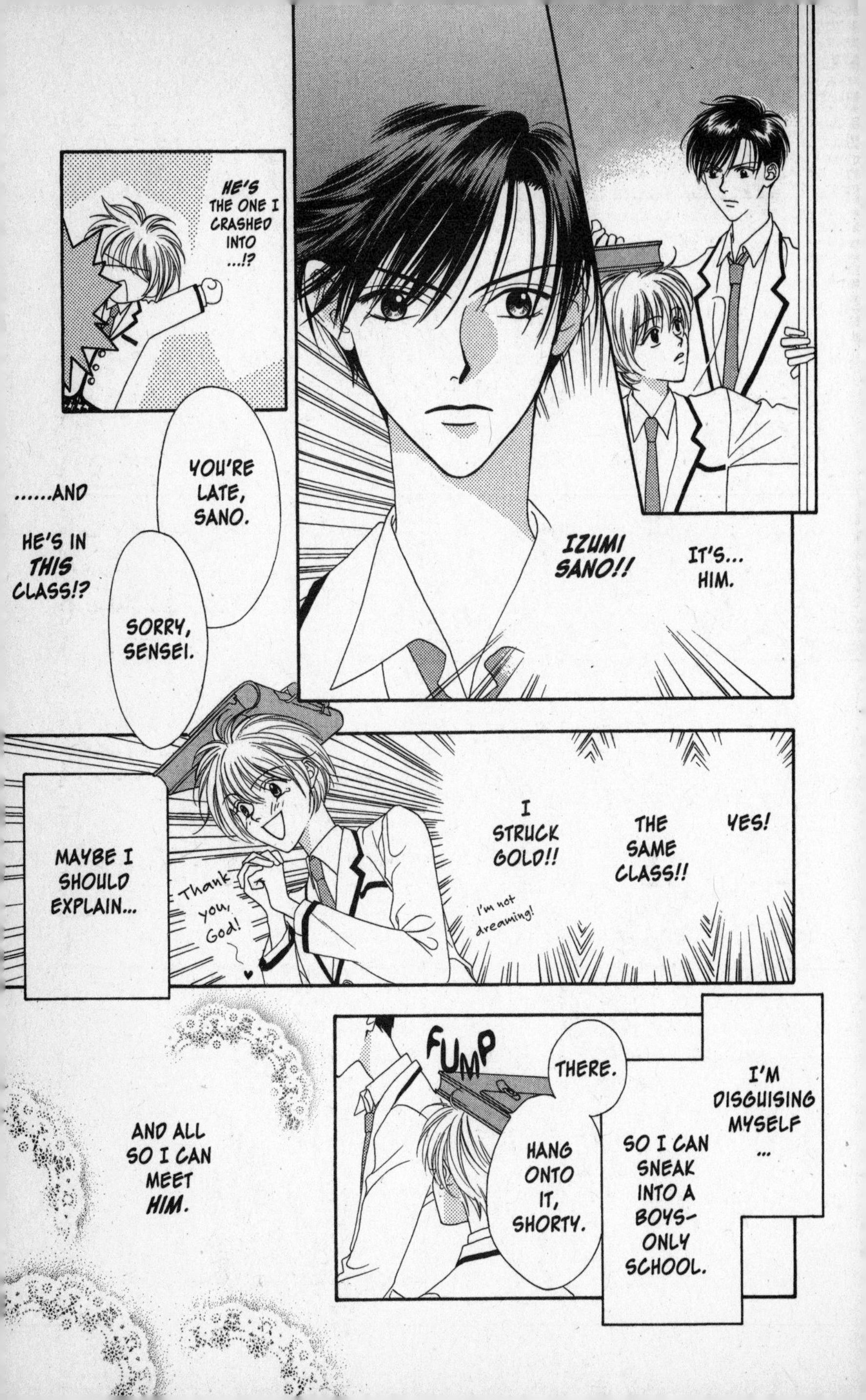
IT'S... HIM.
IZUMI SANO!!
YOU'RE LATE, SANO.
SORRY, SENSEI.
HE'S THE ONE I CRASHED INTO ...!?
......AND HE'S IN THIS CLASS!?
YES!
THE SAME CLASS!!
I STRUCK GOLD!!
I'm not dreaming!
Thank you, God!
MAYBE I SHOULD EXPLAIN...
I'M DISGUISING MYSELF ...
SO I CAN SNEAK INTO A BOYS-ONLY SCHOOL.
FUMP
THERE.
HANG ONTO IT, SHORTY.
AND ALL SO I CAN MEET HIM.

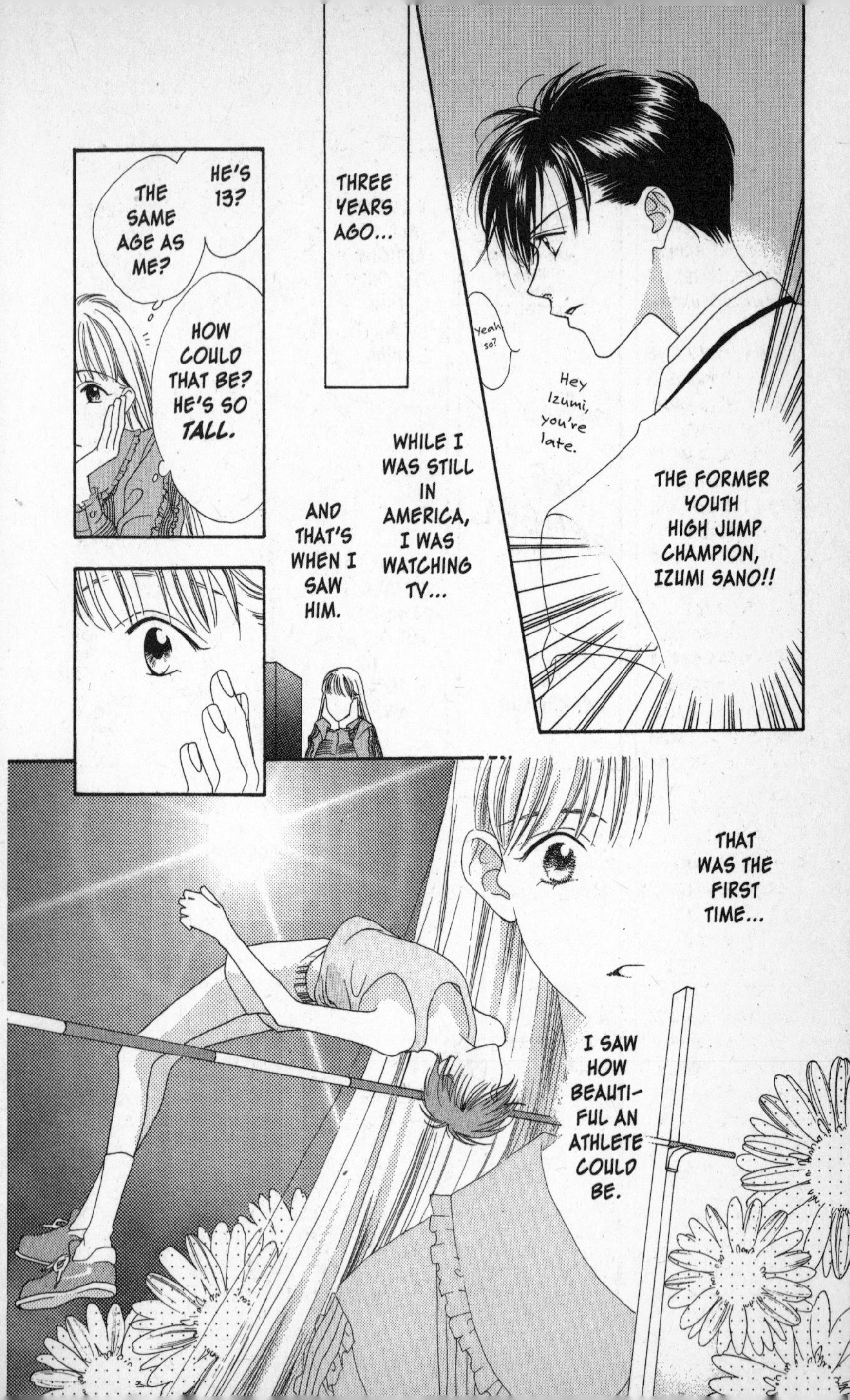
Hey Izumi, you're late.
Yeah so?
THE FORMER YOUTH HIGH JUMP CHAMPION, IZUMI SANO!!
THREE YEARS AGO...
HE'S 13? THE SAME AGE AS ME?
HOW COULD THAT BE? HE'S SO *TALL.*
WHILE I WAS STILL IN AMERICA, I WAS WATCHING TV...
AND THAT'S WHEN I SAW HIM.
THAT WAS THE FIRST TIME...
I SAW HOW BEAUTI-FUL AN ATHLETE COULD BE.

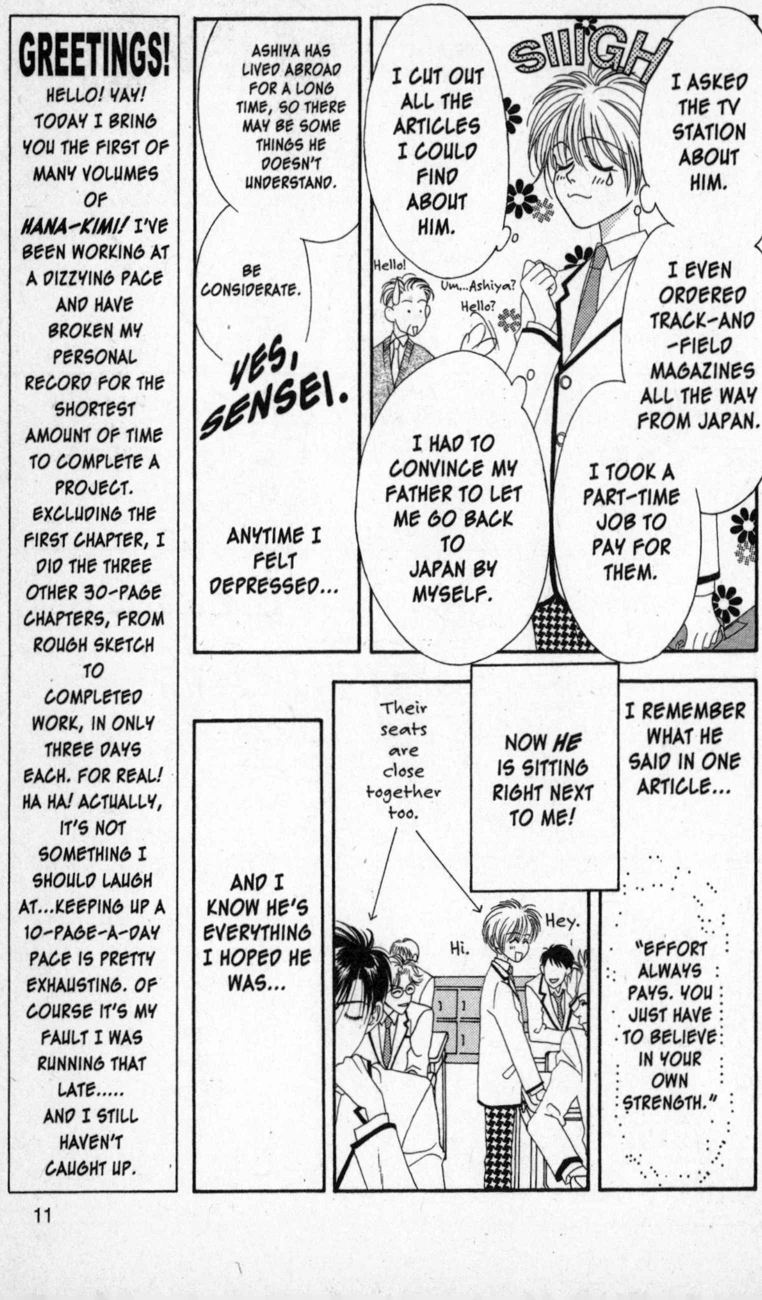
SIIIGH
I ASKED THE TV STATION ABOUT HIM.
I CUT OUT ALL THE ARTICLES I COULD FIND ABOUT HIM.
I EVEN ORDERED TRACK-AND-FIELD MAGAZINES ALL THE WAY FROM JAPAN.
I TOOK A PART-TIME JOB TO PAY FOR THEM.
I HAD TO CONVINCE MY FATHER TO LET ME GO BACK TO JAPAN BY MYSELF.
Um...Ashiya? Hello?
Hello!
ASHIYA HAS LIVED ABROAD FOR A LONG TIME, SO THERE MAY BE SOME THINGS HE DOESN'T UNDERSTAND.
BE CONSIDERATE.
YES, SENSEI.
ANYTIME I FELT DEPRESSED...
I REMEMBER WHAT HE SAID IN ONE ARTICLE...
"EFFORT ALWAYS PAYS. YOU JUST HAVE TO BELIEVE IN YOUR OWN STRENGTH."
NOW HE IS SITTING RIGHT NEXT TO ME!
Hey.
Hi.
Their seats are close together too.
AND I KNOW HE'S EVERYTHING I HOPED HE WAS...

GREETINGS!

HELLO! YAY! TODAY I BRING YOU THE FIRST OF MANY VOLUMES OF *HANA-KIMI!* I'VE BEEN WORKING AT A DIZZYING PACE AND HAVE BROKEN MY PERSONAL RECORD FOR THE SHORTEST AMOUNT OF TIME TO COMPLETE A PROJECT. EXCLUDING THE FIRST CHAPTER, I DID THE THREE OTHER 30-PAGE CHAPTERS, FROM ROUGH SKETCH TO COMPLETED WORK, IN ONLY THREE DAYS EACH. FOR REAL! HA HA! ACTUALLY, IT'S NOT SOMETHING I SHOULD LAUGH AT...KEEPING UP A 10-PAGE-A-DAY PACE IS PRETTY EXHAUSTING. OF COURSE IT'S MY FAULT I WAS RUNNING THAT LATE..... AND I STILL HAVEN'T CAUGHT UP.

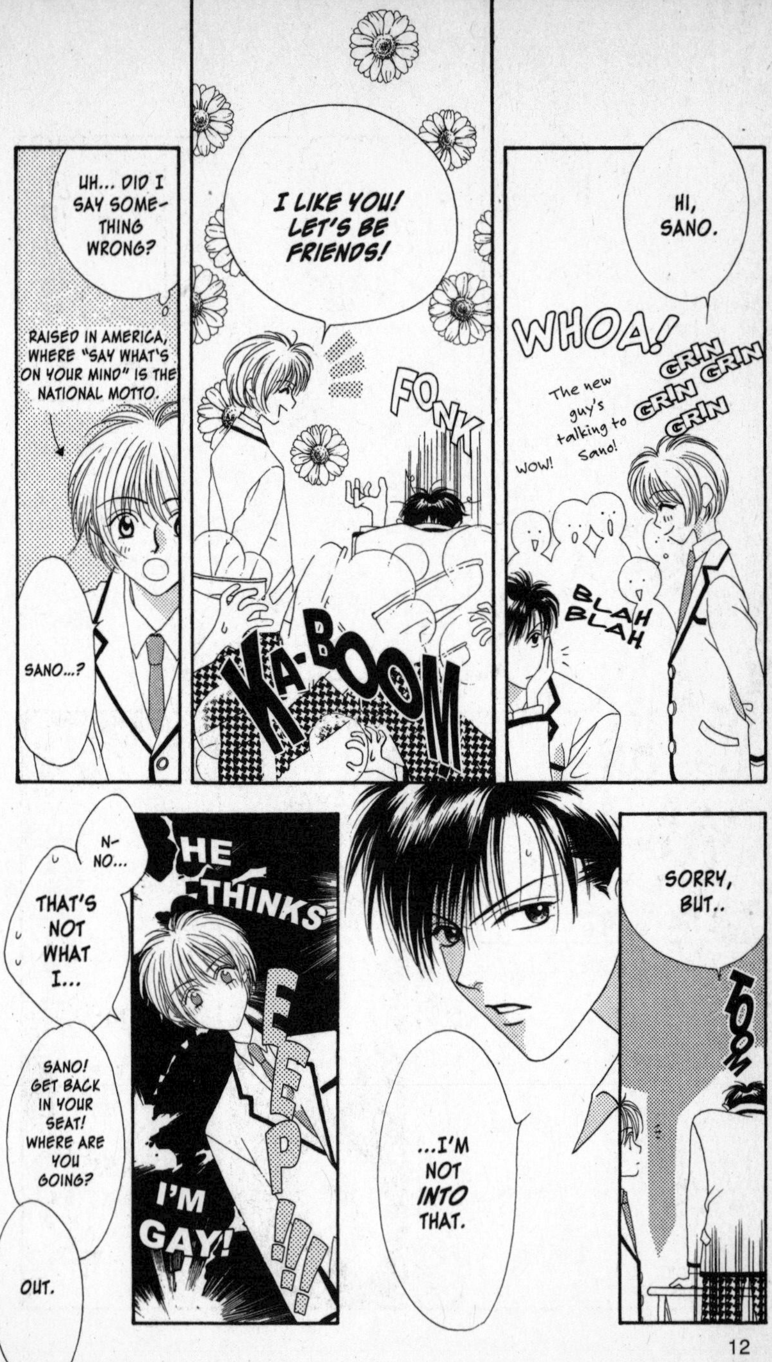
HI, SANO.
WHOA!
GRIN GRIN GRIN GRIN
The new guy's talking to Sano!
WOW!
BLAH BLAH
I LIKE YOU! LET'S BE FRIENDS!
FONK
KA-BOOM!!
UH... DID I SAY SOME-THING WRONG?
RAISED IN AMERICA, WHERE "SAY WHAT'S ON YOUR MIND" IS THE NATIONAL MOTTO.
SANO...?
SORRY, BUT..
TOOM
...I'M NOT INTO THAT.
HE THINKS I'M GAY!
EEEP!!!
N-NO...
THAT'S NOT WHAT I...
SANO! GET BACK IN YOUR SEAT! WHERE ARE YOU GOING?
OUT.

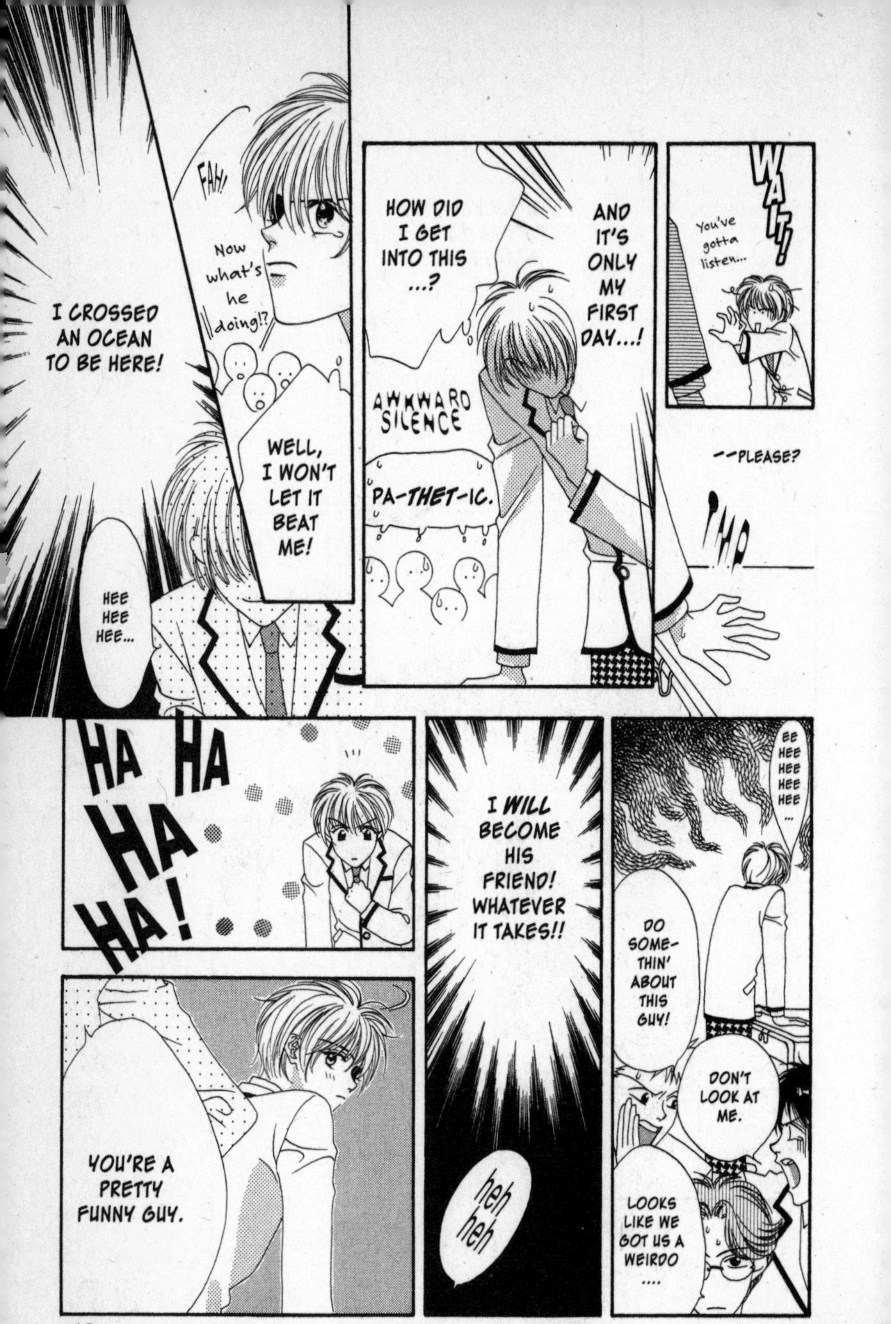
WAIT!
You've gotta listen...
--PLEASE?
THP
AND IT'S ONLY MY FIRST DAY...!
HOW DID I GET INTO THIS ...?
AWKWARD SILENCE
PA-THET-IC.
FAH!
Now what's he doing!?
I CROSSED AN OCEAN TO BE HERE!
WELL, I WON'T LET IT BEAT ME!
HEE HEE HEE...
EE HEE HEE HEE HEE ...
DO SOME-THIN' ABOUT THIS GUY!
DON'T LOOK AT ME.
LOOKS LIKE WE GOT US A WEIRDO ....
I WILL BECOME HIS FRIEND! WHATEVER IT TAKES!!
heh heh
HA HA HA HA!
YOU'RE A PRETTY FUNNY GUY.

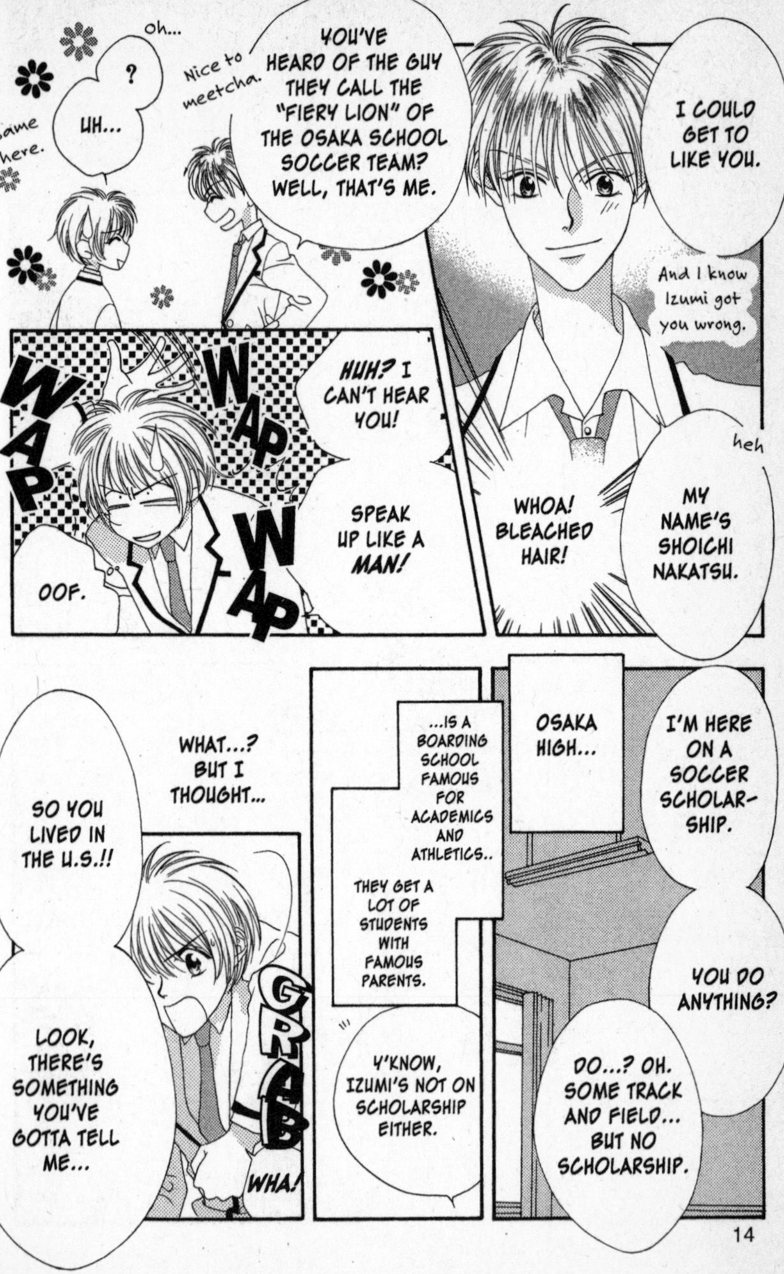
I COULD GET TO LIKE YOU.
And I know Izumi got you wrong.
heh
MY NAME'S SHOICHI NAKATSU.
WHOA! BLEACHED HAIR!
YOU'VE HEARD OF THE GUY THEY CALL THE "FIERY LION" OF THE OSAKA SCHOOL SOCCER TEAM? WELL, THAT'S ME.
Nice to meetcha.
Oh...
?
UH...
Same here.
HUH? I CAN'T HEAR YOU!
SPEAK UP LIKE A MAN!
WAP
WAP
WAP
OOF.
I'M HERE ON A SOCCER SCHOLARSHIP.
OSAKA HIGH...
YOU DO ANYTHING?
DO...? OH. SOME TRACK AND FIELD... BUT NO SCHOLARSHIP.
...IS A BOARDING SCHOOL FAMOUS FOR ACADEMICS AND ATHLETICS..
THEY GET A LOT OF STUDENTS WITH FAMOUS PARENTS.
Y'KNOW, IZUMI'S NOT ON SCHOLARSHIP EITHER.
WHAT...? BUT I THOUGHT...
SO YOU LIVED IN THE U.S.!!
GRAB
WHA!
LOOK, THERE'S SOMETHING YOU'VE GOTTA TELL ME...

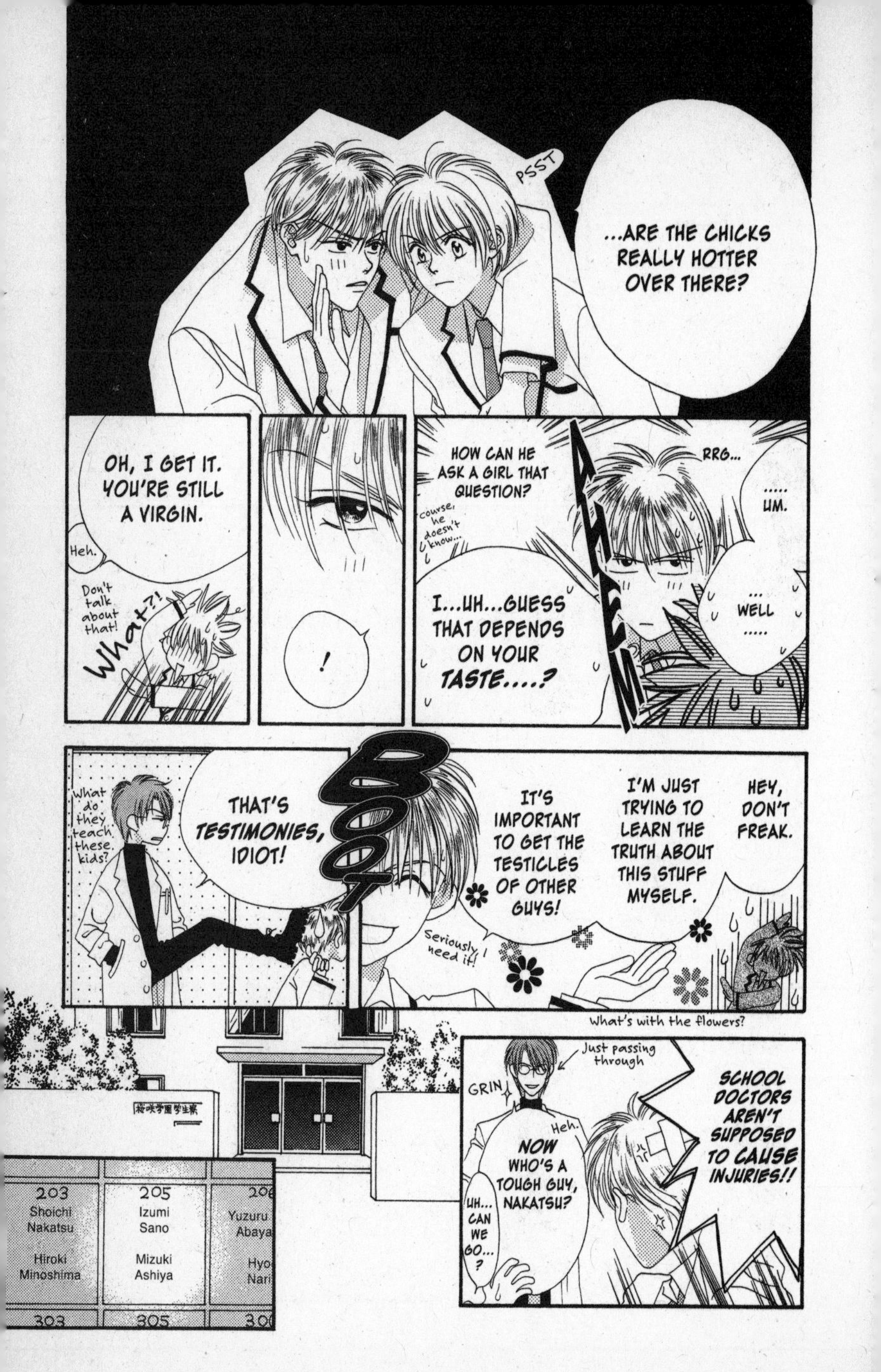
PSST
...ARE THE CHICKS REALLY HOTTER OVER THERE?
RRG...
..... UM.
... WELL .....
HOW CAN HE ASK A GIRL THAT QUESTION?
course, he doesn't know...
I...UH...GUESS THAT DEPENDS ON YOUR TASTE....?
!
OH, I GET IT. YOU'RE STILL A VIRGIN.
Heh.
What?!
Don't talk about that!
HEY, DON'T FREAK.
I'M JUST TRYING TO LEARN THE TRUTH ABOUT THIS STUFF MYSELF.
IT'S IMPORTANT TO GET THE TESTICLES OF OTHER GUYS!
Seriously, I need it!
What's with the flowers?
BOOT
THAT'S TESTIMONIES, IDIOT!
What do they teach these kids?
SCHOOL DOCTORS AREN'T SUPPOSED TO CAUSE INJURIES!!
Just passing through
GRIN
Heh.
NOW WHO'S A TOUGH GUY, NAKATSU?
UH... CAN WE GO...?
203
Shoichi Nakatsu
Hiroki Minoshima
303
205
Izumi Sano
Mizuki Ashiya
305
Yuzuru

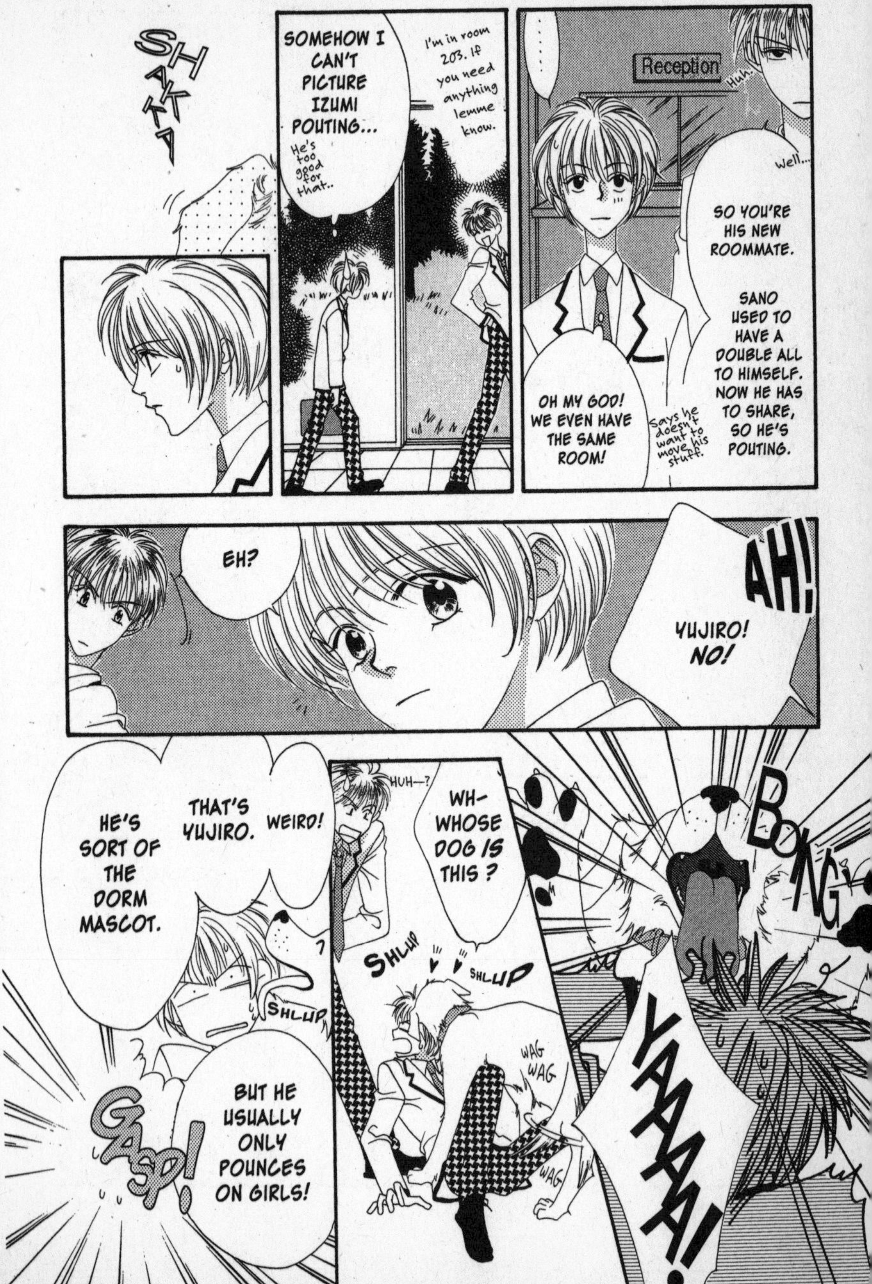
...
Reception
Huh.
Well...
SO YOU'RE HIS NEW ROOMMATE.
SANO USED TO HAVE A DOUBLE ALL TO HIMSELF. NOW HE HAS TO SHARE, SO HE'S POUTING.
Says he doesn't want to move his stuff.
OH MY GOD! WE EVEN HAVE THE SAME ROOM!
I'm in room 203. If you need anything lemme know.
SOMEHOW I CAN'T PICTURE IZUMI POUTING...
He's too good for that..
SHAKA
AH!
YUJIRO! NO!
EH?
BONG
YAAAA!
WH- WHOSE DOG IS THIS ?
HUH—?
SHLUP
SHLUP
WAG WAG
WAG
WEIRD!
THAT'S YUJIRO.
HE'S SORT OF THE DORM MASCOT.
SHLUP
BUT HE USUALLY ONLY POUNCES ON GIRLS!
GASP!

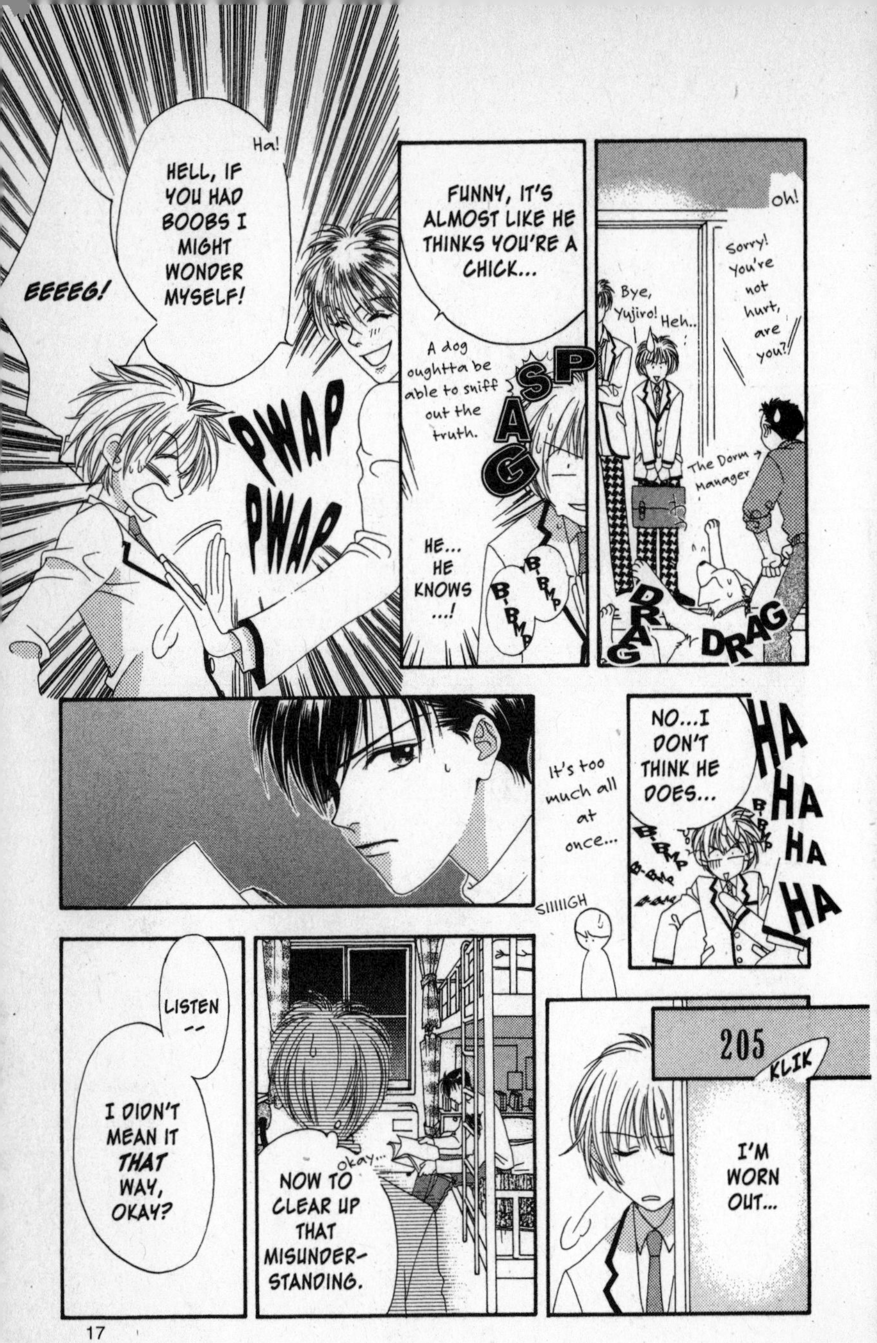
Oh!
Sorry! You're not hurt, are you?
Bye, Yujiro!
Heh..
The Dorm Manager
DRAG DRAG DRAG
FUNNY, IT'S ALMOST LIKE HE THINKS YOU'RE A CHICK...
A dog oughtta be able to sniff out the truth.
SPAG
HE... HE KNOWS ...!
B-BMP B-BMP
Ha!
HELL, IF YOU HAD BOOBS I MIGHT WONDER MYSELF!
EEEEG!
PWAP PWAP
NO...I DON'T THINK HE DOES...
HA HA HA HA
B-BMP B-BMP
It's too much all at once...
SIIIIGH
205
KLIK
I'M WORN OUT...
NOW TO CLEAR UP THAT MISUNDER-STANDING.
okay...
LISTEN --
I DIDN'T MEAN IT *THAT* WAY, OKAY?

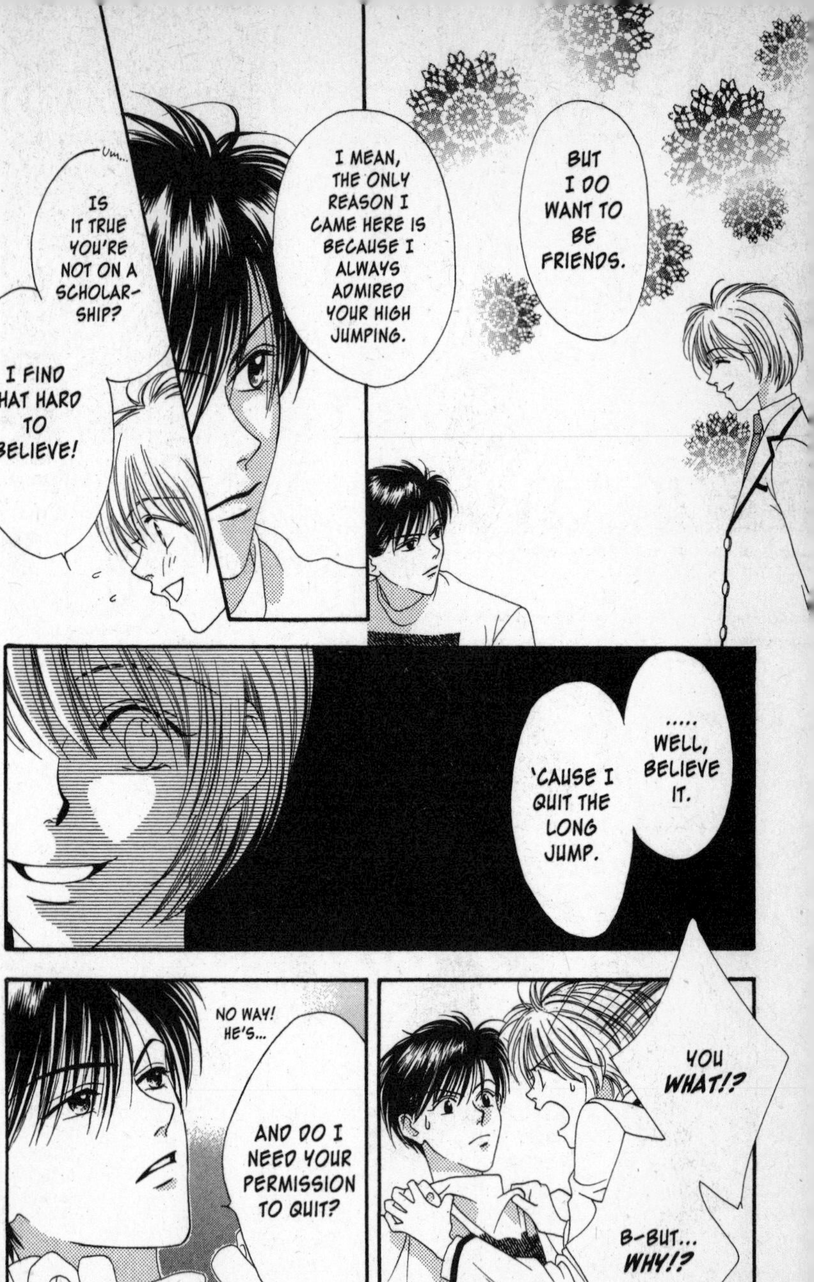
BUT I DO WANT TO BE FRIENDS.
I MEAN, THE ONLY REASON I CAME HERE IS BECAUSE I ALWAYS ADMIRED YOUR HIGH JUMPING.
Um...
IS IT TRUE YOU'RE NOT ON A SCHOLAR-SHIP?
I FIND THAT HARD TO BELIEVE!
..... WELL, BELIEVE IT.
'CAUSE I QUIT THE LONG JUMP.
YOU *WHAT!?*
B-BUT... *WHY!?*
NO WAY! HE'S...
AND DO I NEED YOUR PERMISSION TO QUIT?

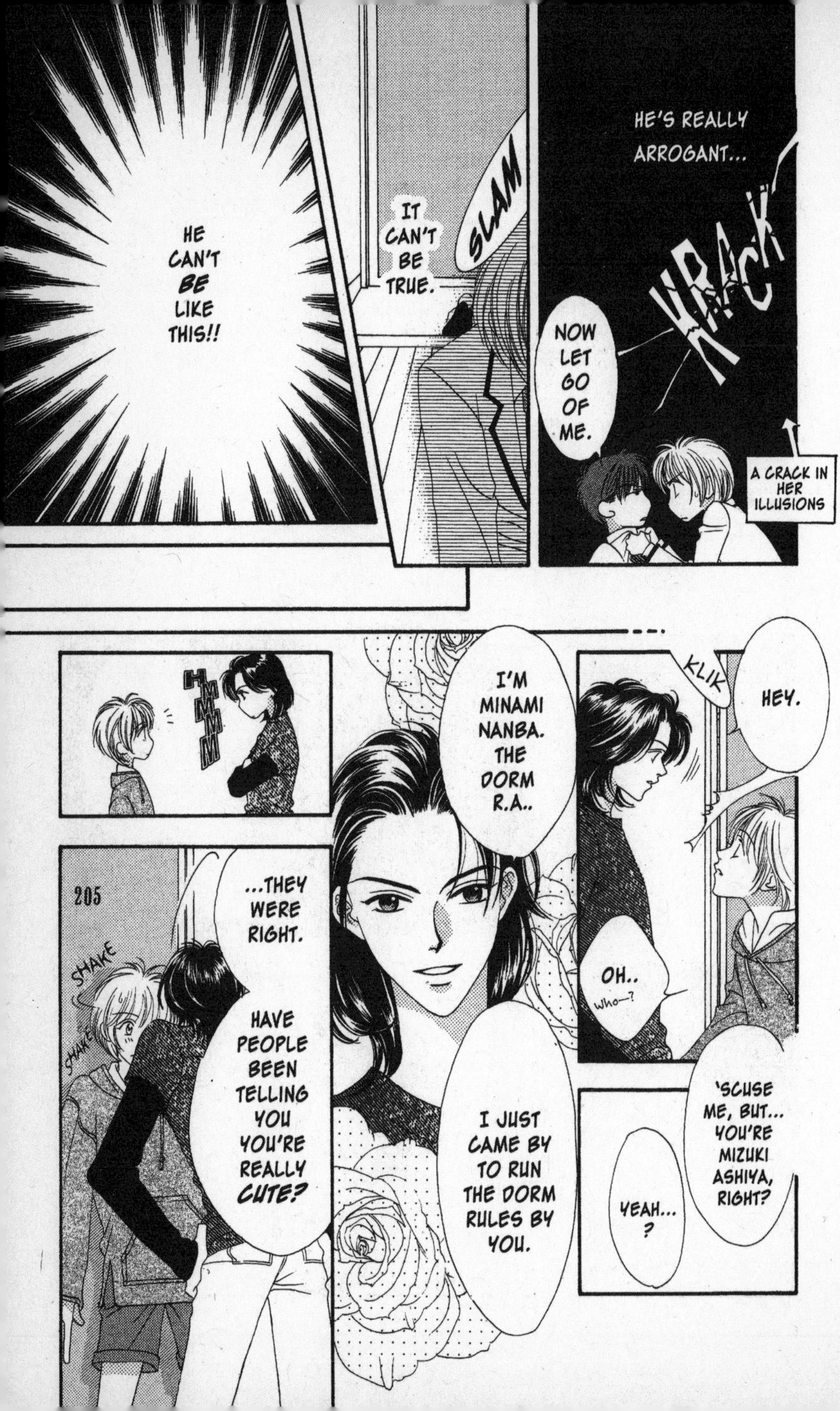

HE'S REALLY ARROGANT...
KRACK
NOW LET GO OF ME.
A CRACK IN HER ILLUSIONS
SLAM
IT CAN'T BE TRUE.
HE CAN'T *BE* LIKE THIS!!
KLIK
HEY.
OH..
who—?
'SCUSE ME, BUT... YOU'RE MIZUKI ASHIYA, RIGHT?
YEAH... ?
I'M MINAMI NANBA. THE DORM R.A..
I JUST CAME BY TO RUN THE DORM RULES BY YOU.
HMMMM
...THEY WERE RIGHT.
HAVE PEOPLE BEEN TELLING YOU YOU'RE REALLY *CUTE?*
SHAKE
SHAKE

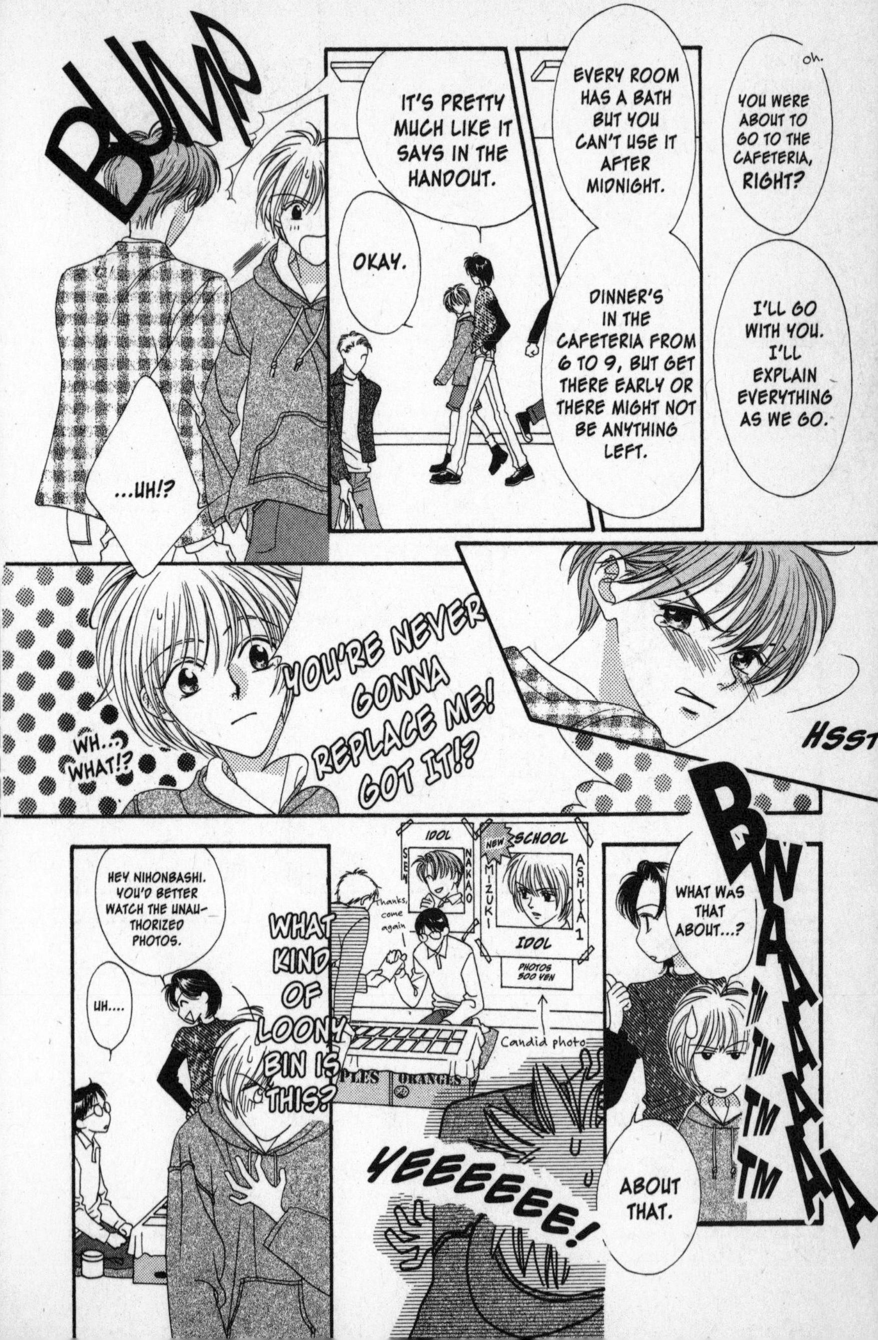

oh.
YOU WERE ABOUT TO GO TO THE CAFETERIA, RIGHT?
I'LL GO WITH YOU. I'LL EXPLAIN EVERYTHING AS WE GO.
EVERY ROOM HAS A BATH BUT YOU CAN'T USE IT AFTER MIDNIGHT.
DINNER'S IN THE CAFETERIA FROM 6 TO 9, BUT GET THERE EARLY OR THERE MIGHT NOT BE ANYTHING LEFT.
IT'S PRETTY MUCH LIKE IT SAYS IN THE HANDOUT.
OKAY.
BUMP
...UH!?
HSST
BWAAAAAA
YOU'RE NEVER GONNA REPLACE ME! GOT IT!?
WH... WHAT!?
WHAT WAS THAT ABOUT...?
ABOUT THAT.
TM TM TM TM
IDOL
NAKAO
NEW SCHOOL IDOL
MIZUKI ASHIYA 1
PHOTOS 500 YEN
Thanks, come again
Candid photo
PLES ORANGES
YEEEEEEE!
HEY NIHONBASHI. YOU'D BETTER WATCH THE UNAUTHORIZED PHOTOS.
UH....
WHAT KIND OF LOONY BIN IS THIS?

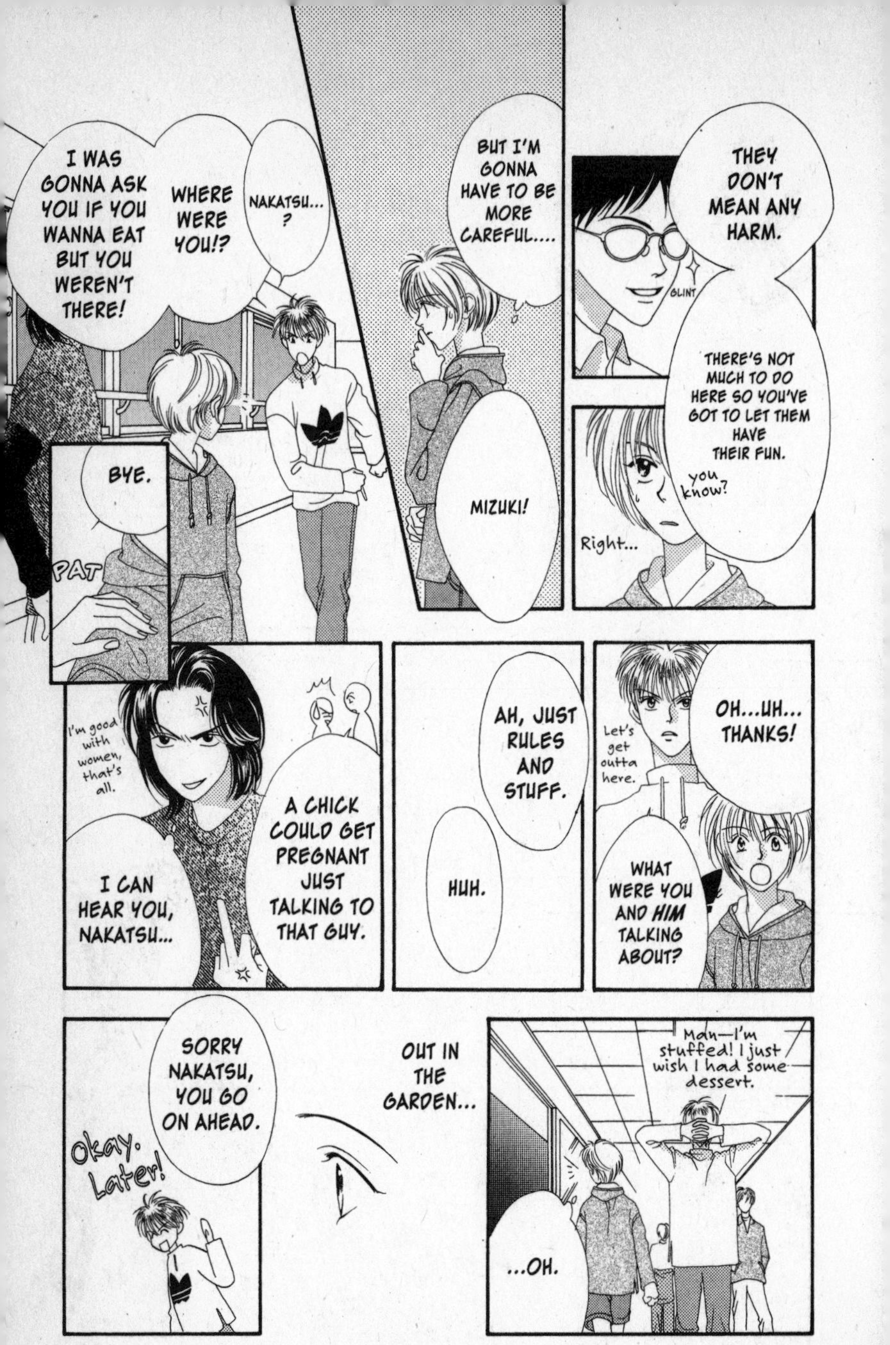
THEY DON'T MEAN ANY HARM.
GLINT
THERE'S NOT MUCH TO DO HERE SO YOU'VE GOT TO LET THEM HAVE THEIR FUN.
you know?
Right...
BUT I'M GONNA HAVE TO BE MORE CAREFUL....
MIZUKI!
NAKATSU...?
WHERE WERE YOU!?
I WAS GONNA ASK YOU IF YOU WANNA EAT BUT YOU WEREN'T THERE!
BYE.
PAT
OH...UH... THANKS!
Let's get outta here.
WHAT WERE YOU AND *HIM* TALKING ABOUT?
AH, JUST RULES AND STUFF.
HUH.
A CHICK COULD GET PREGNANT JUST TALKING TO THAT GUY.
I'm good with women, that's all.
I CAN HEAR YOU, NAKATSU...
Man—I'm stuffed! I just wish I had some dessert.
...OH.
OUT IN THE GARDEN...
SORRY NAKATSU, YOU GO ON AHEAD.
Okay. Later!

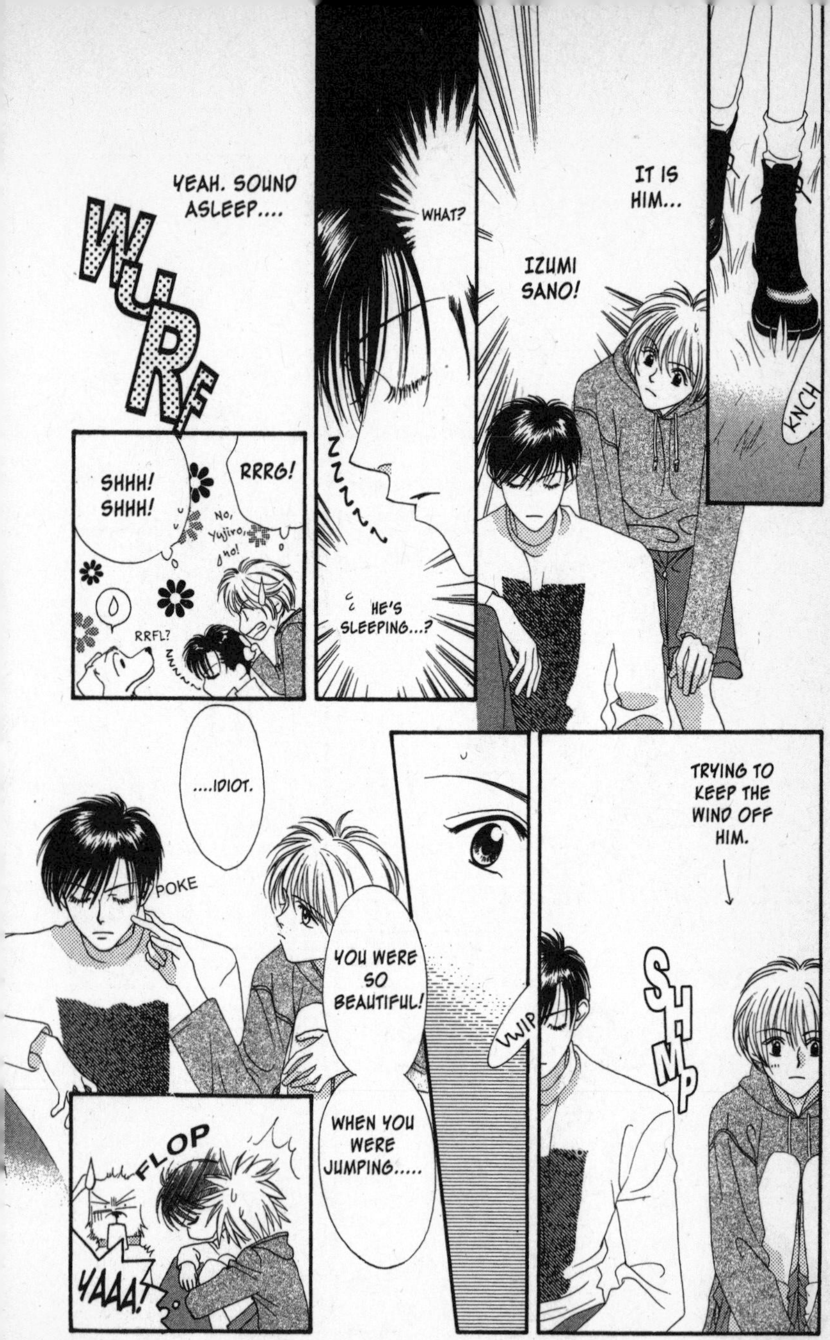
KNCH
IT IS HIM...
IZUMI SANO!
WHAT?
ZZZZZZ
HE'S SLEEPING...?
YEAH. SOUND ASLEEP....
WURF
RRRG!
SHHH! SHHH!
No, Yujiro, no!
RRFL?
TRYING TO KEEP THE WIND OFF HIM.
SHMP
WWIP
....IDIOT.
POKE
YOU WERE SO BEAUTIFUL!
WHEN YOU WERE JUMPING.....
FLOP
YAAA!

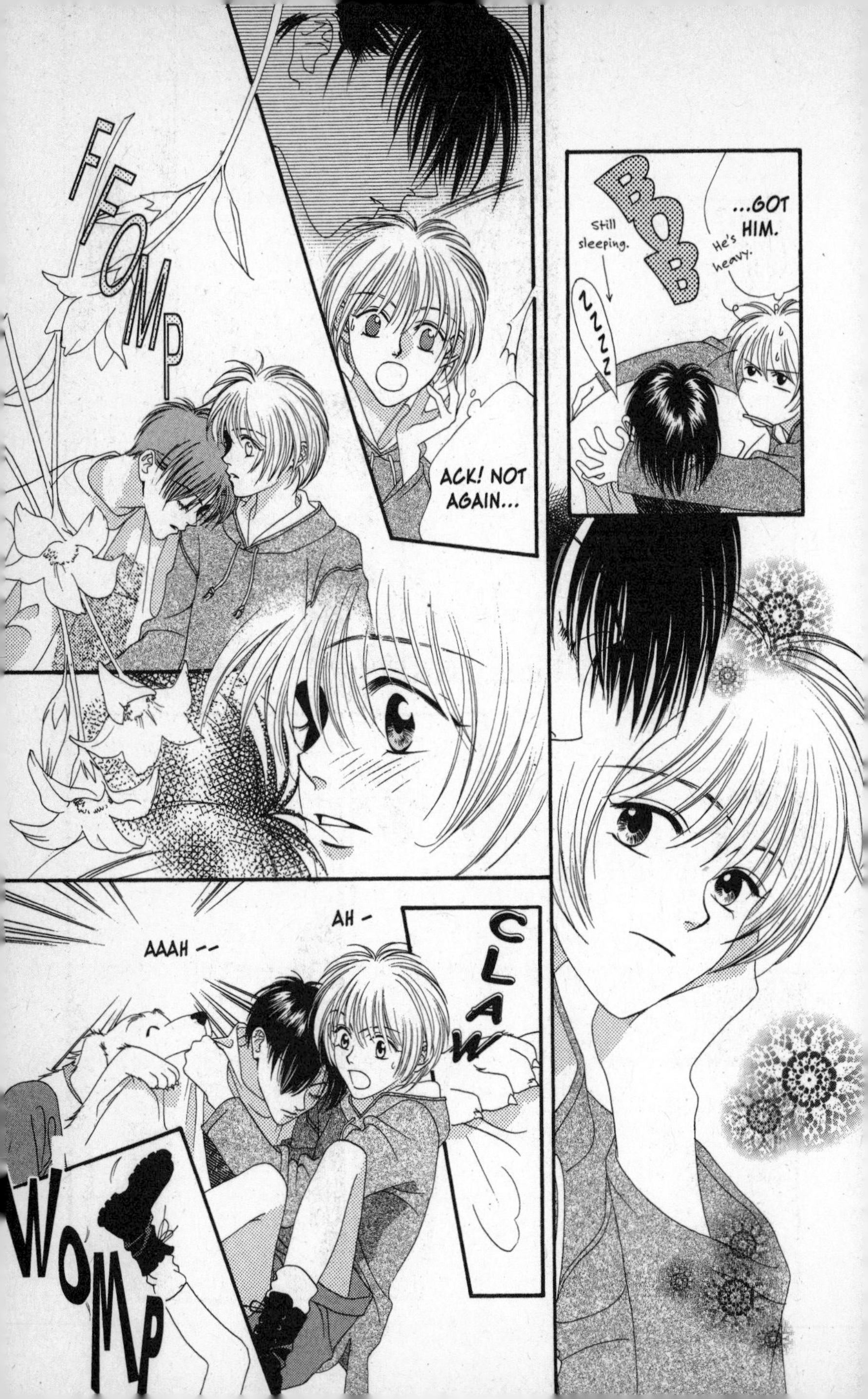
BOB
Still sleeping.
ZZZZ
...GOT HIM.
He's heavy.
ACK! NOT AGAIN...
FFOMP
AH -
AAAH --
CLAW
WOMP

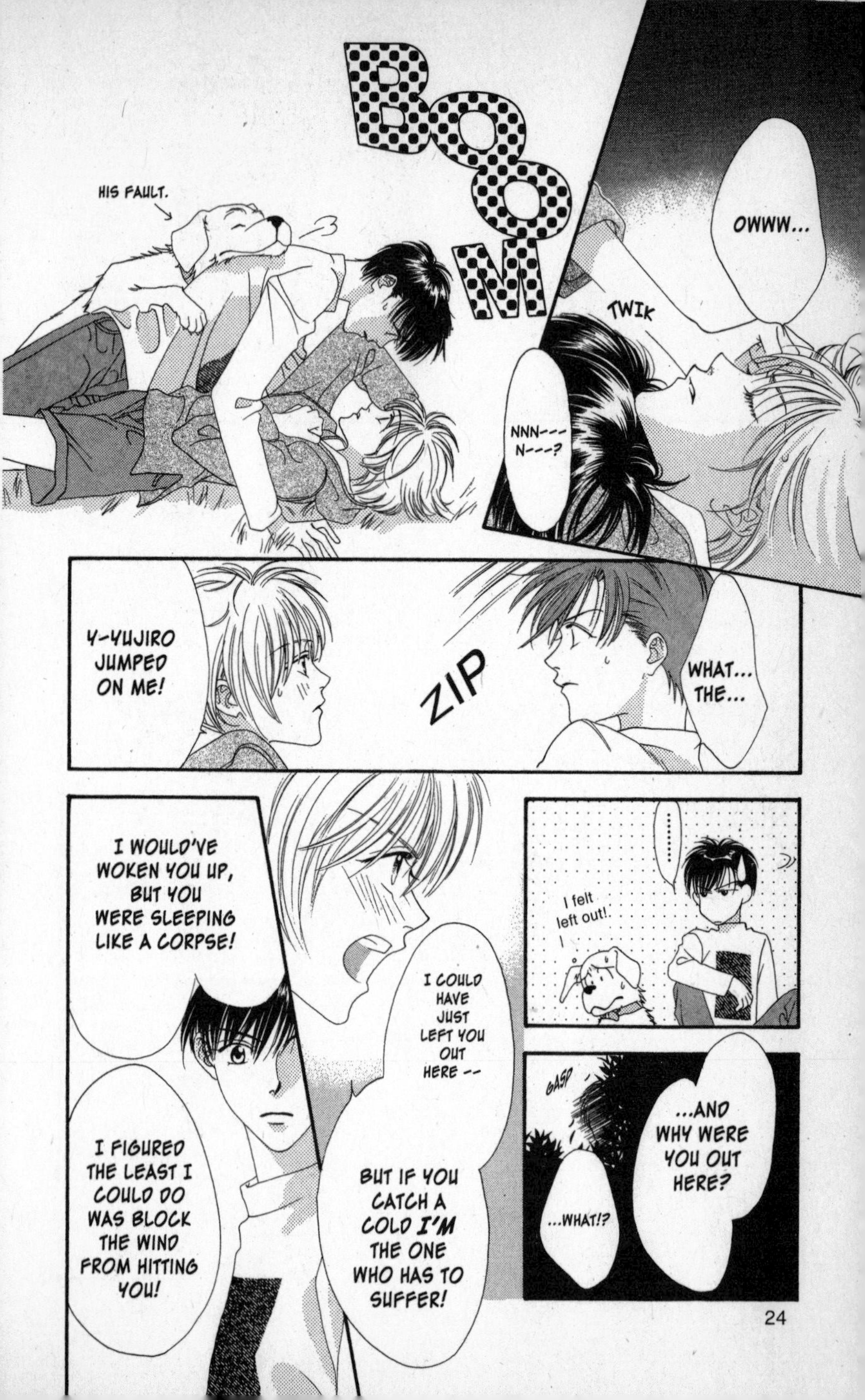
OWWW...
TWIK
NNN---
N---?
BOOM
HIS FAULT.
WHAT...
THE...
ZIP
Y-YUJIRO
JUMPED
ON ME!
......
I felt left out!
...AND WHY WERE YOU OUT HERE?
GASP
...WHAT!?
I WOULD'VE WOKEN YOU UP, BUT YOU WERE SLEEPING LIKE A CORPSE!
I COULD HAVE JUST LEFT YOU OUT HERE --
BUT IF YOU CATCH A COLD ***I'M*** THE ONE WHO HAS TO SUFFER!
I FIGURED THE LEAST I COULD DO WAS BLOCK THE WIND FROM HITTING YOU!

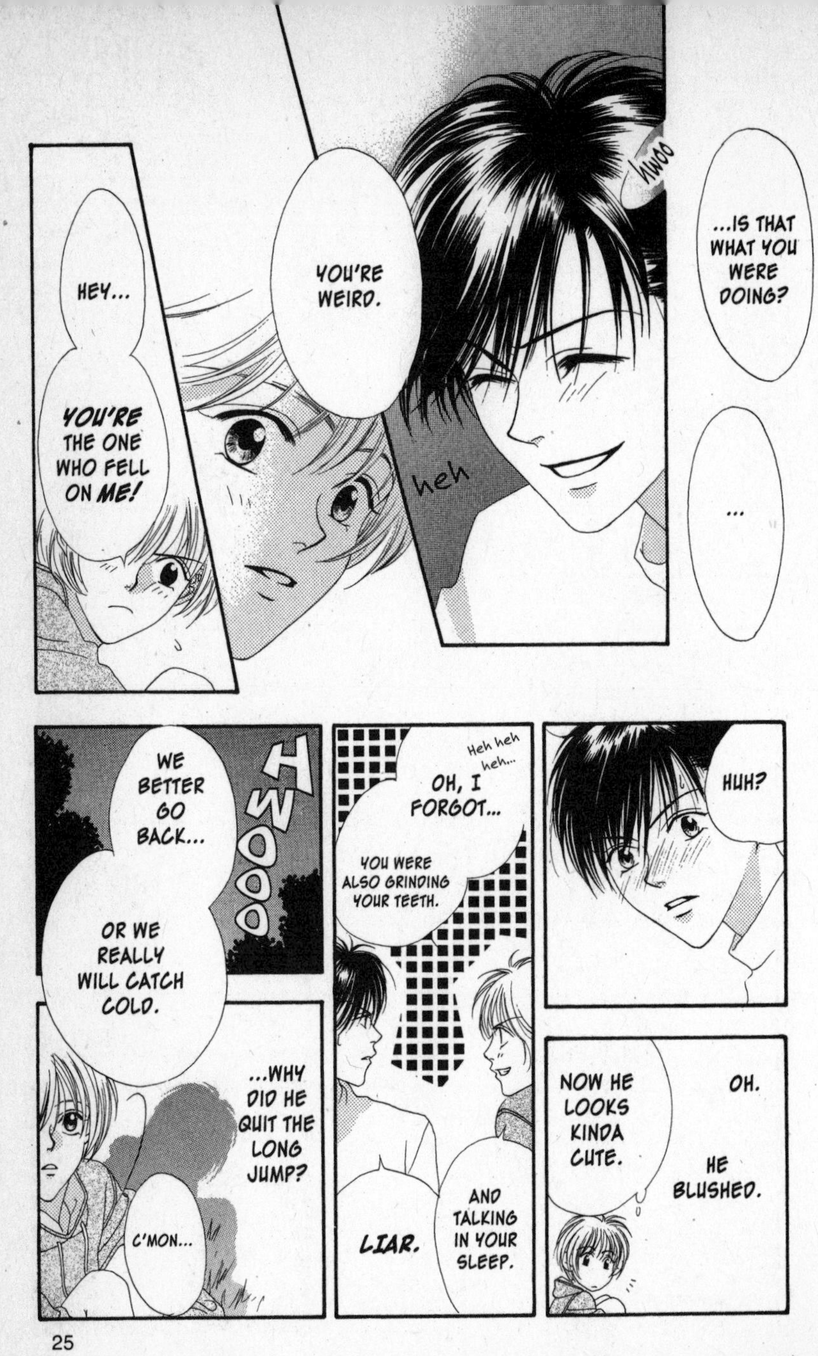
hwoo
...IS THAT WHAT YOU WERE DOING?
...
heh
YOU'RE WEIRD.
HEY...
YOU'RE THE ONE WHO FELL ON ME!
HUH?
OH.
HE BLUSHED.
NOW HE LOOKS KINDA CUTE.
Heh heh heh...
OH, I FORGOT...
YOU WERE ALSO GRINDING YOUR TEETH.
AND TALKING IN YOUR SLEEP.
LIAR.
HWOOO
WE BETTER GO BACK...
OR WE REALLY WILL CATCH COLD.
...WHY DID HE QUIT THE LONG JUMP?
C'MON...

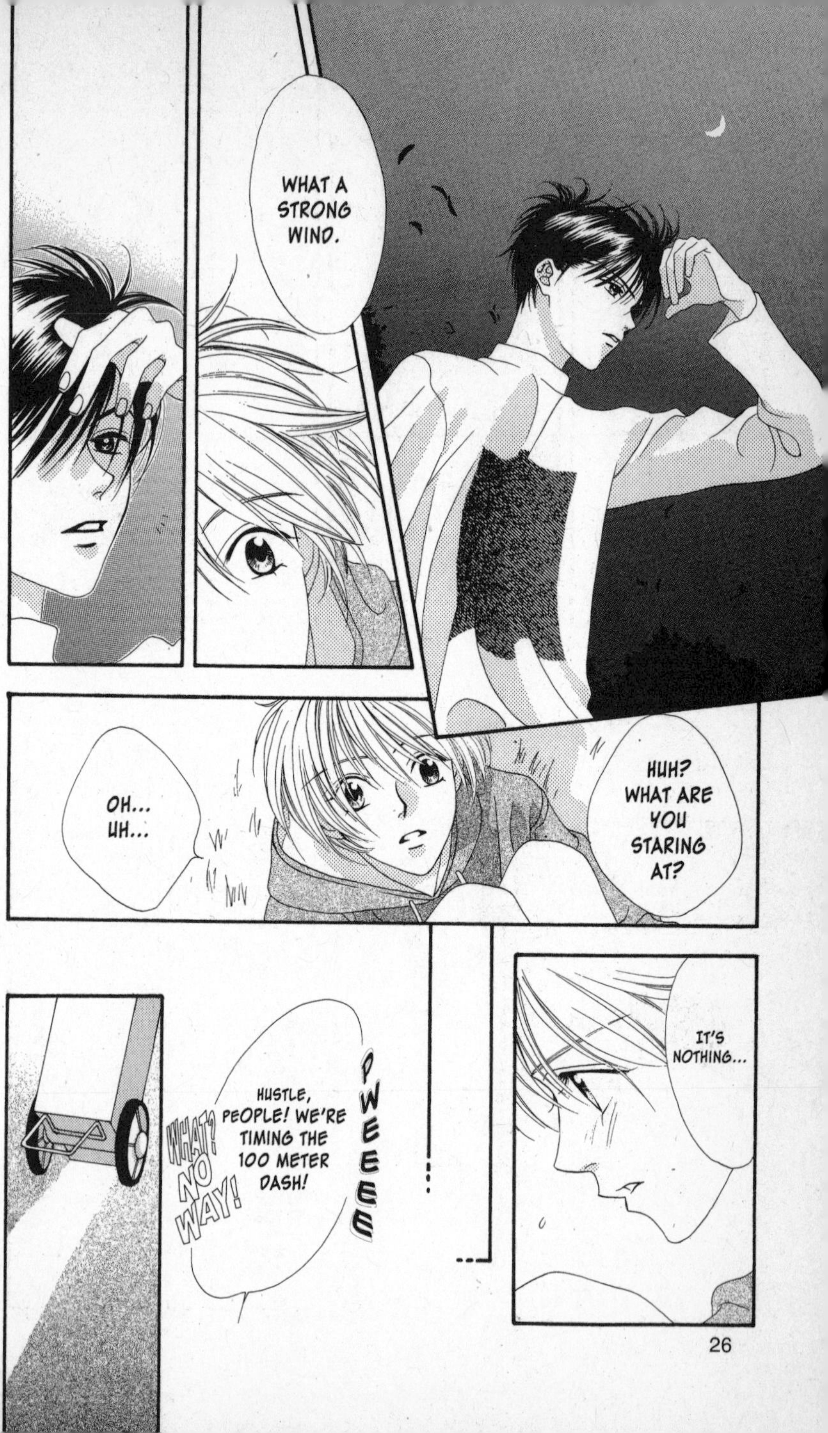
WHAT A STRONG WIND.
HUH? WHAT ARE YOU STARING AT?
OH... UH...
IT'S NOTHING...
...
...
PWEEEE
HUSTLE, PEOPLE! WE'RE TIMING THE 100 METER DASH!
WHAT? NO WAY!

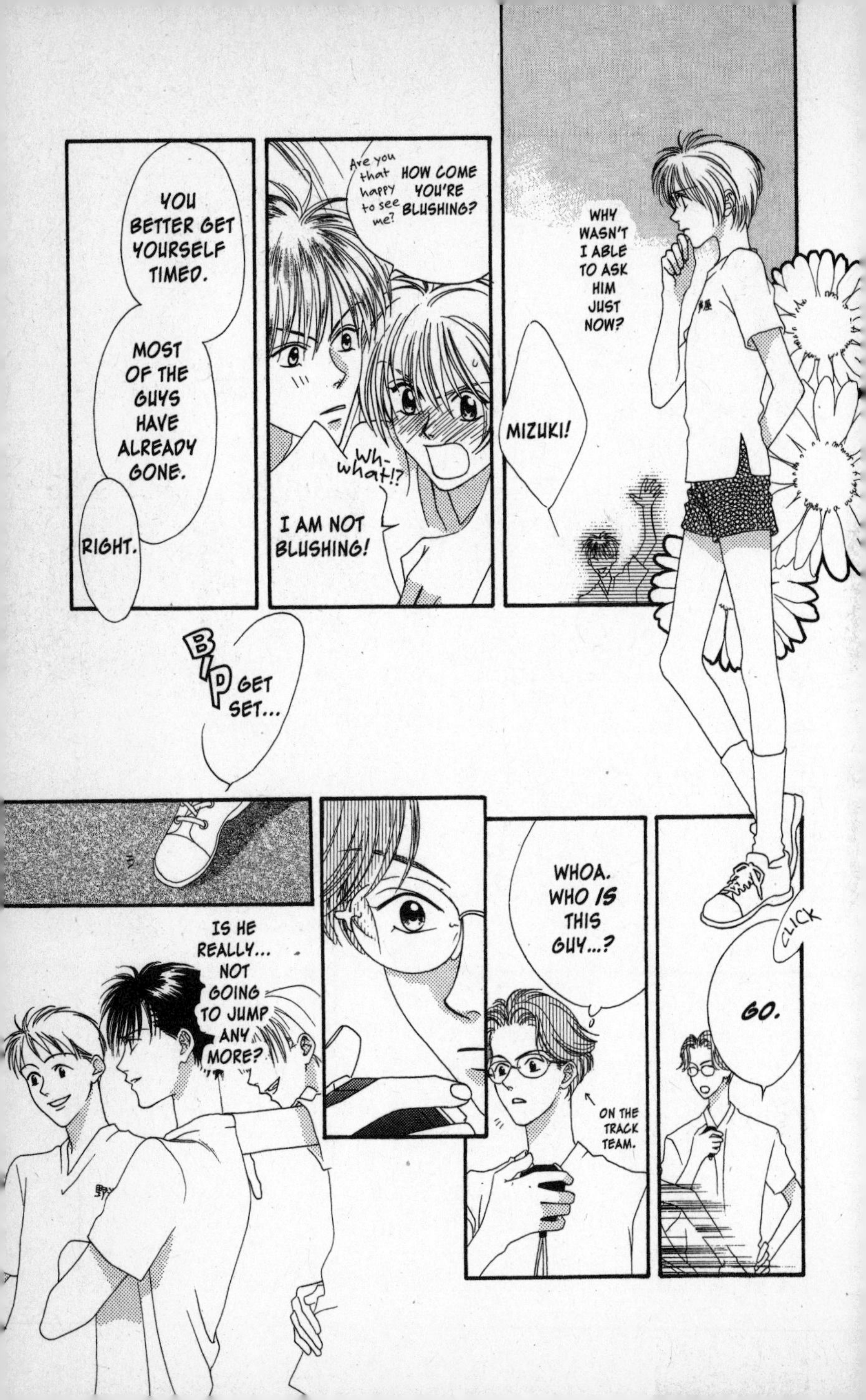
WHY WASN'T I ABLE TO ASK HIM JUST NOW?
MIZUKI!
HOW COME YOU'RE BLUSHING?
Are you that happy to see me?
Wh-what!?
I AM NOT BLUSHING!
YOU BETTER GET YOURSELF TIMED.
MOST OF THE GUYS HAVE ALREADY GONE.
RIGHT.
BIP
GET SET...
CLICK
GO.
WHOA. WHO *IS* THIS GUY...?
ON THE TRACK TEAM.
IS HE REALLY... NOT GOING TO JUMP ANY MORE?

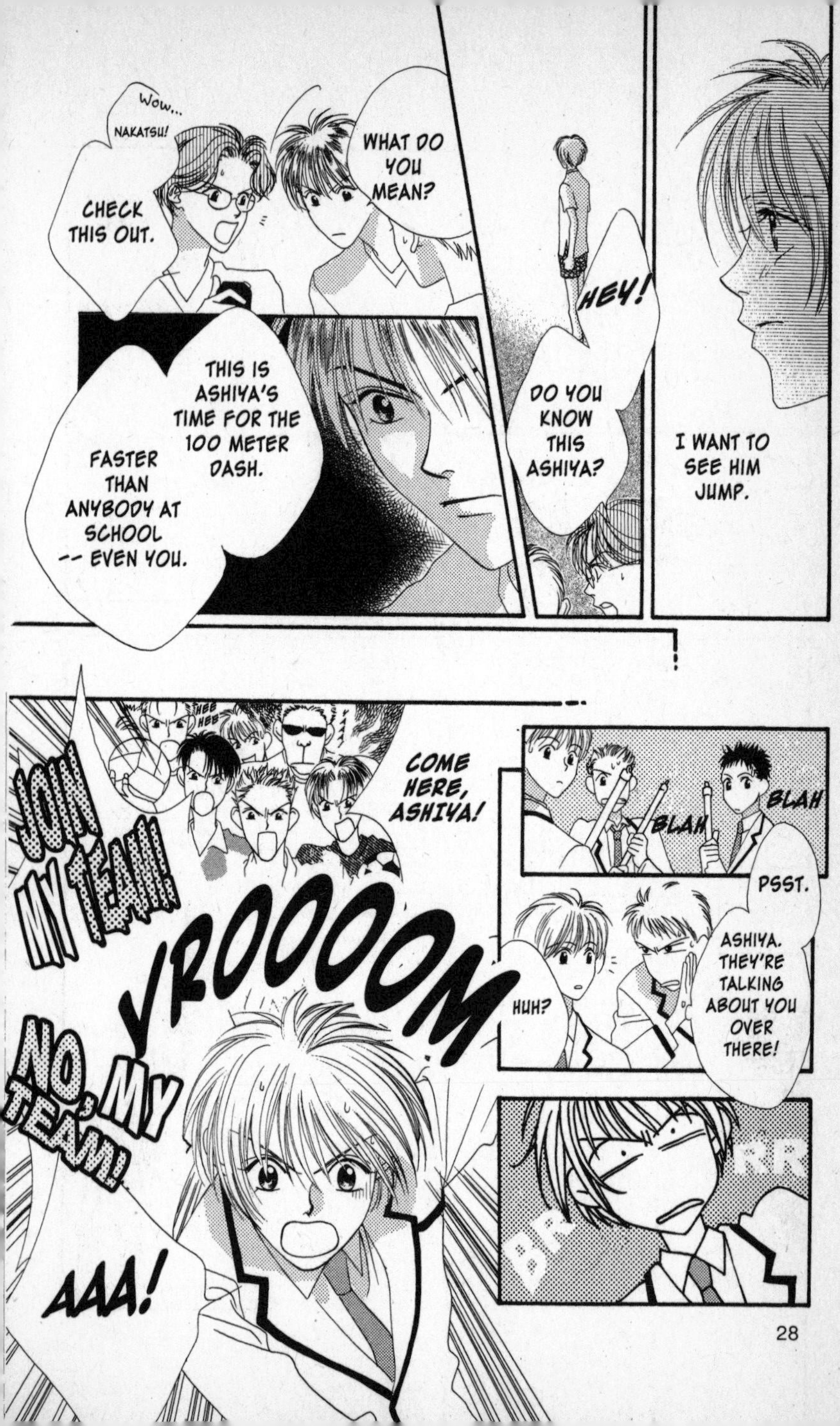
I WANT TO SEE HIM JUMP.
HEY!
DO YOU KNOW THIS ASHIYA?
Wow... NAKATSU!
CHECK THIS OUT.
WHAT DO YOU MEAN?
THIS IS ASHIYA'S TIME FOR THE 100 METER DASH.
FASTER THAN ANYBODY AT SCHOOL -- EVEN YOU.
BLAH
BLAH
PSST.
ASHIYA. THEY'RE TALKING ABOUT YOU OVER THERE!
HUH?
BRRR
COME HERE, ASHIYA!
HEE HEE
JOIN MY TEAM!
VROOOOM
NO, MY TEAM!
AAA!

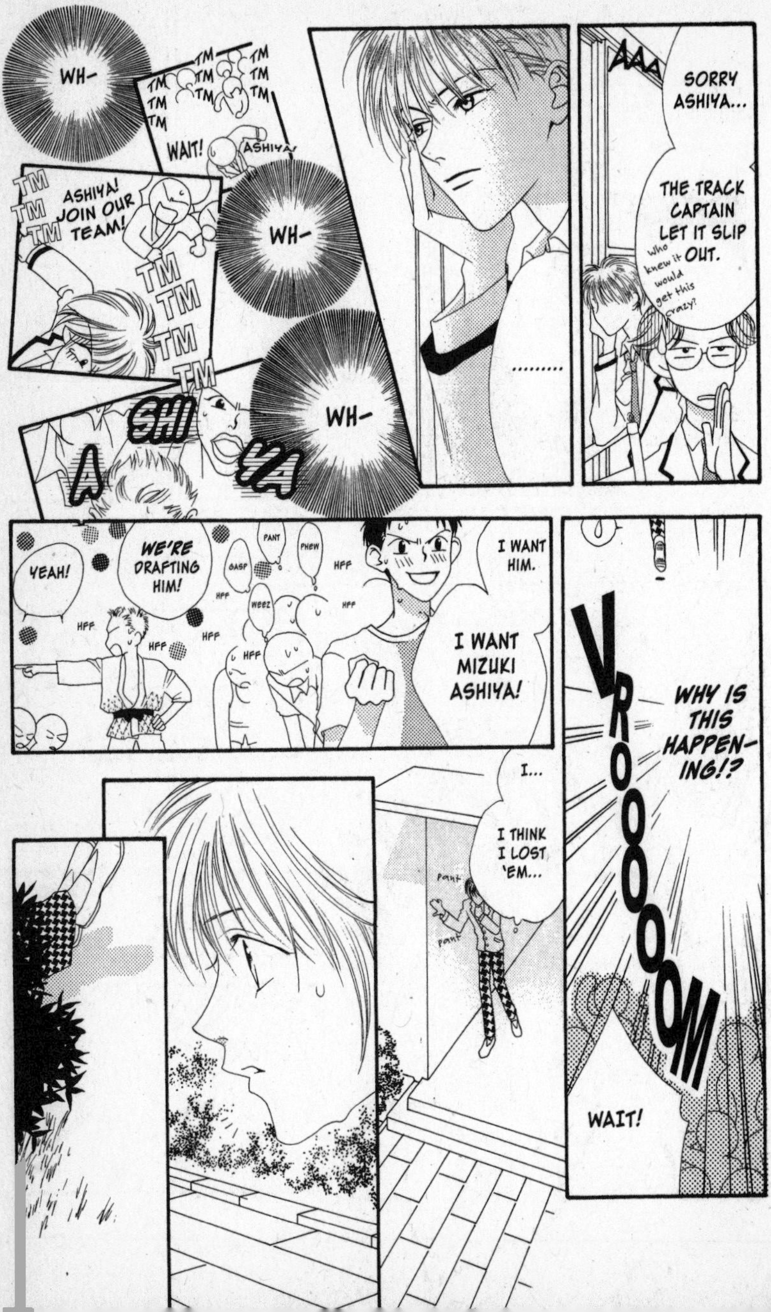
AAA
SORRY ASHIYA...
THE TRACK CAPTAIN LET IT SLIP OUT.
who knew it would get this crazy?
....
WH-
TM TM TM TM TM TM TM TM TM
WAIT!
ASHIYA!
ASHIYA! JOIN OUR TEAM!
TM TM TM
WH-
TM TM TM TM
A SHI YA
WH-
VROOOOOOM
WHY IS THIS HAPPEN-ING!?
WAIT!
I WANT HIM.
I WANT MIZUKI ASHIYA!
PHEW
PANT
GASP
WEEZ
HFF
WE'RE DRAFTING HIM!
YEAH!
I...
I THINK I LOST 'EM...
pant
pant

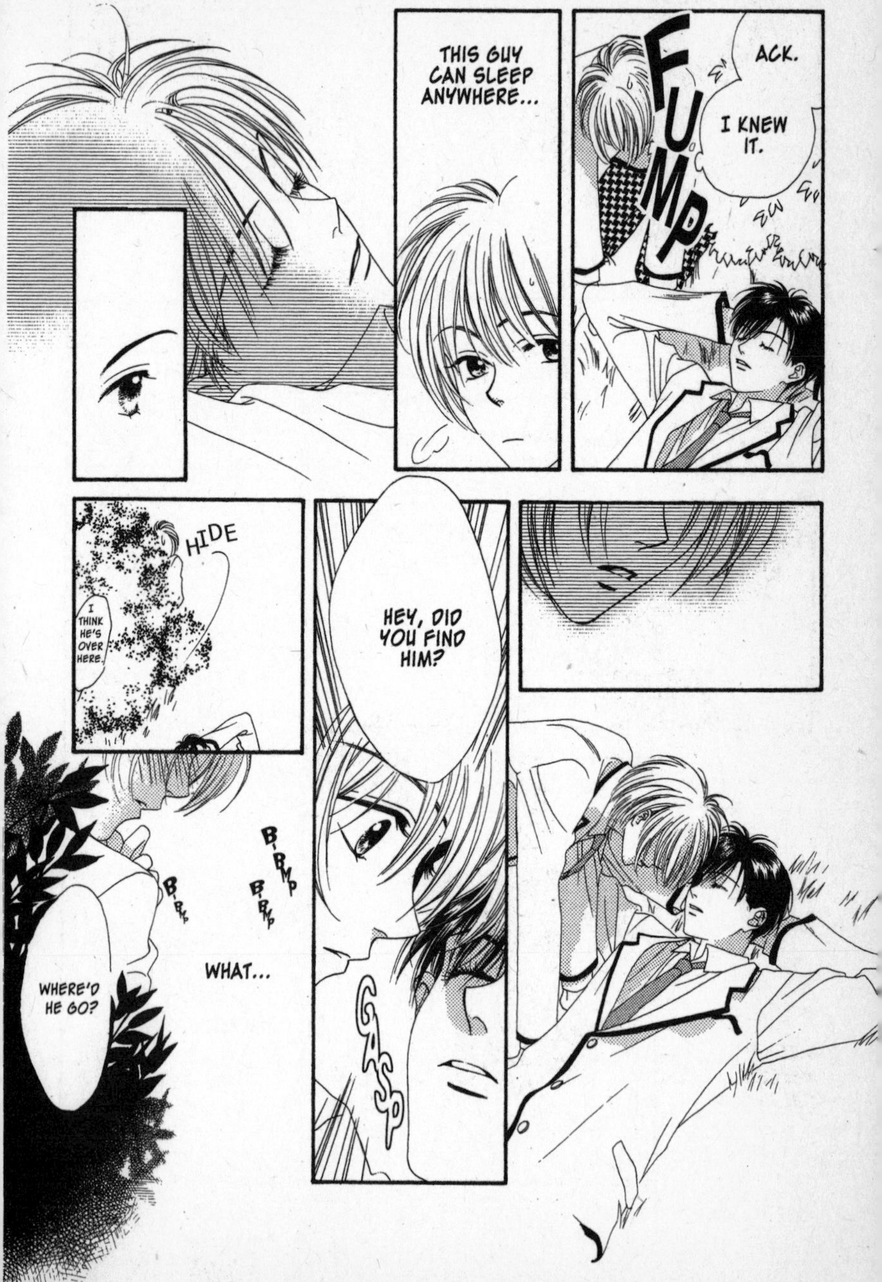
FUMP
ACK.
I KNEW IT.
THIS GUY CAN SLEEP ANYWHERE...
HEY, DID YOU FIND HIM?
GASP
HIDE
I THINK HE'S OVER HERE.
B-BMP
B-BMP
B-BMP
WHAT...
WHERE'D HE GO?

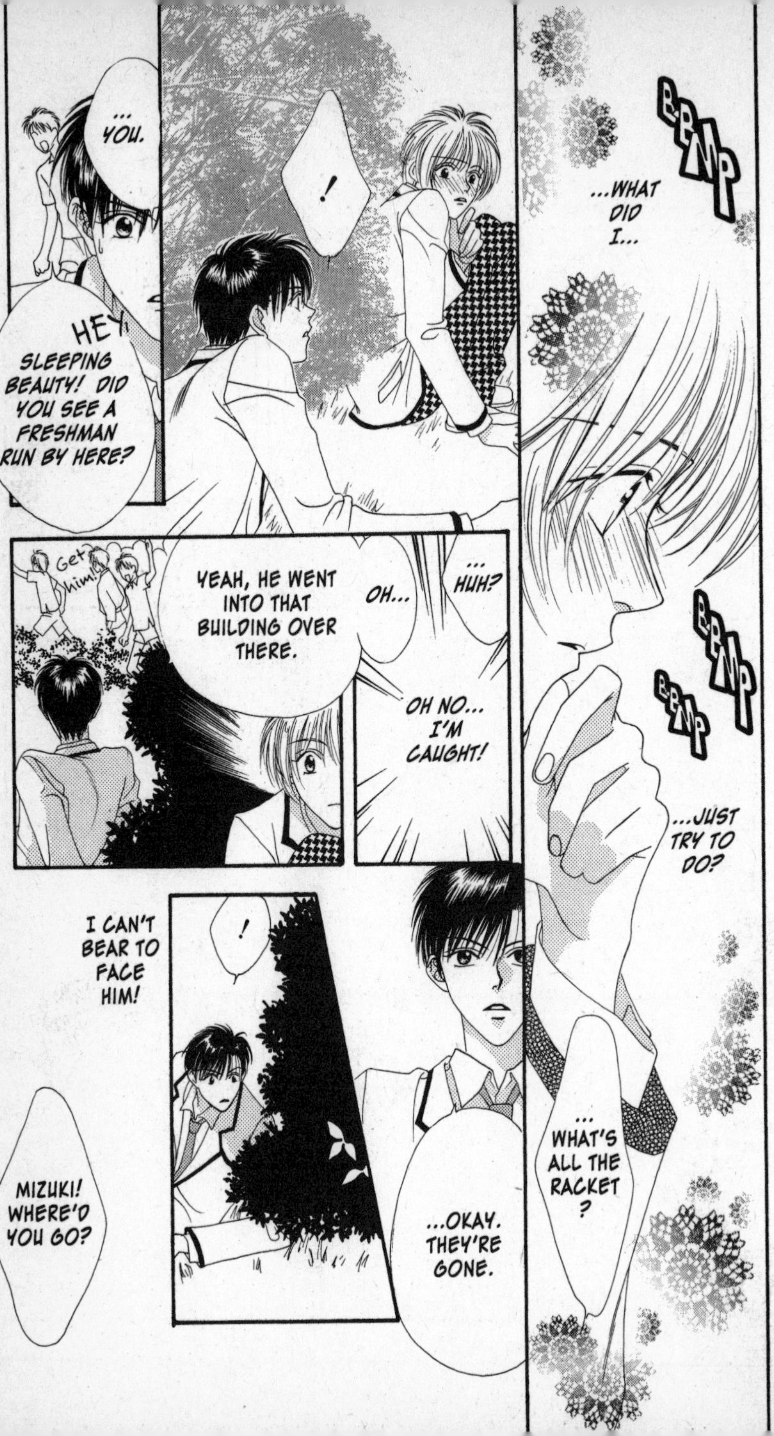
B-BMP
...WHAT DID I...
B-BMP
B-BMP
...JUST TRY TO DO?
!
... YOU.
HEY, SLEEPING BEAUTY! DID YOU SEE A FRESHMAN RUN BY HERE?
... HUH?
OH...
OH NO... I'M CAUGHT!
YEAH, HE WENT INTO THAT BUILDING OVER THERE.
Get him!
... WHAT'S ALL THE RACKET?
...OKAY. THEY'RE GONE.
!
I CAN'T BEAR TO FACE HIM!
MIZUKI! WHERE'D YOU GO?

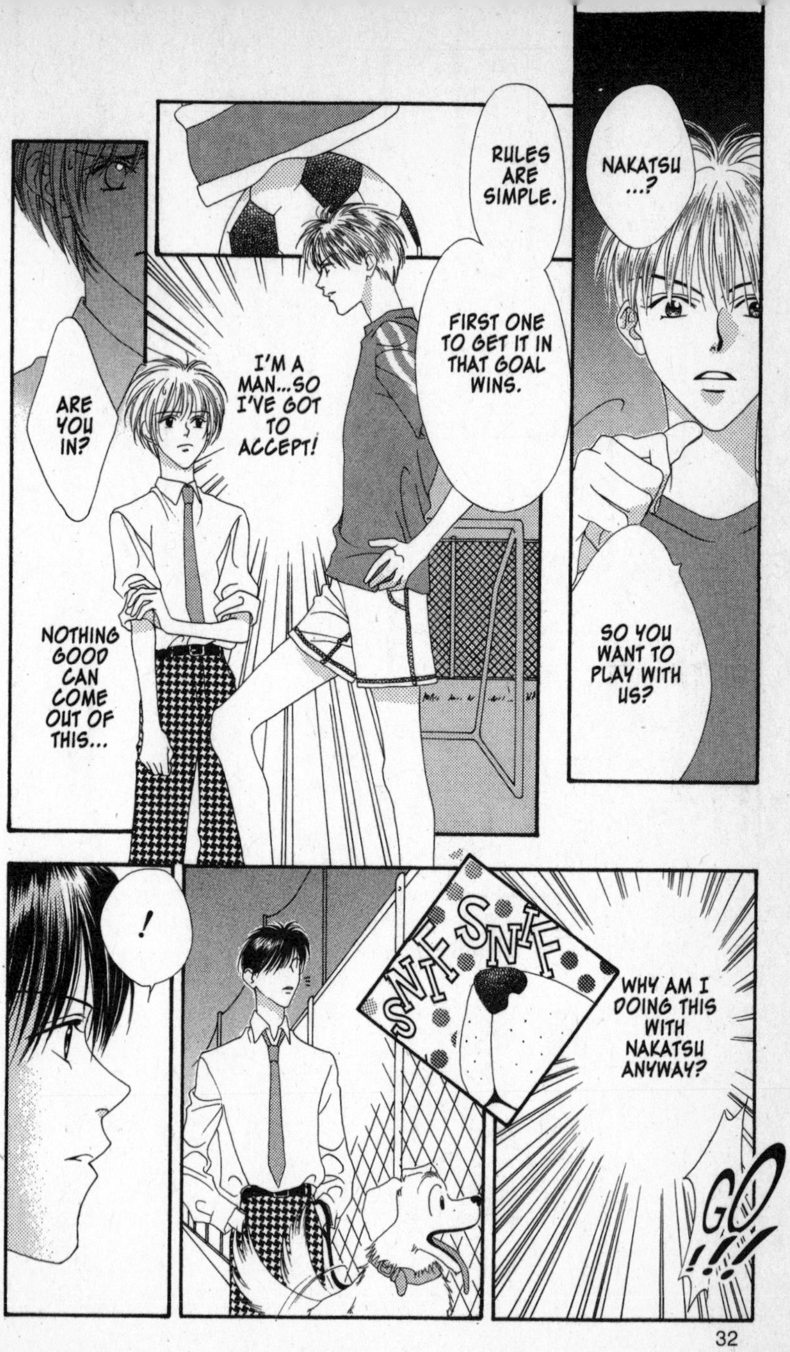

NAKATSU ...?
SO YOU WANT TO PLAY WITH US?
RULES ARE SIMPLE.
FIRST ONE TO GET IT IN THAT GOAL WINS.
ARE YOU IN?
I'M A MAN...SO I'VE GOT TO ACCEPT!
NOTHING GOOD CAN COME OUT OF THIS...
WHY AM I DOING THIS WITH NAKATSU ANYWAY?
GO!!!
SNIFF SNIFF
!

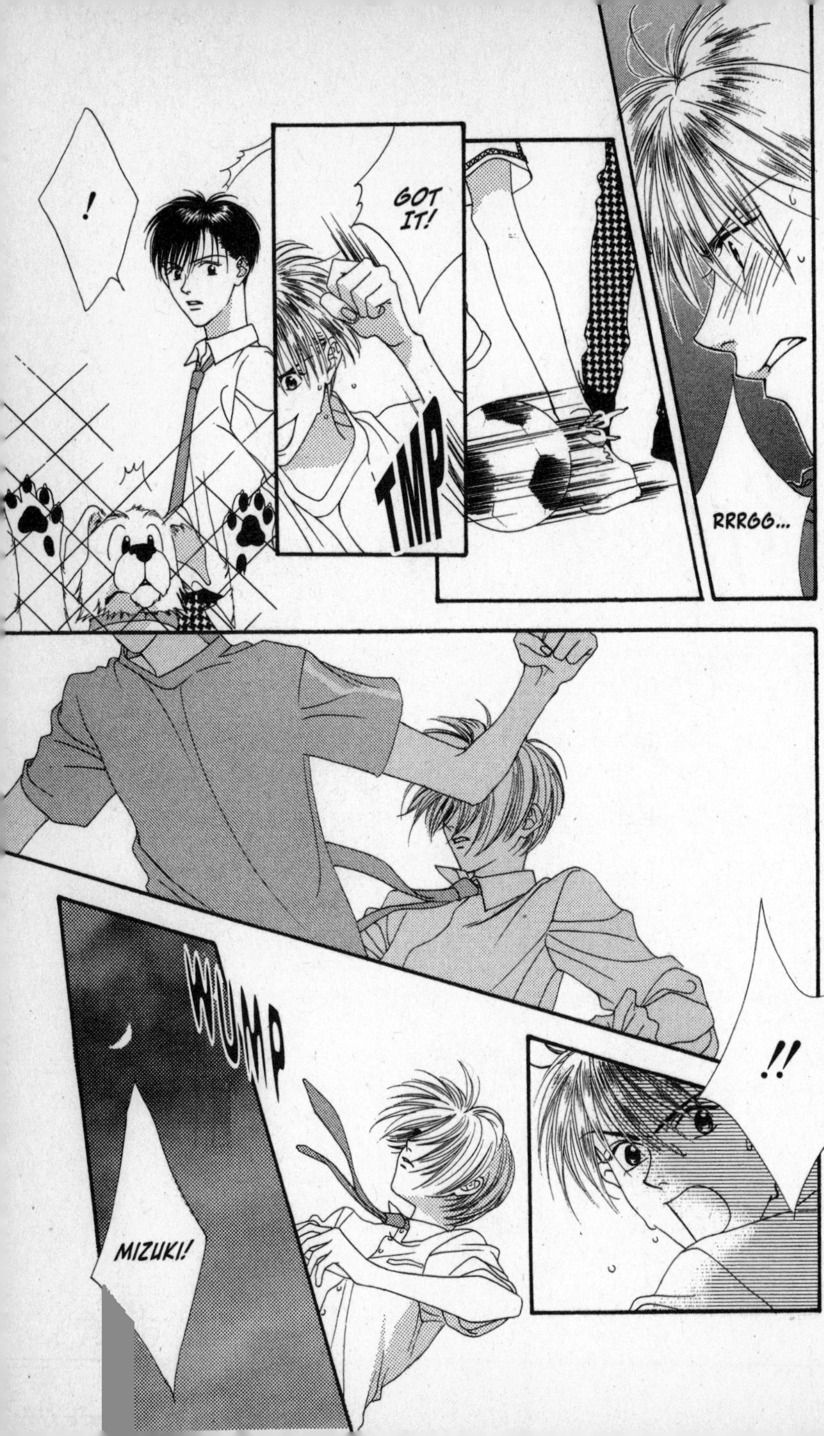
RRRGG...
GOT IT!
TMP
!
!!
WUMP
MIZUKI!

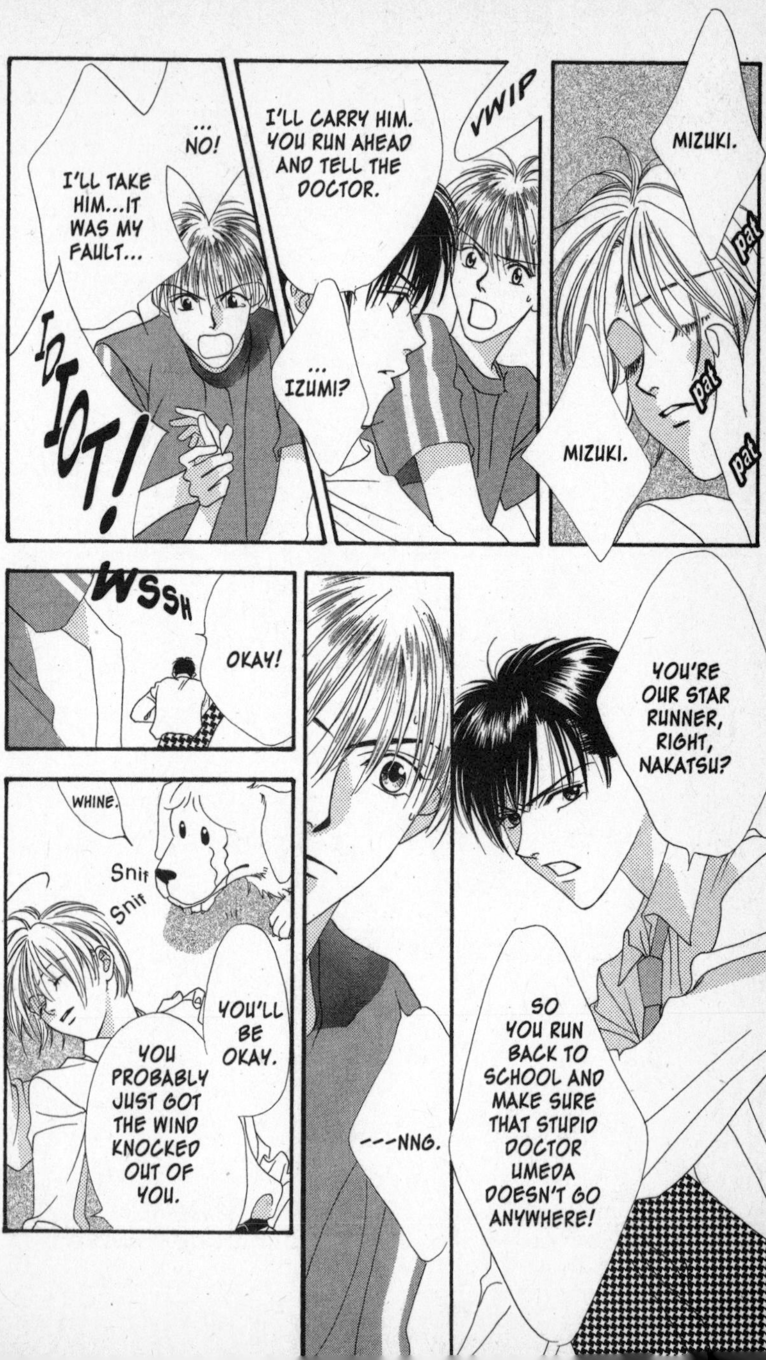
MIZUKI.
pat
pat
pat
MIZUKI.
VWIP
I'LL CARRY HIM. YOU RUN AHEAD AND TELL THE DOCTOR.
... IZUMI?
... NO!
I'LL TAKE HIM...IT WAS MY FAULT...
IDIOT!
YOU'RE OUR STAR RUNNER, RIGHT, NAKATSU?
SO YOU RUN BACK TO SCHOOL AND MAKE SURE THAT STUPID DOCTOR UMEDA DOESN'T GO ANYWHERE!
---NNG.
WSSH
OKAY!
WHINE.
Snif
Snif
YOU'LL BE OKAY.
YOU PROBABLY JUST GOT THE WIND KNOCKED OUT OF YOU.

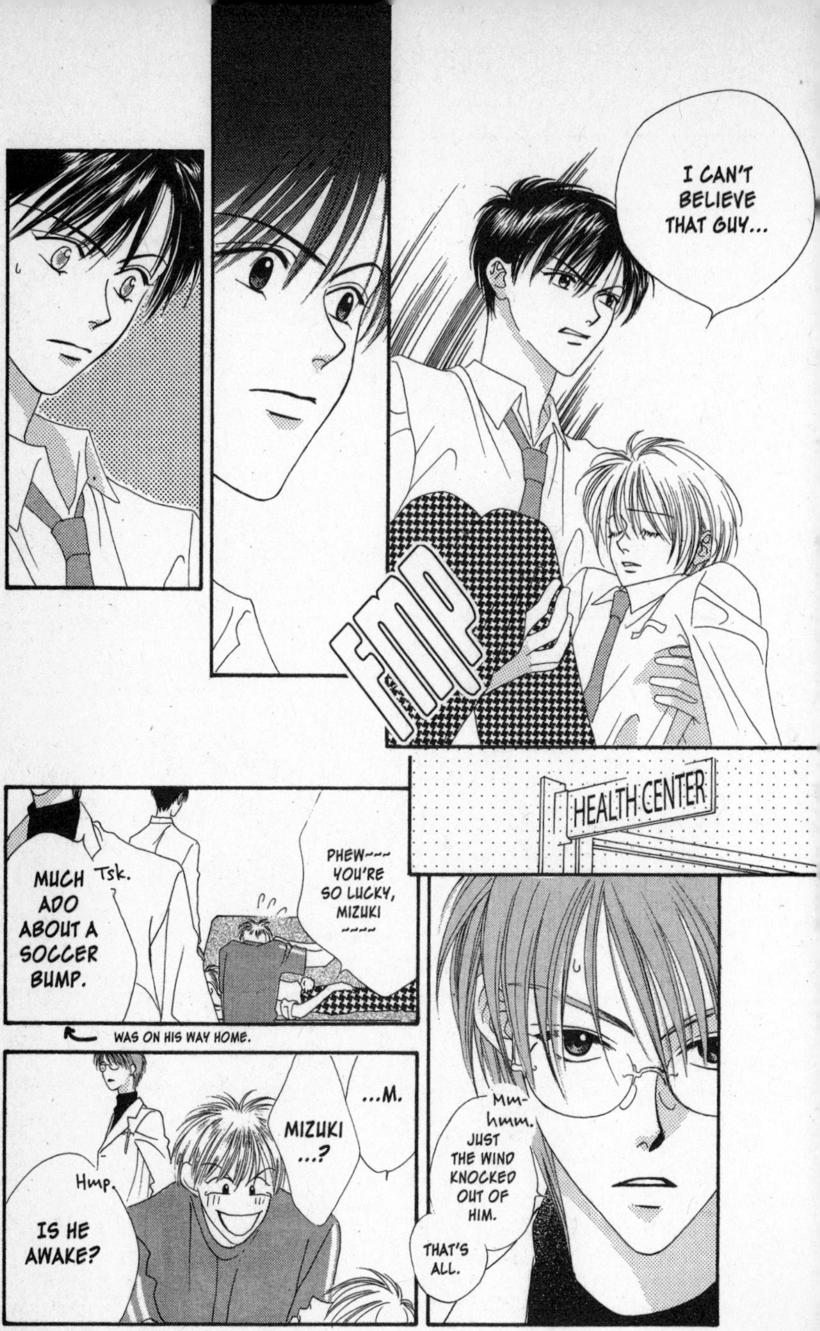
I CAN'T BELIEVE THAT GUY...
FMP
HEALTH CENTER
Mm-hmm.
JUST THE WIND KNOCKED OUT OF HIM.
THAT'S ALL.
PHEW~~~ YOU'RE SO LUCKY, MIZUKI ~~~~
Tsk.
MUCH ADO ABOUT A SOCCER BUMP.
WAS ON HIS WAY HOME.
...M.
MIZUKI ...?
Hmp.
IS HE AWAKE?

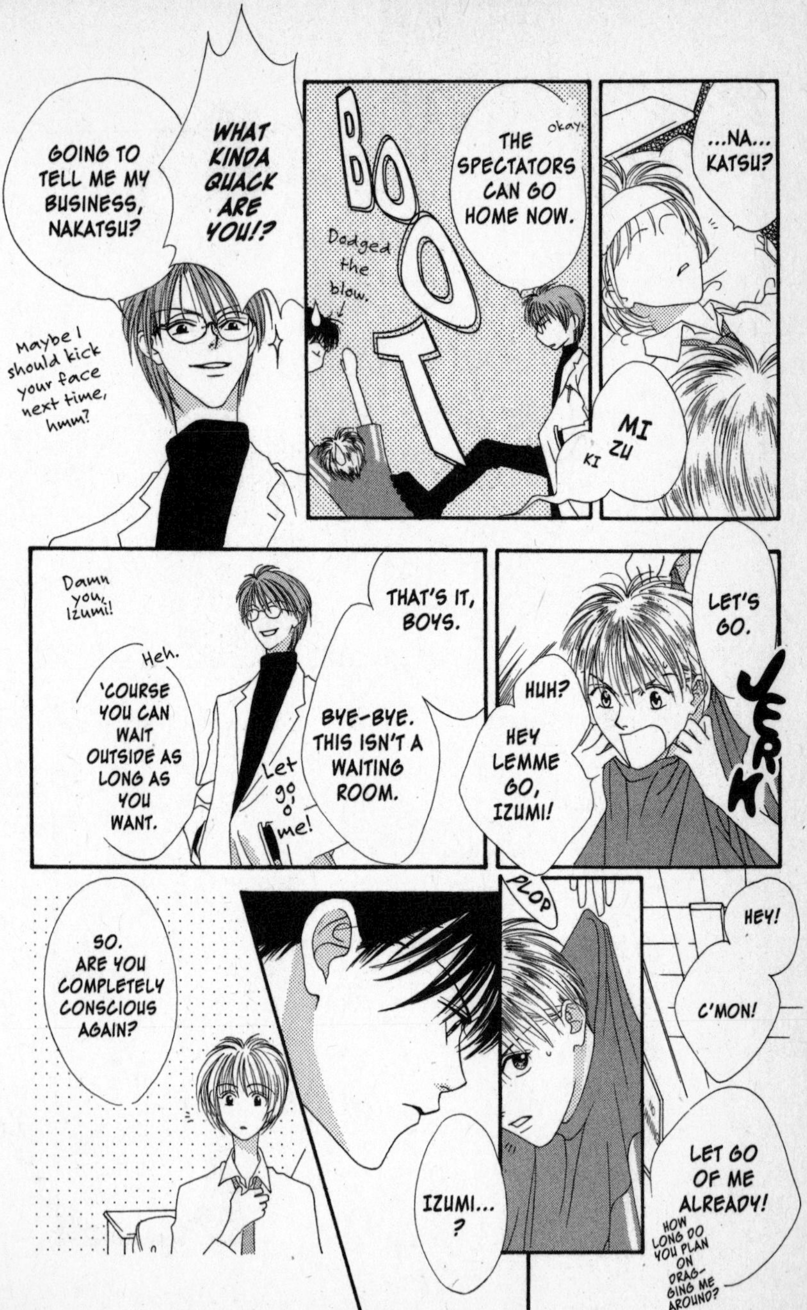
...NA... KATSU?
MI ZU KI
Okay.
THE SPECTATORS CAN GO HOME NOW.
BOOT
Dodged the blow.
WHAT KINDA QUACK ARE YOU!?
GOING TO TELL ME MY BUSINESS, NAKATSU?
Maybe I should kick your face next time, hmm?
LET'S GO.
JERK
HUH?
HEY LEMME GO, IZUMI!
THAT'S IT, BOYS.
BYE-BYE. THIS ISN'T A WAITING ROOM.
Let go o' me!
Damn you, Izumi!
Heh.
'COURSE YOU CAN WAIT OUTSIDE AS LONG AS YOU WANT.
PLOP
HEY!
C'MON!
LET GO OF ME ALREADY!
HOW LONG DO YOU PLAN ON DRAG-GING ME AROUND?
IZUMI...?
SO. ARE YOU COMPLETELY CONSCIOUS AGAIN?

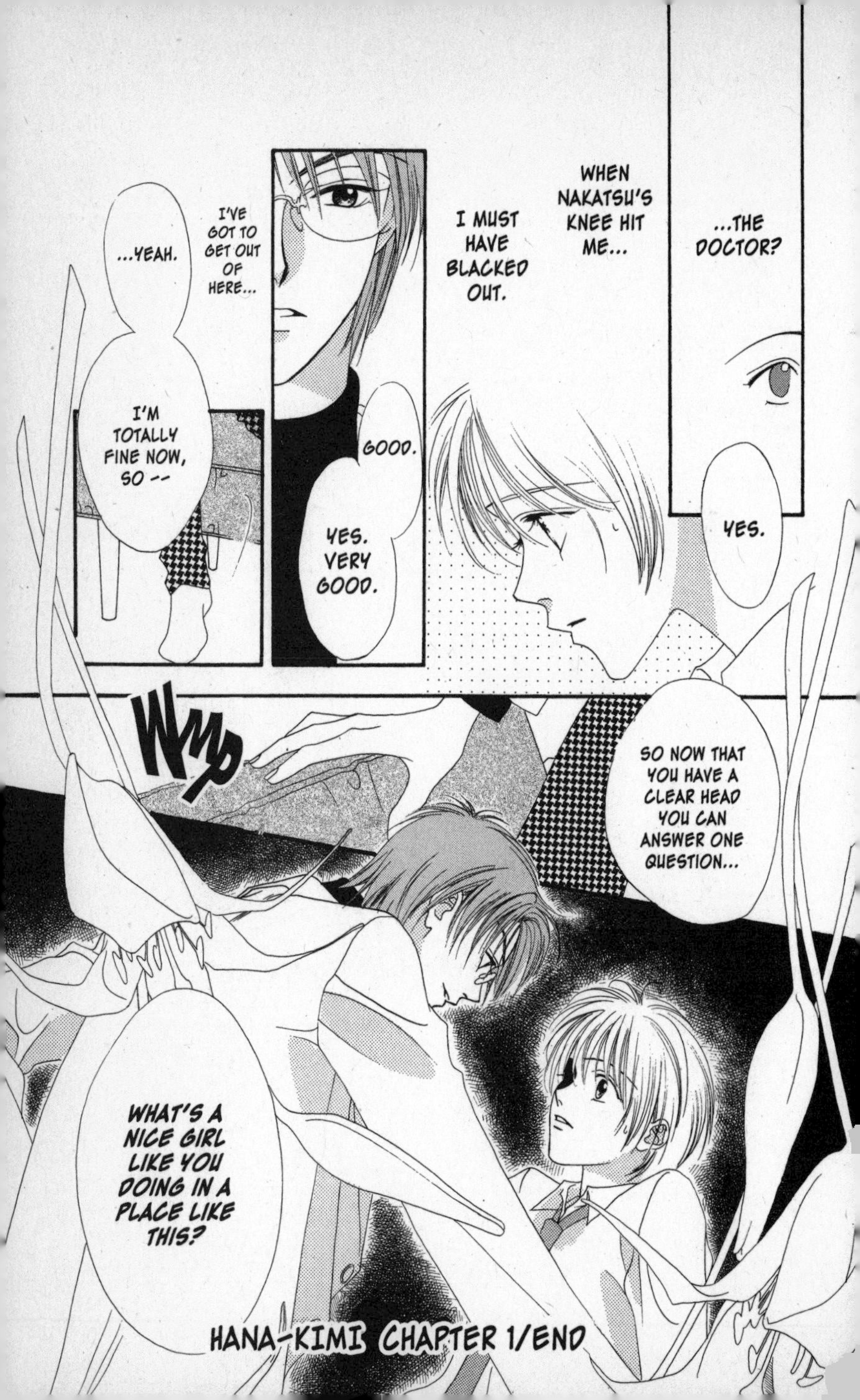
...THE DOCTOR?
YES.
WHEN NAKATSU'S KNEE HIT ME...
I MUST HAVE BLACKED OUT.
GOOD.
YES. VERY GOOD.
I'VE GOT TO GET OUT OF HERE...
...YEAH.
I'M TOTALLY FINE NOW, SO --
WMP
SO NOW THAT YOU HAVE A CLEAR HEAD YOU CAN ANSWER ONE QUESTION...
WHAT'S A NICE GIRL LIKE YOU DOING IN A PLACE LIKE THIS?
HANA-KIMI CHAPTER 1/END

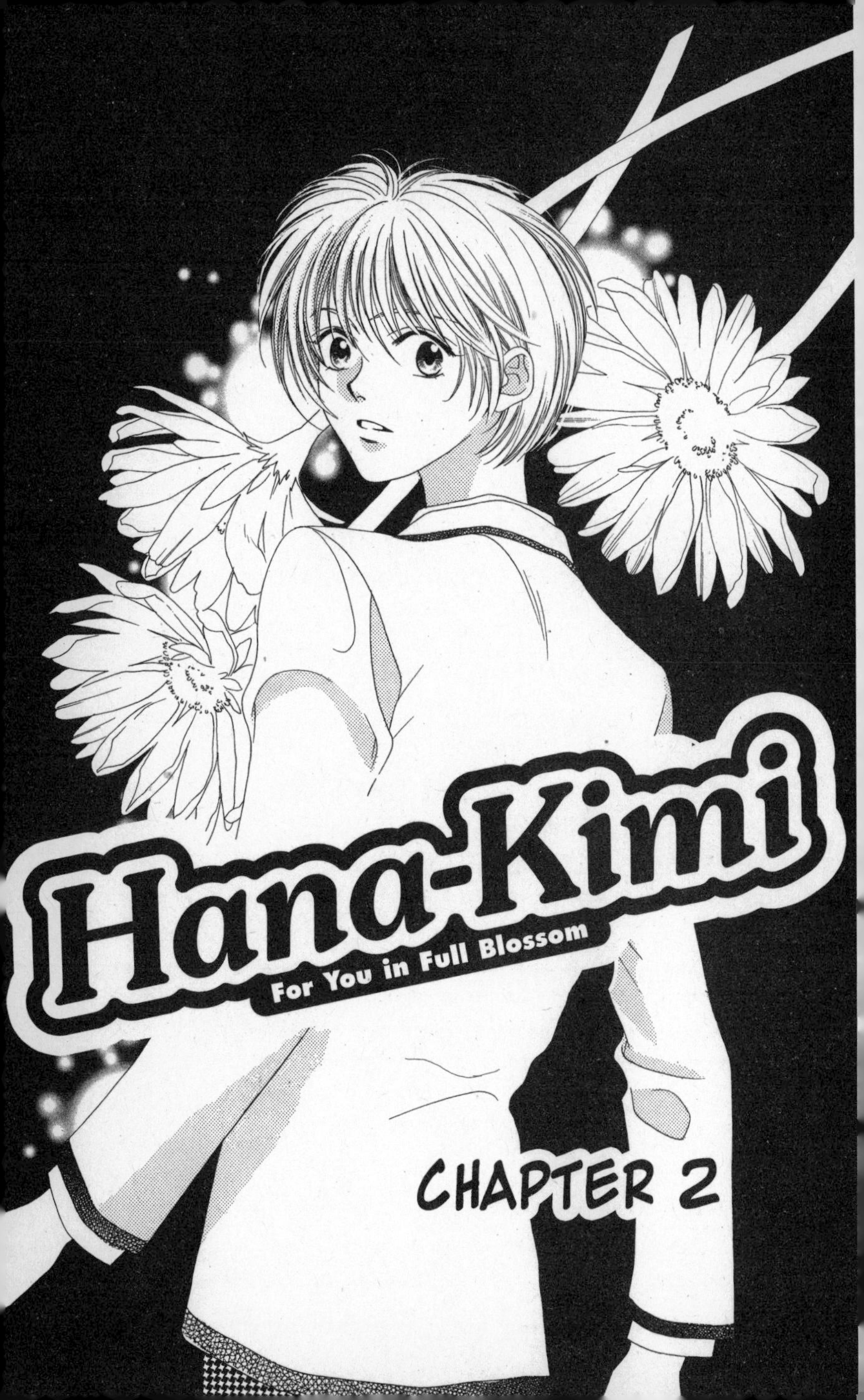
Hana-Kimi
For You in Full Blossom
CHAPTER 2

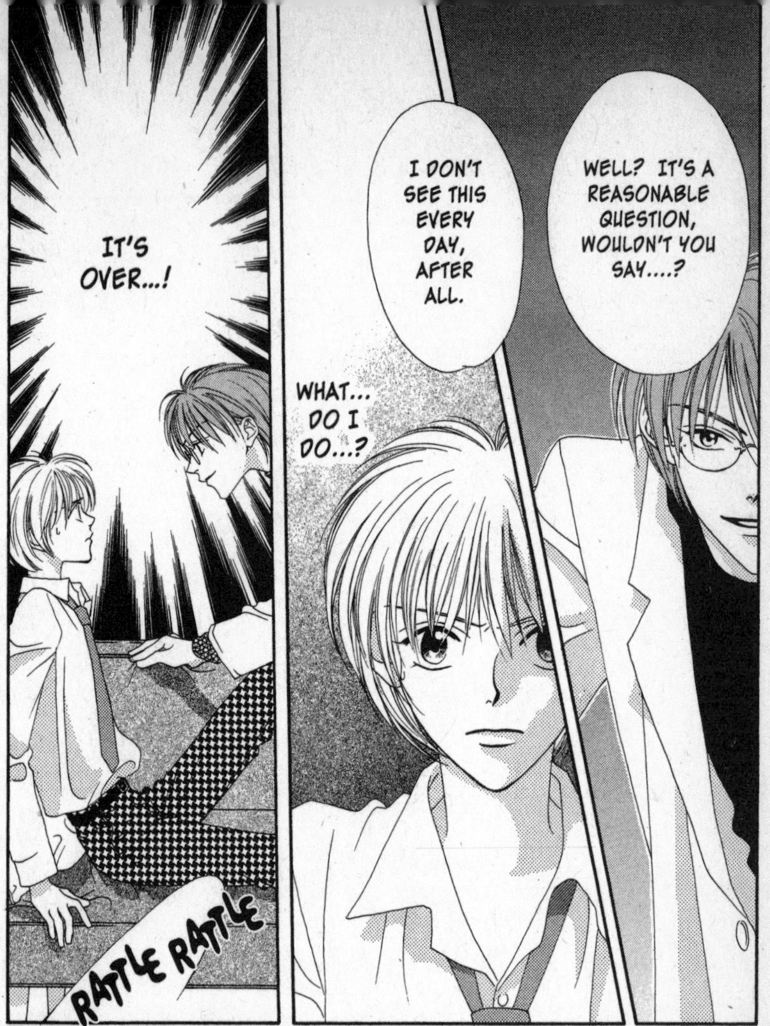
WELL? IT'S A REASONABLE QUESTION, WOULDN'T YOU SAY....?
I DON'T SEE THIS EVERY DAY, AFTER ALL.
WHAT... DO I DO...?
IT'S OVER...!
RATTLE RATTLE

CHARACTER RANKING

WELL, THE VOTES ARE IN AND THE MOST POPULAR CHARACTER IN THIS COMIC IS A GIRL! MIZUKI IS #1. IZUMI, NAKATSU, UMEDA AND YUJIRO TAKE 2ND THROUGH 5TH PLACE RESPECTIVELY. I EXPECTED YOU TO LIKE IZUMI, BUT I WAS SURPRISED AT HOW NICE YOU WERE TO NAKATSU. ACTUALLY, HE'S THE TYPE TO KEEP YELLING "KEEP FIGHTING!" AND "HANG IN THERE (GANBATTE)!" (HA HA). GOOD FOR YOU, NAKATSU!

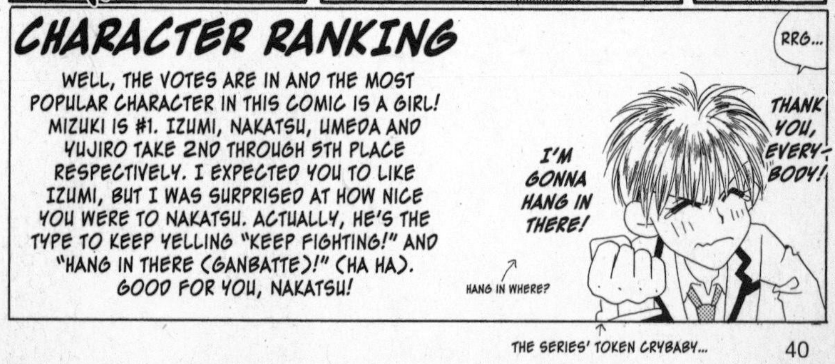
RRG...
THANK YOU, EVERY-BODY!
I'M GONNA HANG IN THERE!
HANG IN WHERE?
THE SERIES' TOKEN CRYBABY...

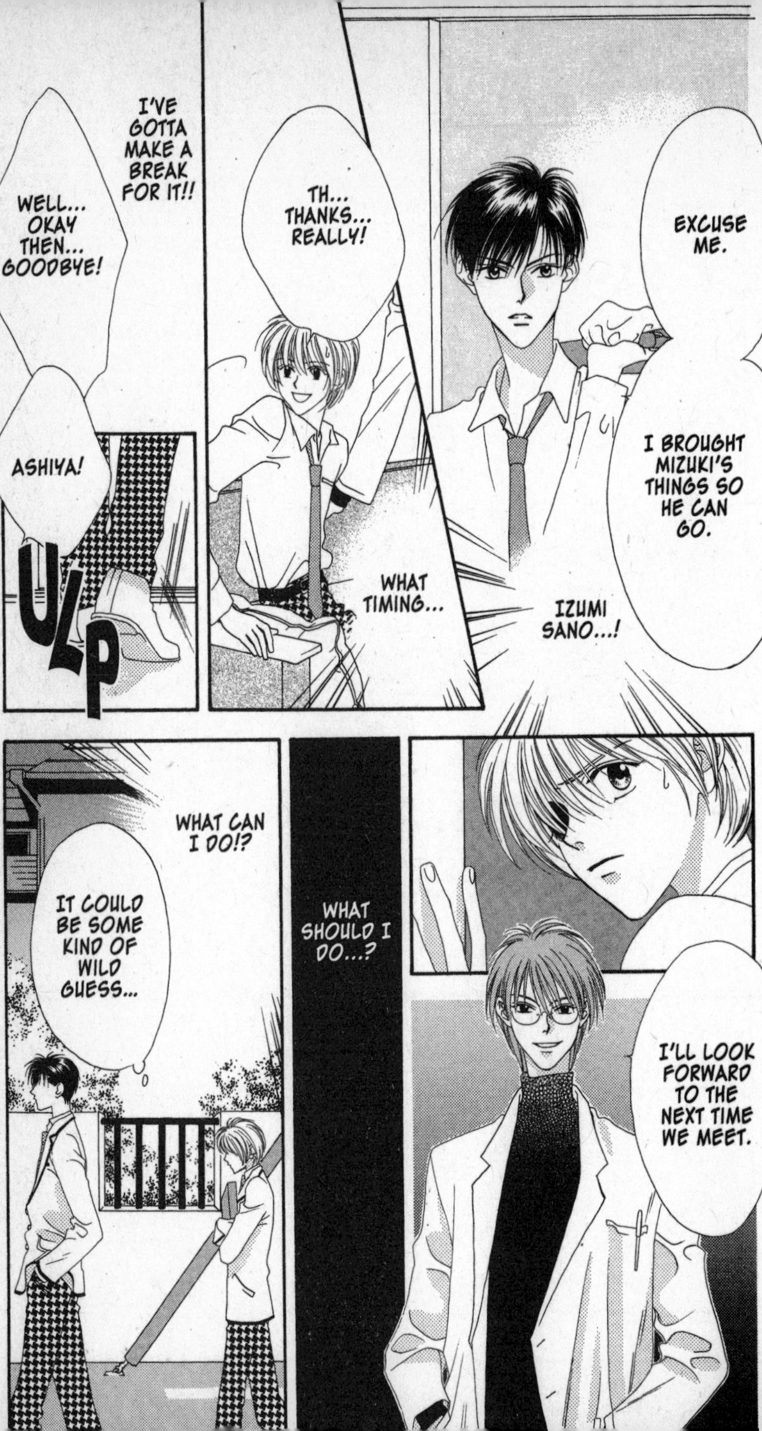
EXCUSE ME.
I BROUGHT MIZUKI'S THINGS SO HE CAN GO.
IZUMI SANO...!
WHAT TIMING...
TH... THANKS... REALLY!
I'VE GOTTA MAKE A BREAK FOR IT!!
WELL... OKAY THEN... GOODBYE!
ASHIYA!
ULP
I'LL LOOK FORWARD TO THE NEXT TIME WE MEET.
WHAT SHOULD I DO...?
WHAT CAN I DO!?
IT COULD BE SOME KIND OF WILD GUESS...

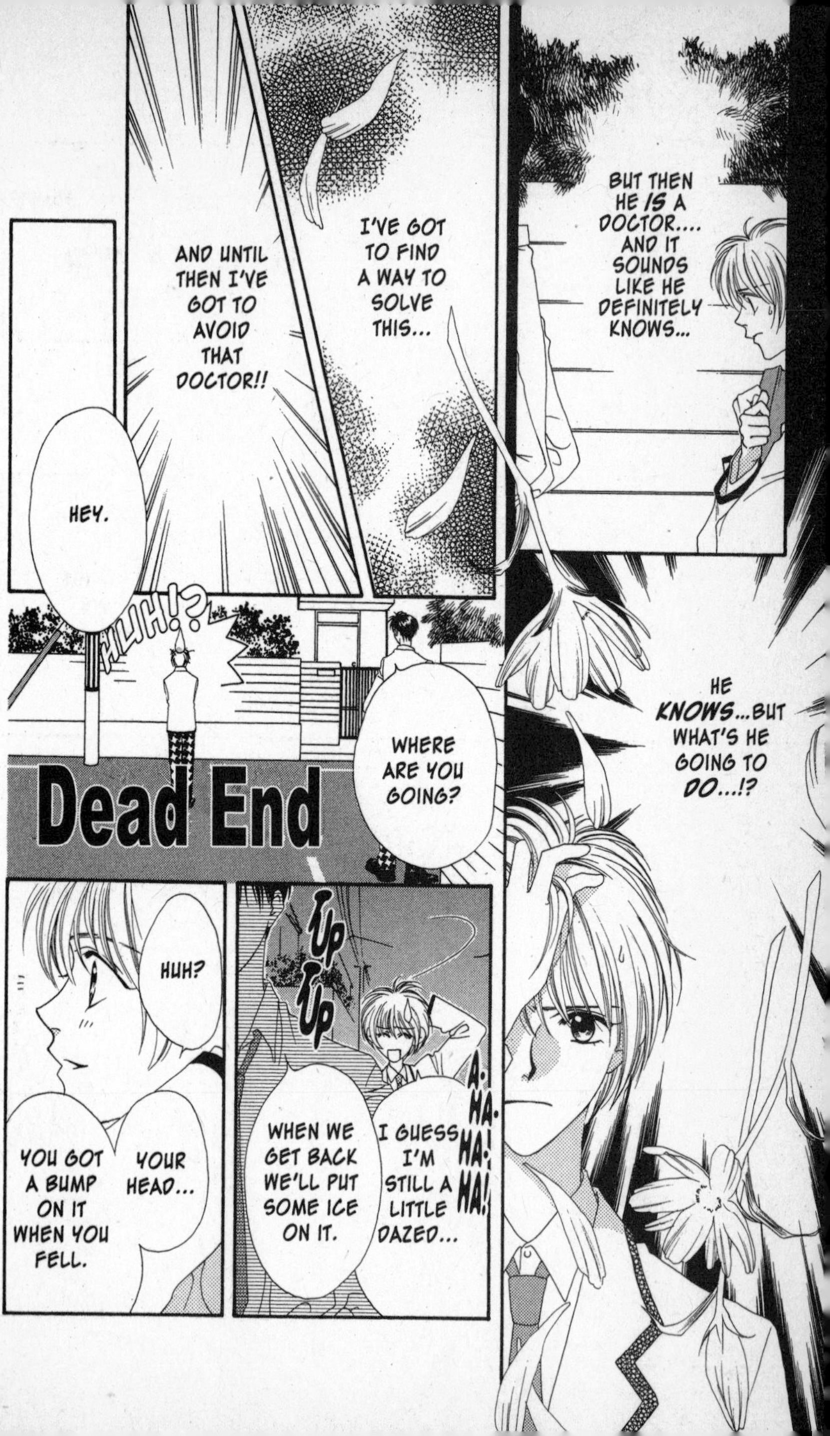
BUT THEN HE IS A DOCTOR.... AND IT SOUNDS LIKE HE DEFINITELY KNOWS...
HE KNOWS...BUT WHAT'S HE GOING TO DO...!?
I'VE GOT TO FIND A WAY TO SOLVE THIS...
AND UNTIL THEN I'VE GOT TO AVOID THAT DOCTOR!!
HEY.
HUH!?
WHERE ARE YOU GOING?
Dead End
UP UP
A-HA-HA-HA!
I GUESS I'M STILL A LITTLE DAZED...
WHEN WE GET BACK WE'LL PUT SOME ICE ON IT.
HUH?
YOUR HEAD...
YOU GOT A BUMP ON IT WHEN YOU FELL.

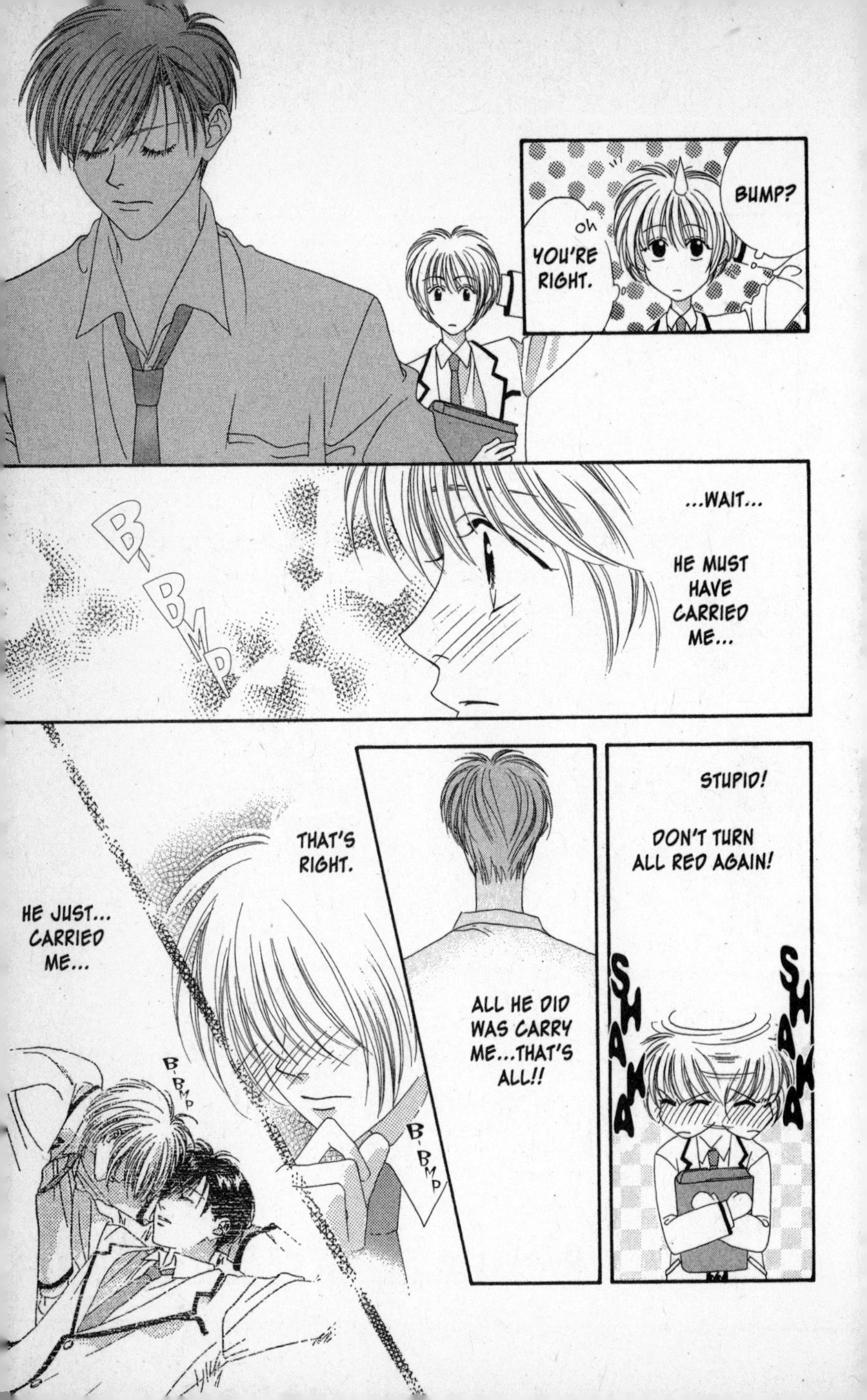
BUMP?
oh
YOU'RE RIGHT.
...WAIT...
HE MUST HAVE CARRIED ME...
B-BMP
STUPID!
DON'T TURN ALL RED AGAIN!
SHAKA
SHAKA
ALL HE DID WAS CARRY ME...THAT'S ALL!!
THAT'S RIGHT.
HE JUST... CARRIED ME...
B-BMP
B-BMP

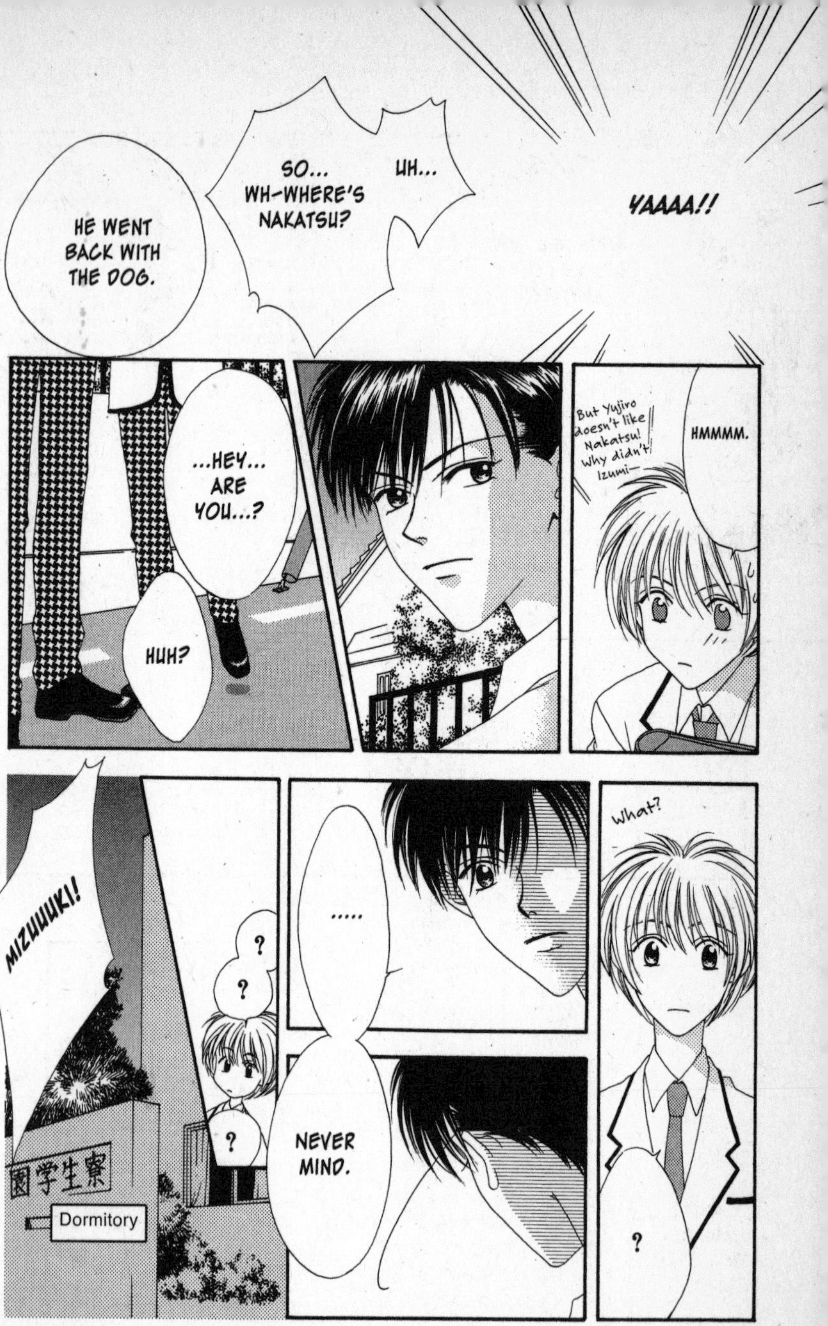
YAAAA!!
UH...
SO... WH-WHERE'S NAKATSU?
HE WENT BACK WITH THE DOG.
HMMMM.
But Yujiro doesn't like Nakatsu! Why didn't Izumi—
...HEY... ARE YOU...?
HUH?
What?
?
.....
NEVER MIND.
?
?
?
MIZUUUKI!
園学生寮
Dormitory

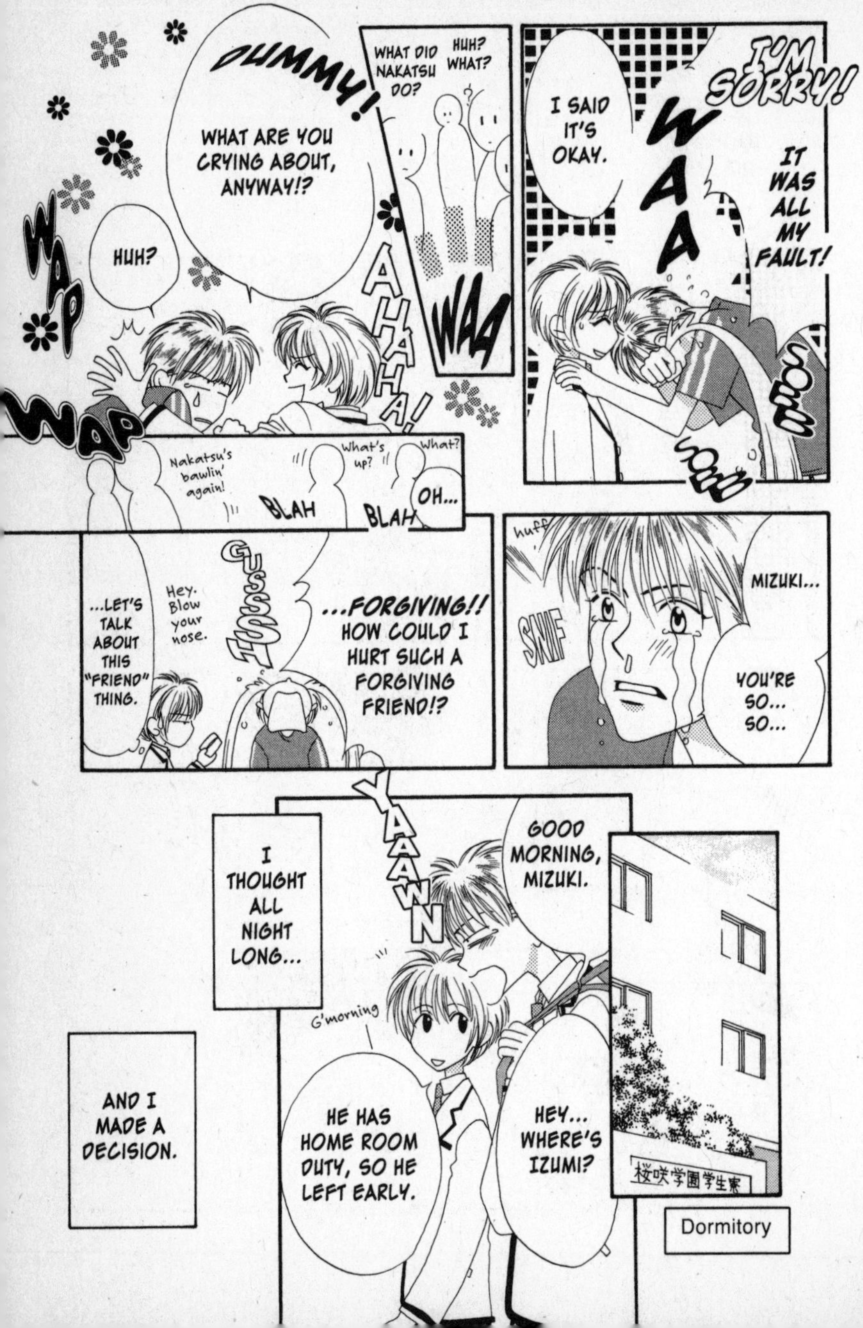
I'M SORRY!
IT WAS ALL MY FAULT!
WAA
I SAID IT'S OKAY.
SOB SOB
WHAT DID NAKATSU DO?
HUH? WHAT?
WAA
DUMMY!
WHAT ARE YOU CRYING ABOUT, ANYWAY!?
AHAHAHA!
HUH?
WAP
WAP
What?
What's up?
OH...
BLAH
BLAH
Nakatsu's bawlin' again!
huff
MIZUKI...
YOU'RE SO... SO...
SNIF
...FORGIVING!! HOW COULD I HURT SUCH A FORGIVING FRIEND!?
GUSSSH
Hey. Blow your nose.
...LET'S TALK ABOUT THIS "FRIEND" THING.
桜咲学園学生寮
Dormitory
GOOD MORNING, MIZUKI.
YAAAWN
HEY... WHERE'S IZUMI?
G'morning
HE HAS HOME ROOM DUTY, SO HE LEFT EARLY.
I THOUGHT ALL NIGHT LONG...
AND I MADE A DECISION.

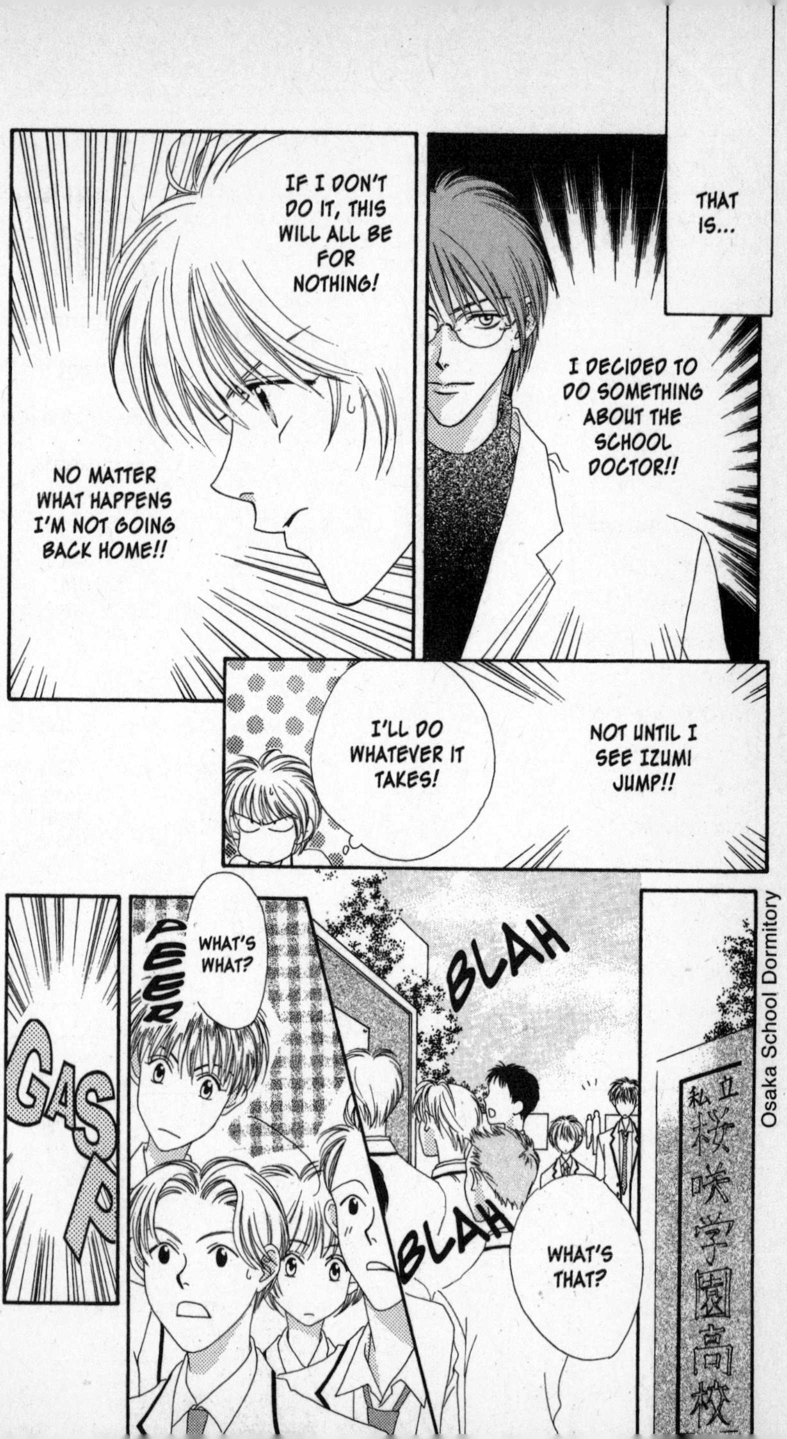
THAT IS...
I DECIDED TO DO SOMETHING ABOUT THE SCHOOL DOCTOR!!
IF I DON'T DO IT, THIS WILL ALL BE FOR NOTHING!
NO MATTER WHAT HAPPENS I'M NOT GOING BACK HOME!!
NOT UNTIL I SEE IZUMI JUMP!!
I'LL DO WHATEVER IT TAKES!
Osaka School Dormitory
私立桜咲学園高校
BLAH
WHAT'S THAT?
BLAH
PEER
WHAT'S WHAT?
GASP

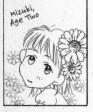

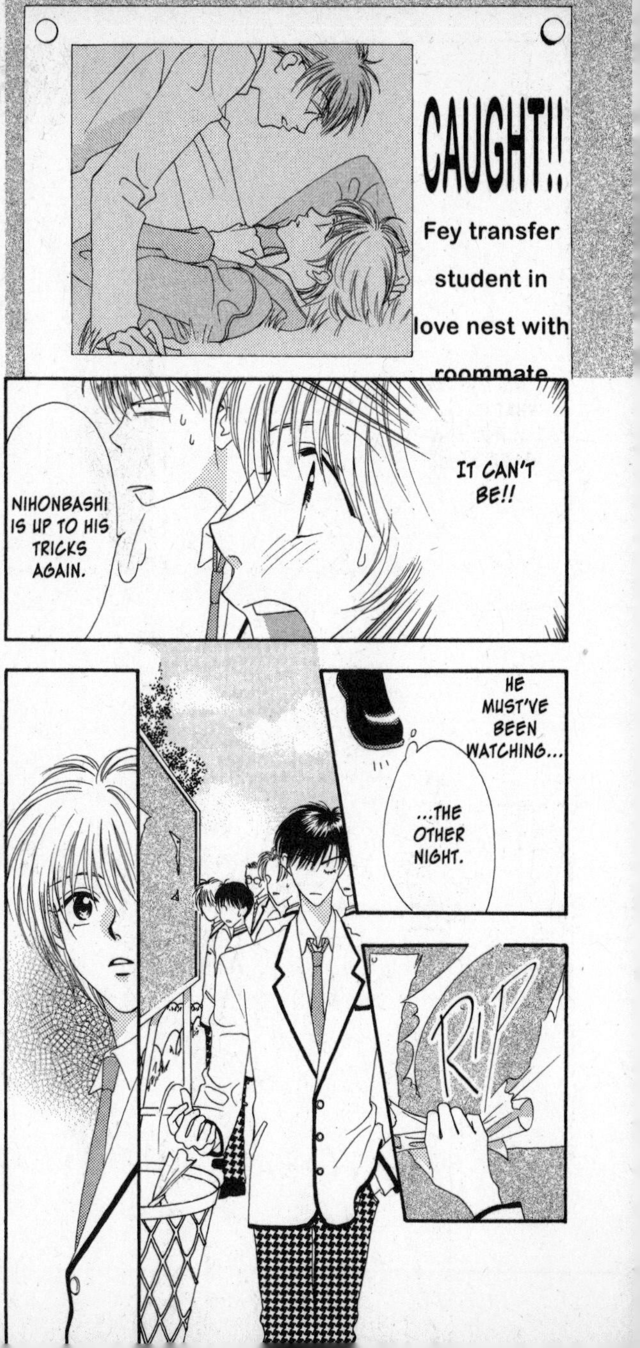
CAUGHT!!
Fey transfer student in love nest with roommate
IT CAN'T BE!!
NIHONBASHI IS UP TO HIS TRICKS AGAIN.
HE MUST'VE BEEN WATCHING...
...THE OTHER NIGHT.
RIP

About Mizuki

ACTUALLY (I KNOW I USE THAT WORD TOO MUCH), I GOT THE NAME MIZUKI FROM THE DAUGHTER OF A FRIEND OF MINE. SHE'S SO CUTE SHE LOOKS JUST LIKE HER MOTHER! I GENERALLY DON'T REALLY LIKE KIDS (BUT FOR SOME REASON THEY LIKE ME). BUT APPARENTLY I'M GOOD AT TAKING CARE OF THEM. I'M LUCKY BECAUSE I GET TO HANG OUT WITH MY FRIENDS' KIDS WITHOUT HAVING MY OWN. EVERY YEAR I GET ALL EXCITED ABOUT WHAT TO GET MIZUKI FOR HER BIRTHDAY.

Mizuki, Age Two

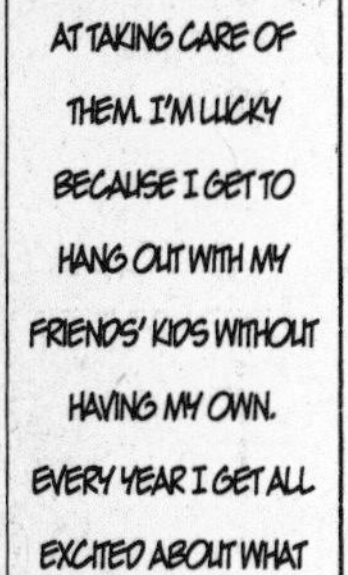

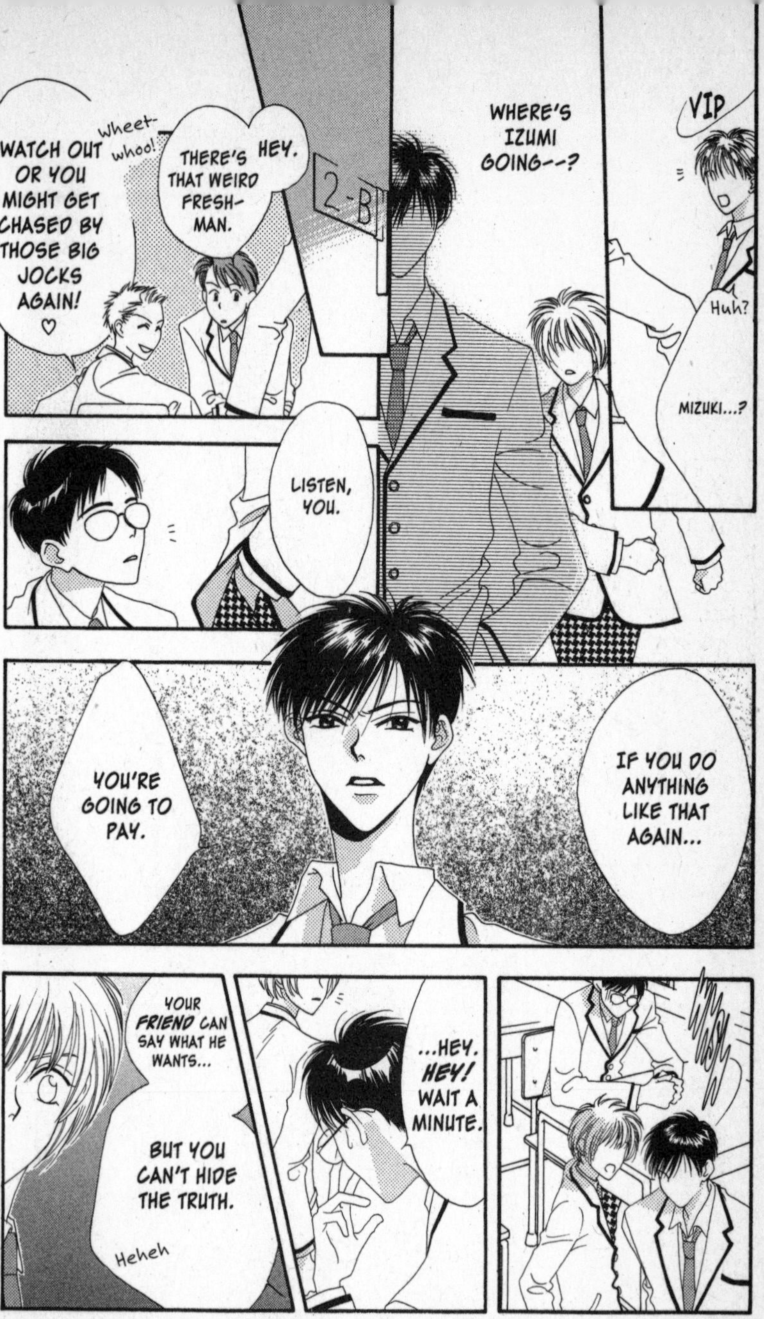
VIP
Huh?
MIZUKI...?
WHERE'S IZUMI GOING--?
HEY.
THERE'S THAT WEIRD FRESHMAN.
Wheet-whoo!
WATCH OUT OR YOU MIGHT GET CHASED BY THOSE BIG JOCKS AGAIN! ♡
LISTEN, YOU.
IF YOU DO ANYTHING LIKE THAT AGAIN...
YOU'RE GOING TO PAY.
...HEY. HEY! WAIT A MINUTE.
YOUR FRIEND CAN SAY WHAT HE WANTS...
BUT YOU CAN'T HIDE THE TRUTH.
Heheh

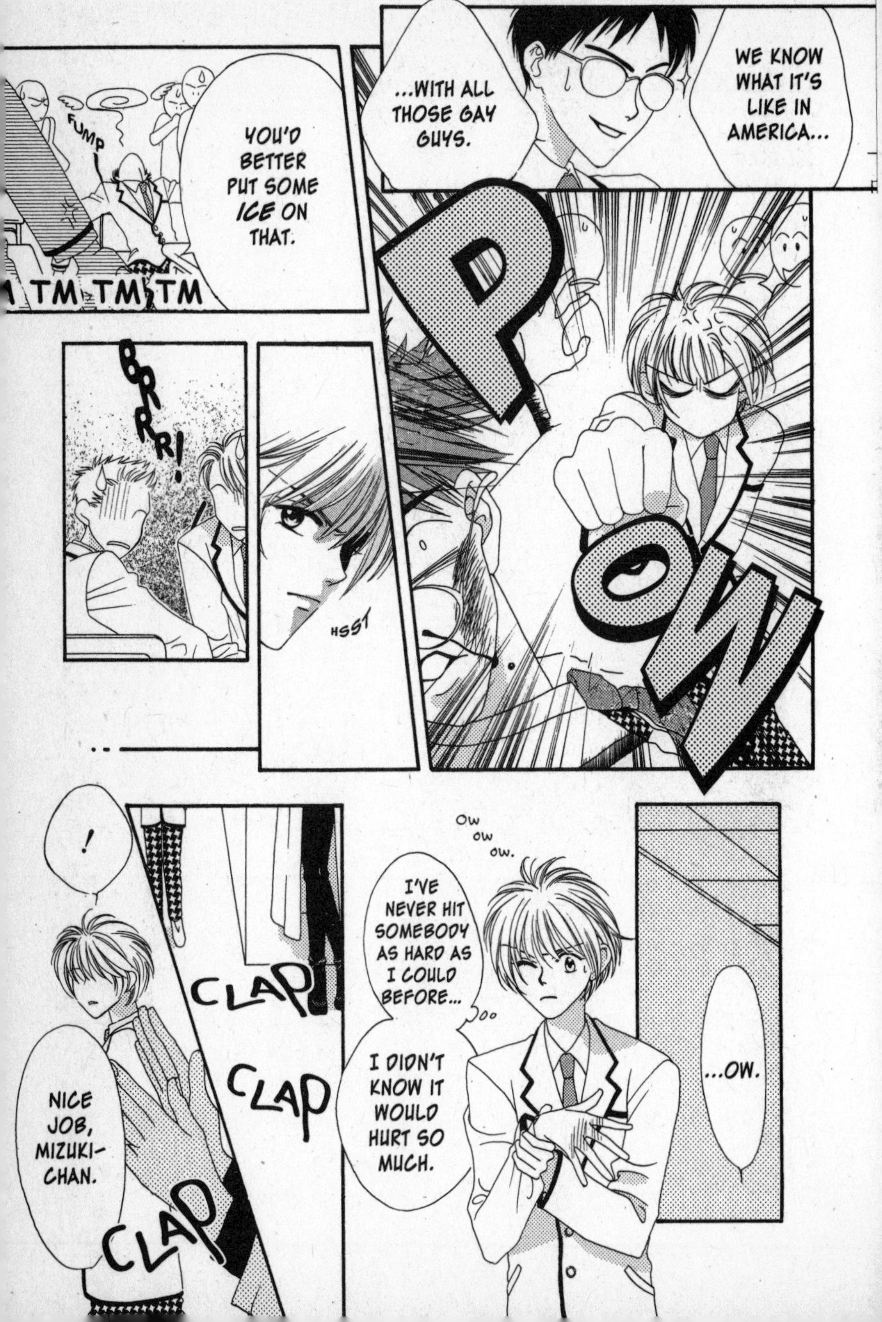
WE KNOW WHAT IT'S LIKE IN AMERICA...
...WITH ALL THOSE GAY GUYS.
POW
YOU'D BETTER PUT SOME ICE ON THAT.
FUMP
TM TM TM TM
HSST
BRRR!
...OW.
OW OW OW.
I'VE NEVER HIT SOMEBODY AS HARD AS I COULD BEFORE...
I DIDN'T KNOW IT WOULD HURT SO MUCH.
CLAP
CLAP
!
NICE JOB, MIZUKI-CHAN.
CLAP

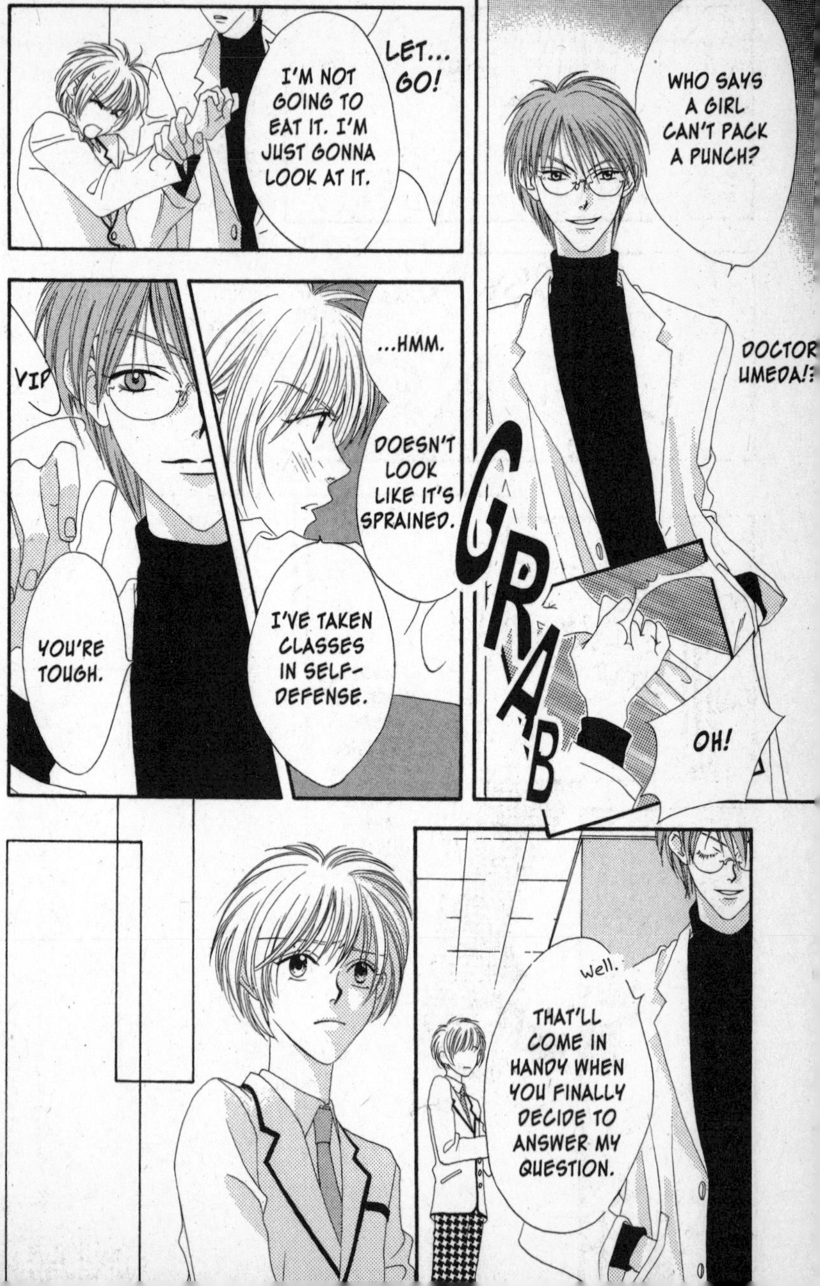
WHO SAYS A GIRL CAN'T PACK A PUNCH?
DOCTOR UMEDA!?
GRAB
OH!
LET... GO!
I'M NOT GOING TO EAT IT. I'M JUST GONNA LOOK AT IT.
...HMM.
DOESN'T LOOK LIKE IT'S SPRAINED.
I'VE TAKEN CLASSES IN SELF-DEFENSE.
VIP
YOU'RE TOUGH.
Well.
THAT'LL COME IN HANDY WHEN YOU FINALLY DECIDE TO ANSWER MY QUESTION.

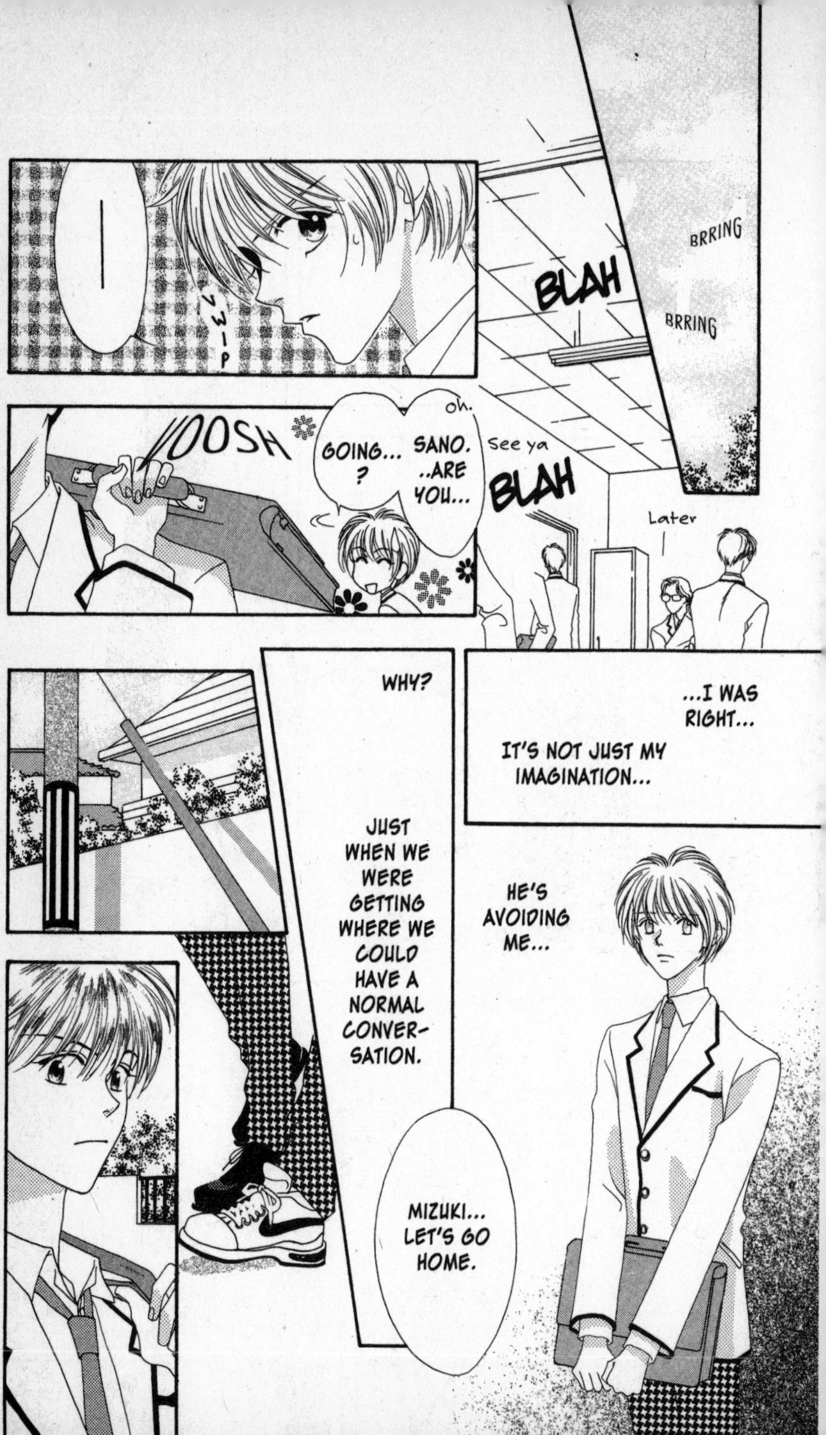
BRRING
BRRING
BLAH
See ya
BLAH
Later
VWIP
VOOSH
oh. SANO. ..ARE YOU... GOING... ?
...I WAS RIGHT...
IT'S NOT JUST MY IMAGINATION...
HE'S AVOIDING ME...
WHY?
JUST WHEN WE WERE GETTING WHERE WE COULD HAVE A NORMAL CONVER-SATION.
MIZUKI... LET'S GO HOME.

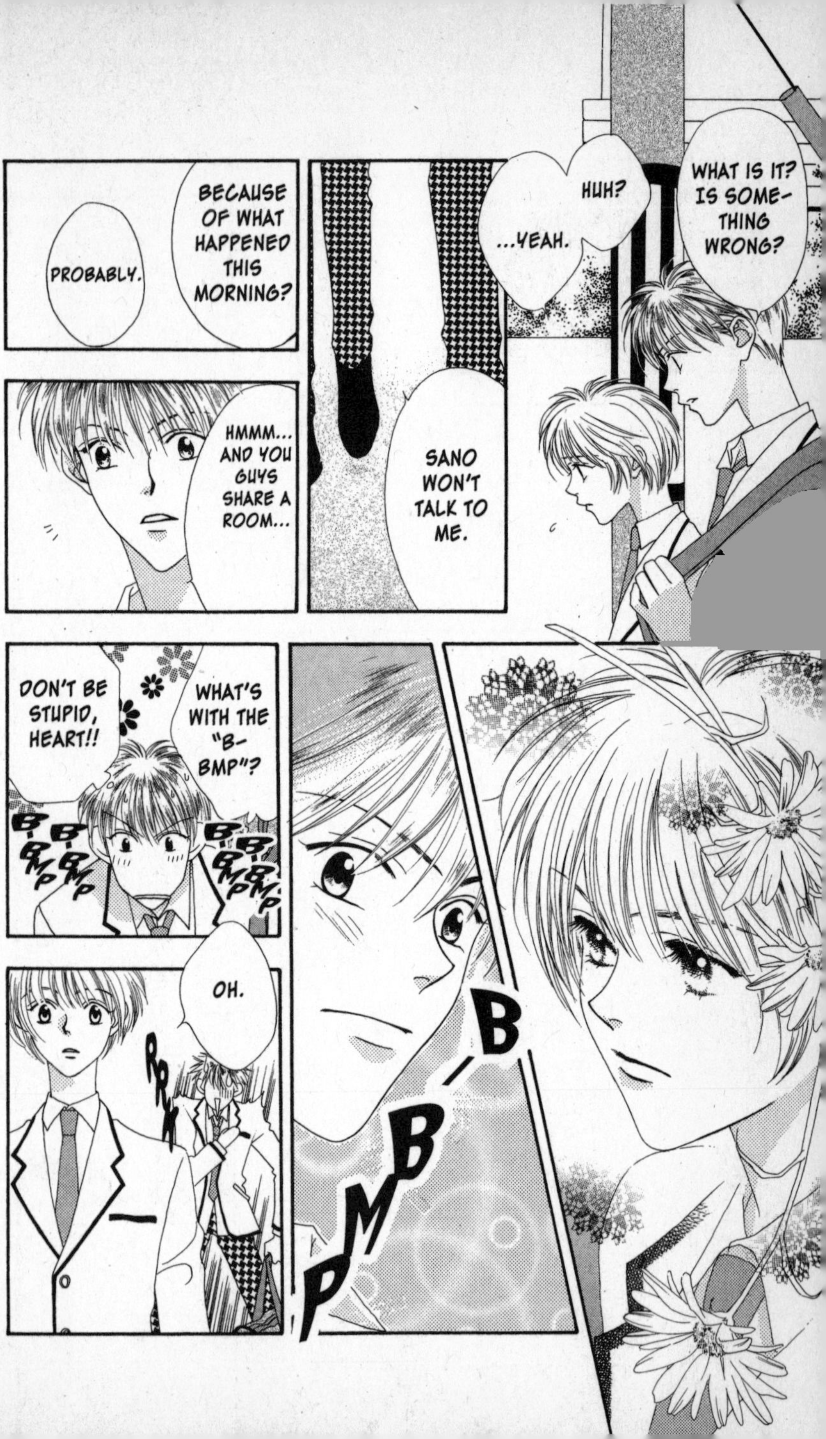
WHAT IS IT? IS SOME-THING WRONG?
HUH?
...YEAH.
SANO WON'T TALK TO ME.
BECAUSE OF WHAT HAPPENED THIS MORNING?
PROBABLY.
HMMM... AND YOU GUYS SHARE A ROOM...
B-BMP
WHAT'S WITH THE "B-BMP"?
DON'T BE STUPID, HEART!!
B-BMP B-BMP
B-BMP B-BMP
OH.
RRUK

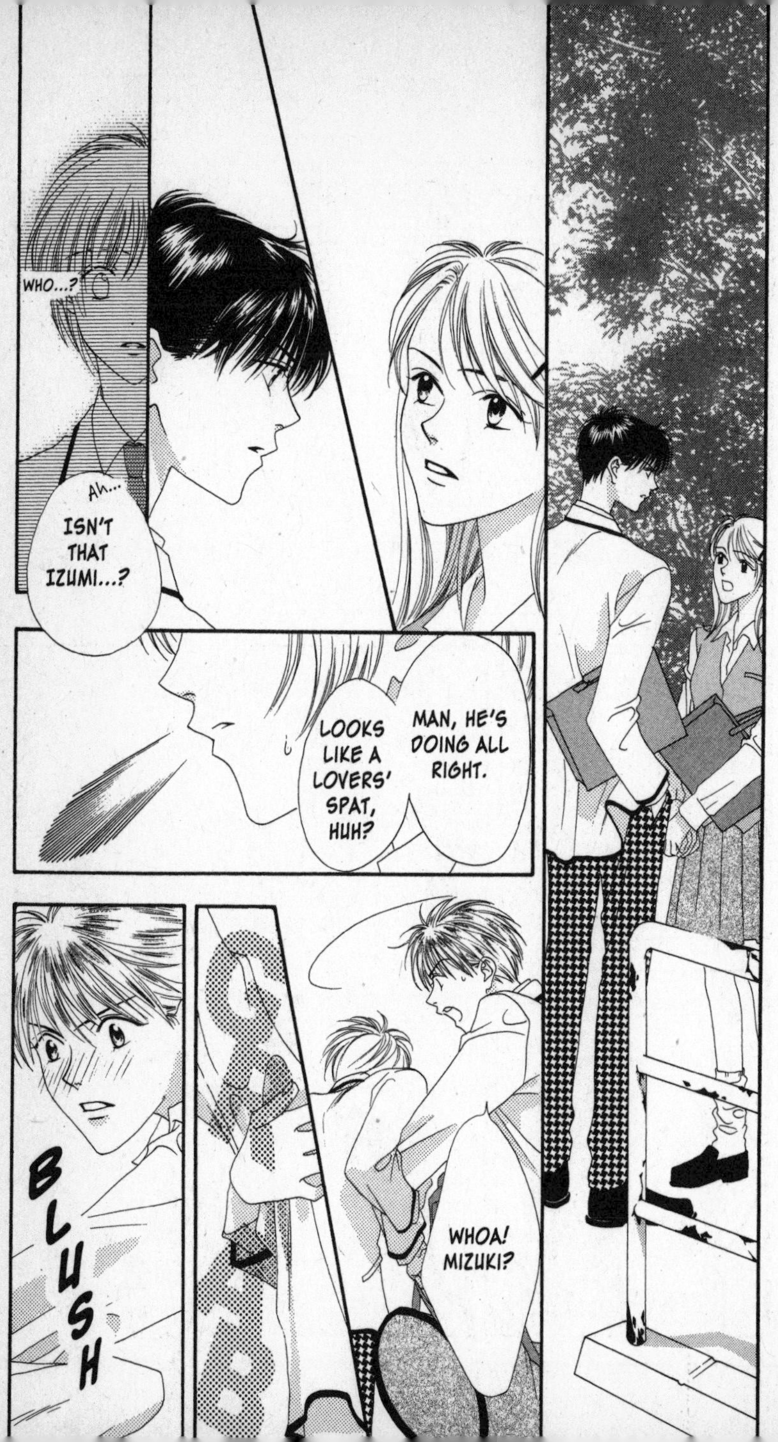
WHO...?
Ah... ISN'T THAT IZUMI...?
MAN, HE'S DOING ALL RIGHT.
LOOKS LIKE A LOVERS' SPAT, HUH?
WHOA! MIZUKI?
BLUSH

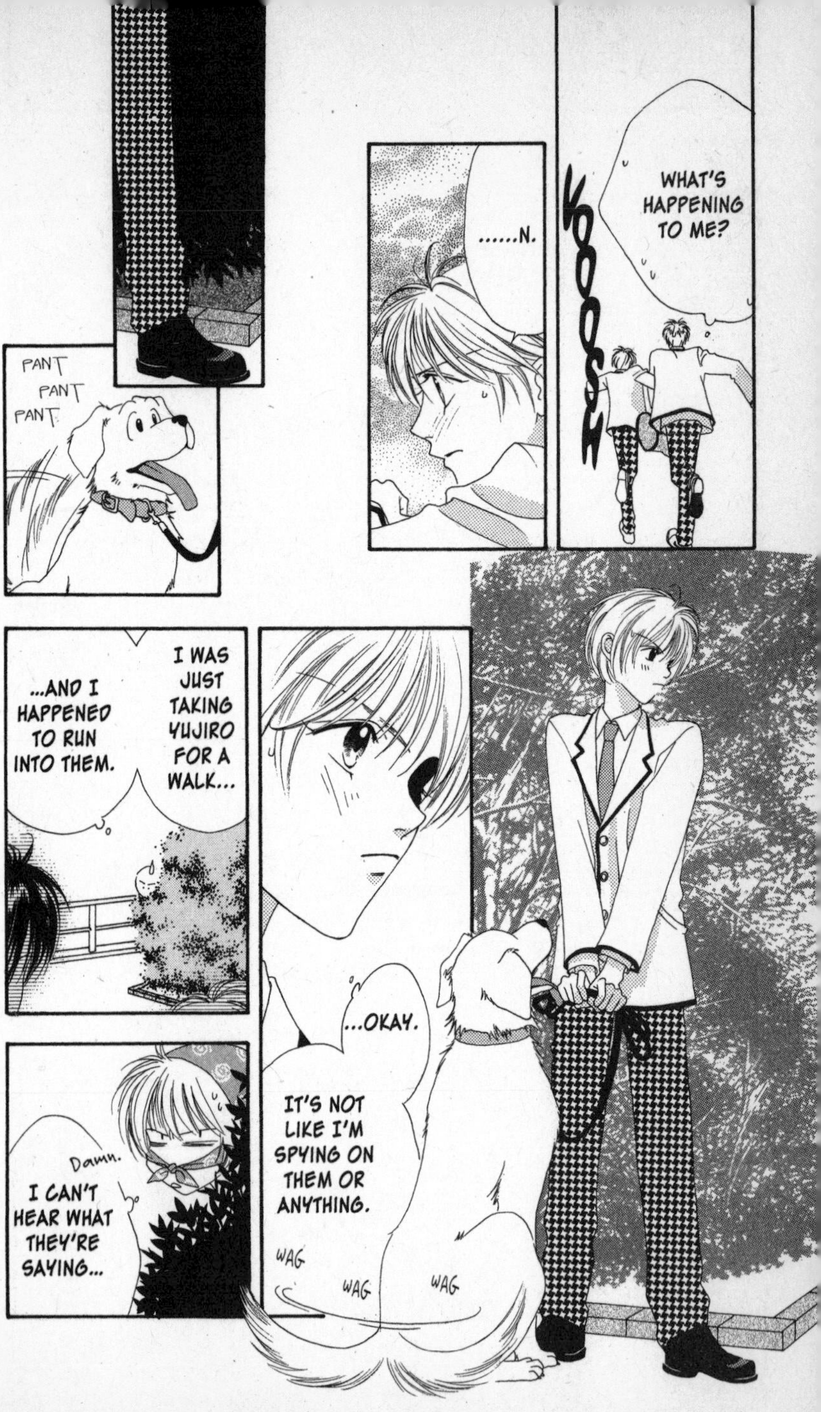
WHAT'S HAPPENING TO ME?
VOOOSH
......N.
PANT PANT PANT
...OKAY.
IT'S NOT LIKE I'M SPYING ON THEM OR ANYTHING.
WAG WAG WAG
I WAS JUST TAKING YUJIRO FOR A WALK...
...AND I HAPPENED TO RUN INTO THEM.
Damn.
I CAN'T HEAR WHAT THEY'RE SAYING...

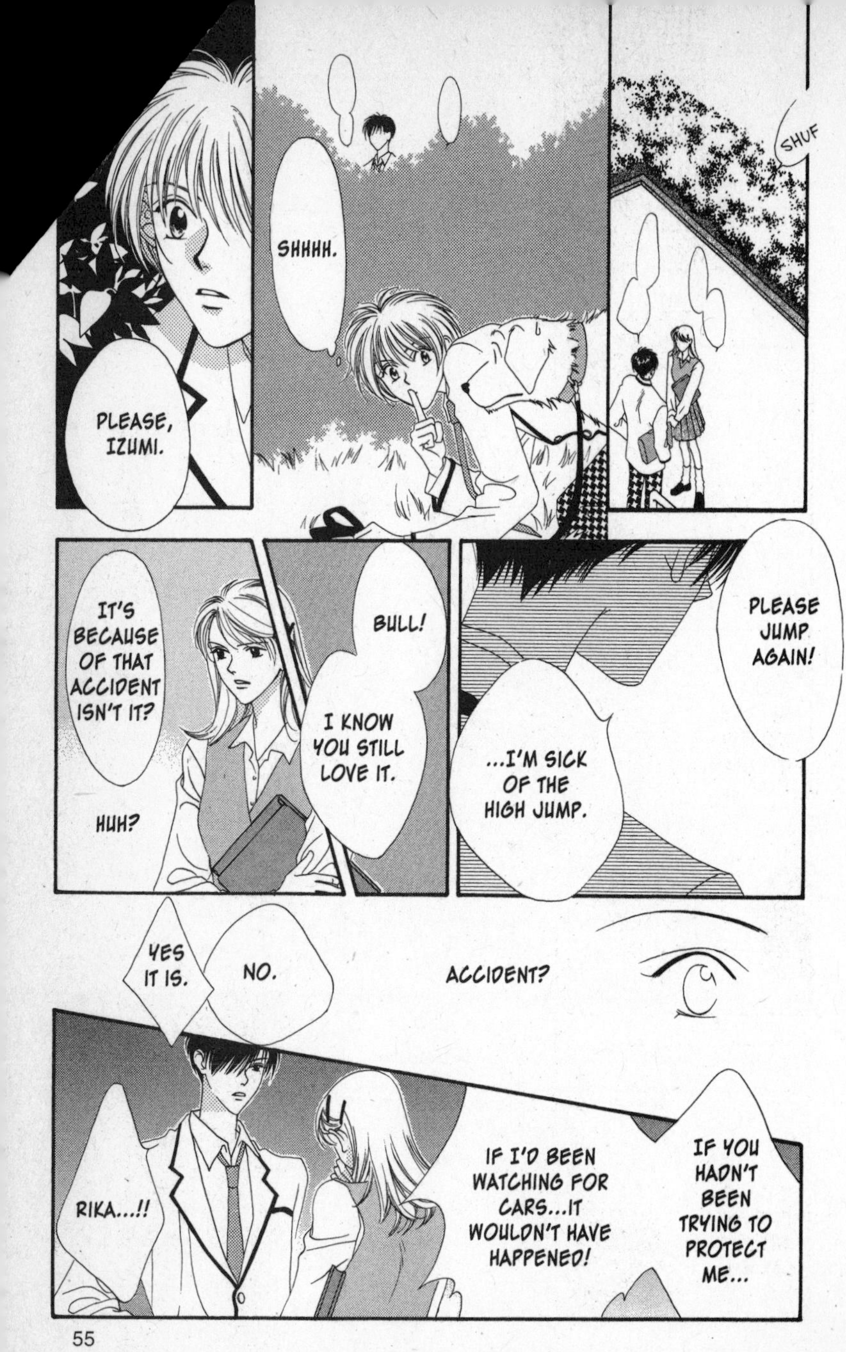
SHUF
SHHHH.
PLEASE, IZUMI.
PLEASE JUMP AGAIN!
...I'M SICK OF THE HIGH JUMP.
BULL!
I KNOW YOU STILL LOVE IT.
IT'S BECAUSE OF THAT ACCIDENT ISN'T IT?
HUH?
ACCIDENT?
NO.
YES IT IS.
IF YOU HADN'T BEEN TRYING TO PROTECT ME...
IF I'D BEEN WATCHING FOR CARS...IT WOULDN'T HAVE HAPPENED!
RIKA...!!

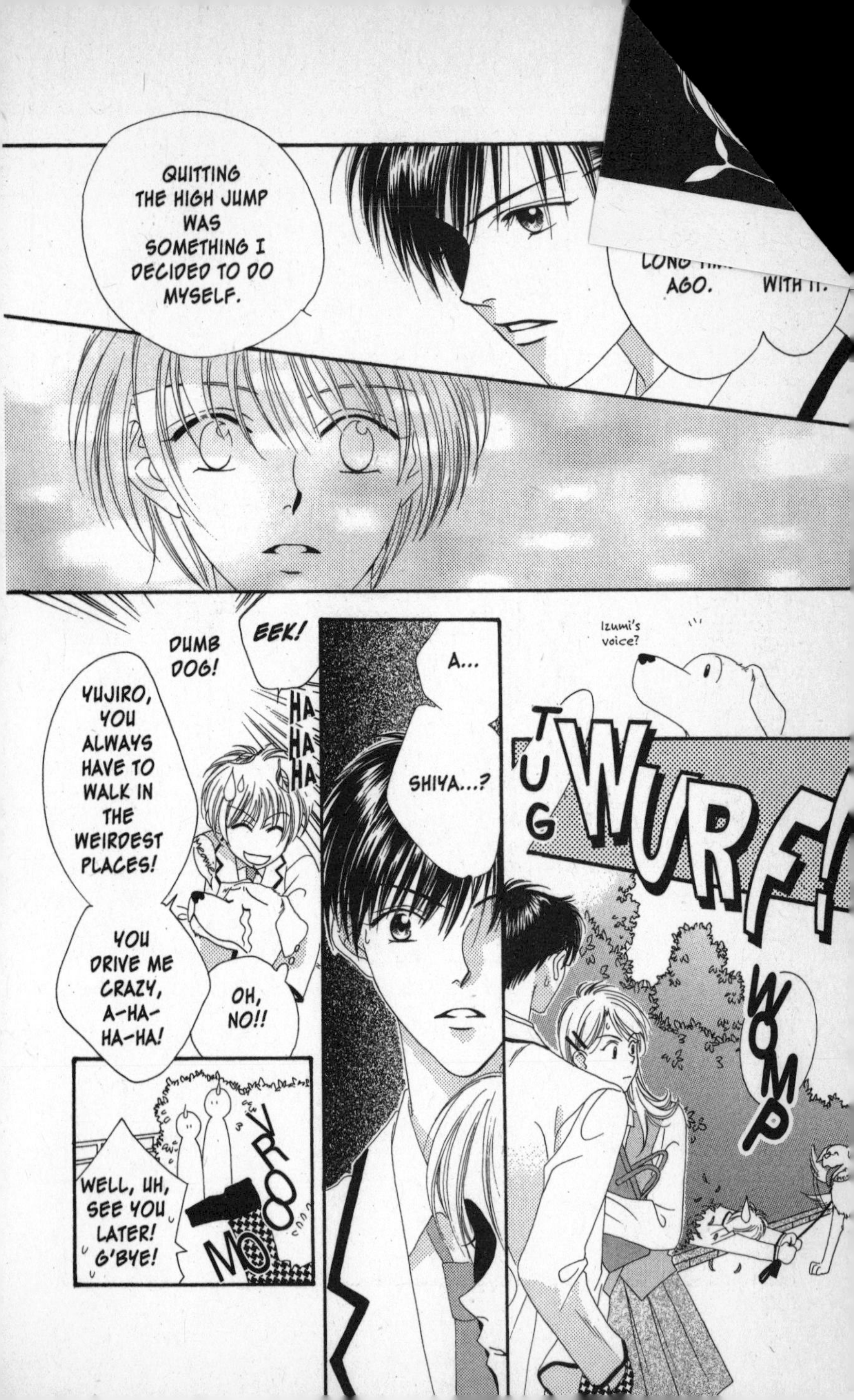
WITH IT.
AGO.
QUITTING THE HIGH JUMP WAS SOMETHING I DECIDED TO DO MYSELF.
Izumi's voice?
TUG
WURF!
WOMP
A...
SHIYA...?
EEK!
DUMB DOG!
HA HA HA
YUJIRO, YOU ALWAYS HAVE TO WALK IN THE WEIRDEST PLACES!
YOU DRIVE ME CRAZY, A-HA-HA-HA!
OH, NO!!
VROOOM
WELL, UH, SEE YOU LATER! G'BYE!

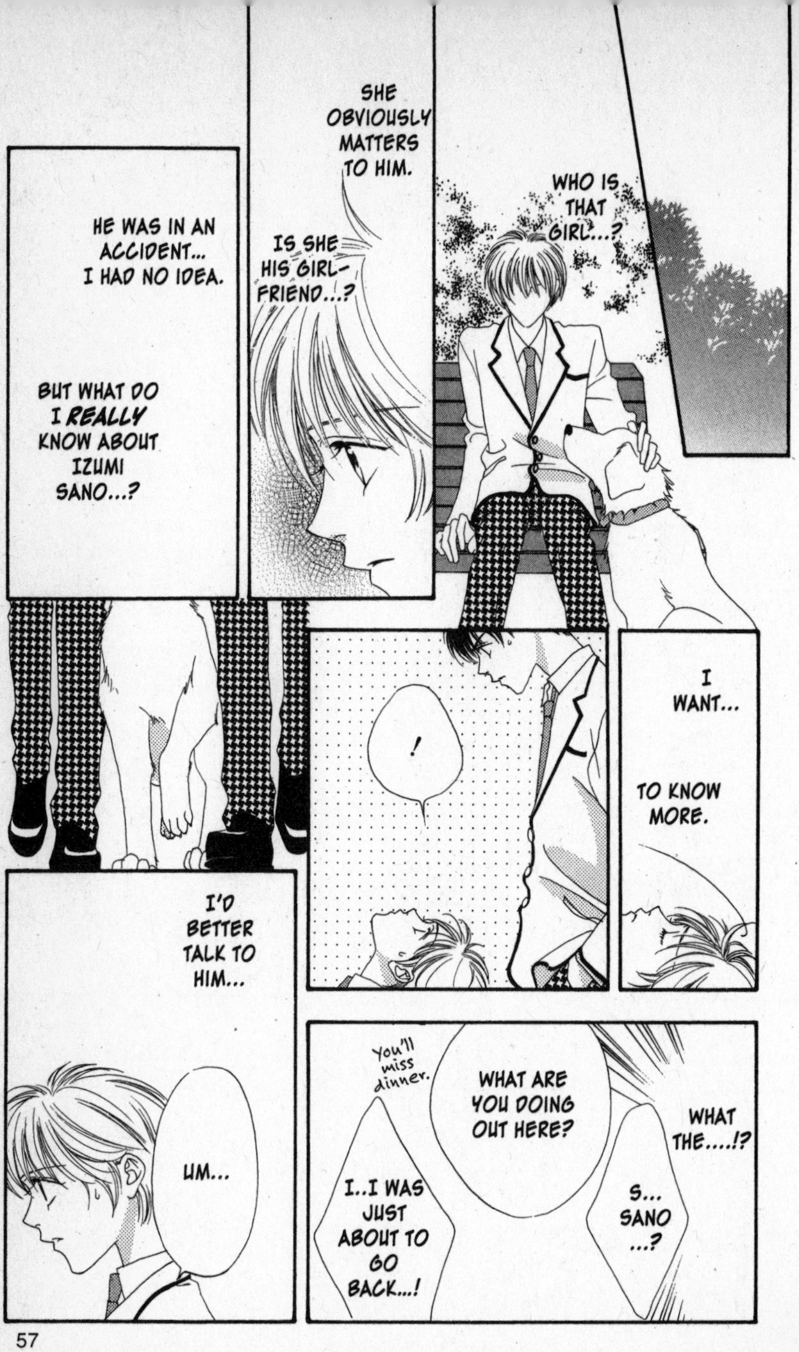
WHO IS THAT GIRL...?
SHE OBVIOUSLY MATTERS TO HIM.
IS SHE HIS GIRL-FRIEND...?
HE WAS IN AN ACCIDENT... I HAD NO IDEA.
BUT WHAT DO I *REALLY* KNOW ABOUT IZUMI SANO...?
I WANT...
TO KNOW MORE.
!
WHAT THE....!?
S... SANO ...?
WHAT ARE YOU DOING OUT HERE?
You'll miss dinner.
I..I WAS JUST ABOUT TO GO BACK...!
I'D BETTER TALK TO HIM...
UM...

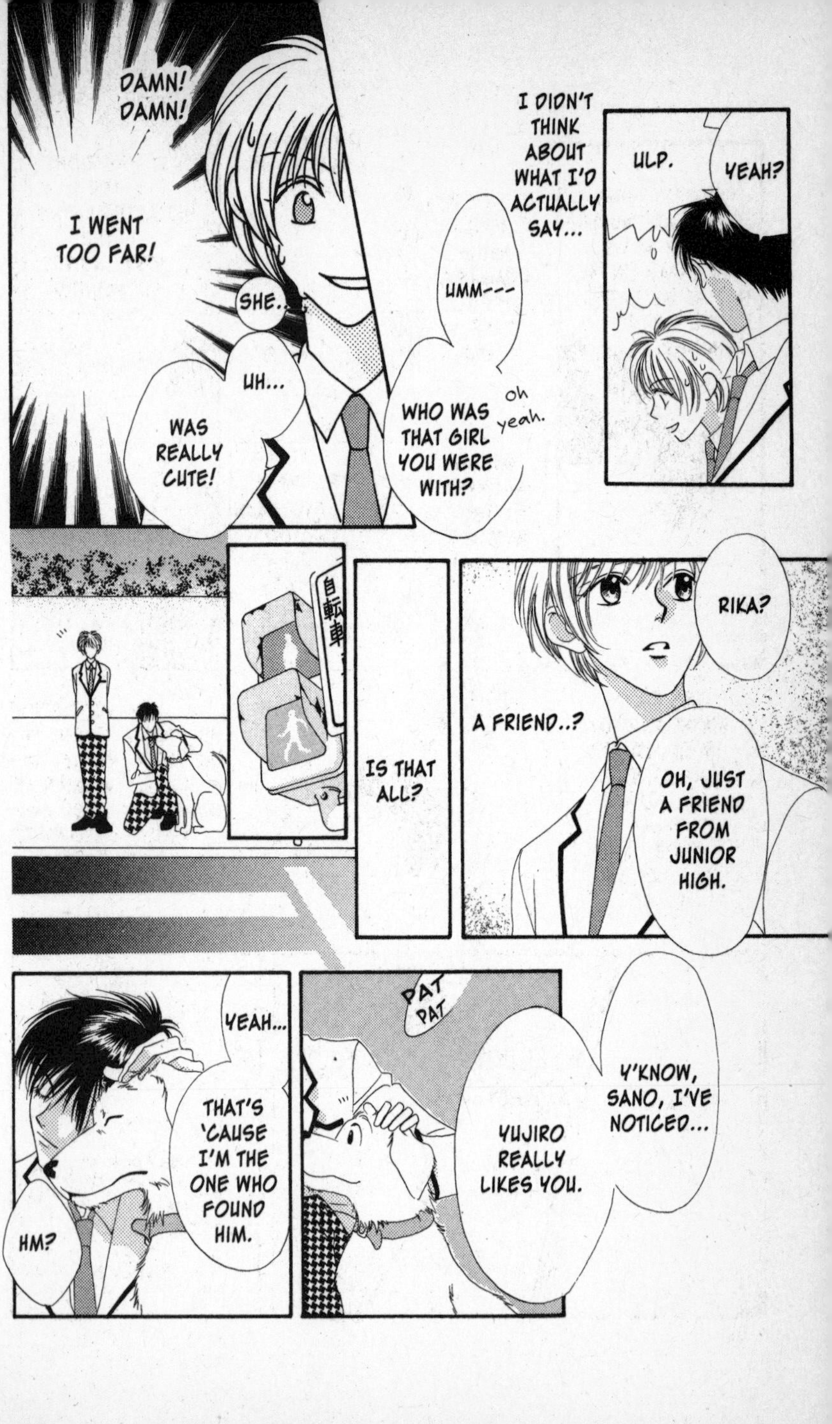
YEAH?
ULP.
I DIDN'T THINK ABOUT WHAT I'D ACTUALLY SAY...
UMM---
WHO WAS THAT GIRL YOU WERE WITH?
oh yeah.
DAMN! DAMN!
I WENT TOO FAR!
SHE...
UH...
WAS REALLY CUTE!
RIKA?
OH, JUST A FRIEND FROM JUNIOR HIGH.
A FRIEND..?
IS THAT ALL?
自転車
Y'KNOW, SANO, I'VE NOTICED...
YUJIRO REALLY LIKES YOU.
PAT PAT
YEAH...
THAT'S 'CAUSE I'M THE ONE WHO FOUND HIM.
HM?

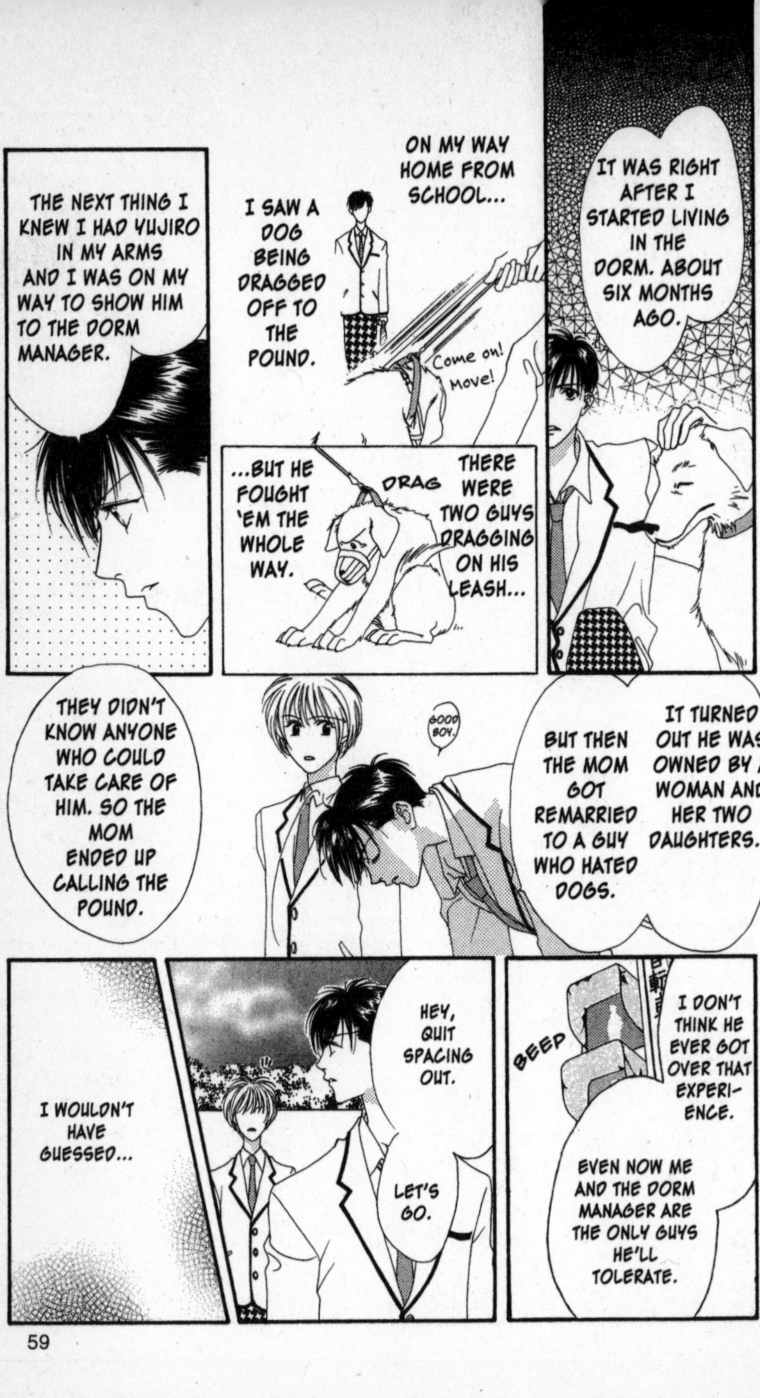
IT WAS RIGHT AFTER I STARTED LIVING IN THE DORM. ABOUT SIX MONTHS AGO.
ON MY WAY HOME FROM SCHOOL...
I SAW A DOG BEING DRAGGED OFF TO THE POUND.
Come on! Move!
THERE WERE TWO GUYS DRAGGING ON HIS LEASH...
DRAG
...BUT HE FOUGHT 'EM THE WHOLE WAY.
THE NEXT THING I KNEW I HAD YUJIRO IN MY ARMS AND I WAS ON MY WAY TO SHOW HIM TO THE DORM MANAGER.
IT TURNED OUT HE WAS OWNED BY A WOMAN AND HER TWO DAUGHTERS...
BUT THEN THE MOM GOT REMARRIED TO A GUY WHO HATED DOGS.
GOOD BOY.
THEY DIDN'T KNOW ANYONE WHO COULD TAKE CARE OF HIM. SO THE MOM ENDED UP CALLING THE POUND.
I DON'T THINK HE EVER GOT OVER THAT EXPERI- ENCE.
BEEP
EVEN NOW ME AND THE DORM MANAGER ARE THE ONLY GUYS HE'LL TOLERATE.
HEY, QUIT SPACING OUT.
LET'S GO.
I WOULDN'T HAVE GUESSED...

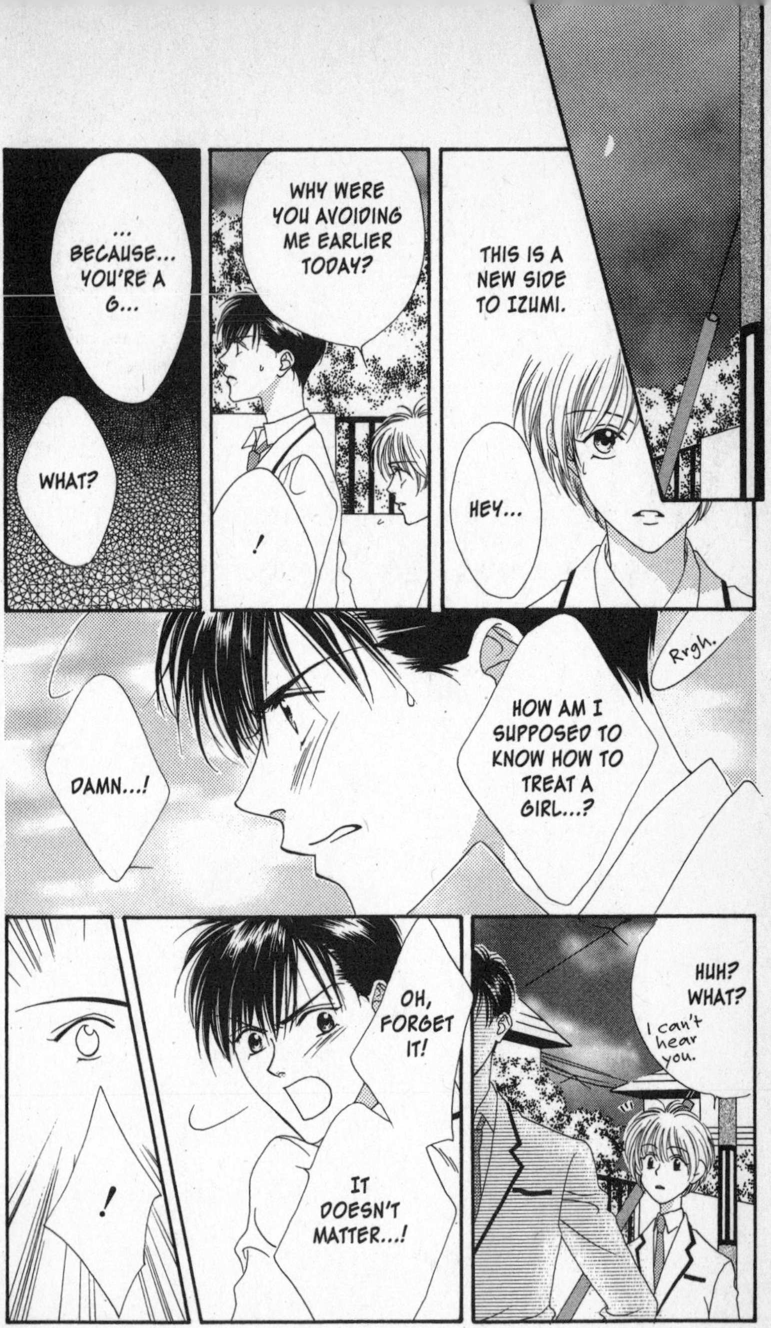
THIS IS A NEW SIDE TO IZUMI.
HEY...
WHY WERE YOU AVOIDING ME EARLIER TODAY?
!
... BECAUSE... YOU'RE A G...
WHAT?
Rrgh.
HOW AM I SUPPOSED TO KNOW HOW TO TREAT A GIRL...?
DAMN...!
HUH? WHAT?
I can't hear you.
OH, FORGET IT!
IT DOESN'T MATTER...!
!

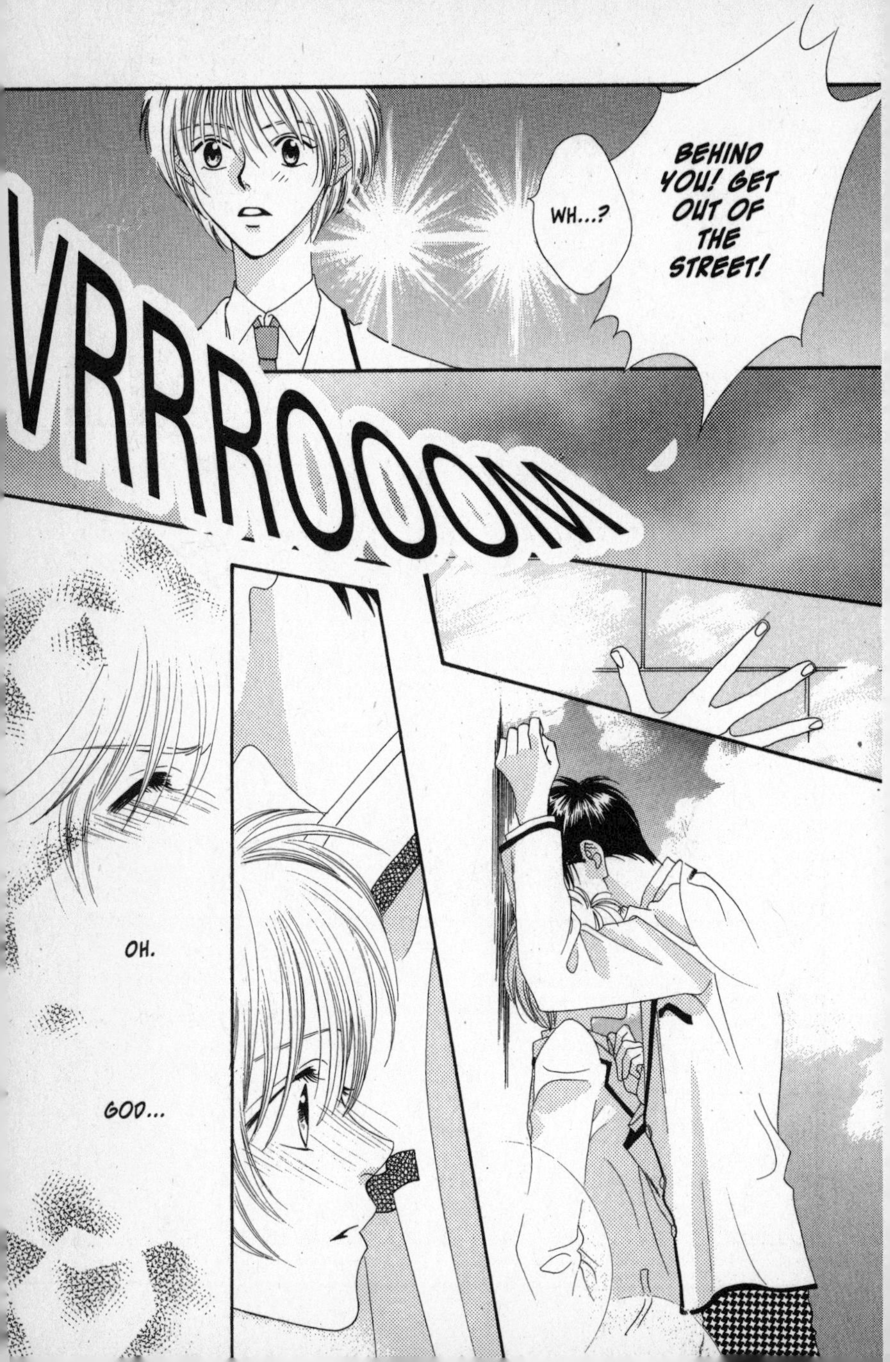
BEHIND YOU! GET OUT OF THE STREET!
WH...?
VRRROOOM
OH.
GOD...

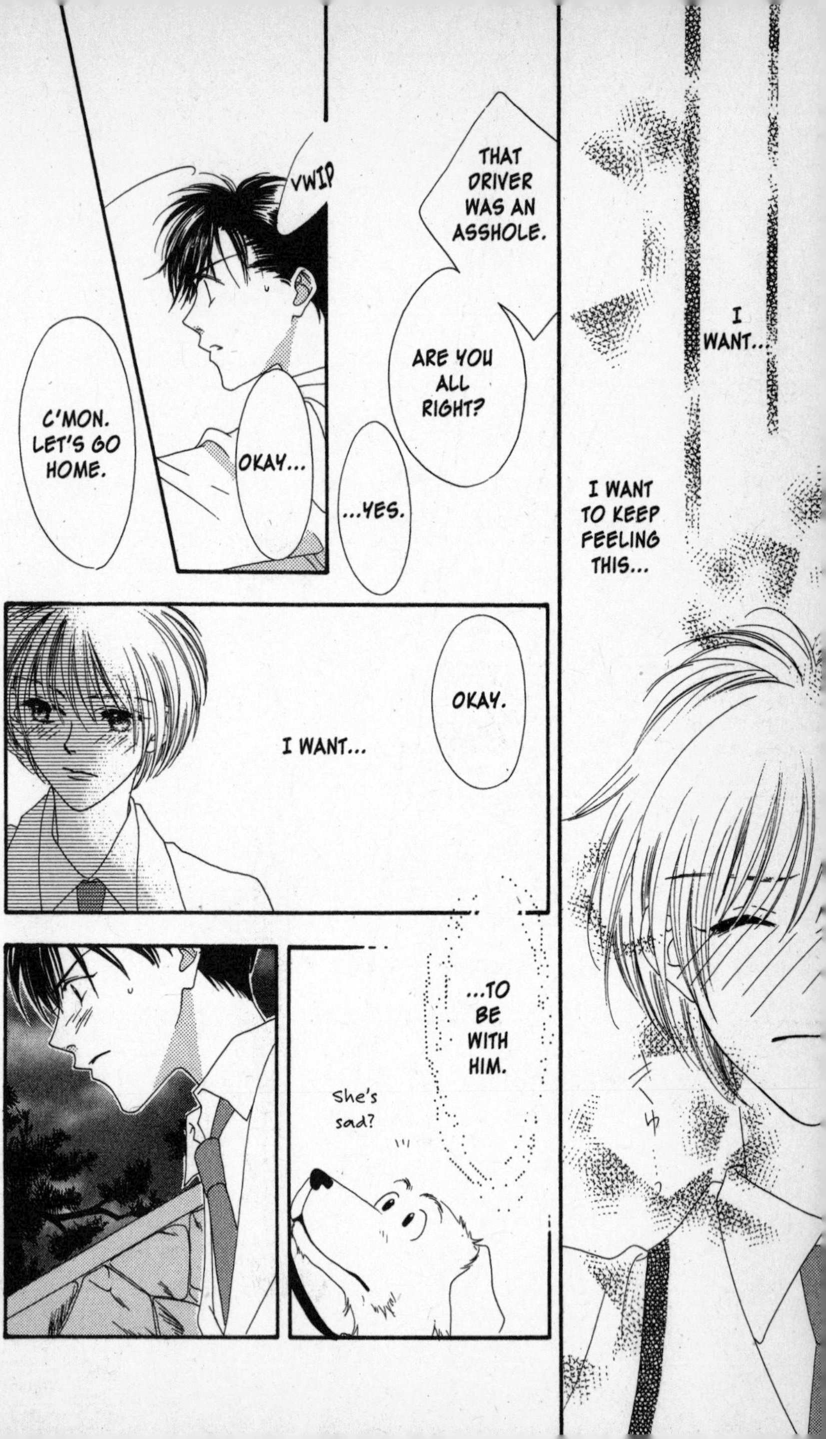
I WANT...
I WANT TO KEEP FEELING THIS...
THAT DRIVER WAS AN ASSHOLE.
VWIP
ARE YOU ALL RIGHT?
...YES.
OKAY...
C'MON. LET'S GO HOME.
OKAY.
I WANT...
...TO BE WITH HIM.
She's sad?

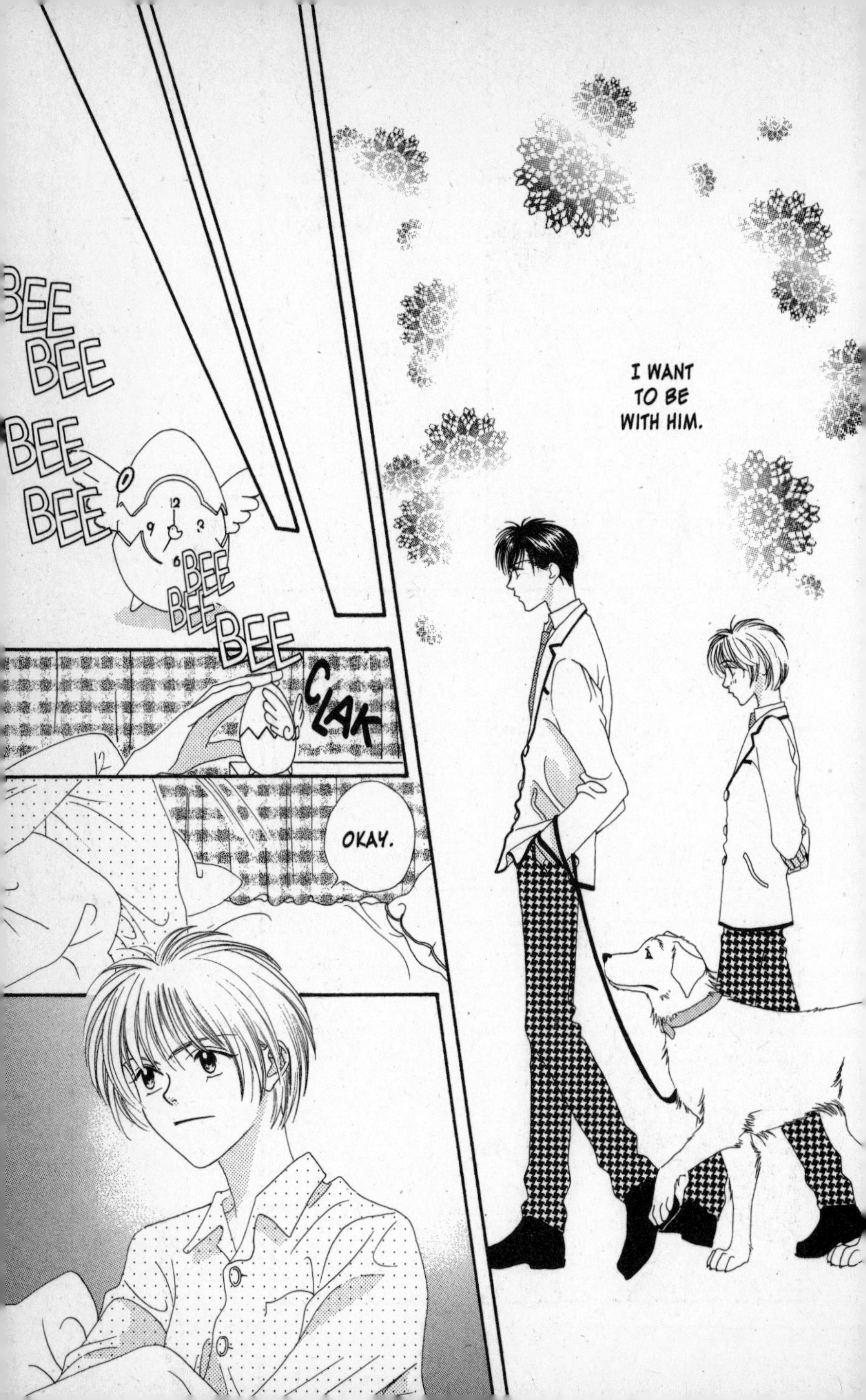
I WANT TO BE WITH HIM.
BEE
BEE
BEE
BEE
BEE
BEE
BEE
CLAK
OKAY.

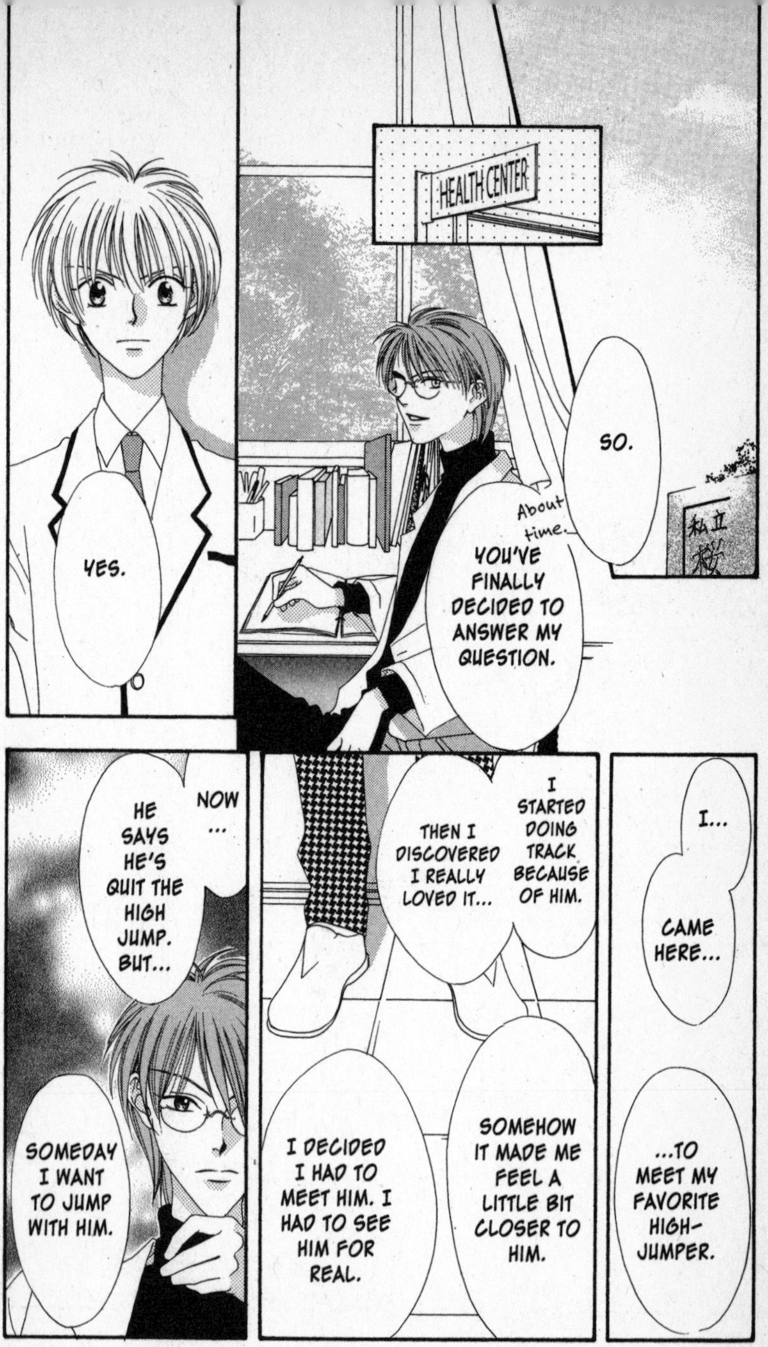
HEALTH CENTER
SO.
About time.
YOU'VE FINALLY DECIDED TO ANSWER MY QUESTION.
YES.
I...
CAME HERE...
...TO MEET MY FAVORITE HIGH-JUMPER.
I STARTED DOING TRACK BECAUSE OF HIM.
THEN I DISCOVERED I REALLY LOVED IT...
SOMEHOW IT MADE ME FEEL A LITTLE BIT CLOSER TO HIM.
I DECIDED I HAD TO MEET HIM. I HAD TO SEE HIM FOR REAL.
NOW...
HE SAYS HE'S QUIT THE HIGH JUMP. BUT...
SOMEDAY I WANT TO JUMP WITH HIM.

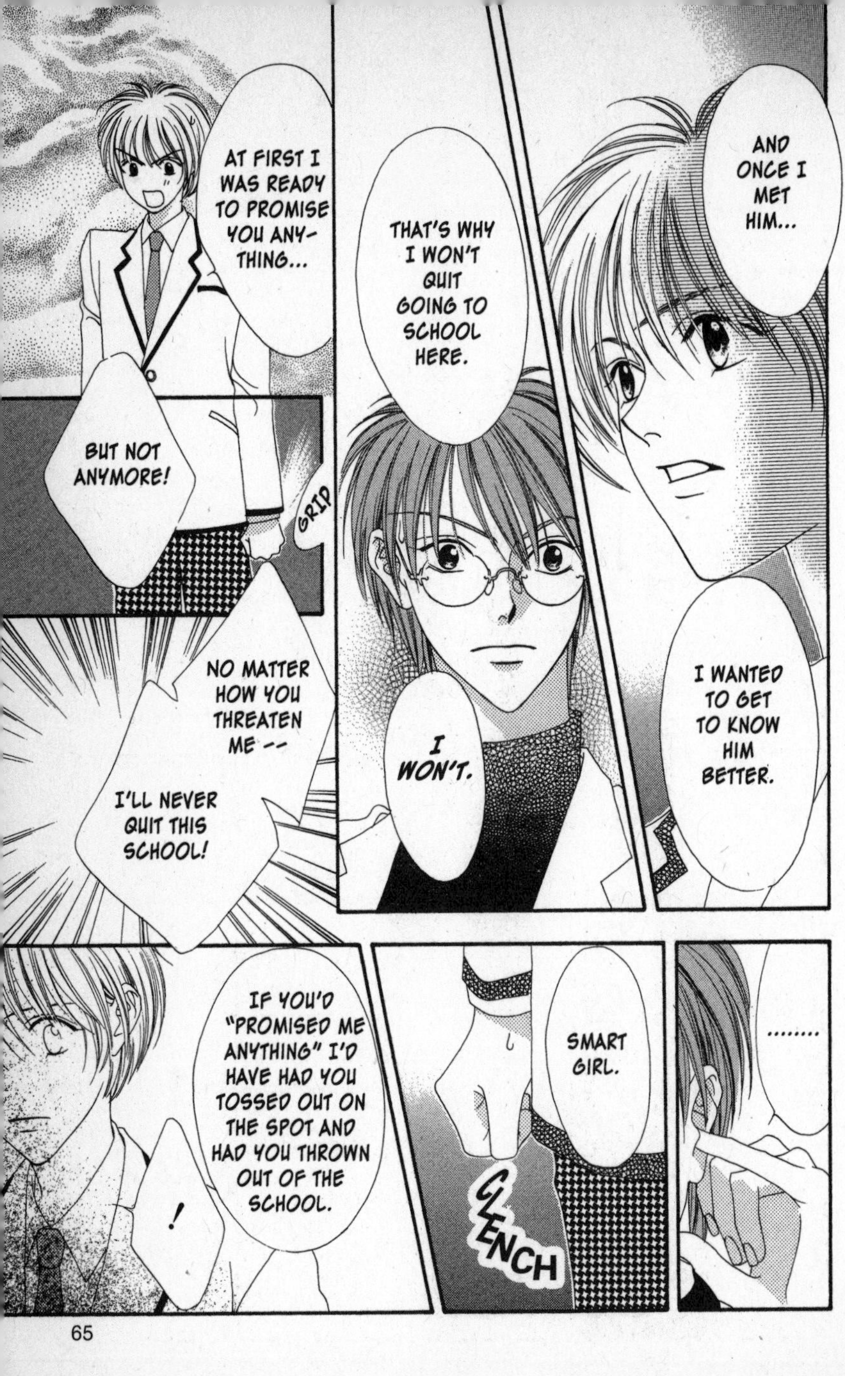

AND ONCE I MET HIM...
I WANTED TO GET TO KNOW HIM BETTER.
THAT'S WHY I WON'T QUIT GOING TO SCHOOL HERE.
I WON'T.
AT FIRST I WAS READY TO PROMISE YOU ANY-THING...
BUT NOT ANYMORE!
GRIP
NO MATTER HOW YOU THREATEN ME --
I'LL NEVER QUIT THIS SCHOOL!
....
SMART GIRL.
CLENCH
IF YOU'D "PROMISED ME ANYTHING" I'D HAVE HAD YOU TOSSED OUT ON THE SPOT AND HAD YOU THROWN OUT OF THE SCHOOL.
!

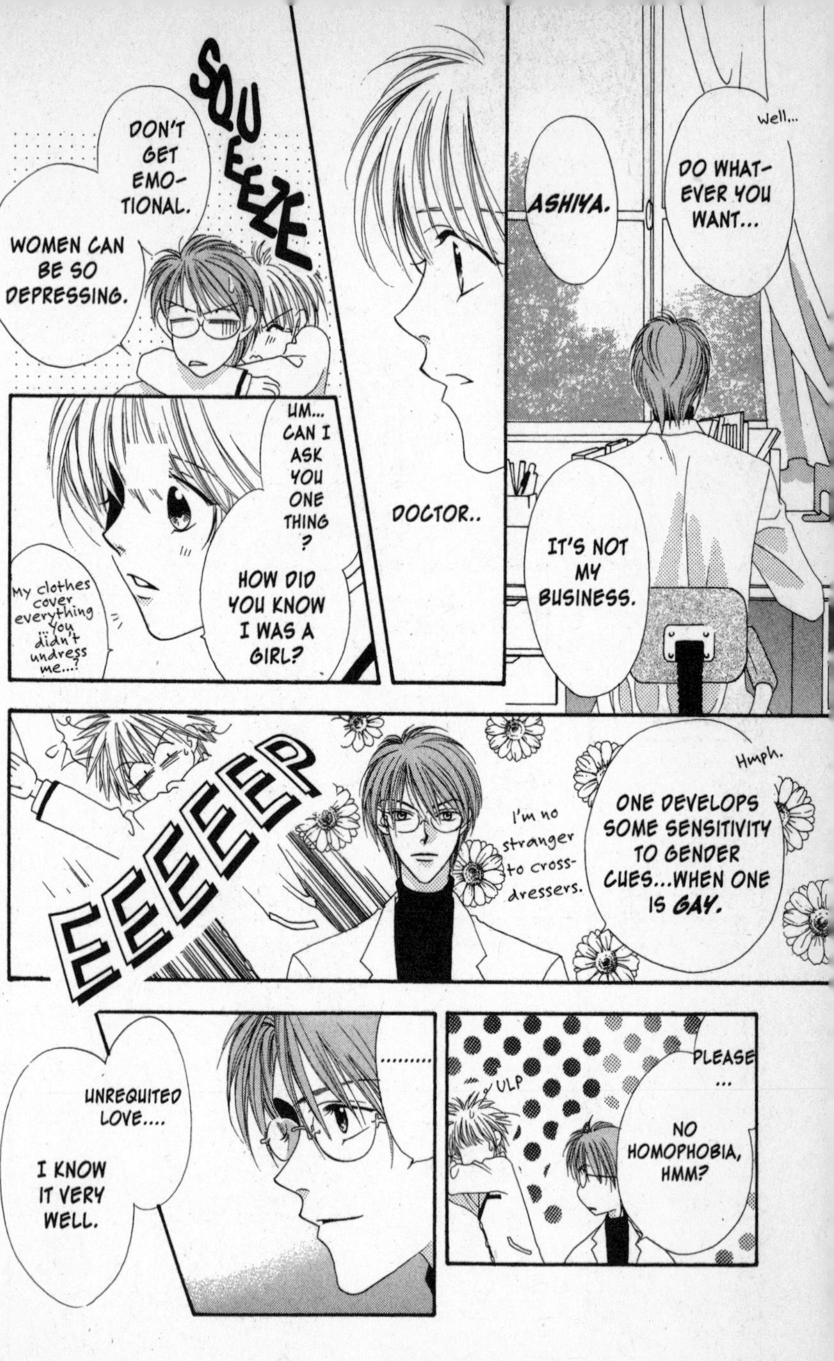
Well...
DO WHATEVER YOU WANT...
ASHIYA.
IT'S NOT MY BUSINESS.
DOCTOR..
SQUEEZE
DON'T GET EMOTIONAL.
WOMEN CAN BE SO DEPRESSING.
UM... CAN I ASK YOU ONE THING?
HOW DID YOU KNOW I WAS A GIRL?
My clothes cover everything ...you didn't undress me...?
Hmph.
ONE DEVELOPS SOME SENSITIVITY TO GENDER CUES...WHEN ONE IS GAY.
I'm no stranger to cross-dressers.
EEEEEEP
PLEASE...
NO HOMOPHOBIA, HMM?
ULP
....
UNREQUITED LOVE....
I KNOW IT VERY WELL.

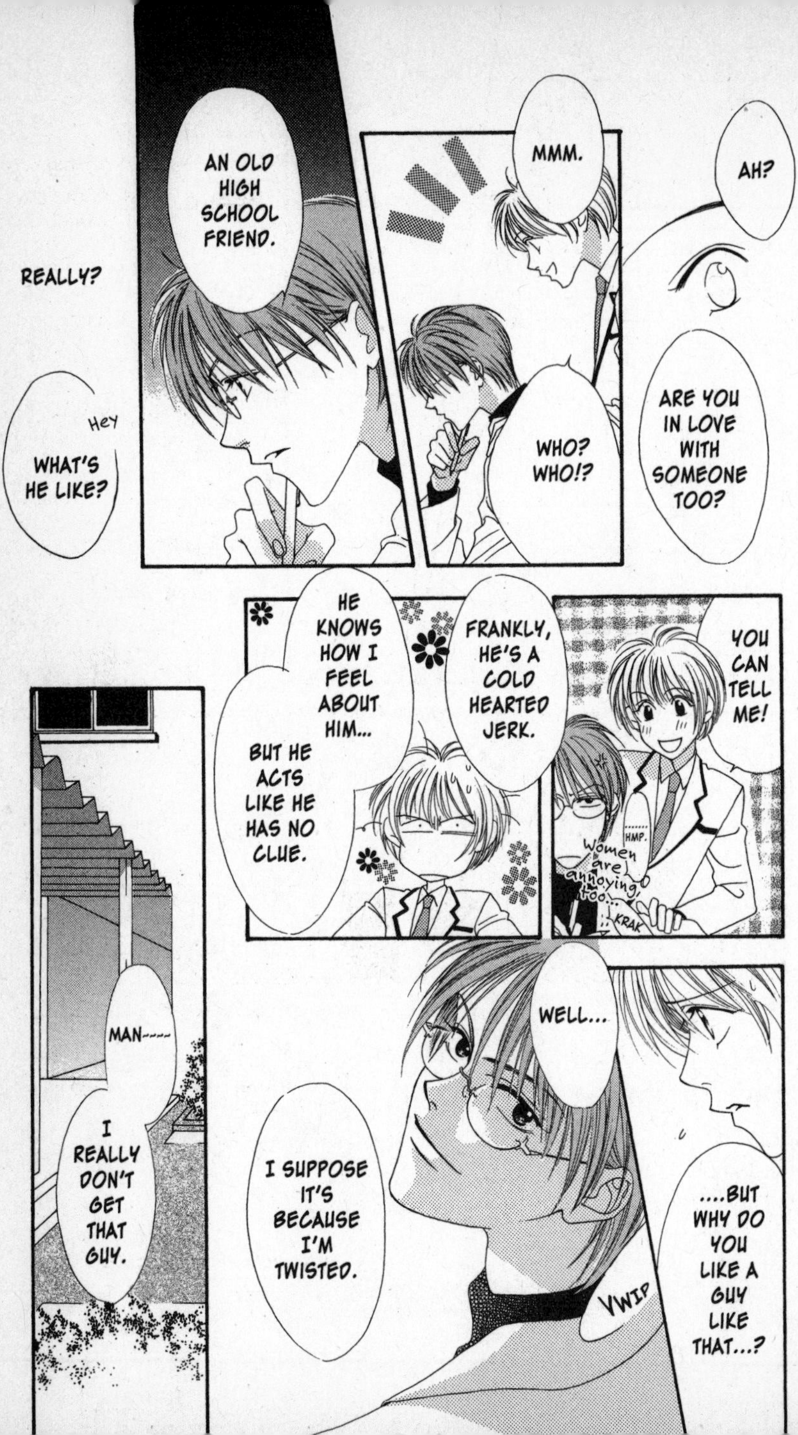
AH?
ARE YOU IN LOVE WITH SOMEONE TOO?
MMM.
WHO? WHO!?
AN OLD HIGH SCHOOL FRIEND.
REALLY?
Hey
WHAT'S HE LIKE?
YOU CAN TELL ME!
......HMP.
Women are annoying, too...
KRAK
FRANKLY, HE'S A COLD HEARTED JERK.
HE KNOWS HOW I FEEL ABOUT HIM...
BUT HE ACTS LIKE HE HAS NO CLUE.
....BUT WHY DO YOU LIKE A GUY LIKE THAT...?
VWIP
WELL...
I SUPPOSE IT'S BECAUSE I'M TWISTED.
MAN----
I REALLY DON'T GET THAT GUY.

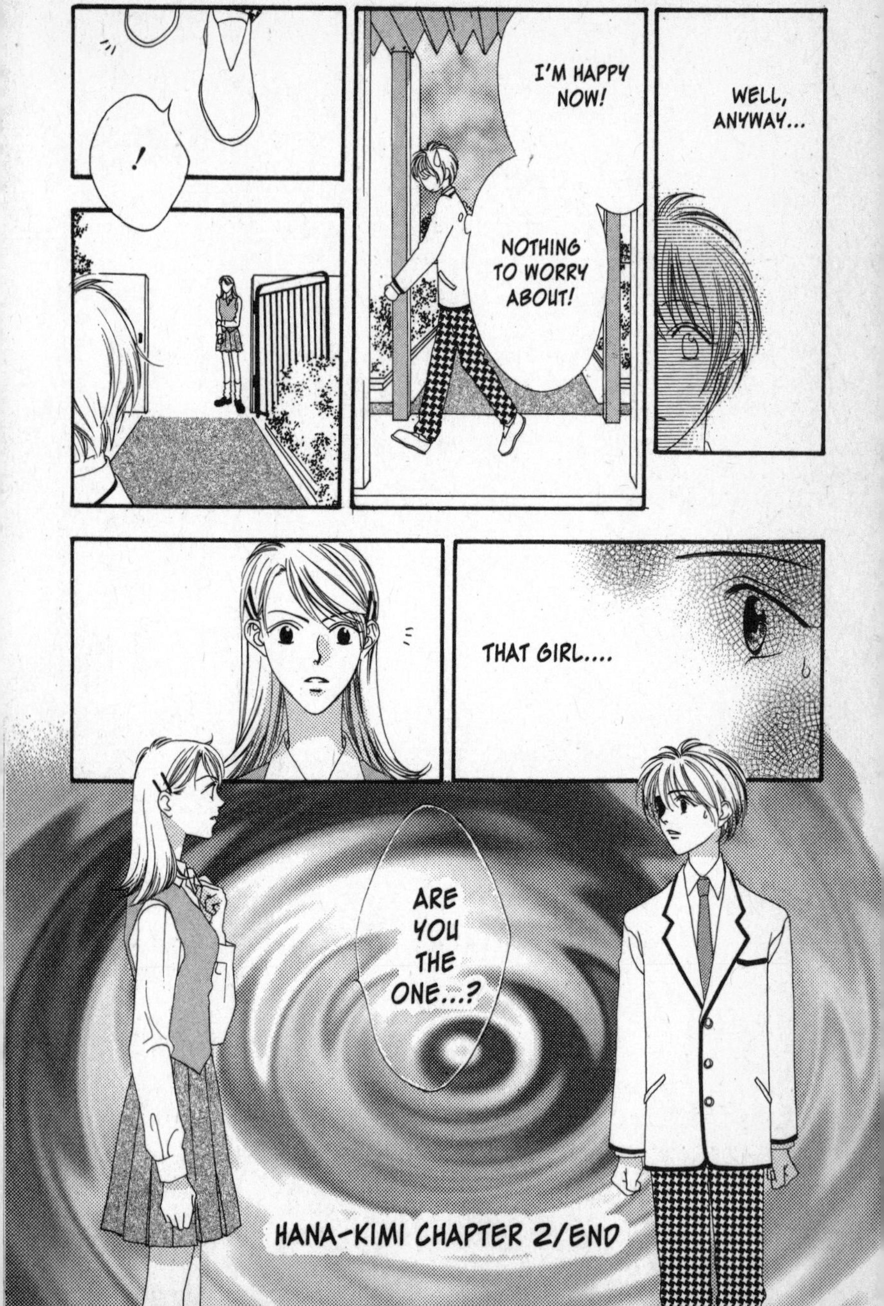
WELL, ANYWAY...
I'M HAPPY NOW!
NOTHING TO WORRY ABOUT!
!
THAT GIRL....
ARE YOU THE ONE...?
HANA-KIMI CHAPTER 2/END

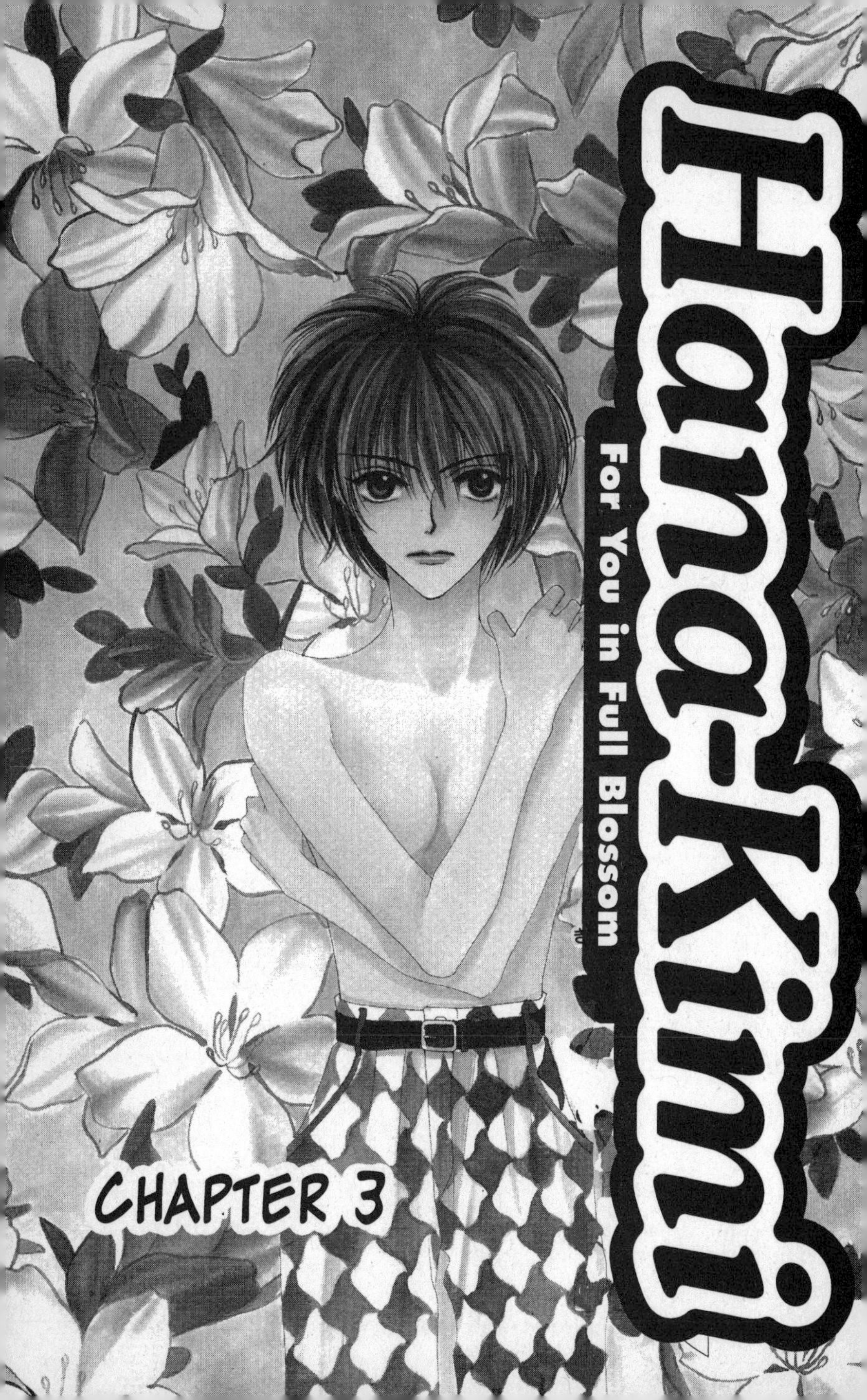
Hana-Kimi
For You in Full Blossom
CHAPTER 3

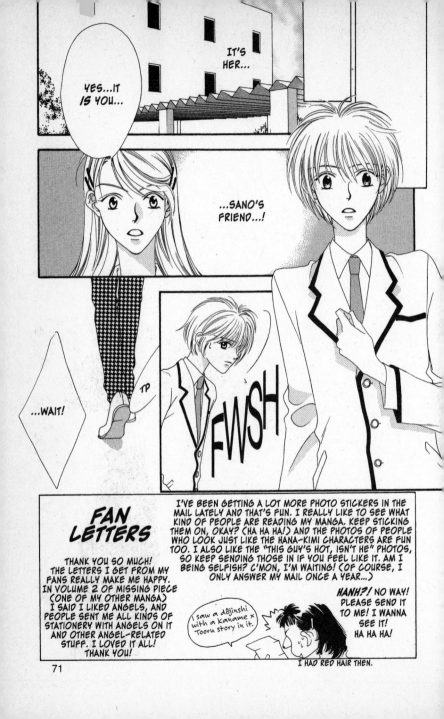

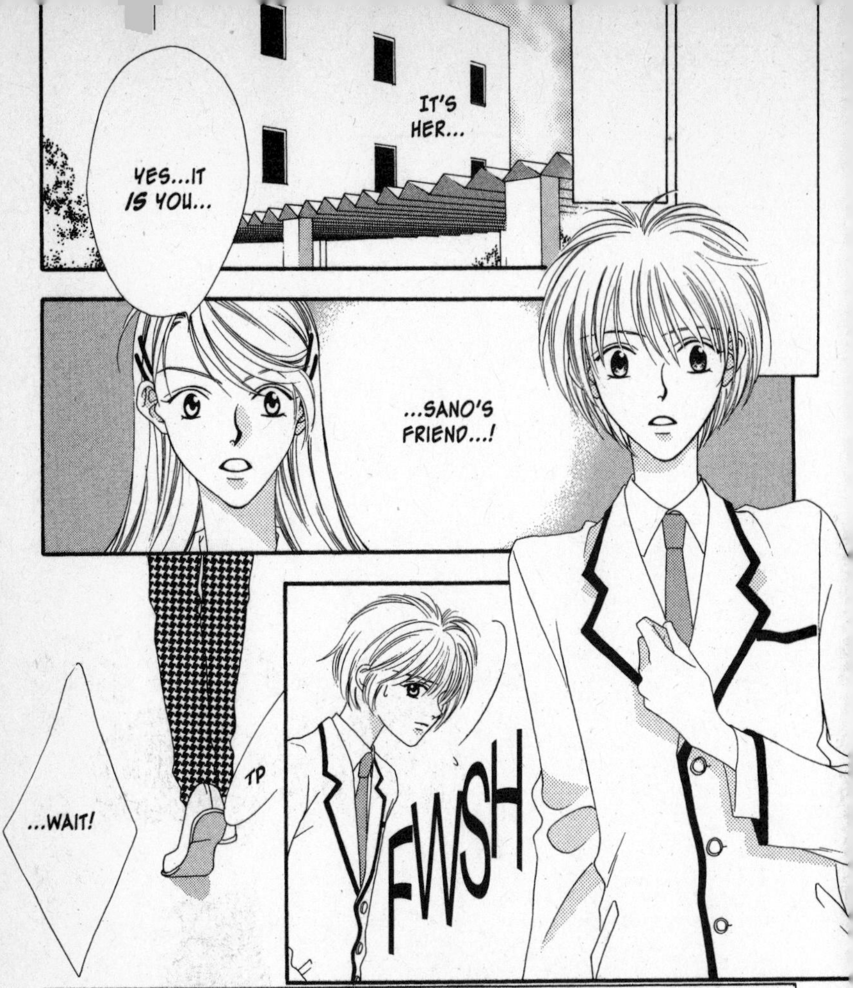
IT'S HER...
YES...IT IS YOU...
...SANO'S FRIEND...!
FWSH
TP
...WAIT!

FAN LETTERS

THANK YOU SO MUCH! THE LETTERS I GET FROM MY FANS REALLY MAKE ME HAPPY. IN VOLUME 2 OF MISSING PIECE (ONE OF MY OTHER MANGA) I SAID I LIKED ANGELS, AND PEOPLE SENT ME ALL KINDS OF STATIONERY WITH ANGELS ON IT AND OTHER ANGEL-RELATED STUFF. I LOVED IT ALL! THANK YOU!

I'VE BEEN GETTING A LOT MORE PHOTO STICKERS IN THE MAIL LATELY AND THAT'S FUN. I REALLY LIKE TO SEE WHAT KIND OF PEOPLE ARE READING MY MANGA. KEEP STICKING THEM ON, OKAY? (HA HA HA!) AND THE PHOTOS OF PEOPLE WHO LOOK JUST LIKE THE HANA-KIMI CHARACTERS ARE FUN TOO. I ALSO LIKE THE "THIS GUY'S HOT, ISN'T HE" PHOTOS, SO KEEP SENDING THOSE IN IF YOU FEEL LIKE IT. AM I BEING SELFISH? C'MON, I'M WAITING! (OF COURSE, I ONLY ANSWER MY MAIL ONCE A YEAR...)

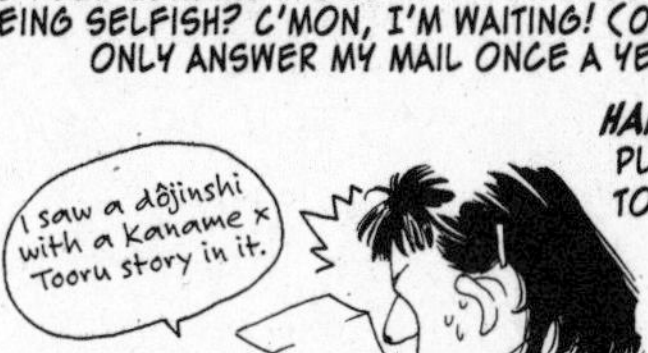
I saw a dôjinshi with a Kaname x Tooru story in it.

HANH?! NO WAY! PLEASE SEND IT TO ME! I WANNA SEE IT! HA HA HA!

I HAD RED HAIR THEN.

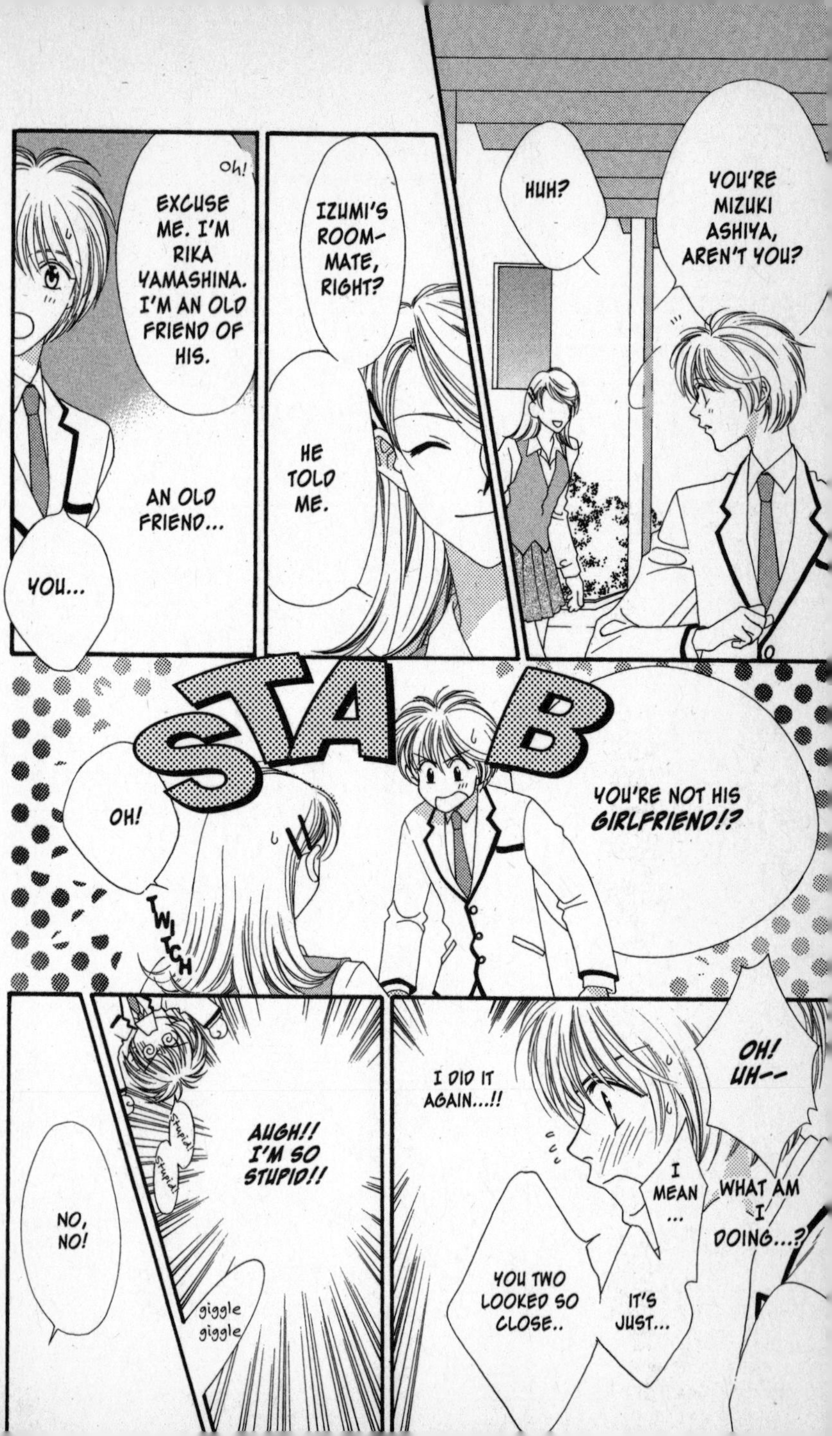
YOU'RE MIZUKI ASHIYA, AREN'T YOU?
HUH?
IZUMI'S ROOM-MATE, RIGHT?
HE TOLD ME.
Oh!
EXCUSE ME. I'M RIKA YAMASHINA. I'M AN OLD FRIEND OF HIS.
AN OLD FRIEND...
YOU...
STAB
YOU'RE NOT HIS GIRLFRIEND!?
OH!
TWITCH
OH! UH--
WHAT AM I DOING...?
I MEAN...
I DID IT AGAIN...!!
IT'S JUST...
YOU TWO LOOKED SO CLOSE..
AUGH!! I'M SO STUPID!!
stupid!
stupid!
giggle giggle
NO, NO!

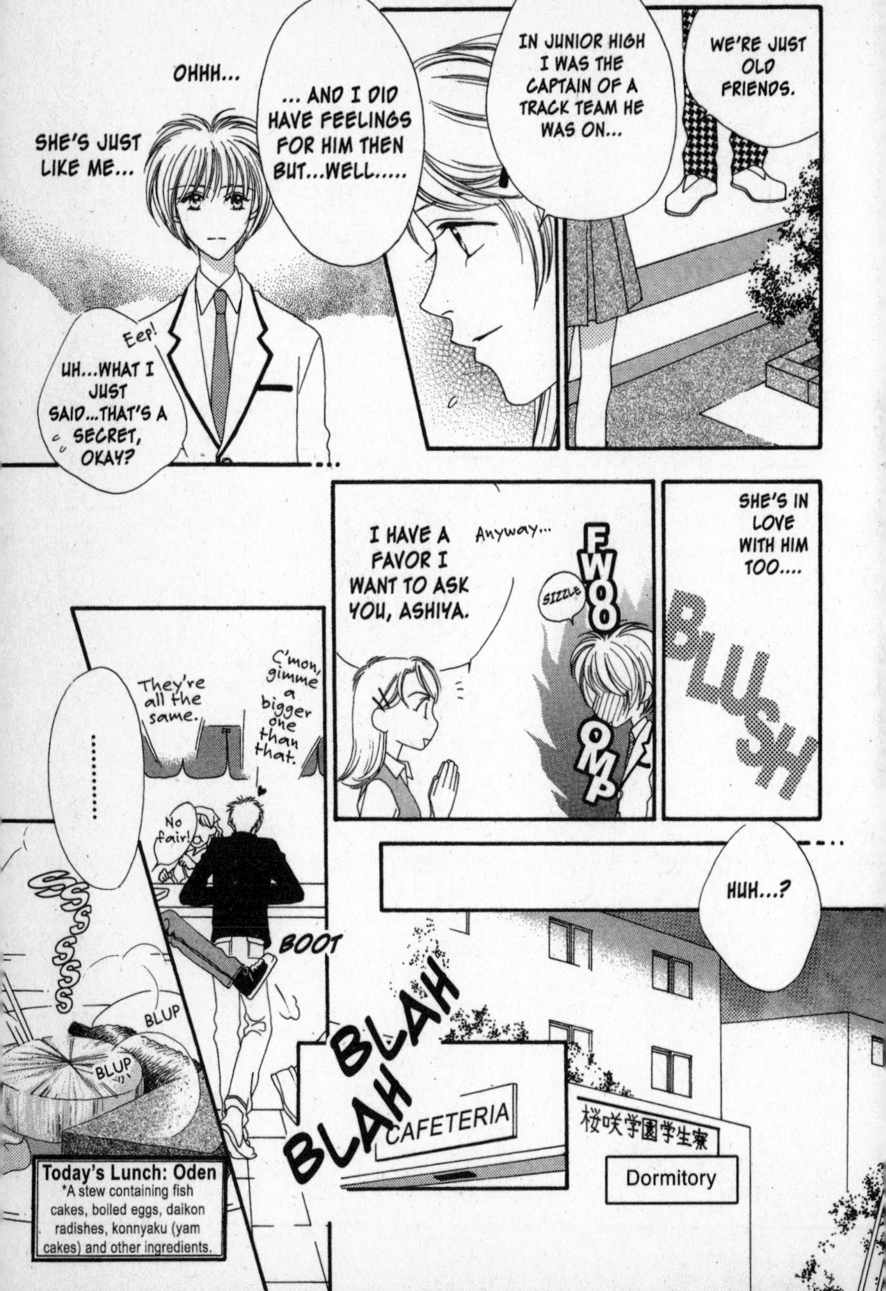
WE'RE JUST OLD FRIENDS.
IN JUNIOR HIGH I WAS THE CAPTAIN OF A TRACK TEAM HE WAS ON...
... AND I DID HAVE FEELINGS FOR HIM THEN BUT...WELL.....
OHHH...
SHE'S JUST LIKE ME...
Eep!
UH...WHAT I JUST SAID...THAT'S A SECRET, OKAY?
...
SHE'S IN LOVE WITH HIM TOO....
BLUSH
FWOOMP
SIZZLE
Anyway...
I HAVE A FAVOR I WANT TO ASK YOU, ASHIYA.
....
They're all the same.
C'mon, gimme a bigger one than that.
No fair!
SSSSSS
BOOT
BLUP
BLUP
Today's Lunch: Oden
*A stew containing fish cakes, boiled eggs, daikon radishes, konnyaku (yam cakes) and other ingredients.
...
HUH...?
BLAH BLAH
CAFETERIA
桜咲学園学生寮
Dormitory

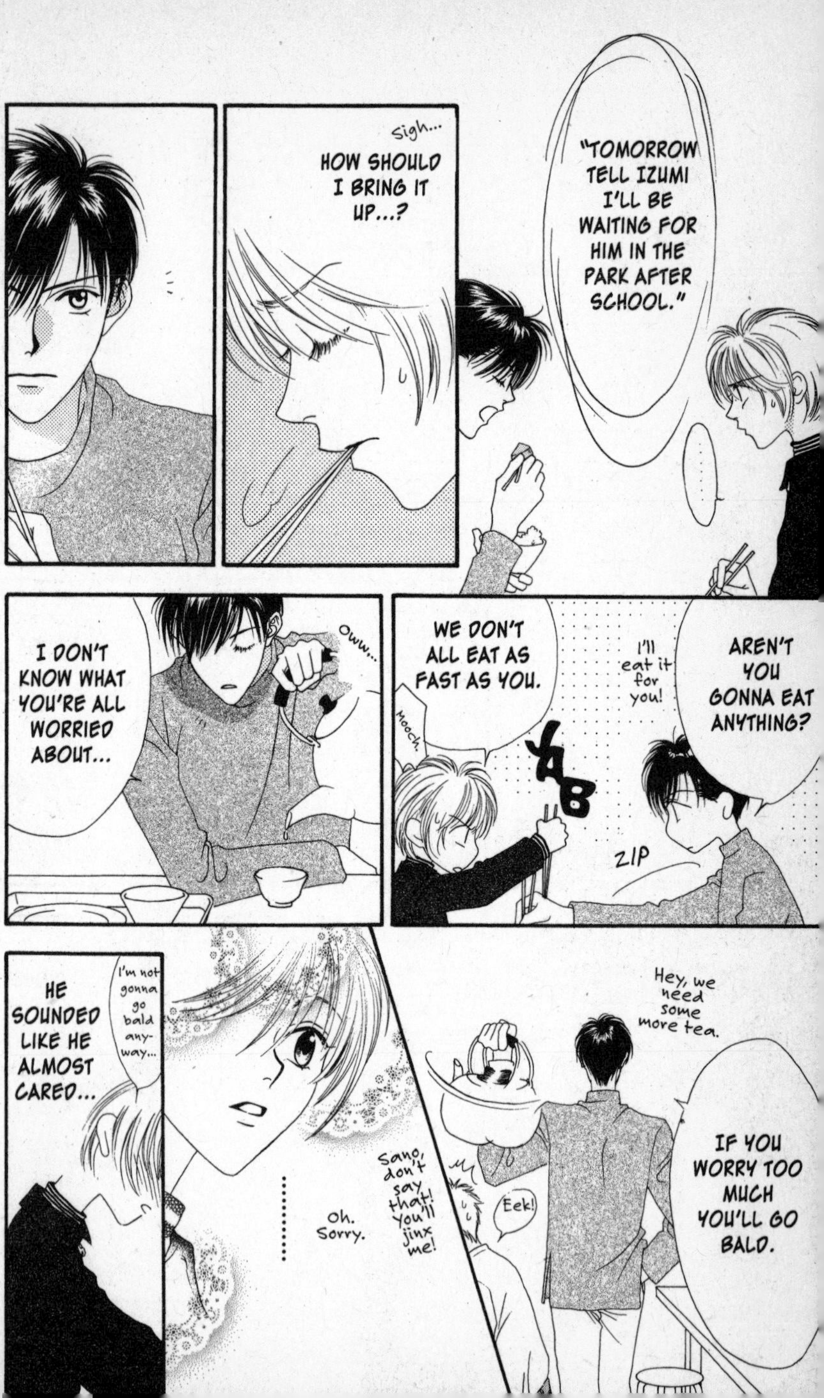
"TOMORROW TELL IZUMI I'LL BE WAITING FOR HIM IN THE PARK AFTER SCHOOL."
Sigh...
HOW SHOULD I BRING IT UP...?
AREN'T YOU GONNA EAT ANYTHING?
I'll eat it for you!
WE DON'T ALL EAT AS FAST AS YOU.
Mooch.
ZIP
Oww...
I DON'T KNOW WHAT YOU'RE ALL WORRIED ABOUT...
Hey, we need some more tea.
IF YOU WORRY TOO MUCH YOU'LL GO BALD.
Eek!
Sano, don't say that! You'll jinx me!
Oh. Sorry.
......
I'm not gonna go bald anyway...
HE SOUNDED LIKE HE ALMOST CARED...

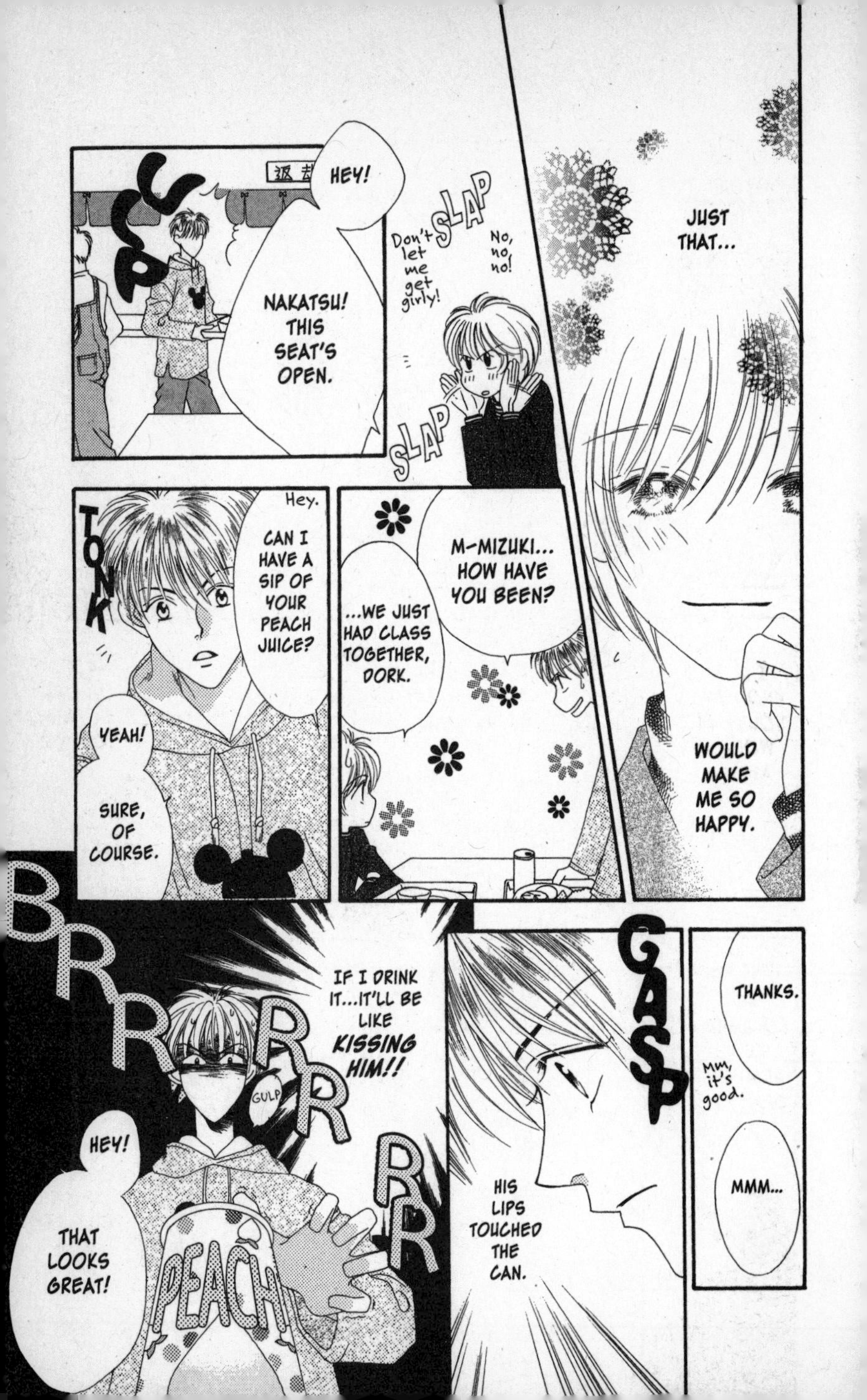
JUST THAT...
WOULD MAKE ME SO HAPPY.
HEY!
NAKATSU! THIS SEAT'S OPEN.
SLAP
No, no, no!
Don't let me get girly!
SLAP
M-MIZUKI... HOW HAVE YOU BEEN?
...WE JUST HAD CLASS TOGETHER, DORK.
Hey.
CAN I HAVE A SIP OF YOUR PEACH JUICE?
TONK
YEAH!
SURE, OF COURSE.
THANKS.
Mm, it's good.
MMM...
GASP
HIS LIPS TOUCHED THE CAN.
IF I DRINK IT...IT'LL BE LIKE *KISSING HIM!!*
BRRRRRR
GULP
HEY!
THAT LOOKS GREAT!
PEACH

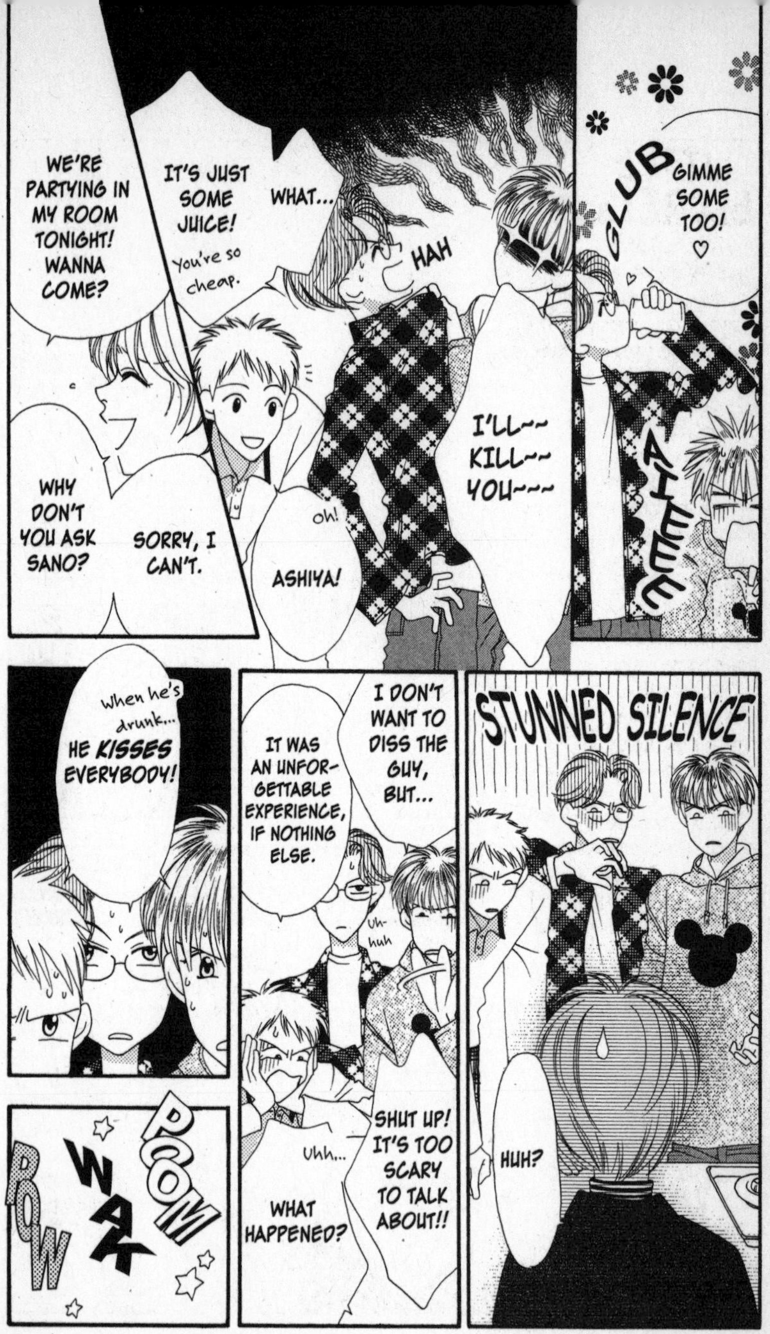
GIMME SOME TOO! ♡
GLUB
AIEEE
WHAT...
HAH
I'LL~~ KILL~~ YOU~~~
IT'S JUST SOME JUICE!
You're so cheap.
WE'RE PARTYING IN MY ROOM TONIGHT! WANNA COME?
SORRY, I CAN'T.
WHY DON'T YOU ASK SANO?
Oh!
ASHIYA!
STUNNED SILENCE
HUH?
I DON'T WANT TO DISS THE GUY, BUT...
IT WAS AN UNFORGETTABLE EXPERIENCE, IF NOTHING ELSE.
Uh-huh
SHUT UP! IT'S TOO SCARY TO TALK ABOUT!!
Uhh...
WHAT HAPPENED?
When he's drunk... HE KISSES EVERYBODY!
POW
WAK
POW

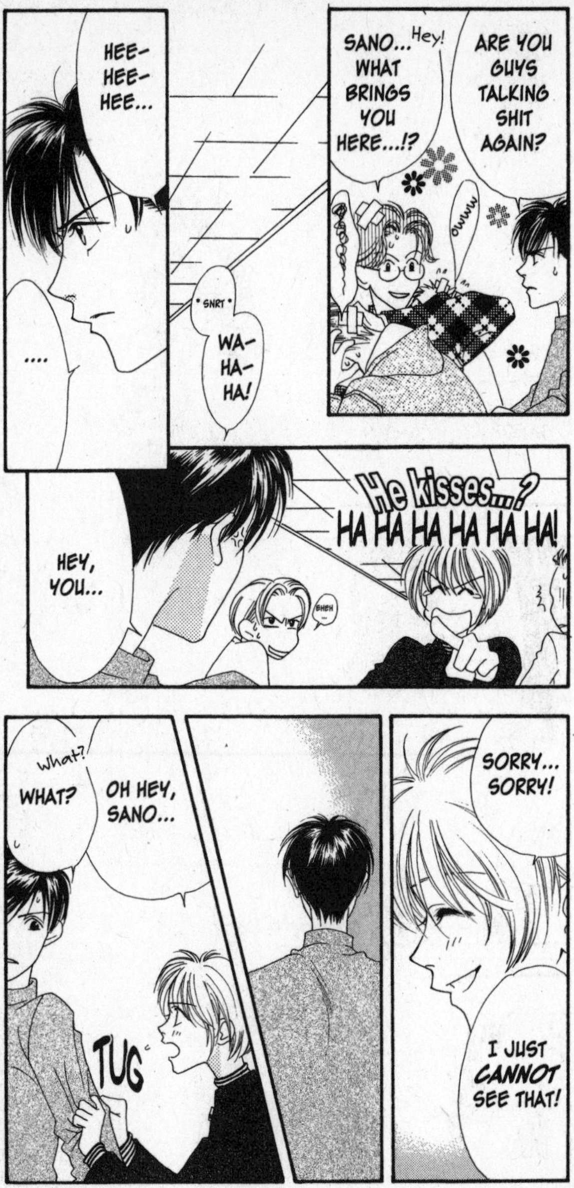
ARE YOU GUYS TALKING SHIT AGAIN?
SANO... WHAT BRINGS YOU HERE...!?
Hey!
owww
HEE-HEE-HEE...
SNRT WA-HA-HA!
....
He kisses...? HA HA HA HA HA HA!
BHEH
HEY, YOU...
SORRY... SORRY!
I JUST CANNOT SEE THAT!
OH HEY, SANO...
WHAT?
What?
TUG

LITTLE SECRETS

A LOT OF READERS HAVE FIGURED THIS OUT, BUT ALL OF THIS MANGA'S CHARACTER NAMES ARE TAKEN FROM PLACES IN THE KANSAI REGION (ESPECIALLY AROUND OSAKA). A LOT OF THEM SOUND LIKE PEOPLE'S NAMES SO I THOUGHT IT WOULD WORK. SOMETIMES THE NAME ACTUALLY HAS SOME CONNECTION WITH THE CHARACTER'S PERSONALITY...LIKE THE CAMERA FANATIC NIHONBASHI (IN TOKYO HE'D BE AKIHABARA). THE NAME KITA UMEDA COMES FROM UMEDA STATION IN OSAKA'S KITA (NORTH) DISTRICT, AND MINAMI NANBA COMES FROM NAMBA STATION IN OSAKA'S MINAMI (SOUTH) DISTRICT. THAT'S WHY IT'S "MINAMI NANBA" AND "KITA UMEDA." SIMPLE, ISN'T IT?

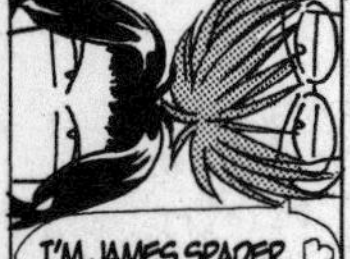
I'M KIMUTAKU. ♡
I'M JAMES SPADER. ♡

THAT'S WHO THEY WERE BASED ON.

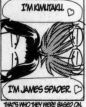

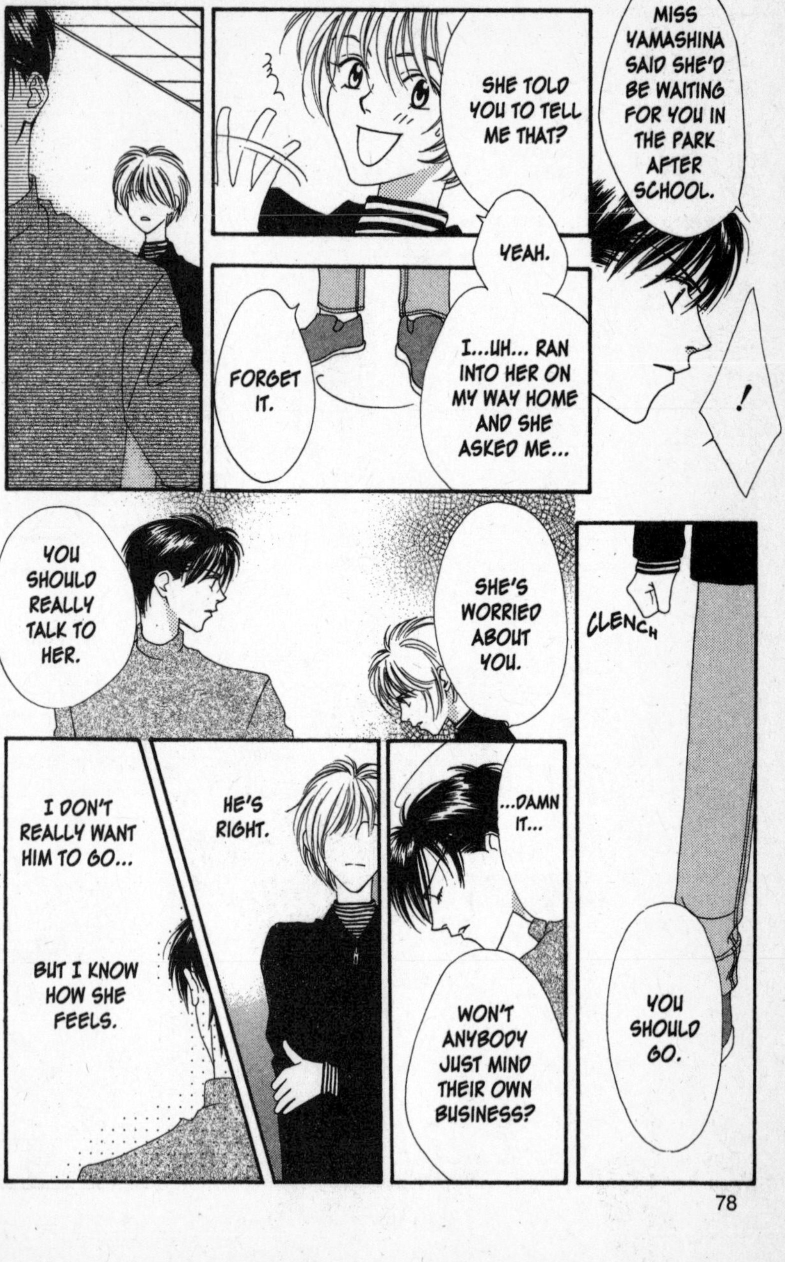
MISS YAMASHINA SAID SHE'D BE WAITING FOR YOU IN THE PARK AFTER SCHOOL.
SHE TOLD YOU TO TELL ME THAT?
YEAH.
!
I...UH... RAN INTO HER ON MY WAY HOME AND SHE ASKED ME...
FORGET IT.
CLENCH
YOU SHOULD GO.
SHE'S WORRIED ABOUT YOU.
YOU SHOULD REALLY TALK TO HER.
...DAMN IT...
WON'T ANYBODY JUST MIND THEIR OWN BUSINESS?
HE'S RIGHT.
I DON'T REALLY WANT HIM TO GO...
BUT I KNOW HOW SHE FEELS.

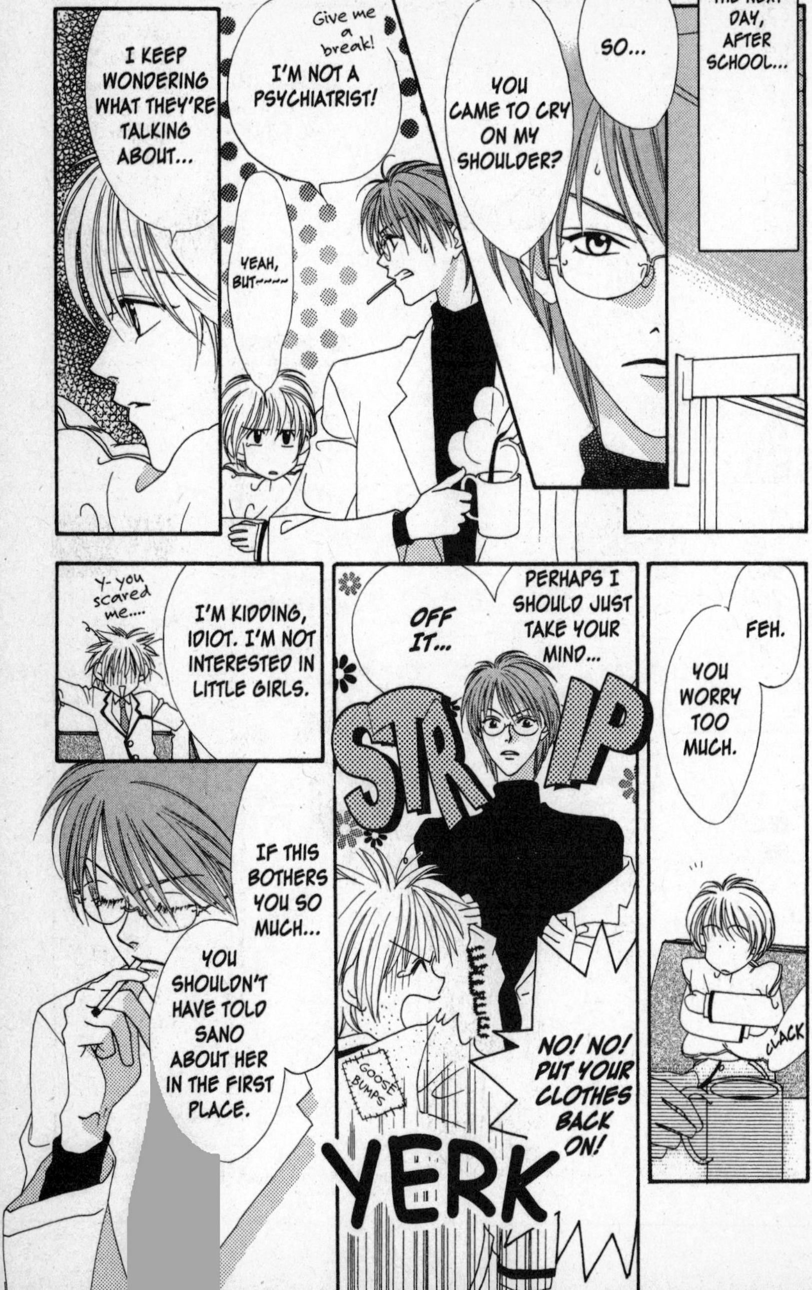
THE NEXT DAY, AFTER SCHOOL...
SO...
YOU CAME TO CRY ON MY SHOULDER?
Give me a break!
I'M NOT A PSYCHIATRIST!
YEAH, BUT~~~~
I KEEP WONDERING WHAT THEY'RE TALKING ABOUT...
FEH.
YOU WORRY TOO MUCH.
CLACK
PERHAPS I SHOULD JUST TAKE YOUR MIND...
OFF IT...
STRIP
GOOSE BUMPS
NO! NO! PUT YOUR CLOTHES BACK ON!
YERK
I'M KIDDING, IDIOT. I'M NOT INTERESTED IN LITTLE GIRLS.
Y-you scared me....
IF THIS BOTHERS YOU SO MUCH...
YOU SHOULDN'T HAVE TOLD SANO ABOUT HER IN THE FIRST PLACE.

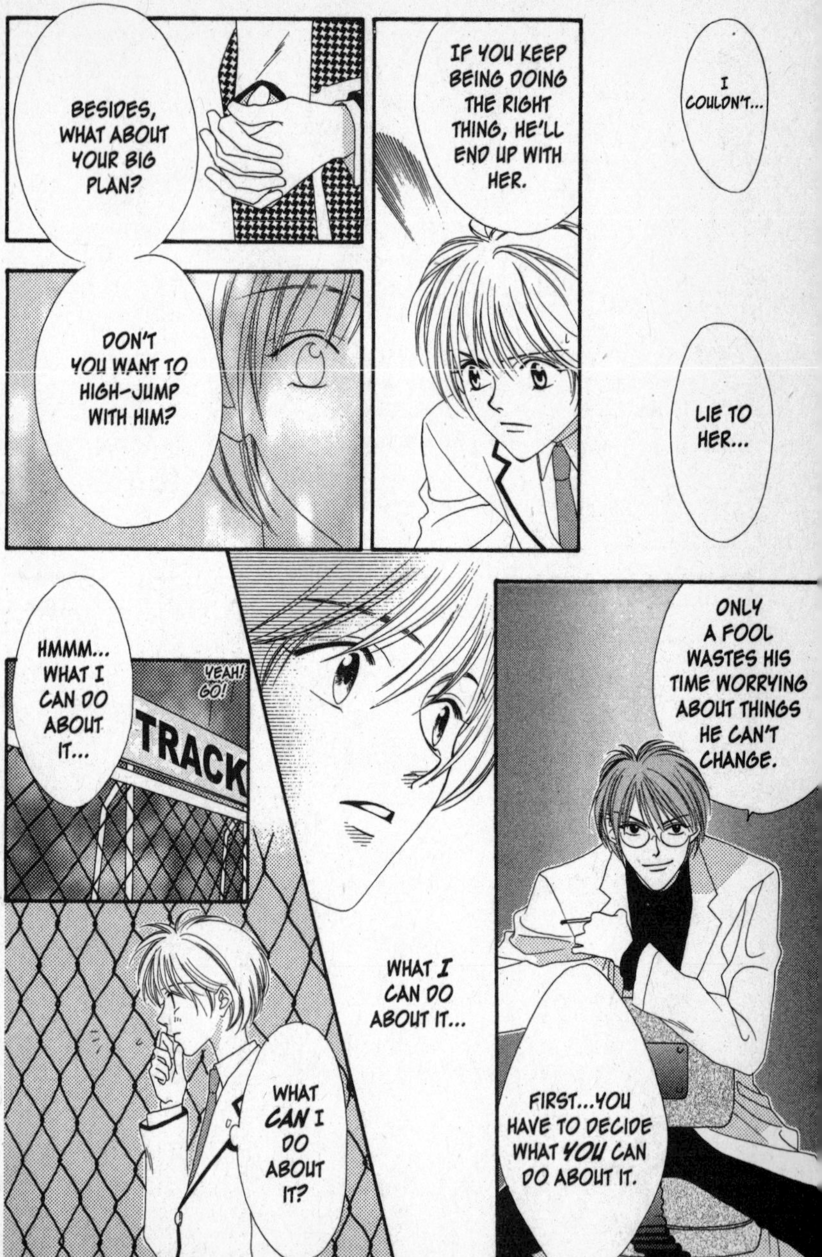
I COULDN'T...
LIE TO HER...
IF YOU KEEP BEING DOING THE RIGHT THING, HE'LL END UP WITH HER.
BESIDES, WHAT ABOUT YOUR BIG PLAN?
DON'T YOU WANT TO HIGH-JUMP WITH HIM?
ONLY A FOOL WASTES HIS TIME WORRYING ABOUT THINGS HE CAN'T CHANGE.
FIRST...YOU HAVE TO DECIDE WHAT *YOU* CAN DO ABOUT IT.
WHAT *I* CAN DO ABOUT IT...
HMMM... WHAT I CAN DO ABOUT IT...
YEAH! GO!
TRACK
WHAT *CAN* I DO ABOUT IT?

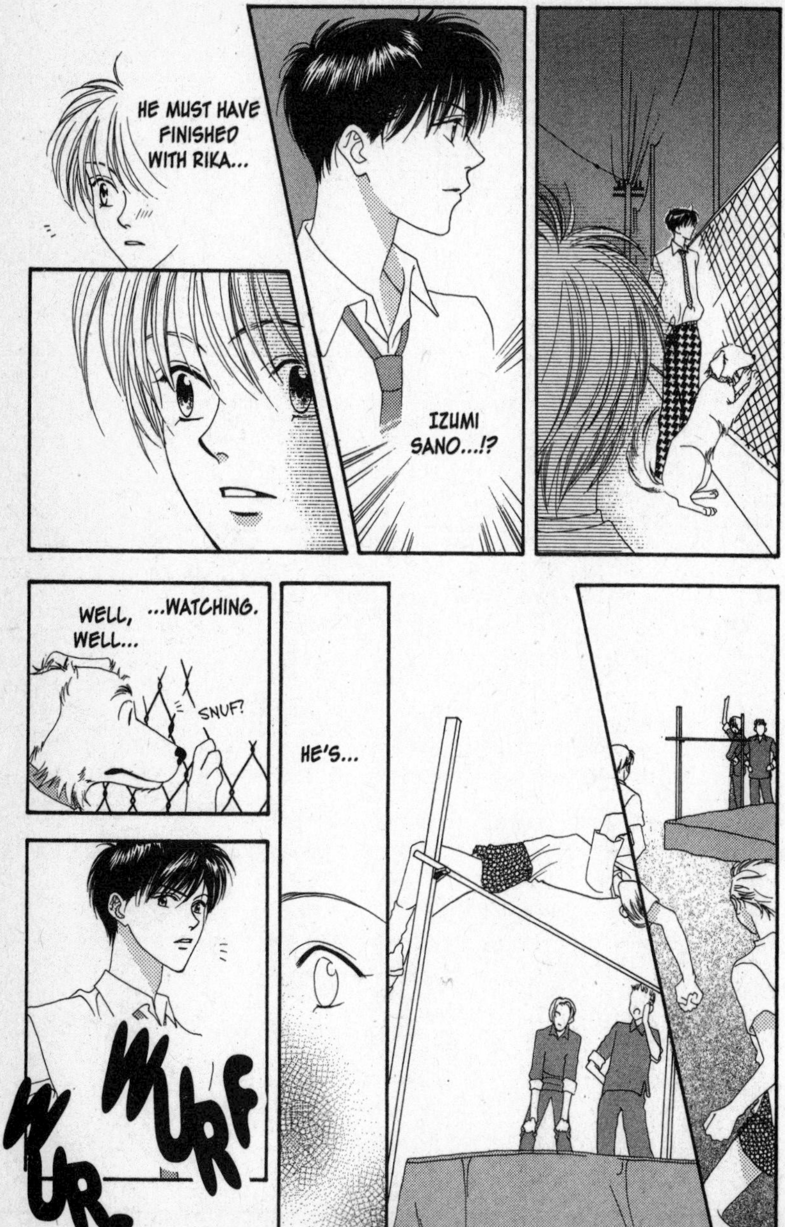
IZUMI SANO...!?
HE MUST HAVE FINISHED WITH RIKA...
HE'S...
...WATCHING.
WELL, WELL...
SNUF?
WURF WURF

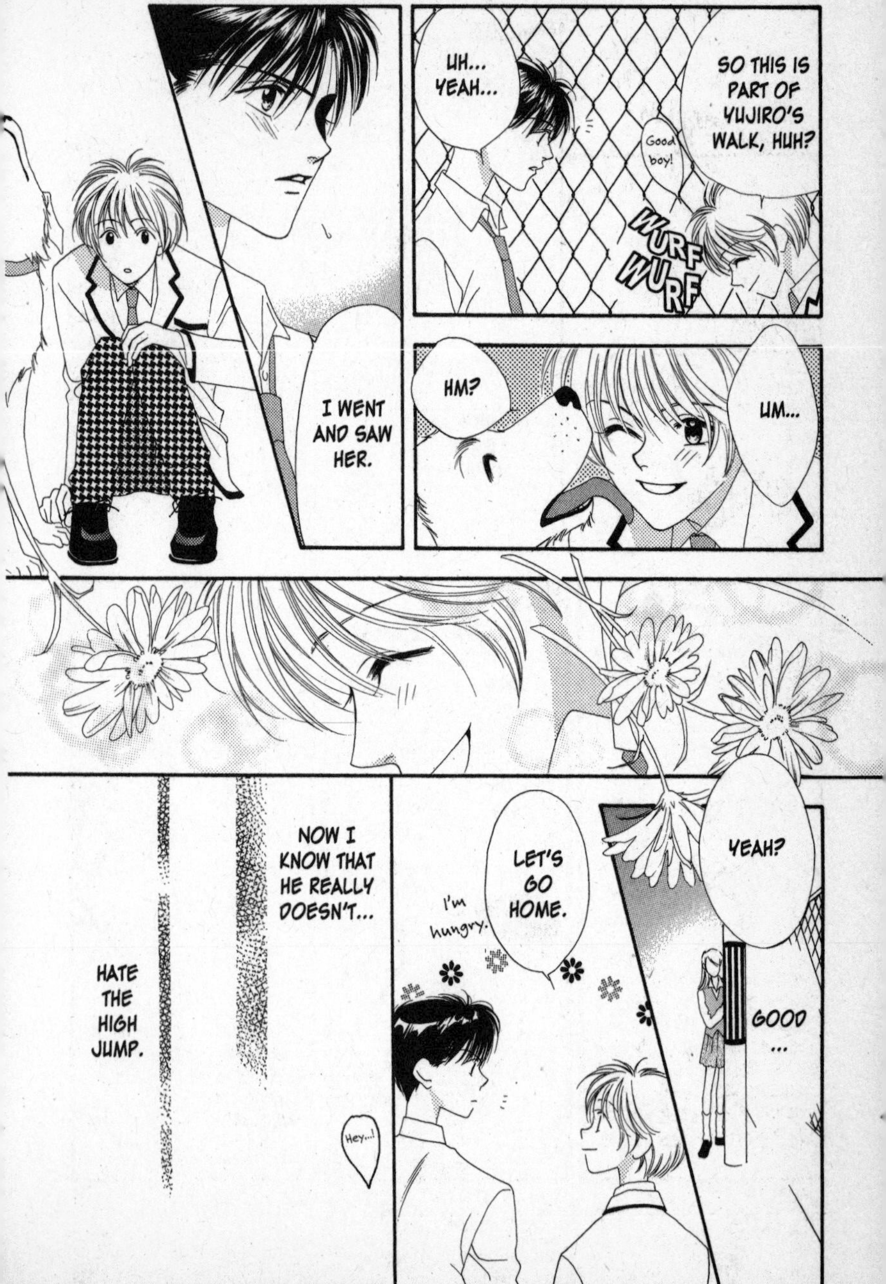
SO THIS IS PART OF YUJIRO'S WALK, HUH?
Good boy!
WURF WURF
UH... YEAH...
UM...
HM?
I WENT AND SAW HER.
YEAH?
GOOD ...
LET'S GO HOME.
I'm hungry.
Hey...!
NOW I KNOW THAT HE REALLY DOESN'T...
HATE THE HIGH JUMP.

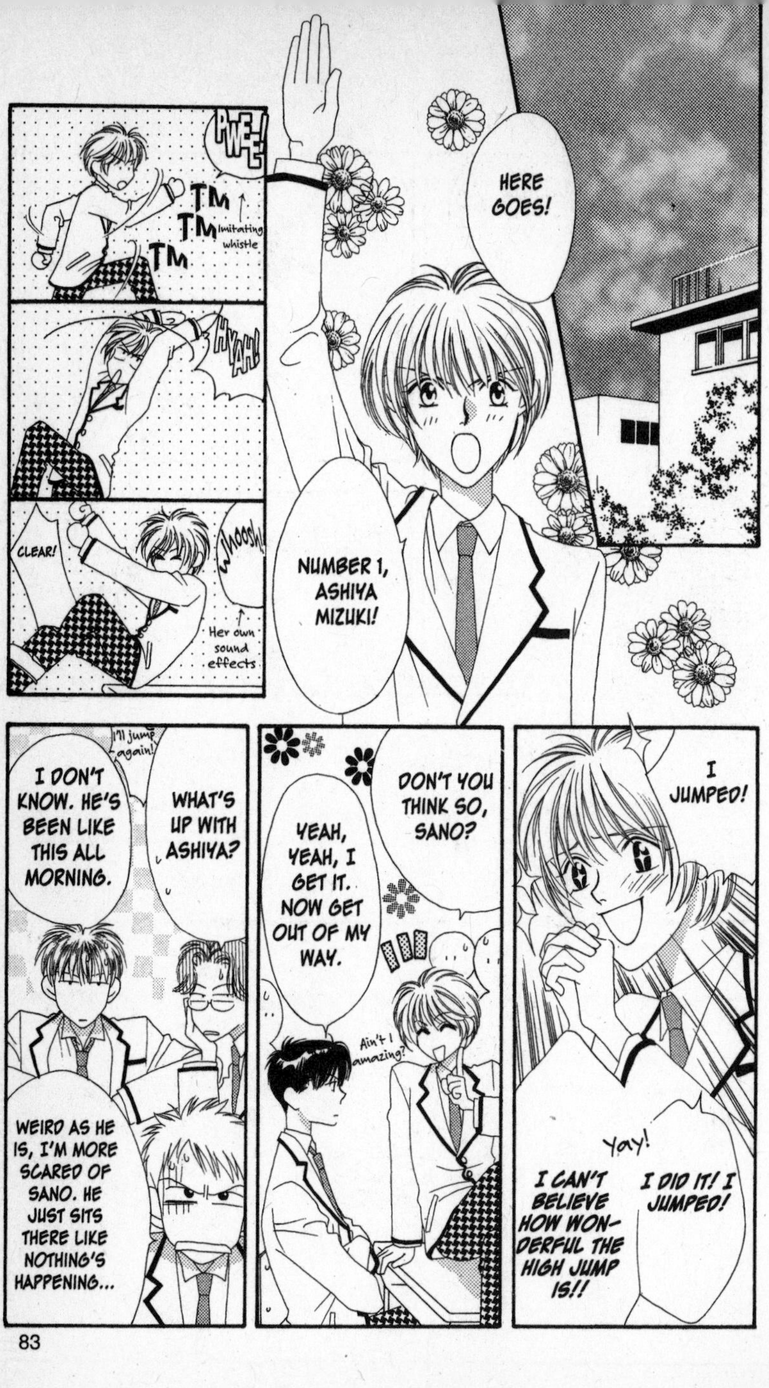
HERE GOES!
NUMBER 1, ASHIYA MIZUKI!
PWEE!
TM TM TM
Imitating whistle
HYAH!
WHOOSH!
CLEAR!
Her own sound effects
I JUMPED!
I DID IT! I JUMPED!
Yay!
I CAN'T BELIEVE HOW WONDERFUL THE HIGH JUMP IS!!
DON'T YOU THINK SO, SANO?
YEAH, YEAH, I GET IT. NOW GET OUT OF MY WAY.
Ain't I amazing?
I'll jump again!
WHAT'S UP WITH ASHIYA?
I DON'T KNOW. HE'S BEEN LIKE THIS ALL MORNING.
WEIRD AS HE IS, I'M MORE SCARED OF SANO. HE JUST SITS THERE LIKE NOTHING'S HAPPENING...

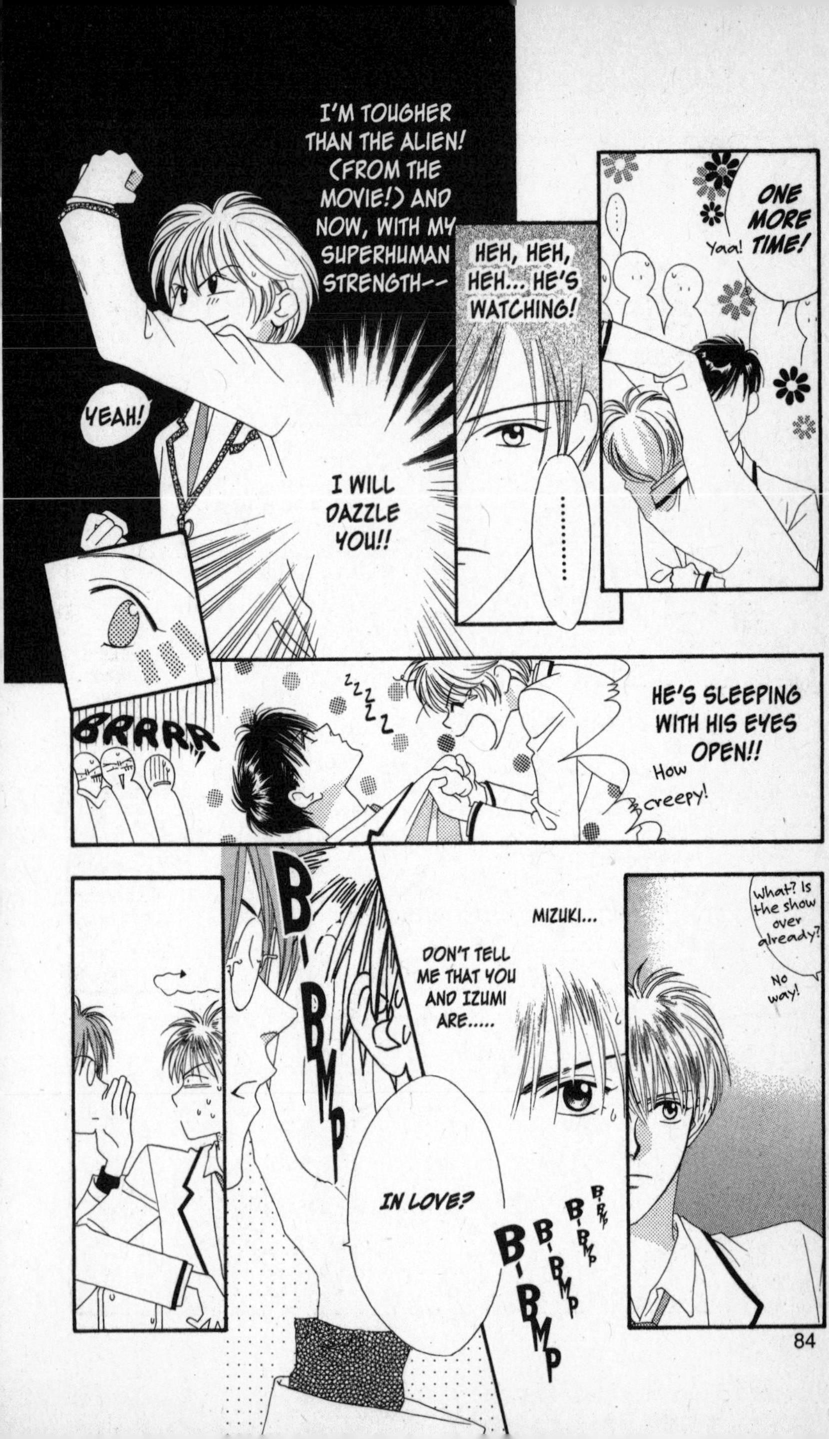
ONE MORE TIME!
Yaa!
...
HEH, HEH, HEH... HE'S WATCHING!
....
I'M TOUGHER THAN THE ALIEN! (FROM THE MOVIE!) AND NOW, WITH MY SUPERHUMAN STRENGTH--
YEAH!
I WILL DAZZLE YOU!!
HE'S SLEEPING WITH HIS EYES OPEN!!
How creepy!
ZZZZZ
BRRRR
What? Is the show over already?
No way!
MIZUKI...
DON'T TELL ME THAT YOU AND IZUMI ARE.....
IN LOVE?
B-BMP
B-BMP
B-BMP
B-BMP
B-BMP

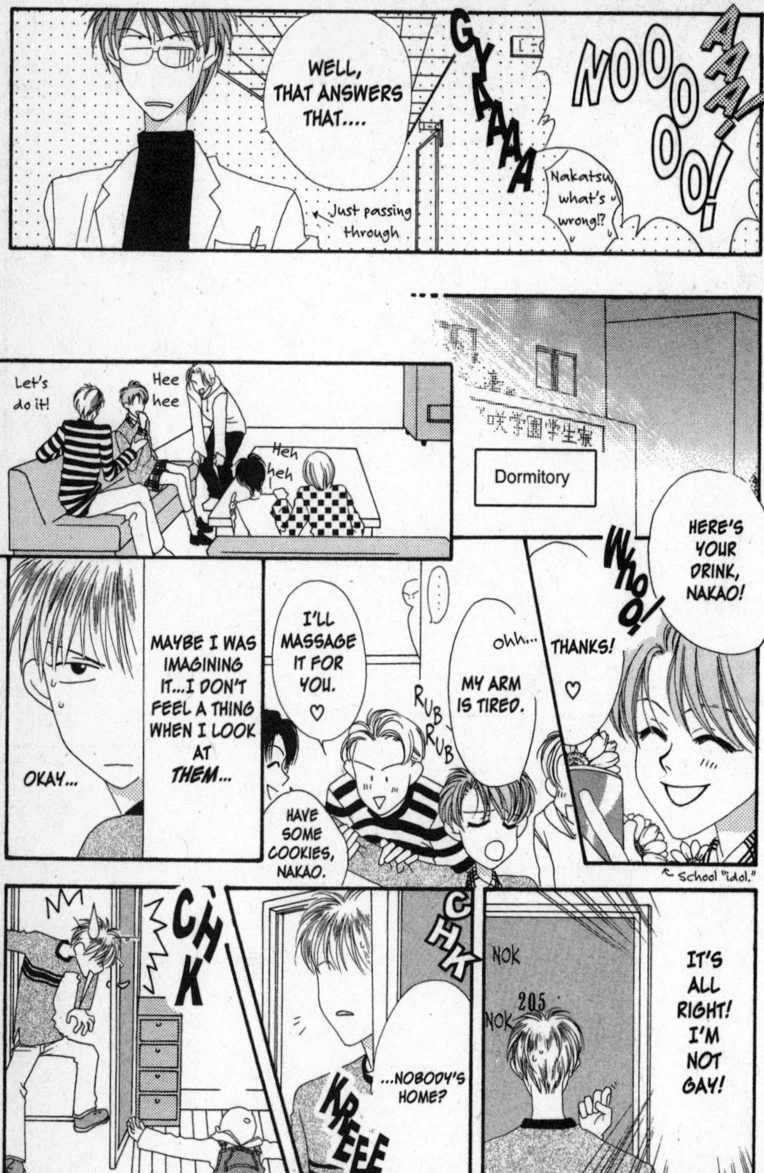
NOOOOOOO!
AAAA!
Nakatsu, what's wrong!?
GYAAAAA
WELL, THAT ANSWERS THAT....
Just passing through
Dormitory
Hee hee
Let's do it!
Heh heh
HERE'S YOUR DRINK, NAKAO!
Whoo!
THANKS!
School "idol."
ohh...
MY ARM IS TIRED.
RUB RUB
I'LL MASSAGE IT FOR YOU.
HAVE SOME COOKIES, NAKAO.
MAYBE I WAS IMAGINING IT...I DON'T FEEL A THING WHEN I LOOK AT THEM...
OKAY...
IT'S ALL RIGHT! I'M NOT GAY!
NOK
NOK
205
CHK
...NOBODY'S HOME?
KREEEE
CHK

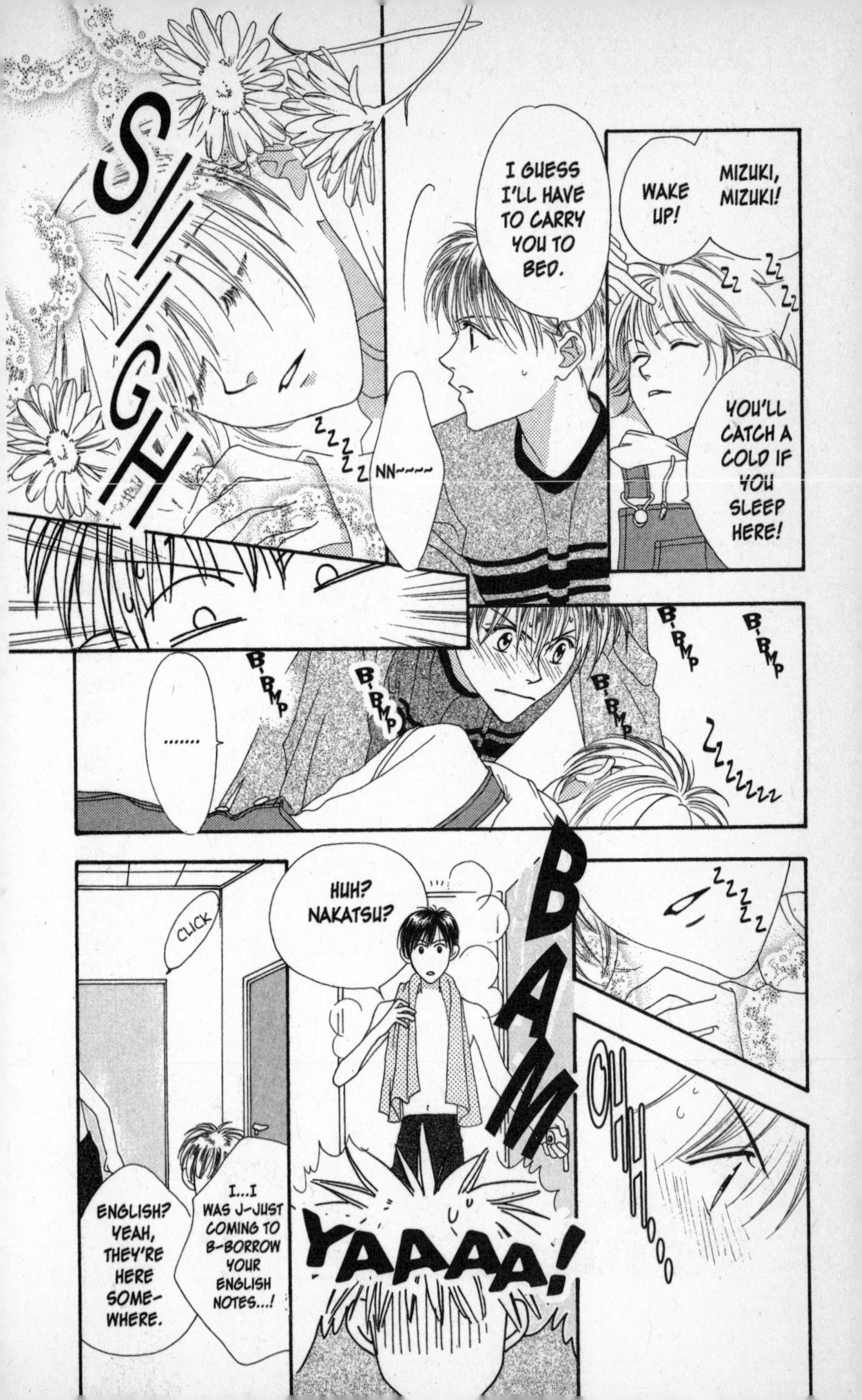
MIZUKI, MIZUKI!
WAKE UP!
ZZ ZZ
YOU'LL CATCH A COLD IF YOU SLEEP HERE!
I GUESS I'LL HAVE TO CARRY YOU TO BED.
NN~~~~
ZZZZZ
SIGH
B-BMP
B-BMP
B-BMP
B-BMP
ZZZZZZZ
....
ZZZZZ
OHHHooo
BAM
HUH? NAKATSU?
YAAAA!
CLICK
I...I WAS J-JUST COMING TO B-BORROW YOUR ENGLISH NOTES...!
ENGLISH? YEAH, THEY'RE HERE SOME-WHERE.

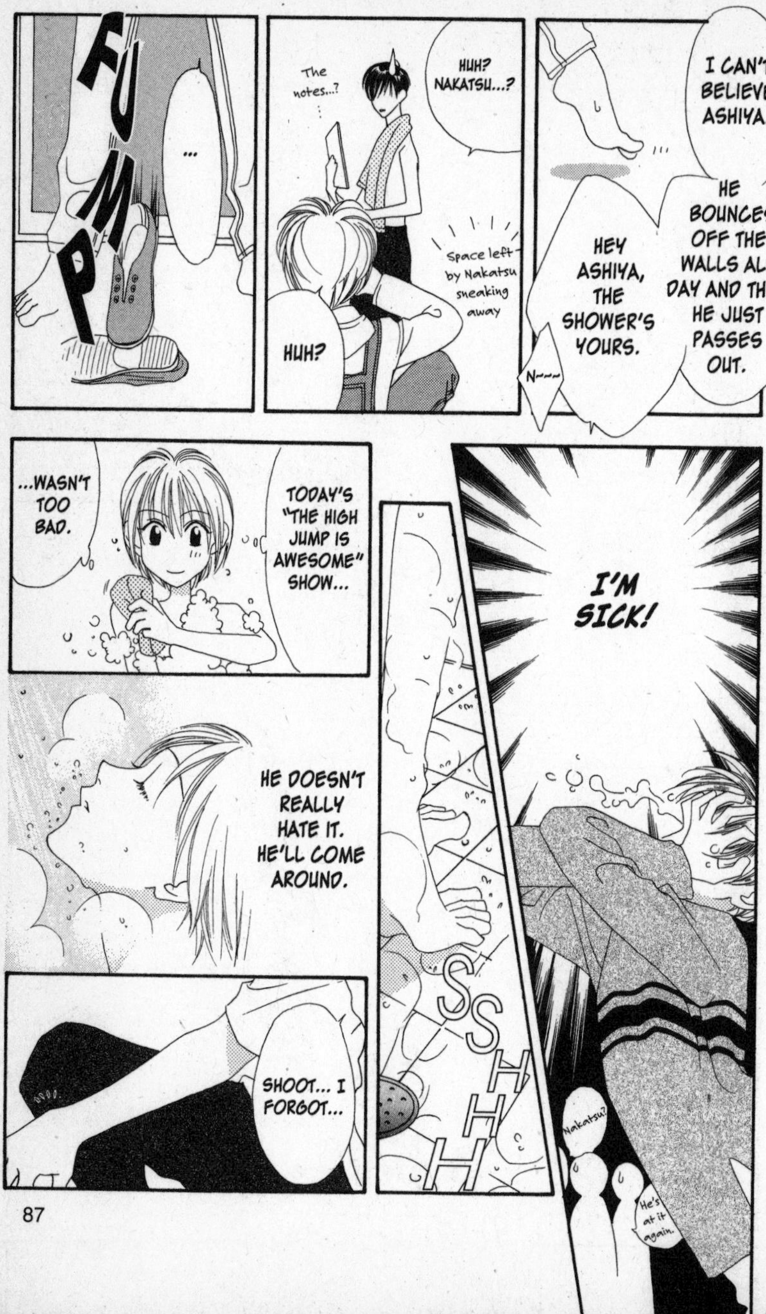
I CAN'T BELIEVE ASHIYA.
HE BOUNCES OFF THE WALLS ALL DAY AND THEN HE JUST PASSES OUT.
HEY ASHIYA, THE SHOWER'S YOURS.
N~~~
HUH? NAKATSU...?
The notes...?
Space left by Nakatsu sneaking away
HUH?
FUMP
...
I'M SICK!
Nakatsu?
He's at it again.
SSHHHH
TODAY'S "THE HIGH JUMP IS AWESOME" SHOW...
...WASN'T TOO BAD.
HE DOESN'T REALLY HATE IT. HE'LL COME AROUND.
SHOOT... I FORGOT...

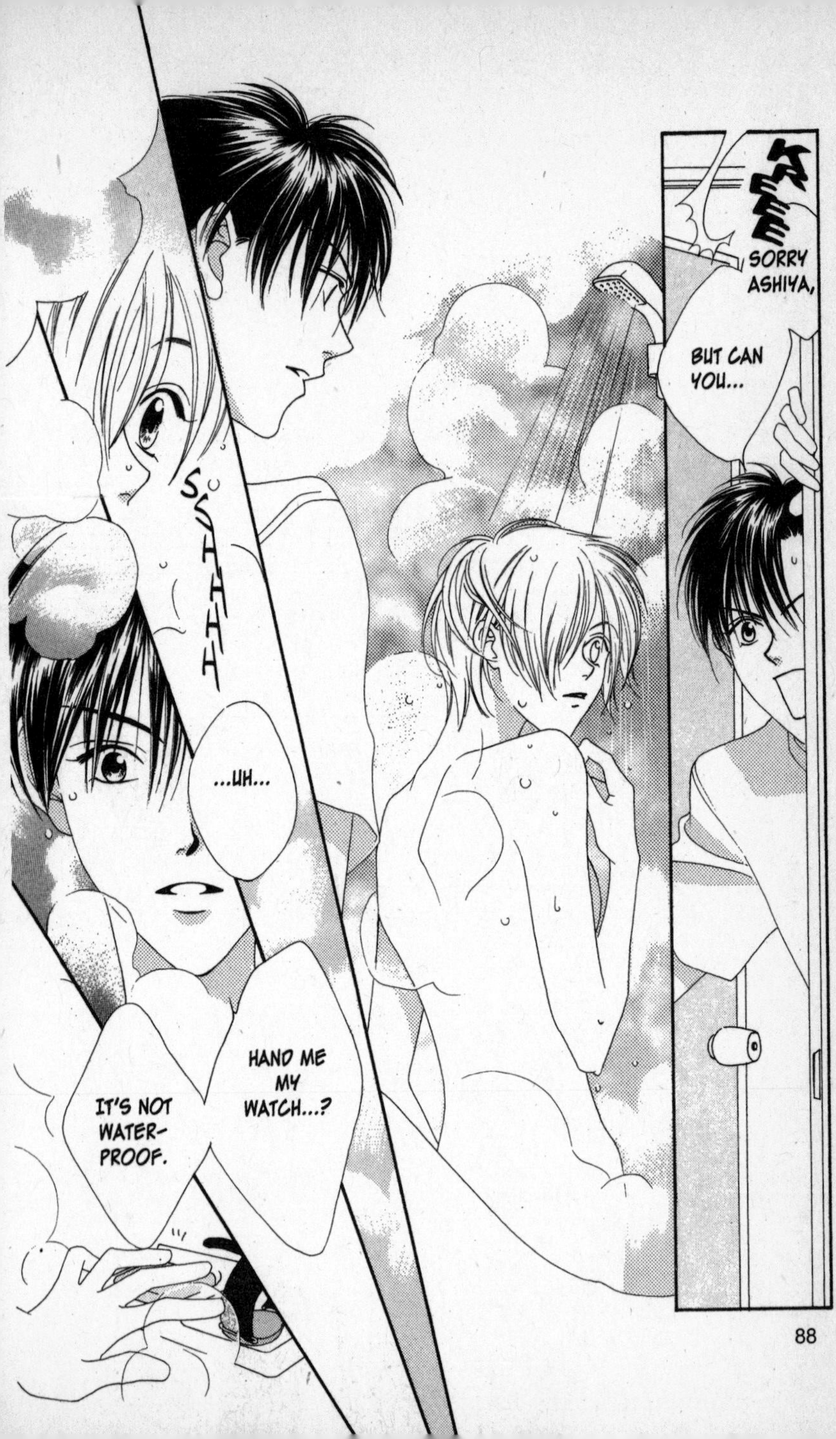
KREEE
SORRY ASHIYA,
BUT CAN YOU...
SSHHHHH
...UH...
HAND ME MY WATCH...?
IT'S NOT WATER-PROOF.

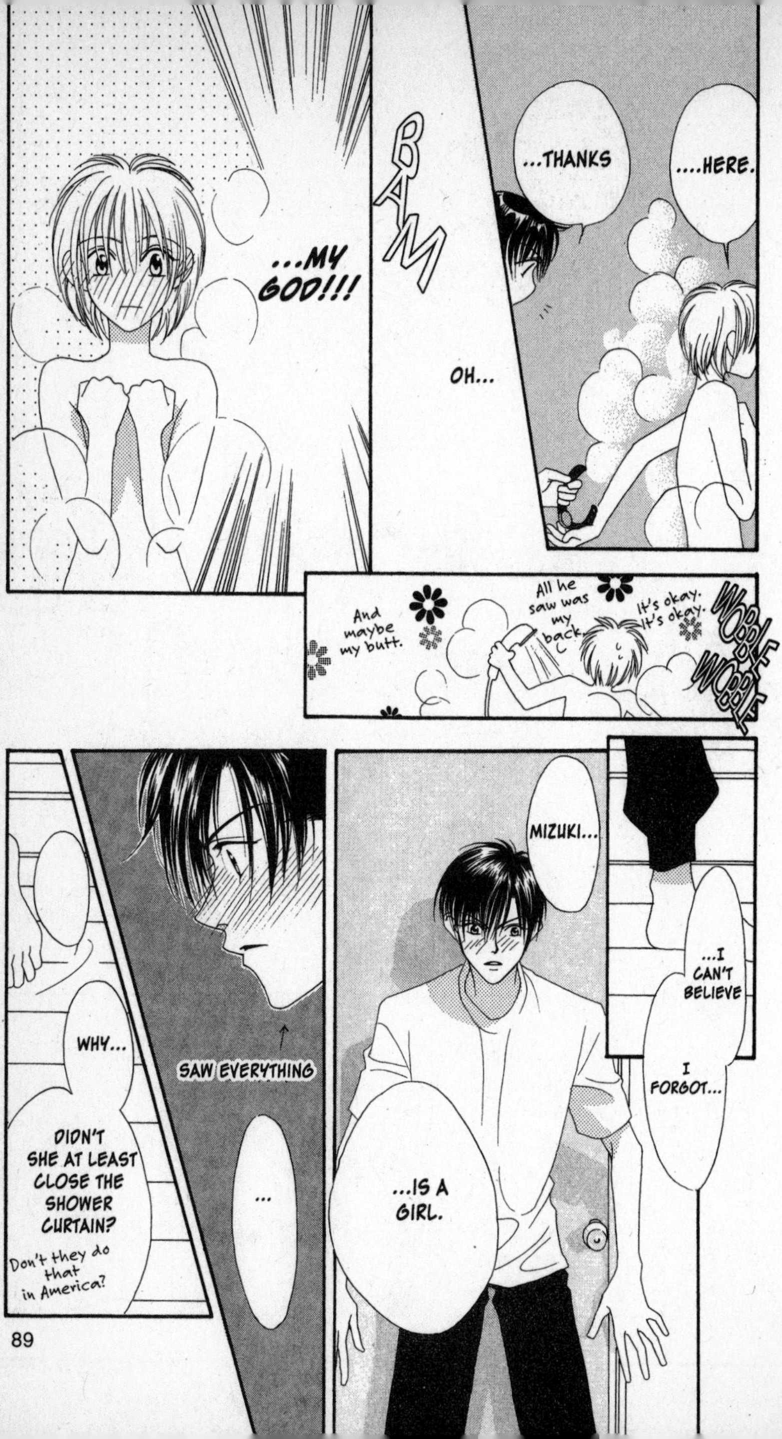
....HERE.
...THANKS
BAM
OH...
...MY GOD!!!
WOBBLE WOBBLE
It's okay. It's okay.
All he saw was my back.
And maybe my butt.
...I CAN'T BELIEVE
I FORGOT...
MIZUKI...
...IS A GIRL.
SAW EVERYTHING
...
WHY...
DIDN'T SHE AT LEAST CLOSE THE SHOWER CURTAIN?
Don't they do that in America?

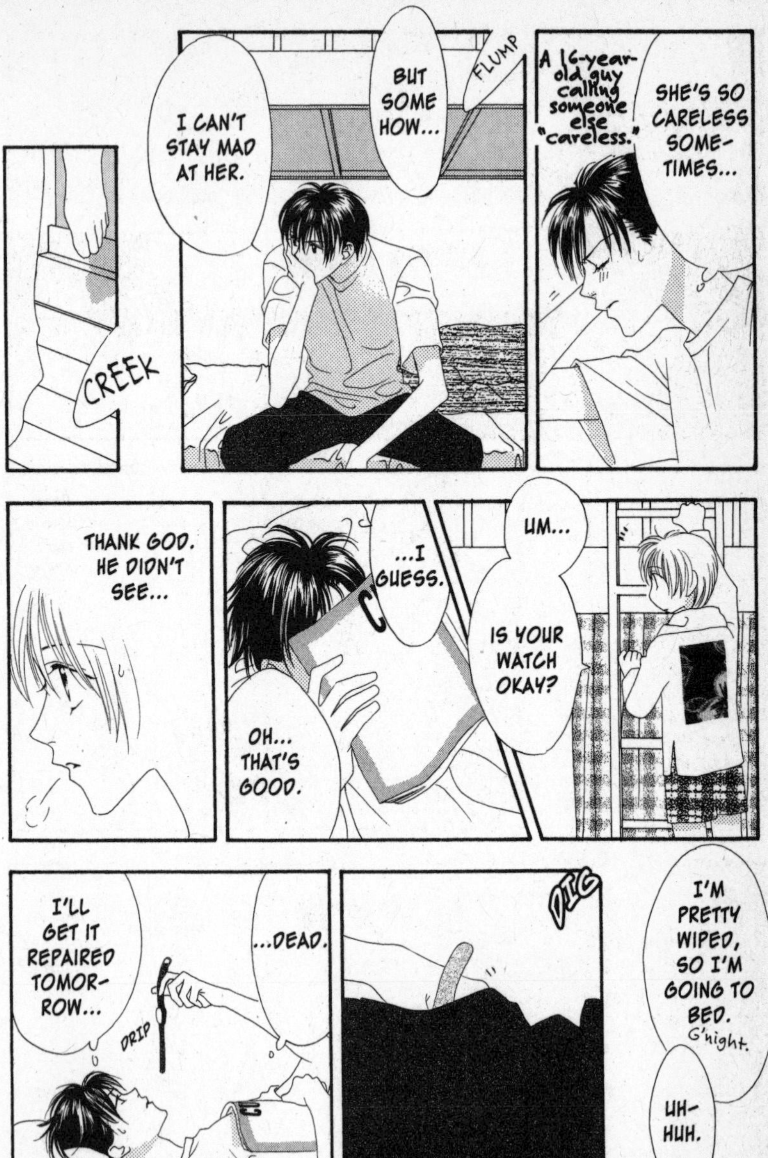
SHE'S SO CARELESS SOME-TIMES...
A 16-year-old guy calling someone else "careless."
FLUMP
BUT SOME HOW...
I CAN'T STAY MAD AT HER.
CREEK
UM...
IS YOUR WATCH OKAY?
...I GUESS.
OH... THAT'S GOOD.
THANK GOD. HE DIDN'T SEE...
I'M PRETTY WIPED, SO I'M GOING TO BED.
G'night.
UH-HUH.
DIG
...DEAD.
I'LL GET IT REPAIRED TOMOR-ROW...
DRIP

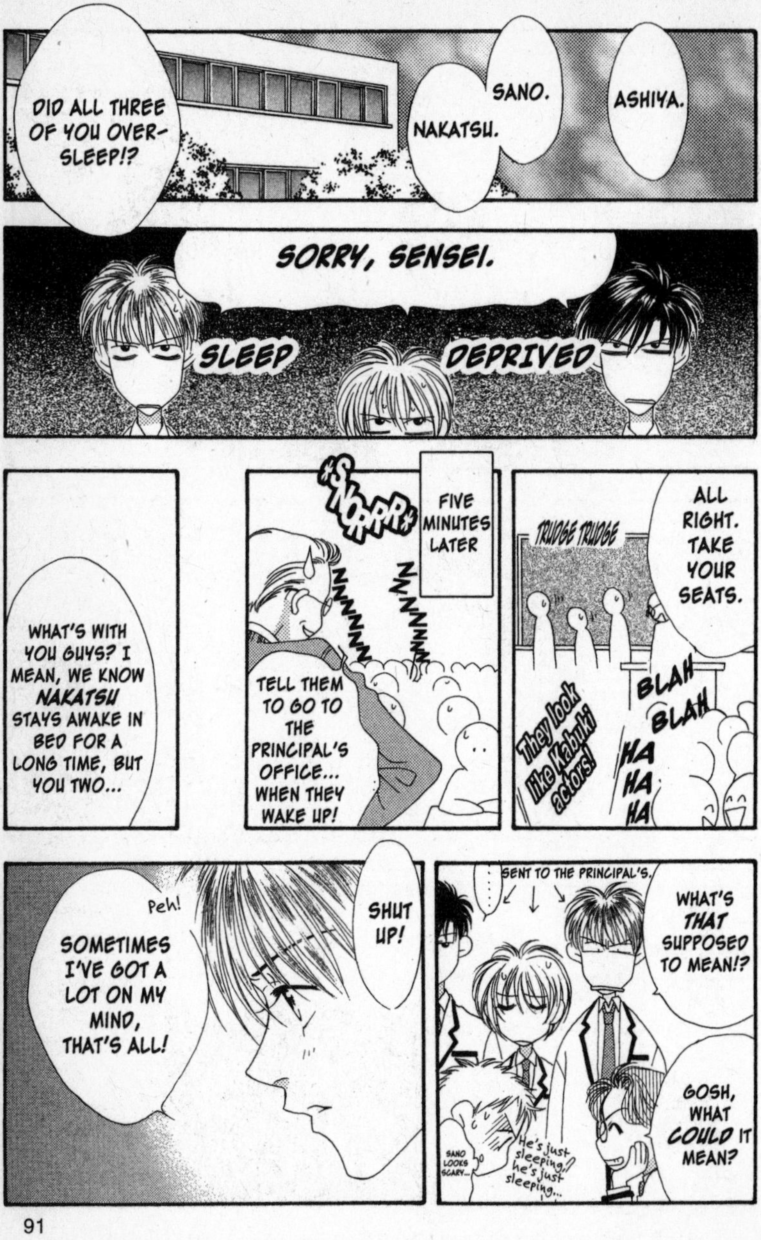
ASHIYA.
SANO.
NAKATSU.
DID ALL THREE OF YOU OVER-SLEEP!?
SORRY, SENSEI.
SLEEP DEPRIVED
ALL RIGHT. TAKE YOUR SEATS.
TRUDGE TRUDGE
BLAH BLAH
HA HA HA
They look like Kabuki actors!
FIVE MINUTES LATER
SNORRR
TELL THEM TO GO TO THE PRINCIPAL'S OFFICE... WHEN THEY WAKE UP!
WHAT'S WITH YOU GUYS? I MEAN, WE KNOW NAKATSU STAYS AWAKE IN BED FOR A LONG TIME, BUT YOU TWO...
WHAT'S THAT SUPPOSED TO MEAN!?
SENT TO THE PRINCIPAL'S.
GOSH, WHAT COULD IT MEAN?
He's just sleeping, he's just sleeping...
SANO LOOKS SCARY...
SHUT UP!
Peh!
SOMETIMES I'VE GOT A LOT ON MY MIND, THAT'S ALL!

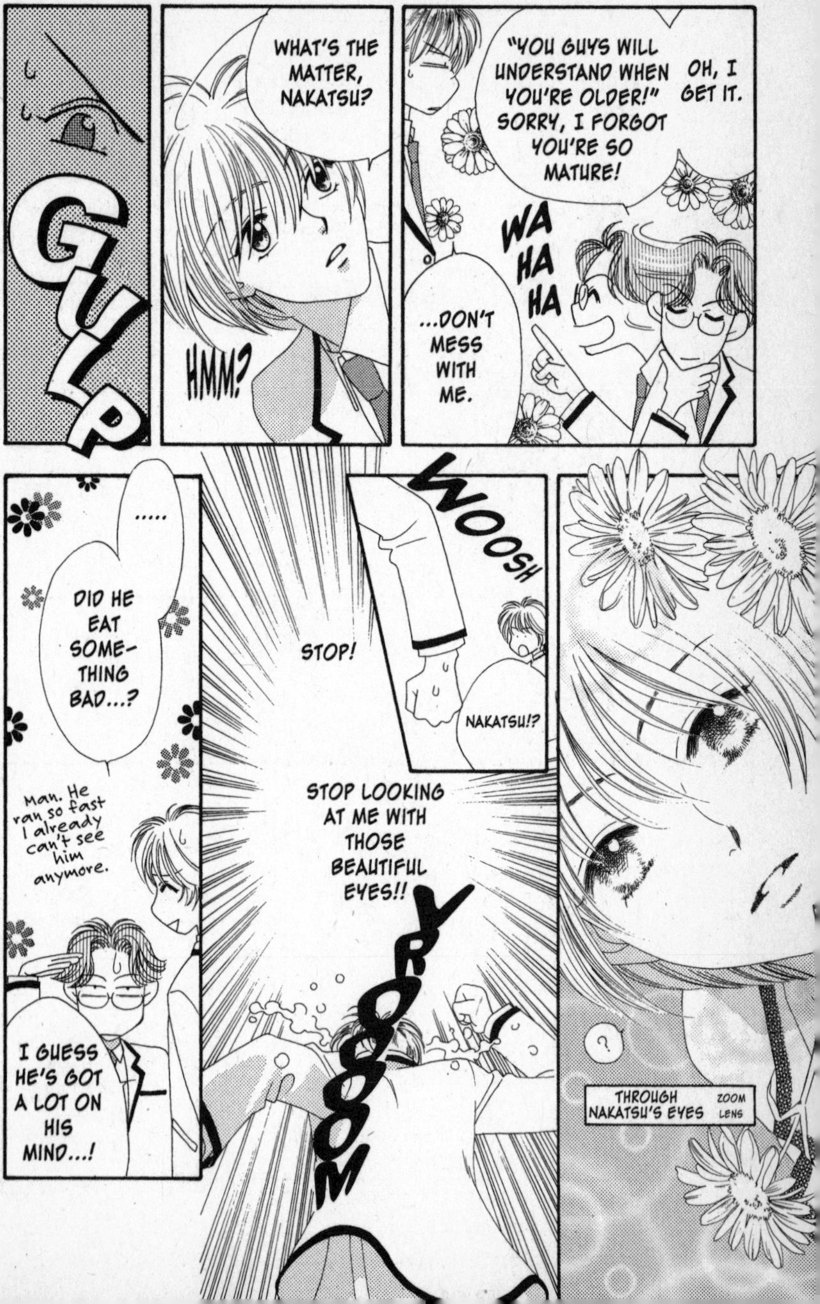
OH, I GET IT.
"YOU GUYS WILL UNDERSTAND WHEN YOU'RE OLDER!" SORRY, I FORGOT YOU'RE SO MATURE!
WA HA HA
...DON'T MESS WITH ME.
WHAT'S THE MATTER, NAKATSU?
HMM?
GULP
?
THROUGH NAKATSU'S EYES
ZOOM LENS
WOOSH
NAKATSU!?
STOP!
STOP LOOKING AT ME WITH THOSE BEAUTIFUL EYES!!
VROOOOOM
.....
DID HE EAT SOMETHING BAD...?
Man. He ran so fast I already can't see him anymore.
I GUESS HE'S GOT A LOT ON HIS MIND...!

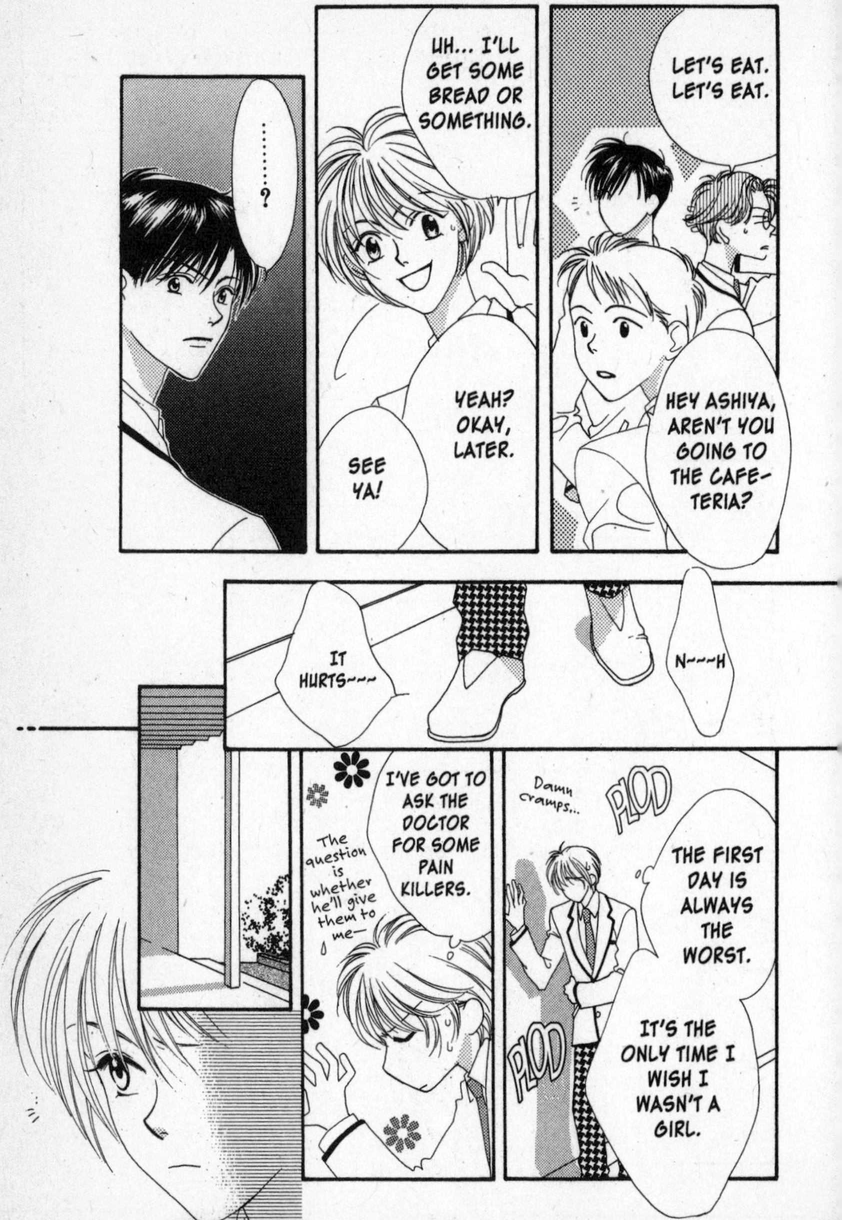
LET'S EAT. LET'S EAT.
HEY ASHIYA, AREN'T YOU GOING TO THE CAFETERIA?
UH... I'LL GET SOME BREAD OR SOMETHING.
YEAH? OKAY, LATER.
SEE YA!
......?
N---H
IT HURTS---
PLOD
Damn cramps...
THE FIRST DAY IS ALWAYS THE WORST.
IT'S THE ONLY TIME I WISH I WASN'T A GIRL.
PLOD
I'VE GOT TO ASK THE DOCTOR FOR SOME PAIN KILLERS.
The question is whether he'll give them to me—

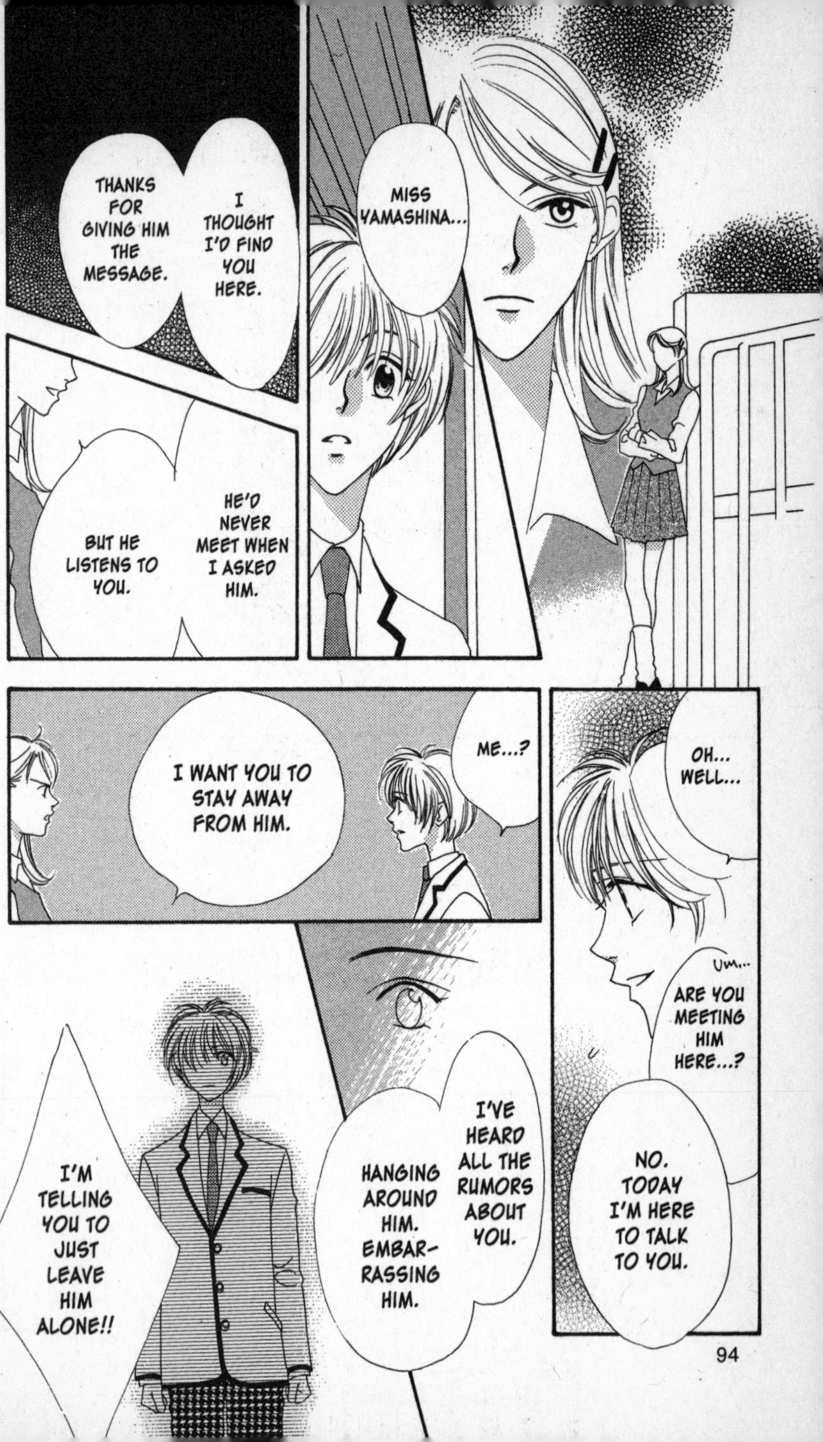
MISS YAMASHINA...
I THOUGHT I'D FIND YOU HERE.
THANKS FOR GIVING HIM THE MESSAGE.
HE'D NEVER MEET WHEN I ASKED HIM.
BUT HE LISTENS TO YOU.
OH... WELL...
UM...
ARE YOU MEETING HIM HERE...?
NO. TODAY I'M HERE TO TALK TO YOU.
ME...?
I WANT YOU TO STAY AWAY FROM HIM.
I'VE HEARD ALL THE RUMORS ABOUT YOU.
HANGING AROUND HIM. EMBAR-RASSING HIM.
I'M TELLING YOU TO JUST LEAVE HIM ALONE!!

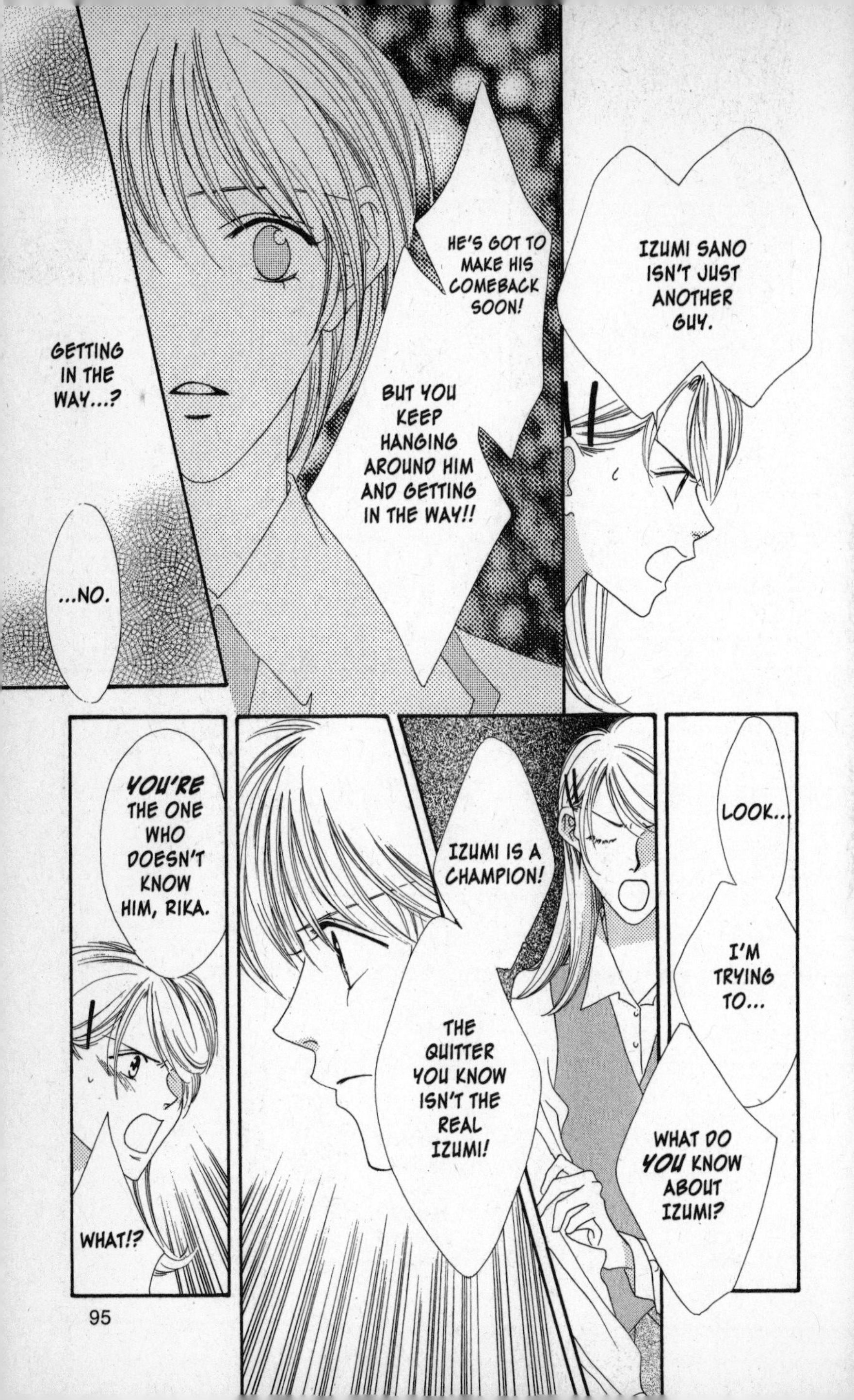
IZUMI SANO ISN'T JUST ANOTHER GUY.
HE'S GOT TO MAKE HIS COMEBACK SOON!
BUT YOU KEEP HANGING AROUND HIM AND GETTING IN THE WAY!!
GETTING IN THE WAY...?
...NO.
LOOK...
I'M TRYING TO...
WHAT DO *YOU* KNOW ABOUT IZUMI?
IZUMI IS A CHAMPION!
THE QUITTER YOU KNOW ISN'T THE REAL IZUMI!
YOU'RE THE ONE WHO DOESN'T KNOW HIM, RIKA.
WHAT!?

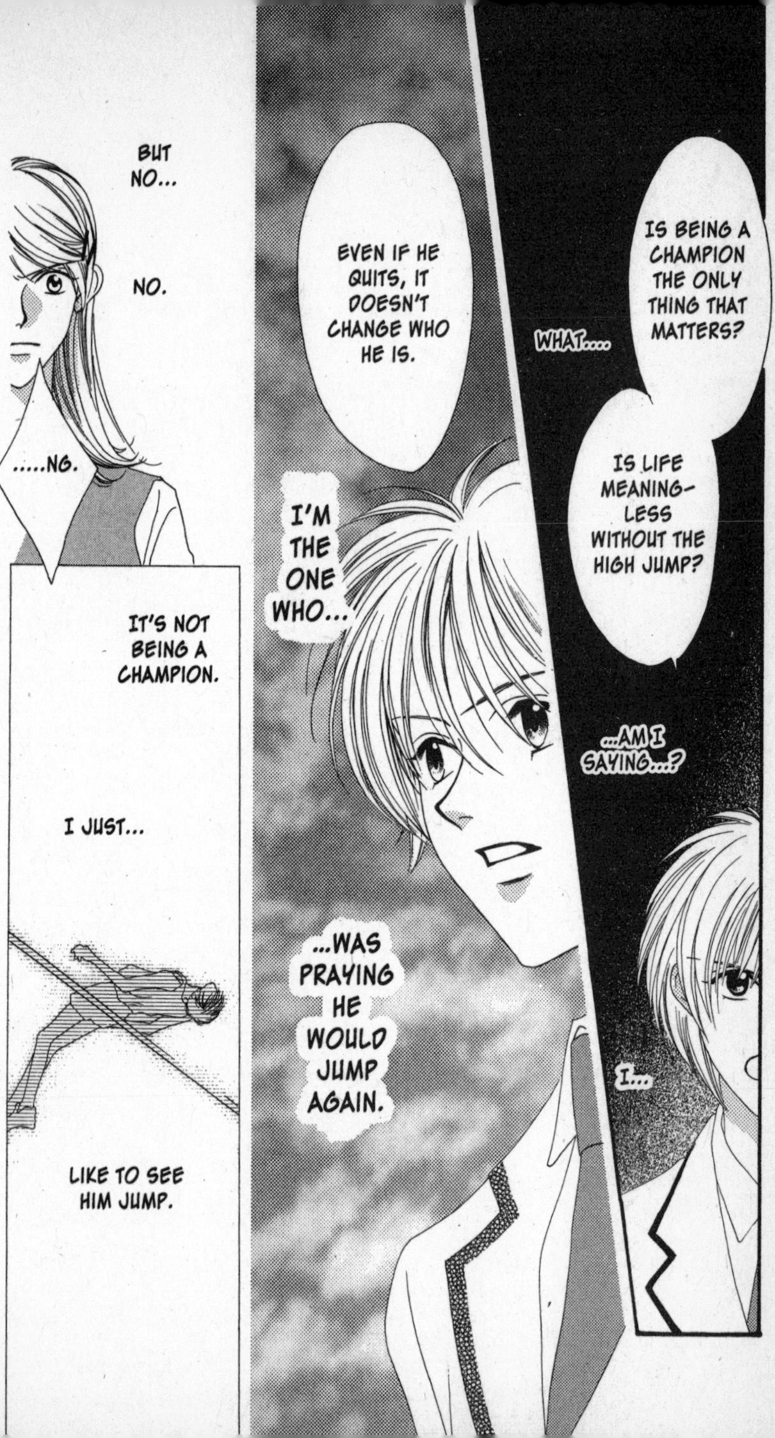

IS BEING A CHAMPION THE ONLY THING THAT MATTERS?
WHAT....
IS LIFE MEANING-LESS WITHOUT THE HIGH JUMP?
...AM I SAYING...?
I...
EVEN IF HE QUITS, IT DOESN'T CHANGE WHO HE IS.
I'M THE ONE WHO...
...WAS PRAYING HE WOULD JUMP AGAIN.
BUT NO...
NO.
.....NG.
IT'S NOT BEING A CHAMPION.
I JUST...
LIKE TO SEE HIM JUMP.

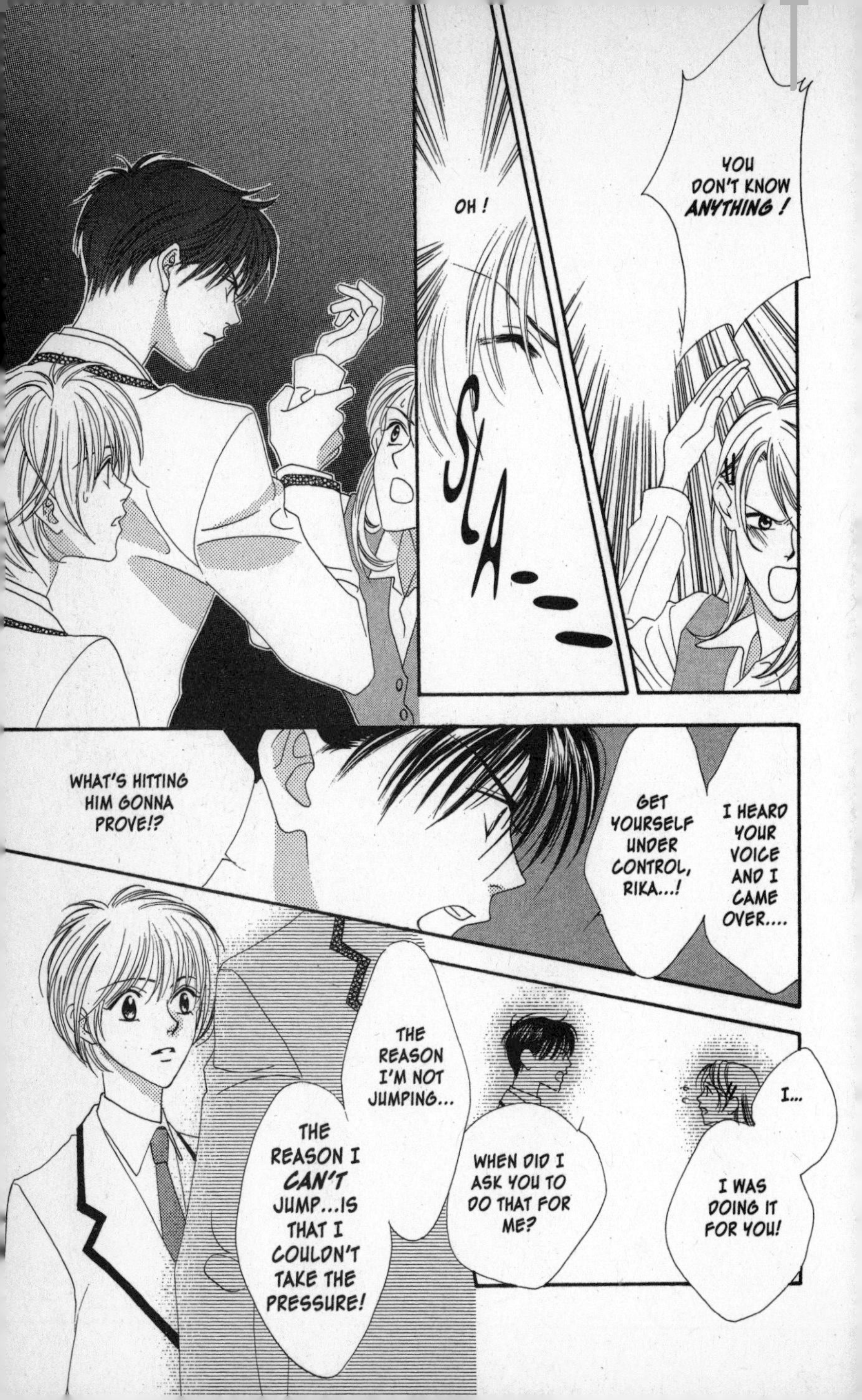
YOU DON'T KNOW ANYTHING !
OH !
SLA---
I HEARD YOUR VOICE AND I CAME OVER....
GET YOURSELF UNDER CONTROL, RIKA...!
WHAT'S HITTING HIM GONNA PROVE!?
I...
I WAS DOING IT FOR YOU!
WHEN DID I ASK YOU TO DO THAT FOR ME?
THE REASON I'M NOT JUMPING...
THE REASON I CAN'T JUMP...IS THAT I COULDN'T TAKE THE PRESSURE!

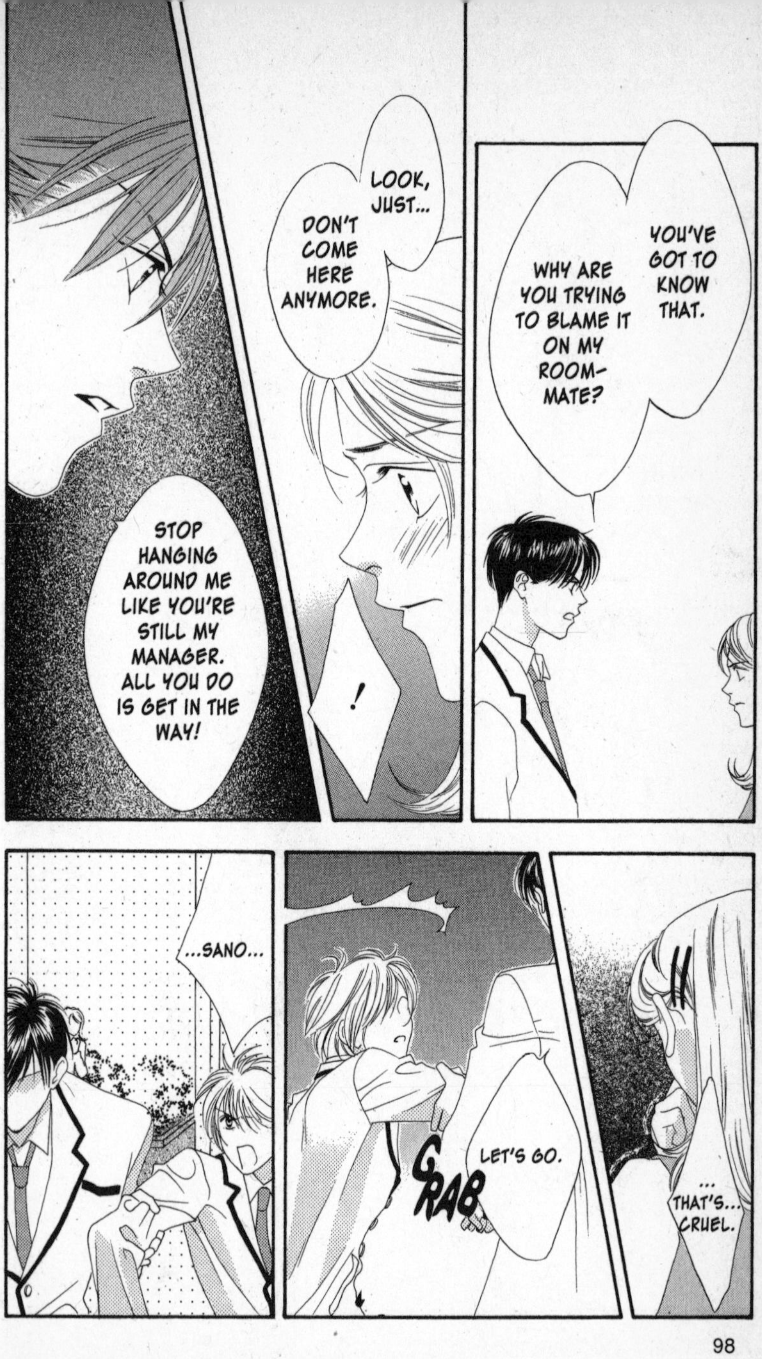
YOU'VE GOT TO KNOW THAT.
WHY ARE YOU TRYING TO BLAME IT ON MY ROOM-MATE?
LOOK, JUST...
DON'T COME HERE ANYMORE.
!
STOP HANGING AROUND ME LIKE YOU'RE STILL MY MANAGER. ALL YOU DO IS GET IN THE WAY!
...THAT'S... CRUEL.
LET'S GO.
GRAB
...SANO...

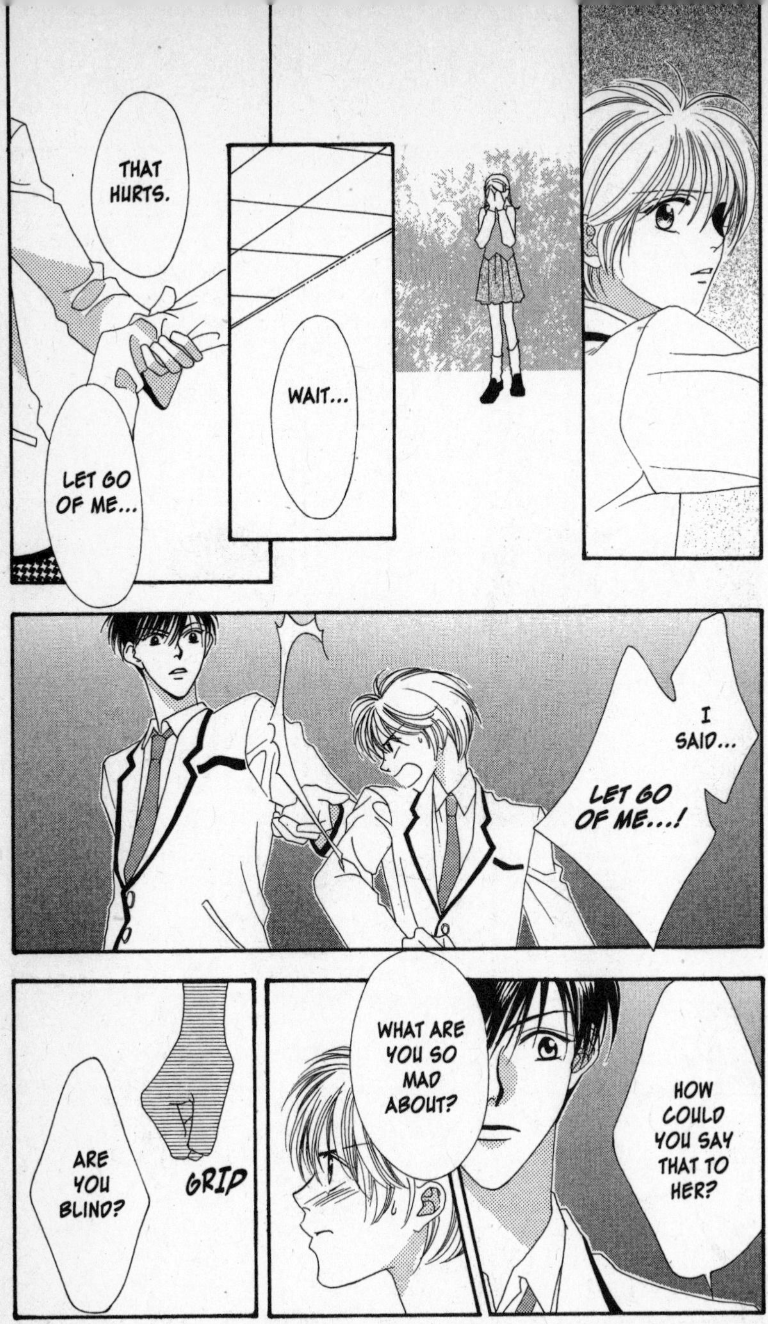
WAIT...
THAT HURTS.
LET GO OF ME...
I SAID...
LET GO OF ME...!
HOW COULD YOU SAY THAT TO HER?
WHAT ARE YOU SO MAD ABOUT?
GRIP
ARE YOU BLIND?

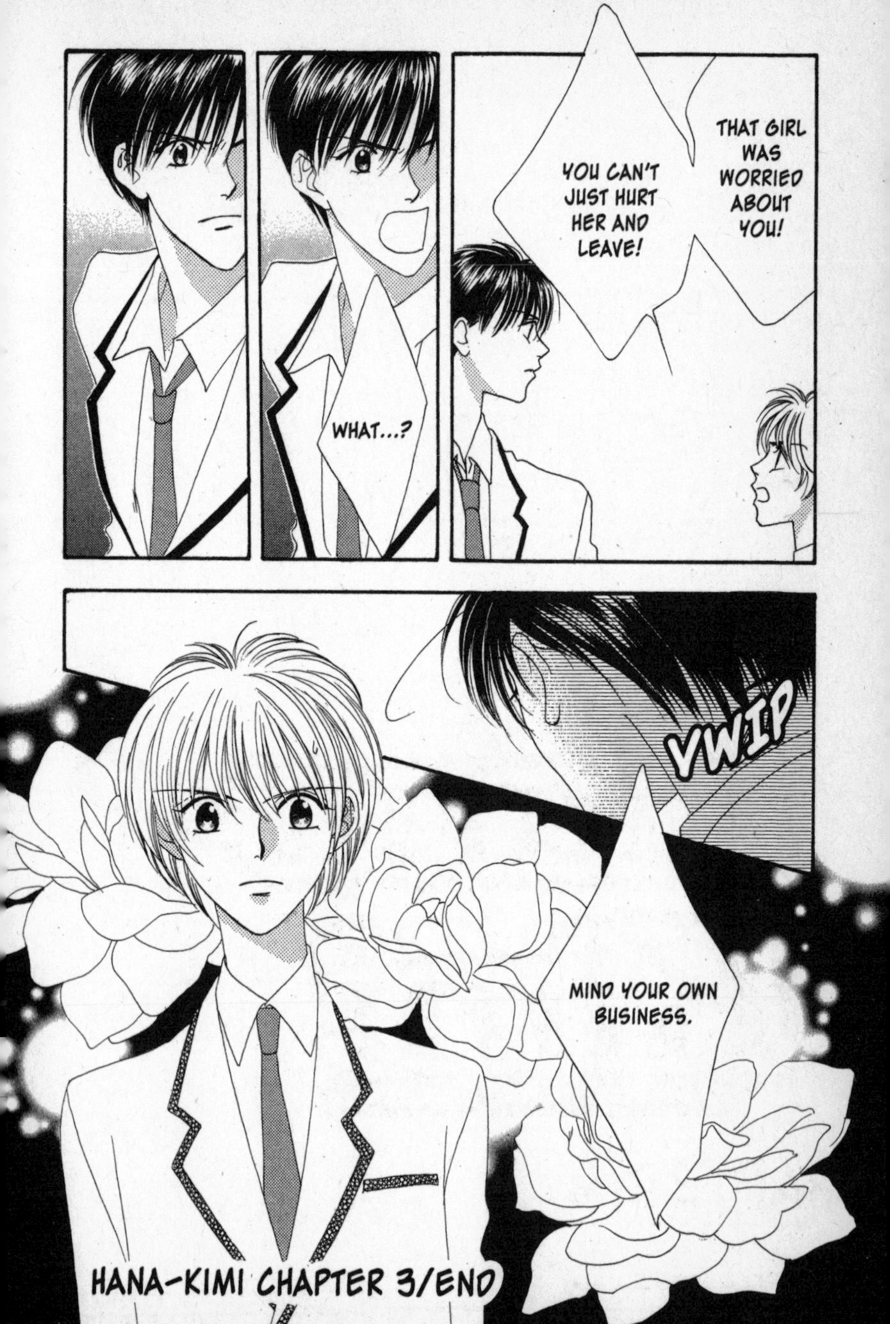
THAT GIRL WAS WORRIED ABOUT YOU!
YOU CAN'T JUST HURT HER AND LEAVE!
WHAT...?
VWIP
MIND YOUR OWN BUSINESS.
HANA-KIMI CHAPTER 3/END

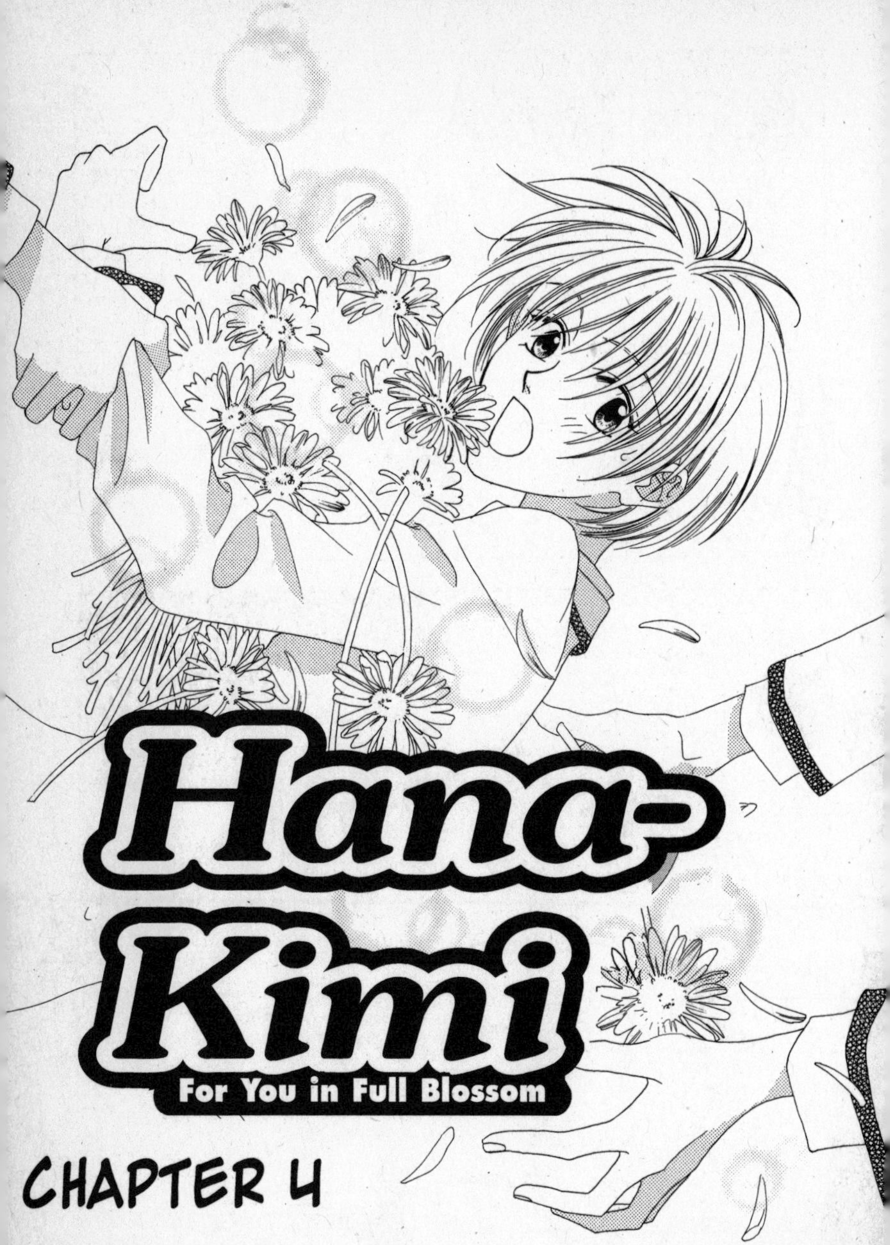
Hana-Kimi
For You in Full Blossom
CHAPTER 4

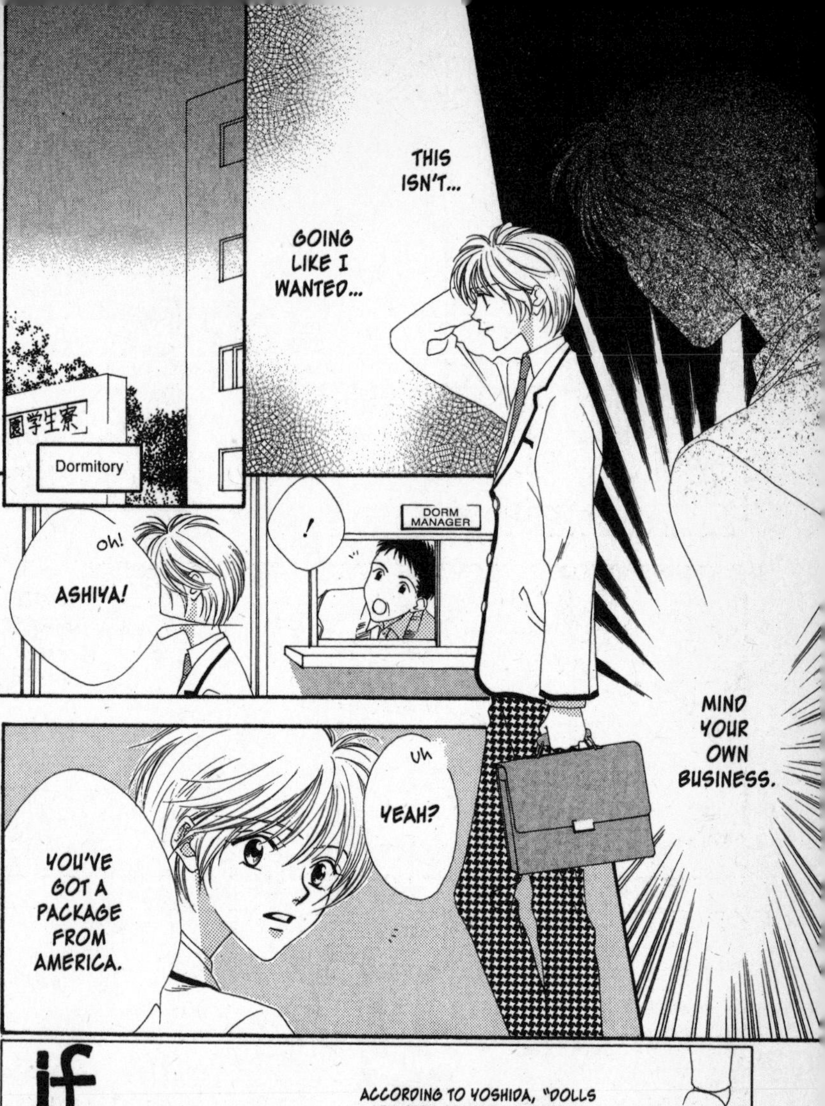
THIS ISN'T...
GOING LIKE I WANTED...
MIND YOUR OWN BUSINESS.
園学生寮
Dormitory
DORM MANAGER
!
oh! ASHIYA!
uh YEAH?
YOU'VE GOT A PACKAGE FROM AMERICA.

if

IF I HADN'T GOTTEN THIS JOB, I WAS THINKING OF BEING A DOLL MAKER. I'VE ALWAYS BEEN VERY IMPRESSED WITH THE DOLLS OF SHIMON YOTSUYA, RYOICHI YOSHIDA AND THE VERY BUSY KAORI TENNO. I MIGHT HAVE TRIED TO GET INTO YOTSUYA'S DOLL SCHOOL. EVENTUALLY I CHOSE COMICS, BUT I WAS REALLY SERIOUS ABOUT DOLLS AT ONE POINT (HEH).

ACCORDING TO YOSHIDA, "DOLLS ARE VERY BEAUTIFUL AND ALSO VERY FRIGHTENING, BECAUSE WE CAN SEE DEATH IN THEM." I GUESS THE CLOSER YOU GET TO SOMEONE THE CLOSER YOU FEEL TO DEATH. BUT THAT'S WHERE THE ATTRACTION LIES.

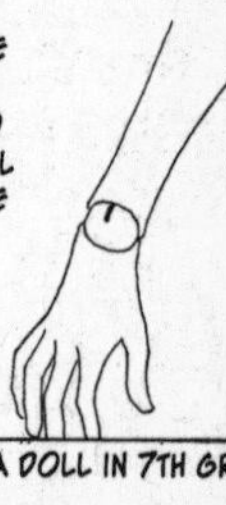

I ACTUALLY MADE A DOLL IN 7TH GRADE.

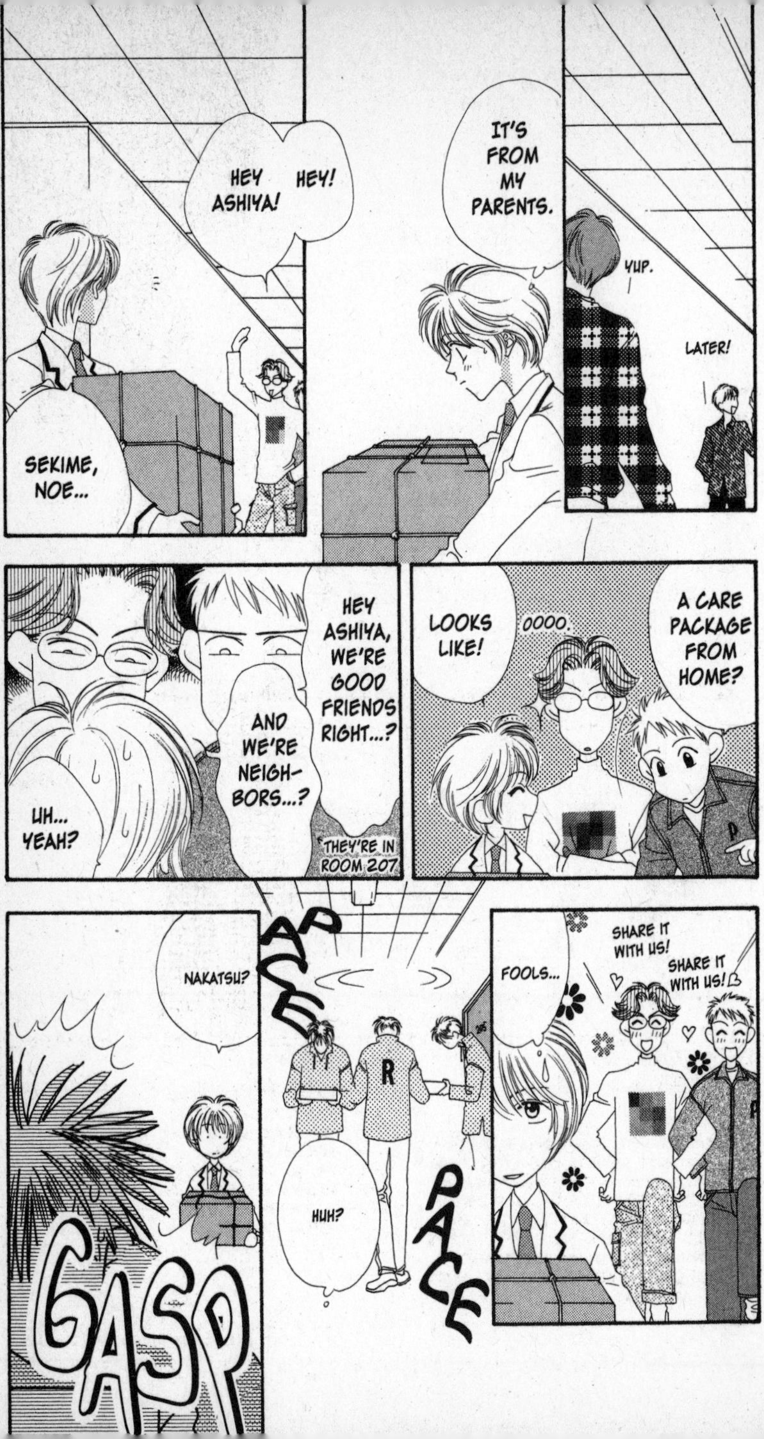
YUP.
LATER!
IT'S FROM MY PARENTS.
HEY ASHIYA!
HEY!
SEKIME, NOE...
A CARE PACKAGE FROM HOME?
OOOO.
LOOKS LIKE!
HEY ASHIYA, WE'RE GOOD FRIENDS RIGHT...?
AND WE'RE NEIGHBORS...?
THEY'RE IN ROOM 207
UH... YEAH?
SHARE IT WITH US!
SHARE IT WITH US!
FOOLS...
PACE
PACE
HUH?
NAKATSU?
GASP

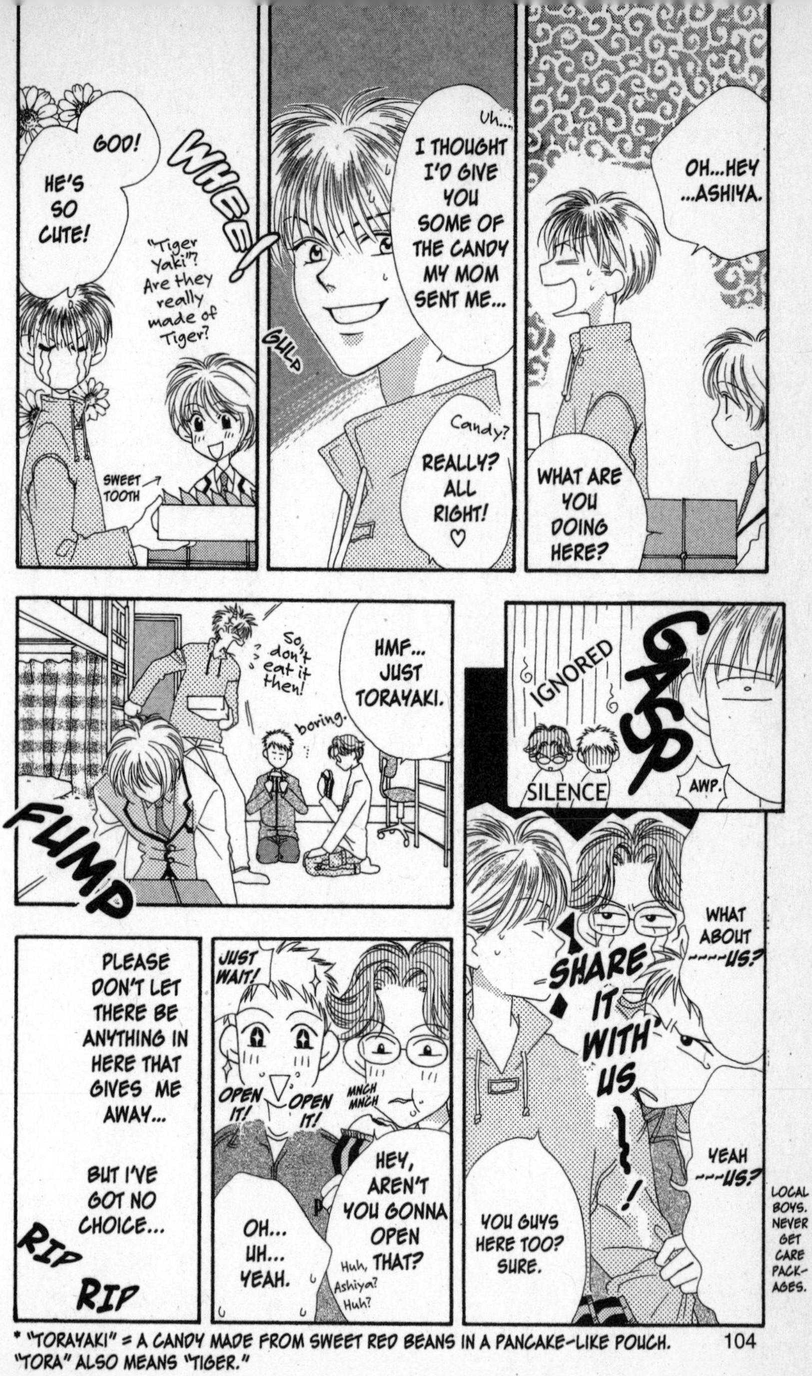
OH...HEY ...ASHIYA.
WHAT ARE YOU DOING HERE?
Uh...
I THOUGHT I'D GIVE YOU SOME OF THE CANDY MY MOM SENT ME...
GULP
Candy?
REALLY? ALL RIGHT! ♡
WHEE!
GOD! HE'S SO CUTE!
"Tiger Yaki"? Are they really made of Tiger?
SWEET TOOTH
GASP
IGNORED
SILENCE
AWP.
HMF... JUST TORAYAKI.
So, don't eat it then!
boring.
FUMP
WHAT ABOUT ---US?
SHARE IT WITH US!
YEAH ---US?
LOCAL BOYS. NEVER GET CARE PACKAGES.
YOU GUYS HERE TOO? SURE.
JUST WAIT!
OPEN IT! OPEN IT!
MNCH MNCH
HEY, AREN'T YOU GONNA OPEN THAT?
OH... UH... YEAH.
Huh, Ashiya? Huh?
PLEASE DON'T LET THERE BE ANYTHING IN HERE THAT GIVES ME AWAY...
BUT I'VE GOT NO CHOICE...
RIP
RIP

* "TORAYAKI" = A CANDY MADE FROM SWEET RED BEANS IN A PANCAKE-LIKE POUCH. "TORA" ALSO MEANS "TIGER."

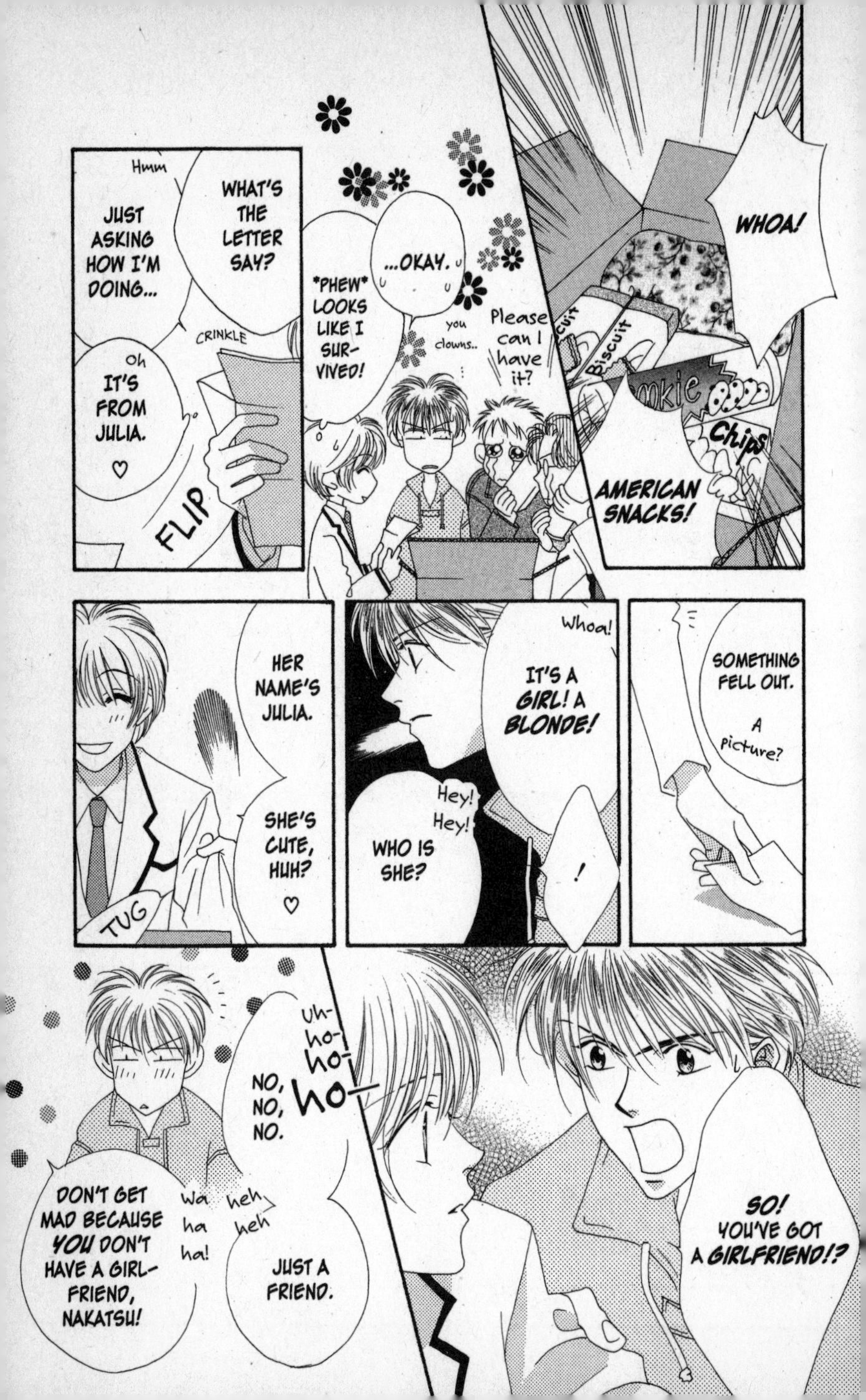
WHOA!
Biscuit
Chips
AMERICAN SNACKS!
...OKAY.
PHEW LOOKS LIKE I SURVIVED!
you clowns..
Please can I have it?
WHAT'S THE LETTER SAY?
Hmm
JUST ASKING HOW I'M DOING...
CRINKLE
Oh IT'S FROM JULIA. ♡
FLIP
SOMETHING FELL OUT.
A picture?
Whoa!
IT'S A GIRL! A BLONDE!
!
Hey! Hey!
WHO IS SHE?
HER NAME'S JULIA.
SHE'S CUTE, HUH? ♡
TUG
SO! YOU'VE GOT A GIRLFRIEND!?
Uh-ho-ho-ho
NO, NO, NO.
heh heh
JUST A FRIEND.
Wa ha ha!
DON'T GET MAD BECAUSE YOU DON'T HAVE A GIRL-FRIEND, NAKATSU!

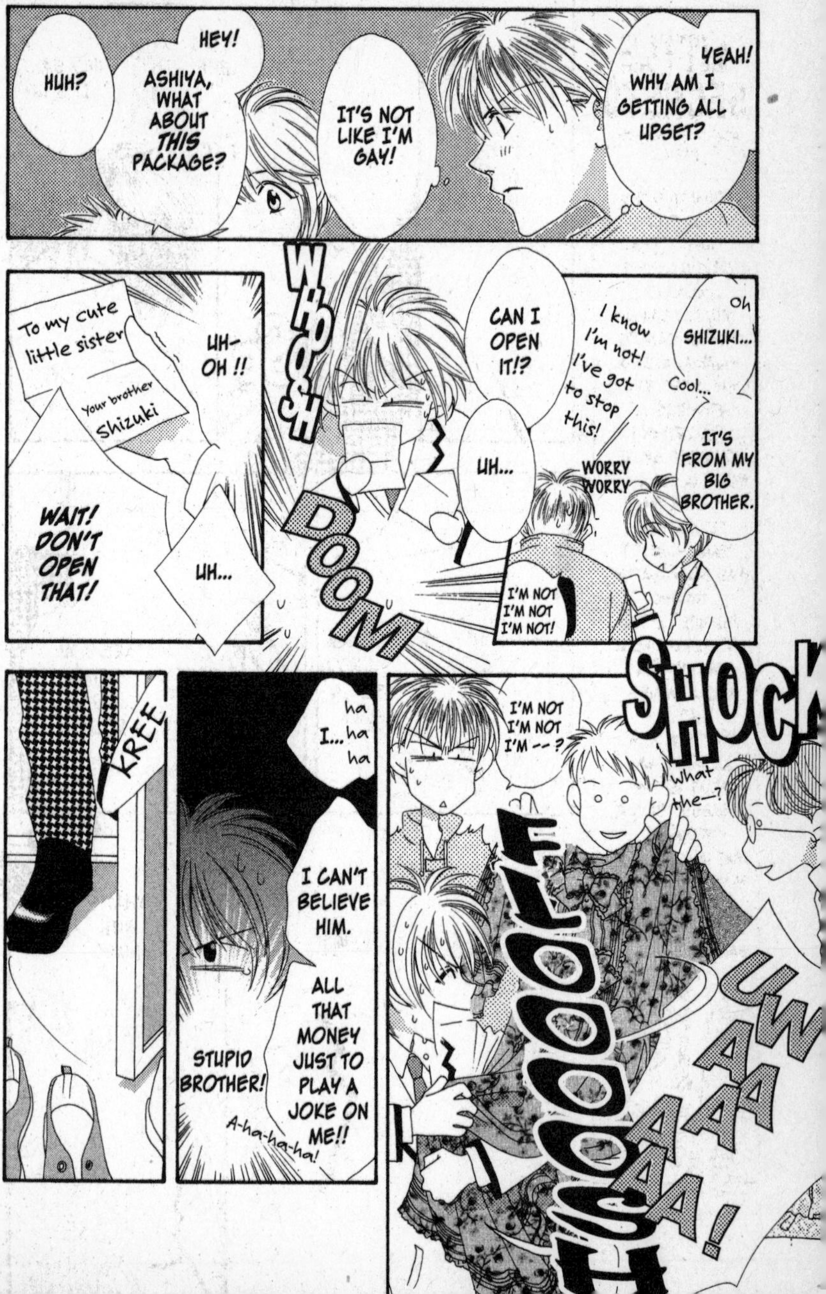
YEAH! WHY AM I GETTING ALL UPSET?
IT'S NOT LIKE I'M GAY!
HEY!
ASHIYA, WHAT ABOUT THIS PACKAGE?
HUH?
Oh SHIZUKI... Cool...
IT'S FROM MY BIG BROTHER.
I know I'm not! I've got to stop this!
CAN I OPEN IT!?
WORRY WORRY
I'M NOT I'M NOT I'M NOT!
UH...
WHOOSH
DOOOM
To my cute little sister
Your brother Shizuki
UH-OH !!
UH...
WAIT! DON'T OPEN THAT!
SHOCK
I'M NOT I'M NOT I'M -- ?
what the--?
UWAAAAAA!
FLOOOOOSH
ha I... ha ha
I CAN'T BELIEVE HIM.
ALL THAT MONEY JUST TO PLAY A JOKE ON ME!!
STUPID BROTHER!
A-ha-ha-ha!
KREE

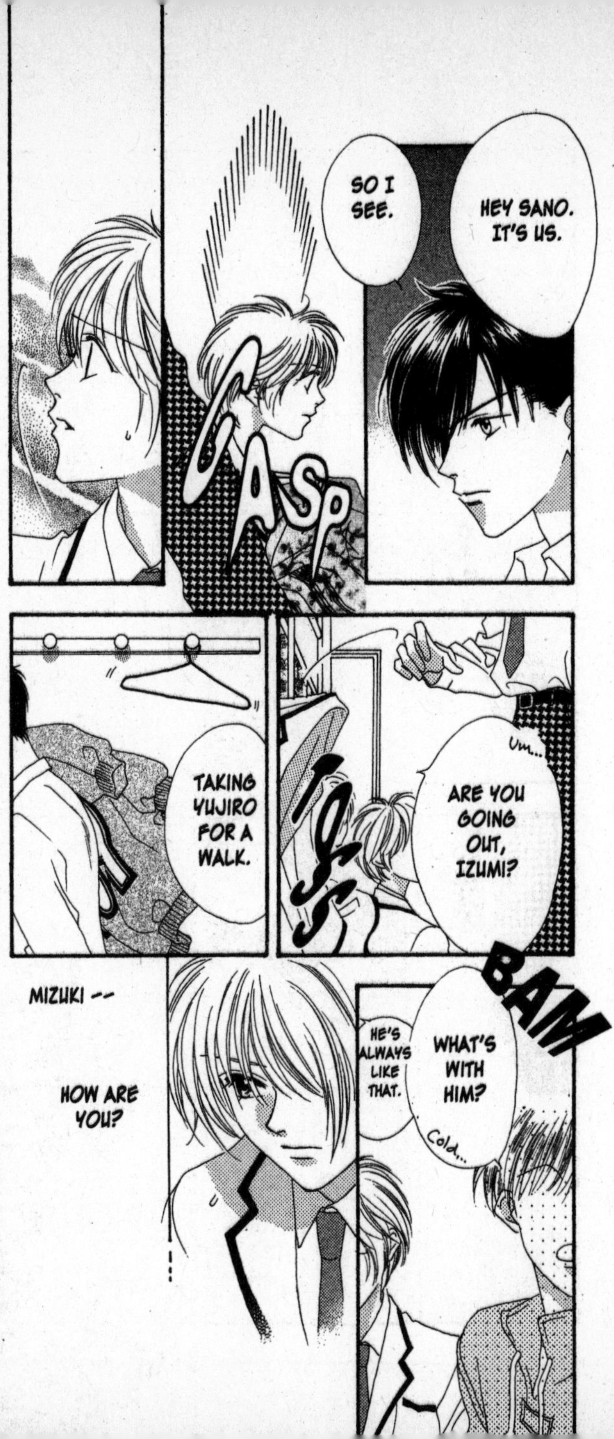
HEY SANO. IT'S US.
SO I SEE.
GASP
Um...
ARE YOU GOING OUT, IZUMI?
TAKING YUJIRO FOR A WALK.
BAM
WHAT'S WITH HIM?
HE'S ALWAYS LIKE THAT.
Cold...
MIZUKI --
HOW ARE YOU?
...

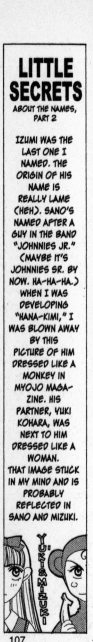

LITTLE SECRETS

ABOUT THE NAMES, PART 2

IZUMI WAS THE LAST ONE I NAMED. THE ORIGIN OF HIS NAME IS REALLY LAME (HEH). SANO'S NAMED AFTER A GUY IN THE BAND "JOHNNIES JR." (MAYBE IT'S JOHNNIES SR. BY NOW. HA-HA-HA.) WHEN I WAS DEVELOPING "HANA-KIMI," I WAS BLOWN AWAY BY THIS PICTURE OF HIM DRESSED LIKE A MONKEY IN MYOJO MAGAZINE. HIS PARTNER, YUKI KOHARA, WAS NEXT TO HIM DRESSED LIKE A WOMAN. THAT IMAGE STUCK IN MY MIND AND IS PROBABLY REFLECTED IN SANO AND MIZUKI.

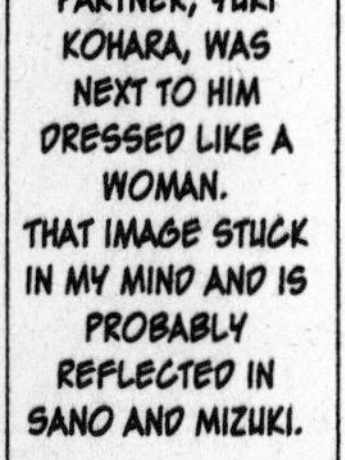
YUKI & MIZUKI

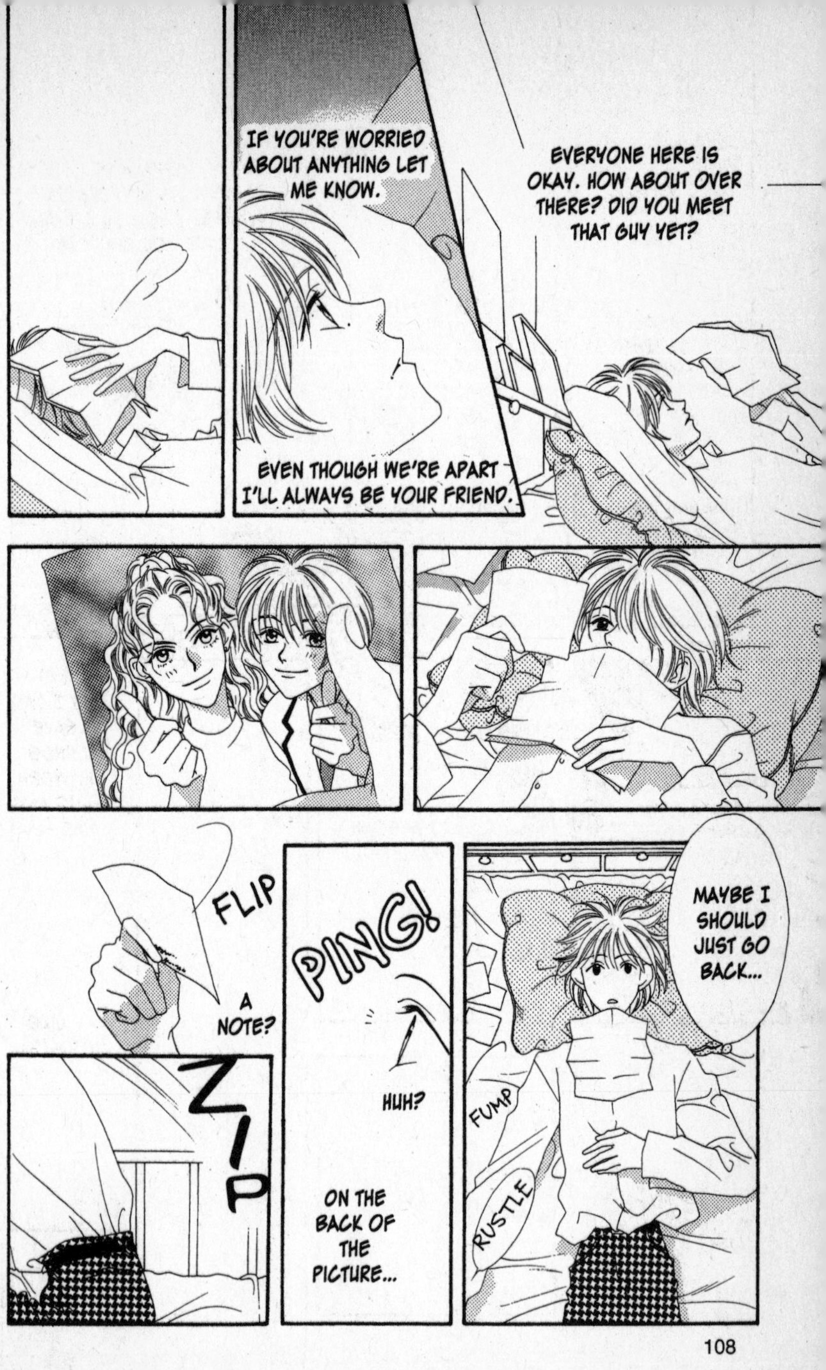
EVERYONE HERE IS OKAY. HOW ABOUT OVER THERE? DID YOU MEET THAT GUY YET?
IF YOU'RE WORRIED ABOUT ANYTHING LET ME KNOW.
EVEN THOUGH WE'RE APART I'LL ALWAYS BE YOUR FRIEND.
MAYBE I SHOULD JUST GO BACK...
FUMP
RUSTLE
PING!
HUH?
ON THE BACK OF THE PICTURE...
FLIP
A NOTE?
ZIP

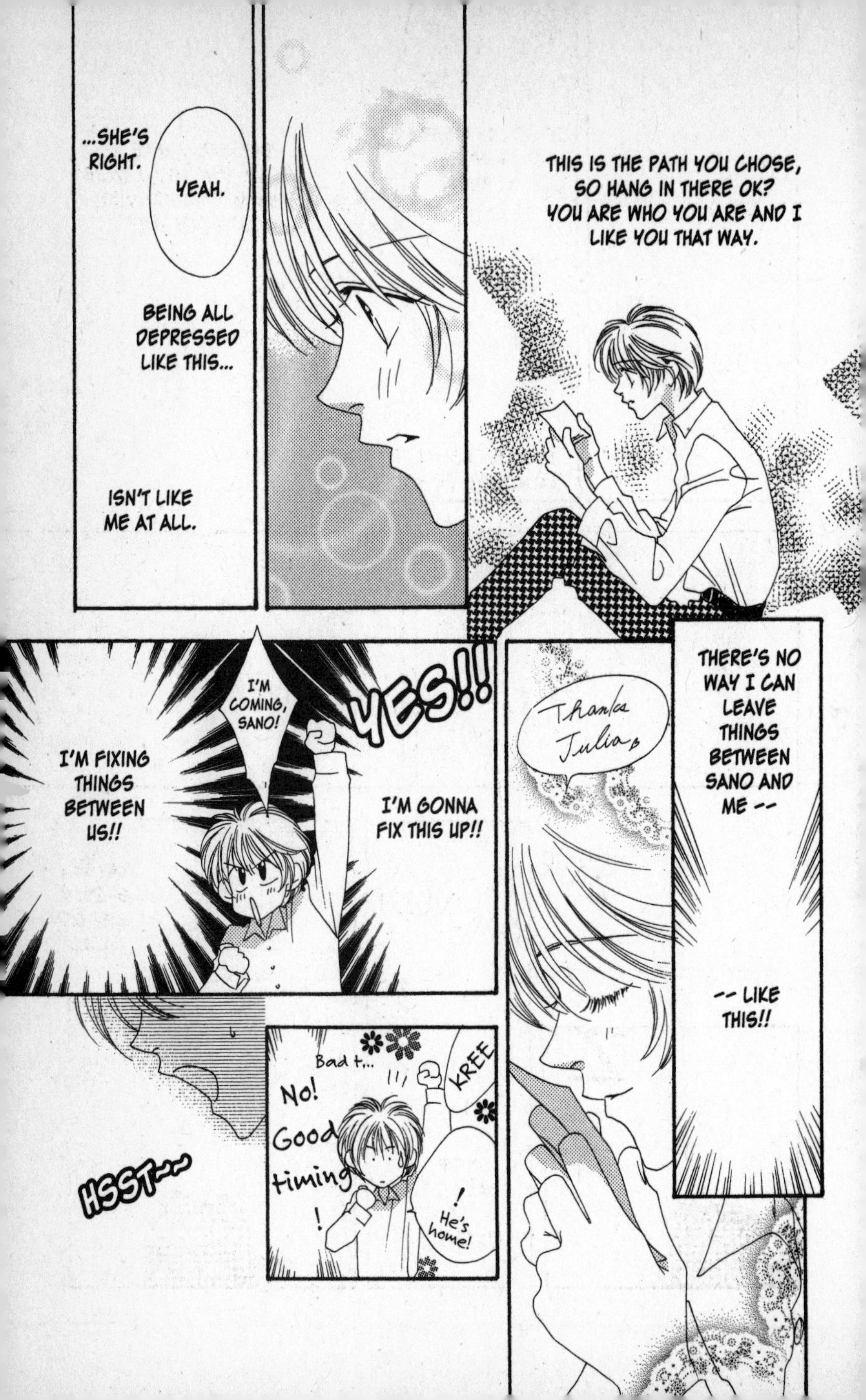
THIS IS THE PATH YOU CHOSE, SO HANG IN THERE OK? YOU ARE WHO YOU ARE AND I LIKE YOU THAT WAY.
YEAH.
...SHE'S RIGHT.
BEING ALL DEPRESSED LIKE THIS...
ISN'T LIKE ME AT ALL.
THERE'S NO WAY I CAN LEAVE THINGS BETWEEN SANO AND ME --
Thanks Julia
-- LIKE THIS!!
YES!!
I'M GONNA FIX THIS UP!!
I'M COMING, SANO!
I'M FIXING THINGS BETWEEN US!!
KREE
Bad t...
No! Good timing!
! He's home!
HSST--

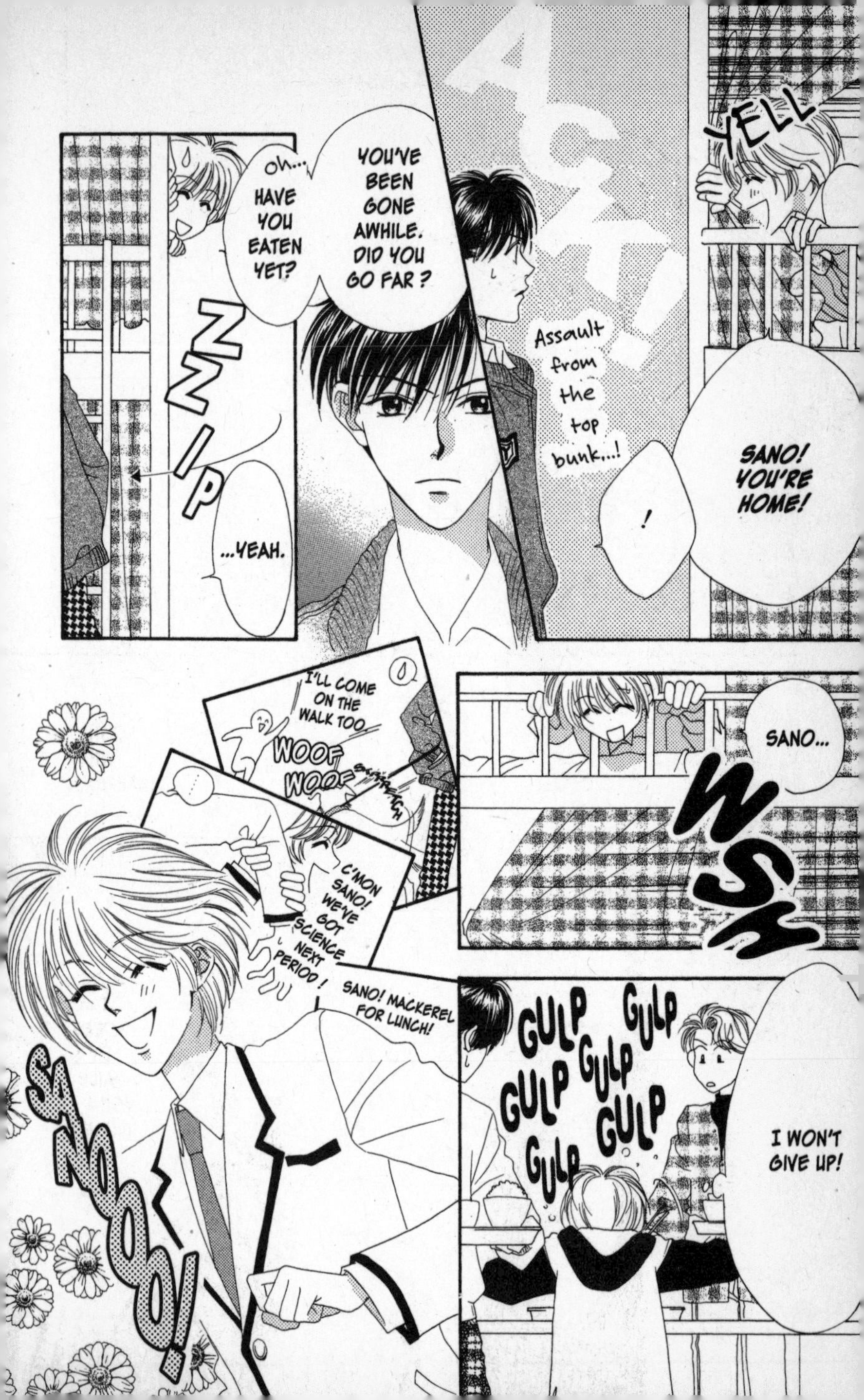
YELL
SANO! YOU'RE HOME!
!
Assault from the top bunk...!
YOU'VE BEEN GONE AWHILE. DID YOU GO FAR?
Oh... HAVE YOU EATEN YET?
ZZIP
...YEAH.
SANO...
WSH
GULP GULP GULP GULP GULP GULP
I WON'T GIVE UP!
I'LL COME ON THE WALK TOO.
WOOF WOOF
...
C'MON SANO! WE'VE GOT SCIENCE NEXT PERIOD!
SANO! MACKEREL FOR LUNCH!
SANOOO!

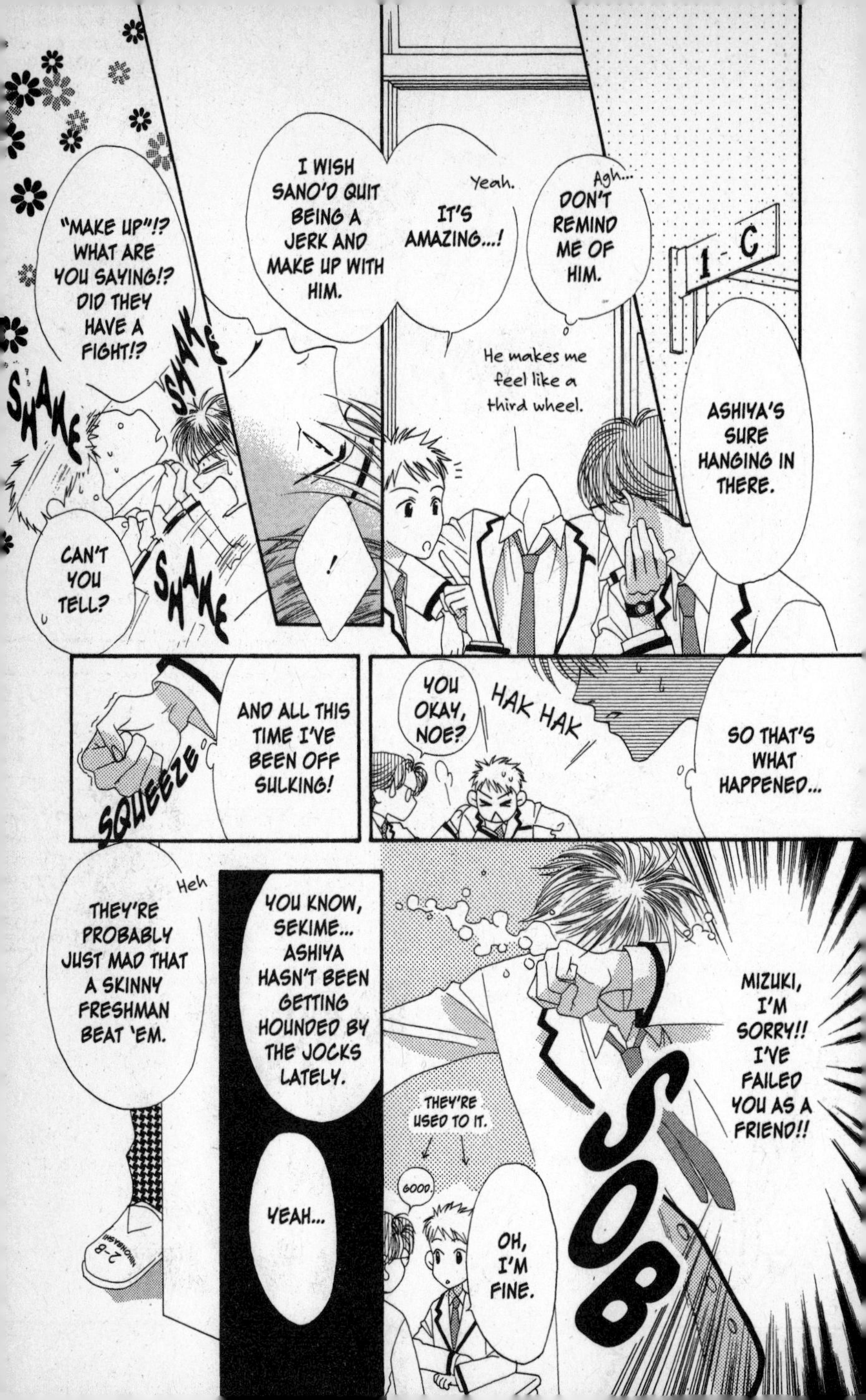
1-C
ASHIYA'S SURE HANGING IN THERE.
Yeah. IT'S AMAZING...!
Agh... DON'T REMIND ME OF HIM.
He makes me feel like a third wheel.
I WISH SANO'D QUIT BEING A JERK AND MAKE UP WITH HIM.
!
"MAKE UP"!? WHAT ARE YOU SAYING!? DID THEY HAVE A FIGHT!?
SHAKE SHAKE SHAKE
CAN'T YOU TELL?
SO THAT'S WHAT HAPPENED...
HAK HAK
YOU OKAY, NOE?
AND ALL THIS TIME I'VE BEEN OFF SULKING!
SQUEEZE
MIZUKI, I'M SORRY!! I'VE FAILED YOU AS A FRIEND!!
SOB
THEY'RE USED TO IT.
GOOD.
OH, I'M FINE.
YOU KNOW, SEKIME... ASHIYA HASN'T BEEN GETTING HOUNDED BY THE JOCKS LATELY.
YEAH...
Heh
THEY'RE PROBABLY JUST MAD THAT A SKINNY FRESHMAN BEAT 'EM.
2-B

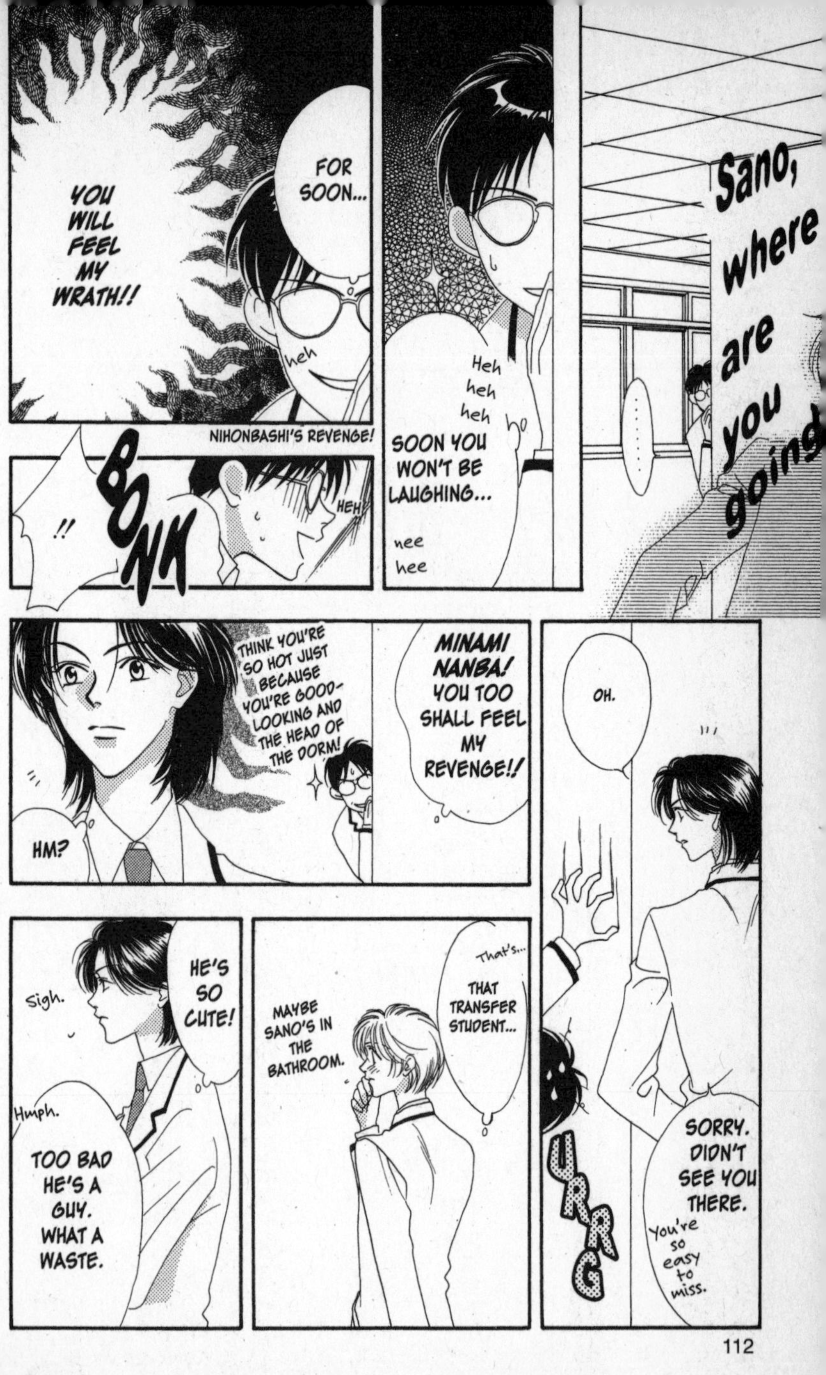

Sano, where are you going
......
Heh heh heh
SOON YOU WON'T BE LAUGHING...
nee hee
FOR SOON...
YOU WILL FEEL MY WRATH!!
heh
NIHONBASHI'S REVENGE!
BONK
!!
HEH
OH.
URRG
SORRY. DIDN'T SEE YOU THERE.
You're so easy to miss.
MINAMI NANBA! YOU TOO SHALL FEEL MY REVENGE!!
THINK YOU'RE SO HOT JUST BECAUSE YOU'RE GOOD-LOOKING AND THE HEAD OF THE DORM!
HM?
That's...
THAT TRANSFER STUDENT...
MAYBE SANO'S IN THE BATHROOM.
Sigh.
HE'S SO CUTE!
Hmph.
TOO BAD HE'S A GUY. WHAT A WASTE.

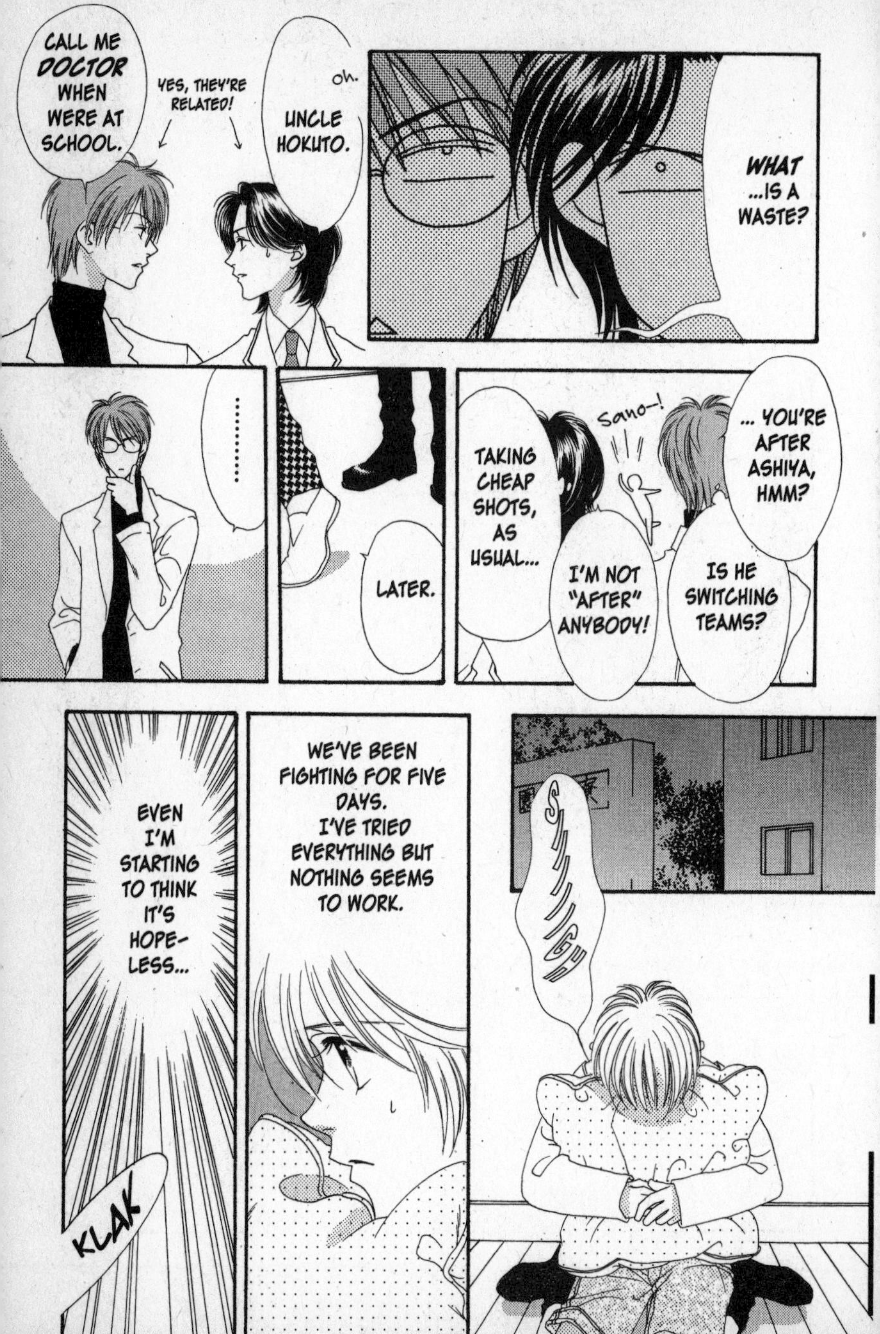
WHAT ...IS A WASTE?
Oh.
UNCLE HOKUTO.
YES, THEY'RE RELATED!
CALL ME DOCTOR WHEN WERE AT SCHOOL.
... YOU'RE AFTER ASHIYA, HMM?
Sano-!
TAKING CHEAP SHOTS, AS USUAL...
IS HE SWITCHING TEAMS?
I'M NOT "AFTER" ANYBODY!
LATER.
....
SIIIIGH
WE'VE BEEN FIGHTING FOR FIVE DAYS. I'VE TRIED EVERYTHING BUT NOTHING SEEMS TO WORK.
EVEN I'M STARTING TO THINK IT'S HOPE-LESS...
KLAK

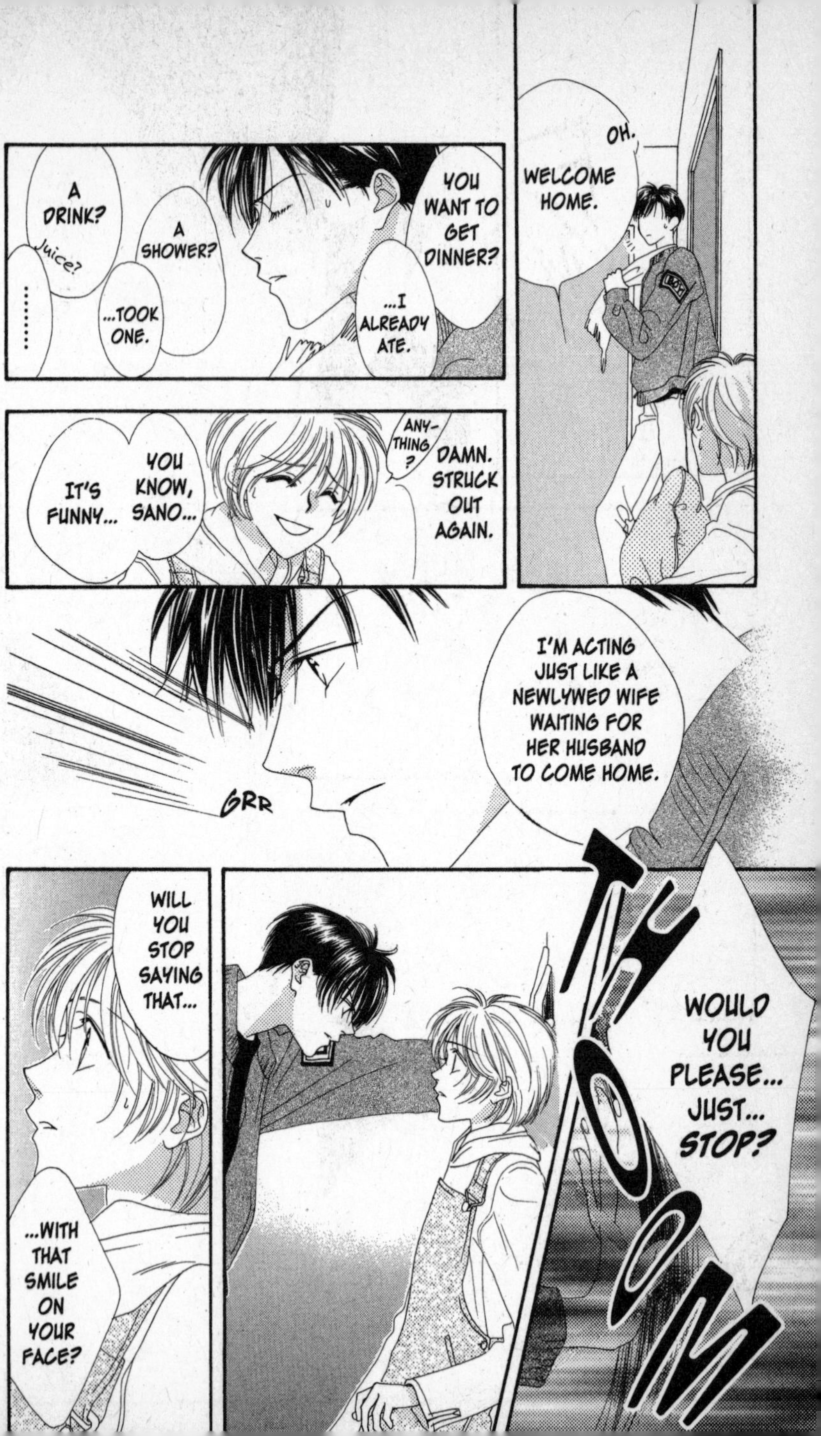
OH.
WELCOME HOME.
YOU WANT TO GET DINNER?
...I ALREADY ATE.
A SHOWER?
...TOOK ONE.
A DRINK?
Juice?
....
ANY-THING?
DAMN. STRUCK OUT AGAIN.
YOU KNOW, SANO...
IT'S FUNNY...
I'M ACTING JUST LIKE A NEWLYWED WIFE WAITING FOR HER HUSBAND TO COME HOME.
GRR
THOOM
WOULD YOU PLEASE... JUST... STOP?
WILL YOU STOP SAYING THAT...
...WITH THAT SMILE ON YOUR FACE?

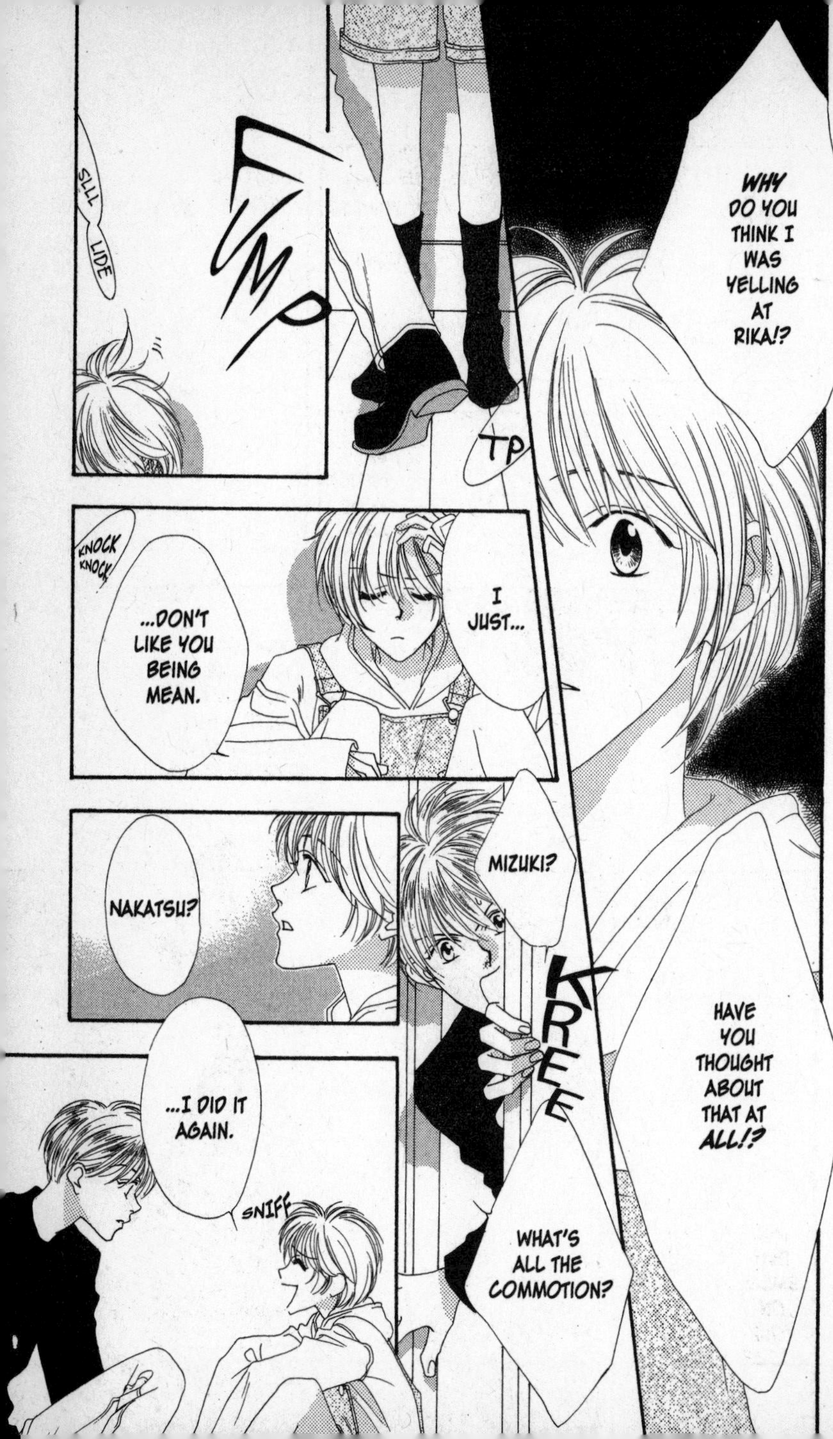
WHY DO YOU THINK I WAS YELLING AT RIKA!?
HAVE YOU THOUGHT ABOUT THAT AT ALL!?
TP
LUMP
SLLL LIDE
I JUST...
...DON'T LIKE YOU BEING MEAN.
KNOCK KNOCK
MIZUKI?
KREE
NAKATSU?
WHAT'S ALL THE COMMOTION?
...I DID IT AGAIN.
SNIFF

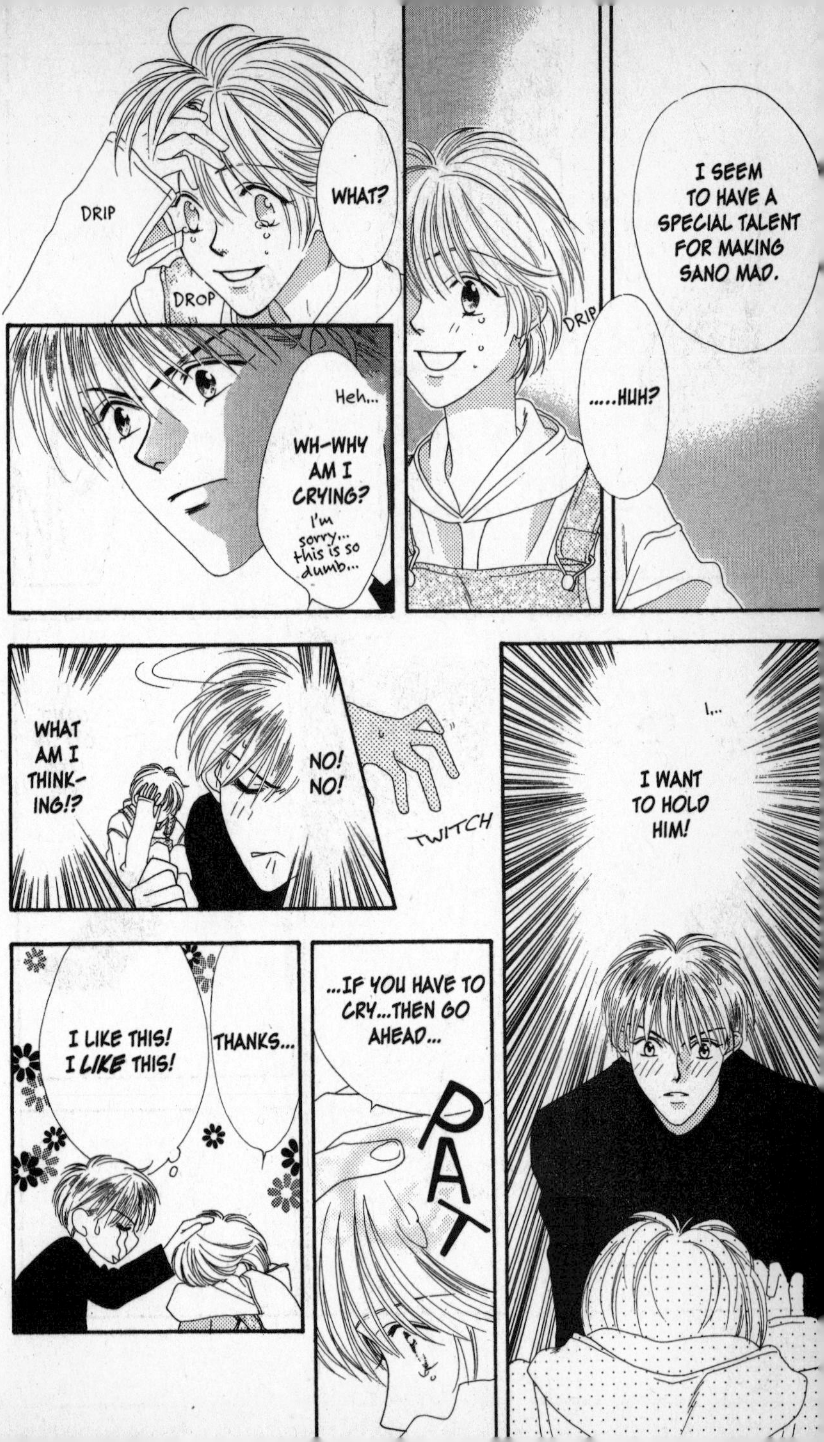

I SEEM TO HAVE A SPECIAL TALENT FOR MAKING SANO MAD.
.....HUH?
DRIP
WHAT?
DRIP
DROP
Heh...
WH-WHY AM I CRYING?
I'm sorry... this is so dumb...
I...
I WANT TO HOLD HIM!
NO! NO!
TWITCH
WHAT AM I THINK-ING!?
...IF YOU HAVE TO CRY...THEN GO AHEAD...
PAT
THANKS...
I LIKE THIS! I *LIKE* THIS!

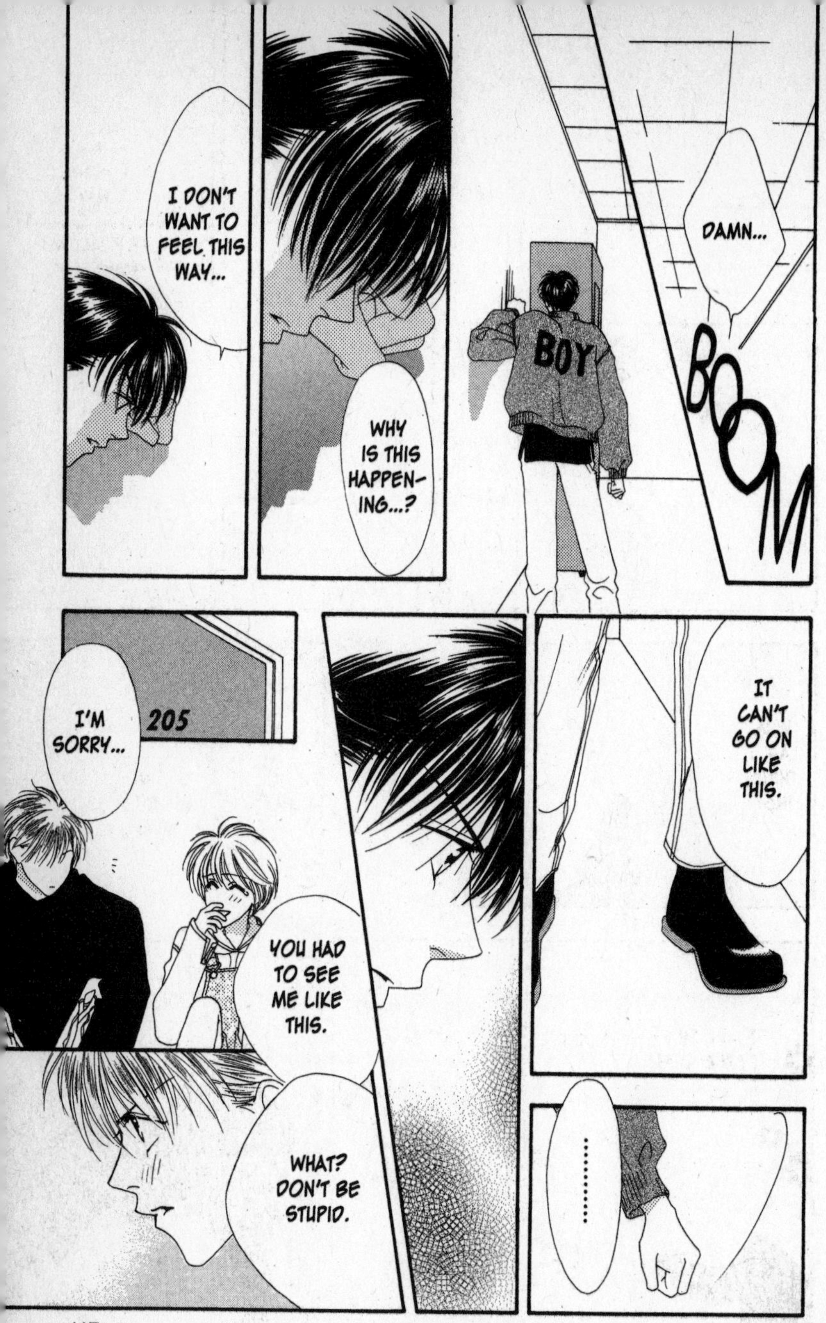
DAMN...
BOOM
WHY IS THIS HAPPENING...?
I DON'T WANT TO FEEL THIS WAY...
IT CAN'T GO ON LIKE THIS.
....
I'M SORRY...
205
YOU HAD TO SEE ME LIKE THIS.
WHAT? DON'T BE STUPID.

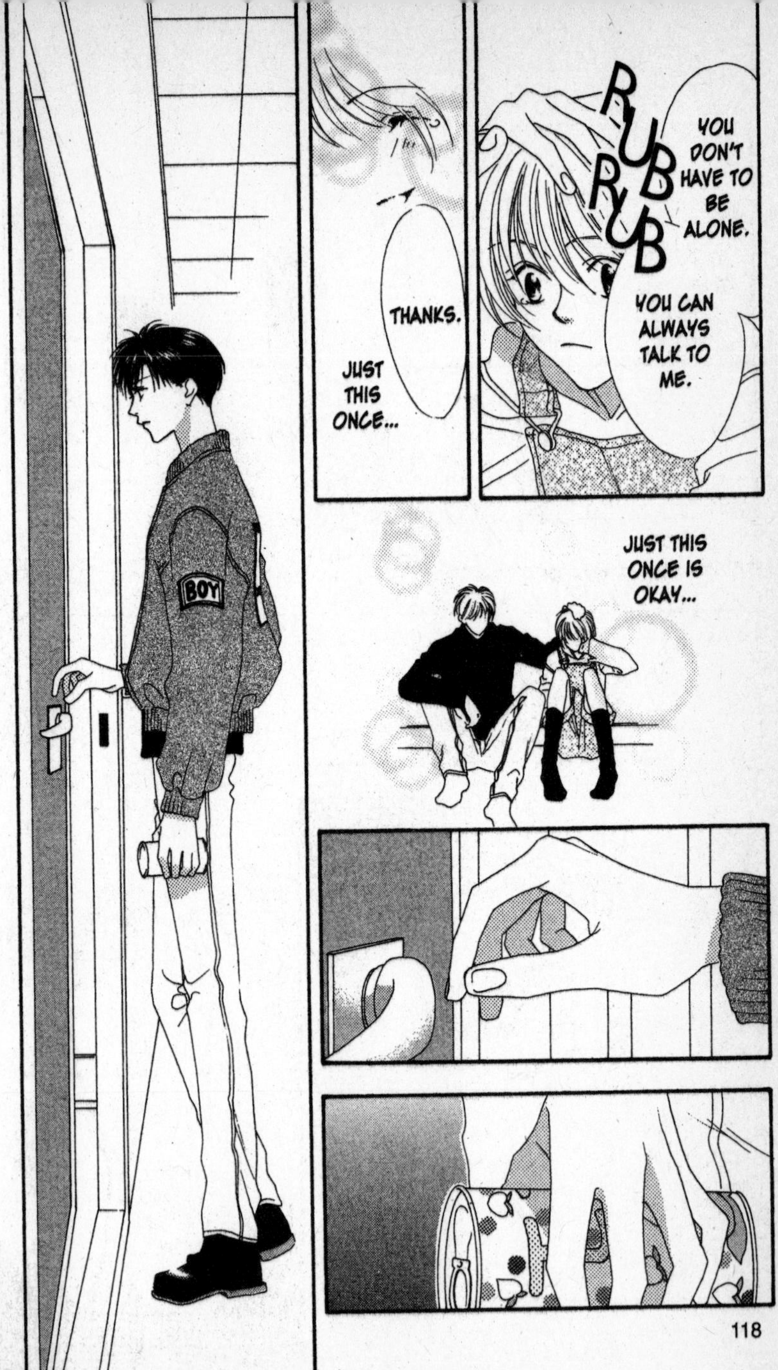
RUB RUB
YOU DON'T HAVE TO BE ALONE.
YOU CAN ALWAYS TALK TO ME.
THANKS.
JUST THIS ONCE...
JUST THIS ONCE IS OKAY...

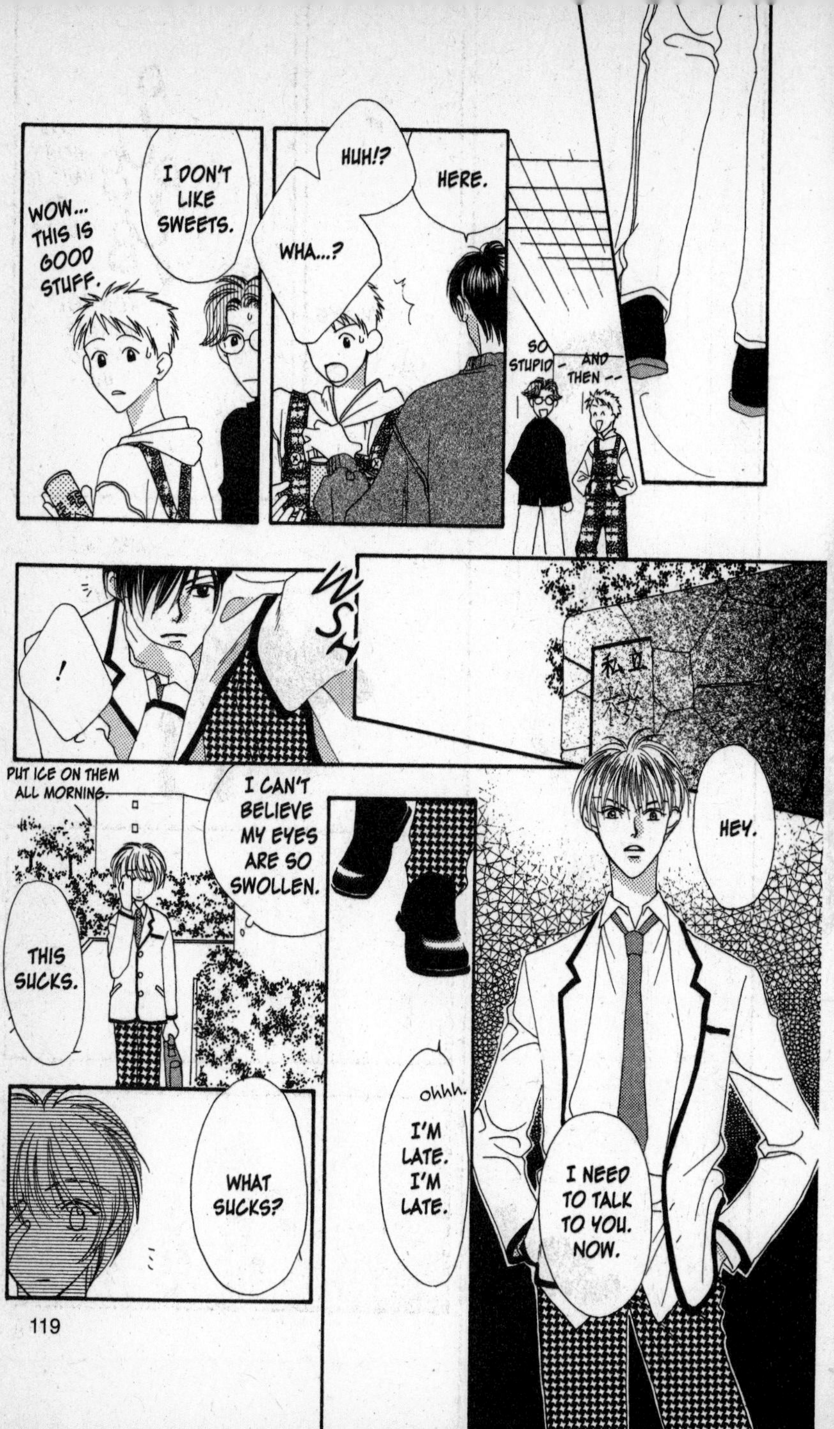
SO STUPID -
AND THEN --
HERE.
HUH!?
WHA...?
I DON'T LIKE SWEETS.
WOW... THIS IS GOOD STUFF.
HEY.
WSH
!
I NEED TO TALK TO YOU. NOW.
ohhh.
I'M LATE. I'M LATE.
I CAN'T BELIEVE MY EYES ARE SO SWOLLEN.
PUT ICE ON THEM ALL MORNING.
THIS SUCKS.
WHAT SUCKS?

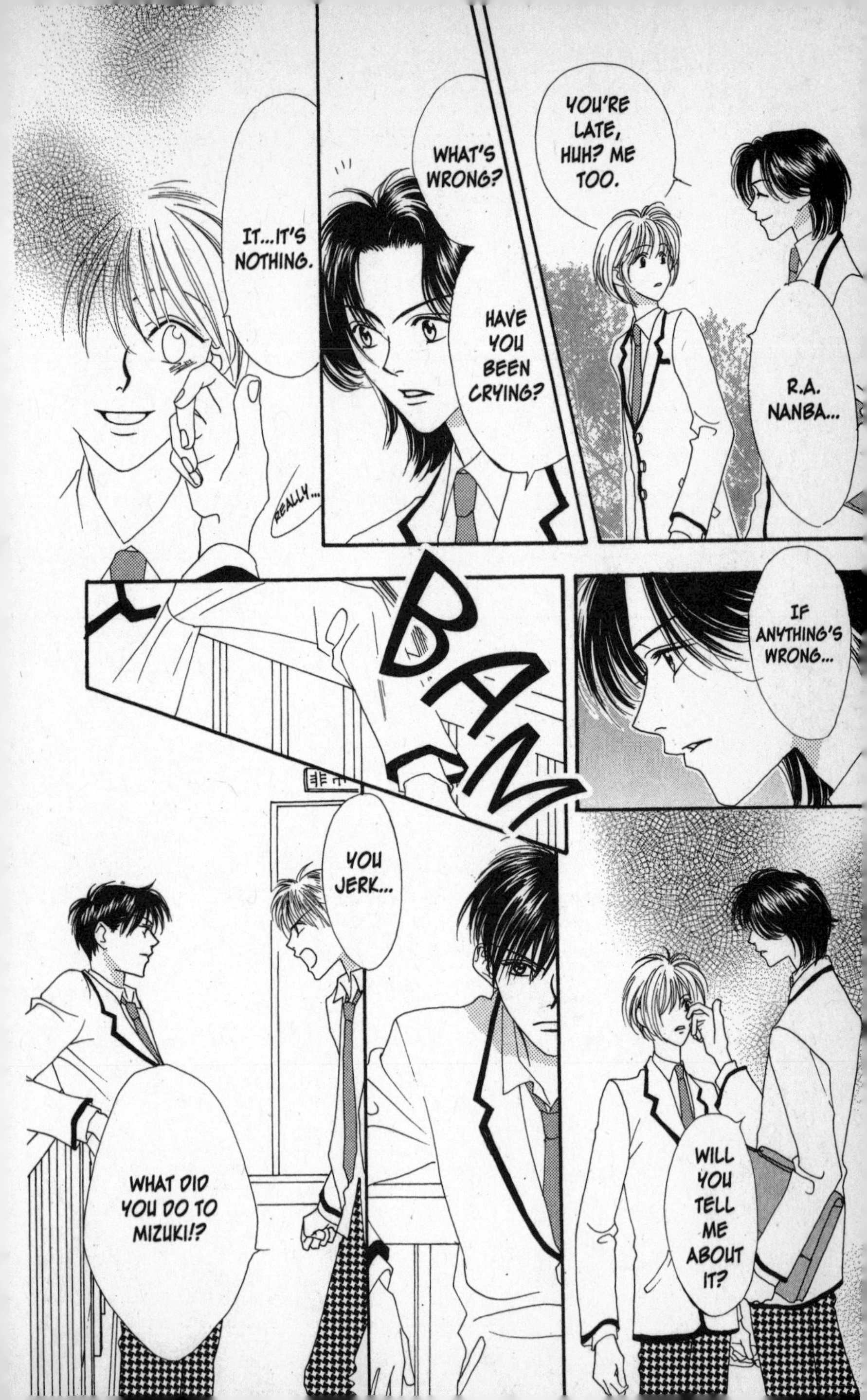
YOU'RE LATE, HUH? ME TOO.
R.A. NANBA...
WHAT'S WRONG?
HAVE YOU BEEN CRYING?
IT...IT'S NOTHING.
REALLY...
IF ANYTHING'S WRONG...
WILL YOU TELL ME ABOUT IT?
BAM
YOU JERK...
WHAT DID YOU DO TO MIZUKI!?

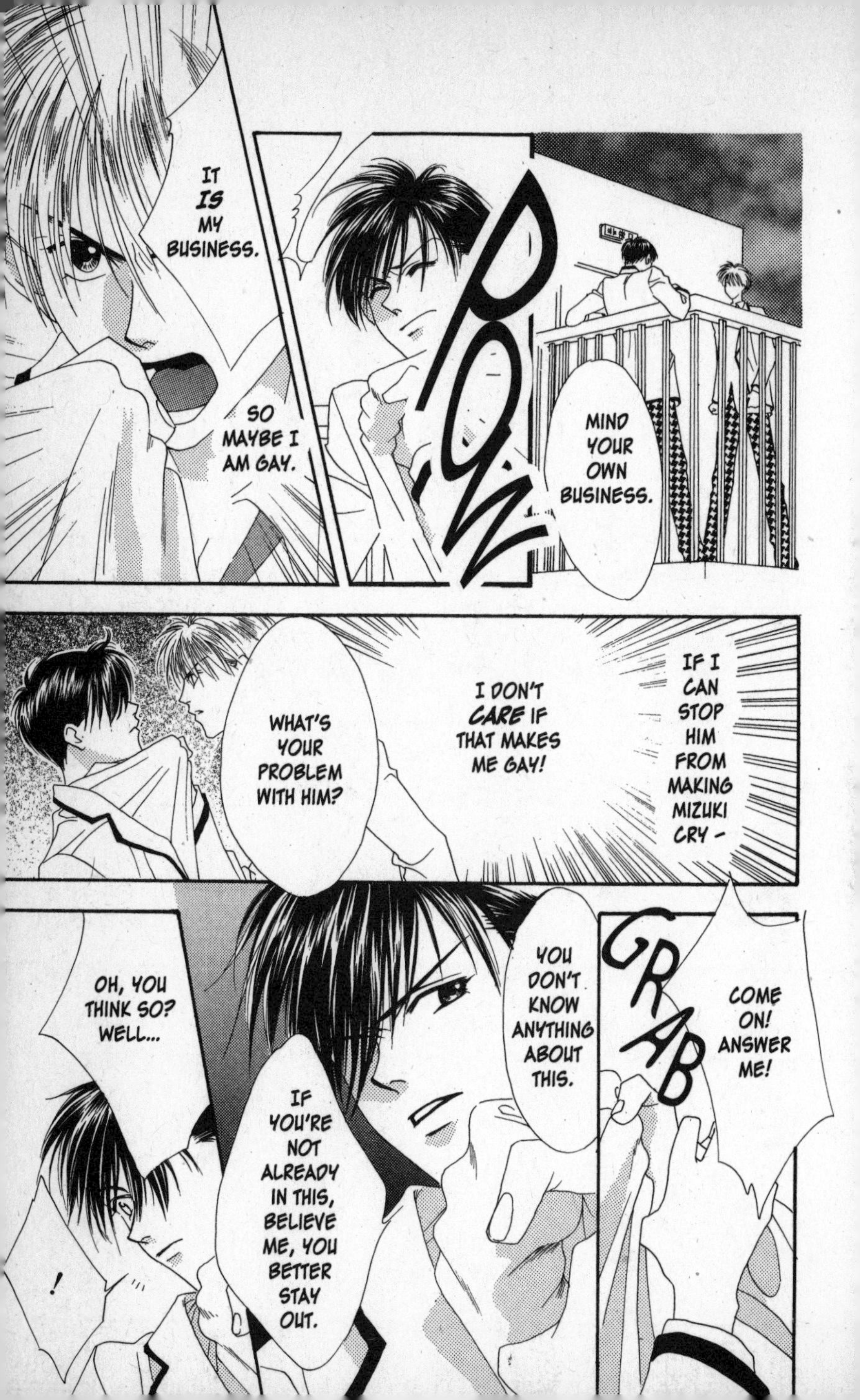
POW
MIND YOUR OWN BUSINESS.
IT IS MY BUSINESS.
SO MAYBE I AM GAY.
IF I CAN STOP HIM FROM MAKING MIZUKI CRY –
I DON'T CARE IF THAT MAKES ME GAY!
WHAT'S YOUR PROBLEM WITH HIM?
GRAB
COME ON! ANSWER ME!
YOU DON'T KNOW ANYTHING ABOUT THIS.
OH, YOU THINK SO? WELL...
IF YOU'RE NOT ALREADY IN THIS, BELIEVE ME, YOU BETTER STAY OUT.
!

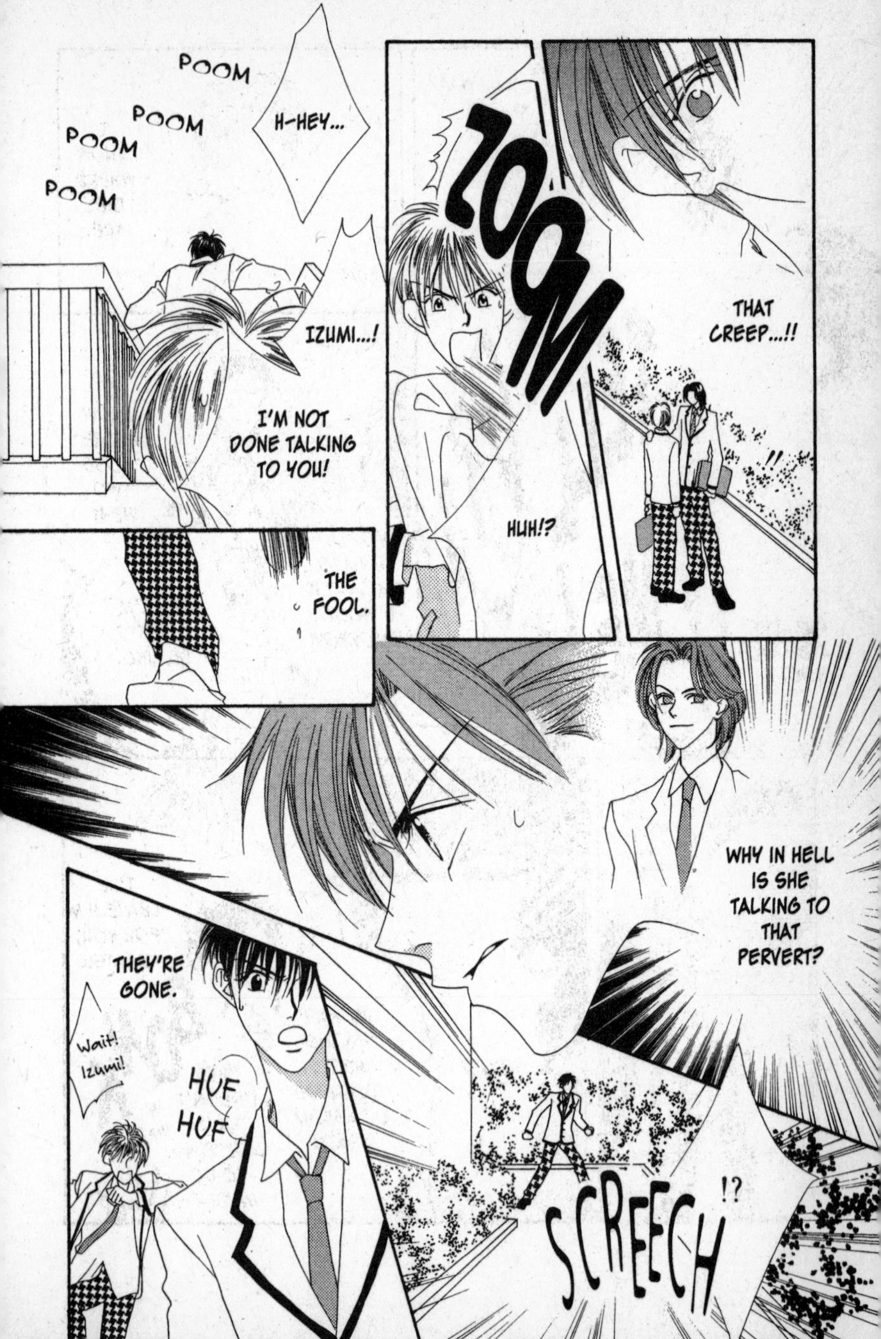
THAT CREEP...!!
!!
ZOOM
HUH!?
POOM
POOM
POOM
POOM
H-HEY...
IZUMI...!
I'M NOT DONE TALKING TO YOU!
THE FOOL.
WHY IN HELL IS SHE TALKING TO THAT PERVERT?
SCREECH
!?
THEY'RE GONE.
Wait! Izumi!
HUF HUF

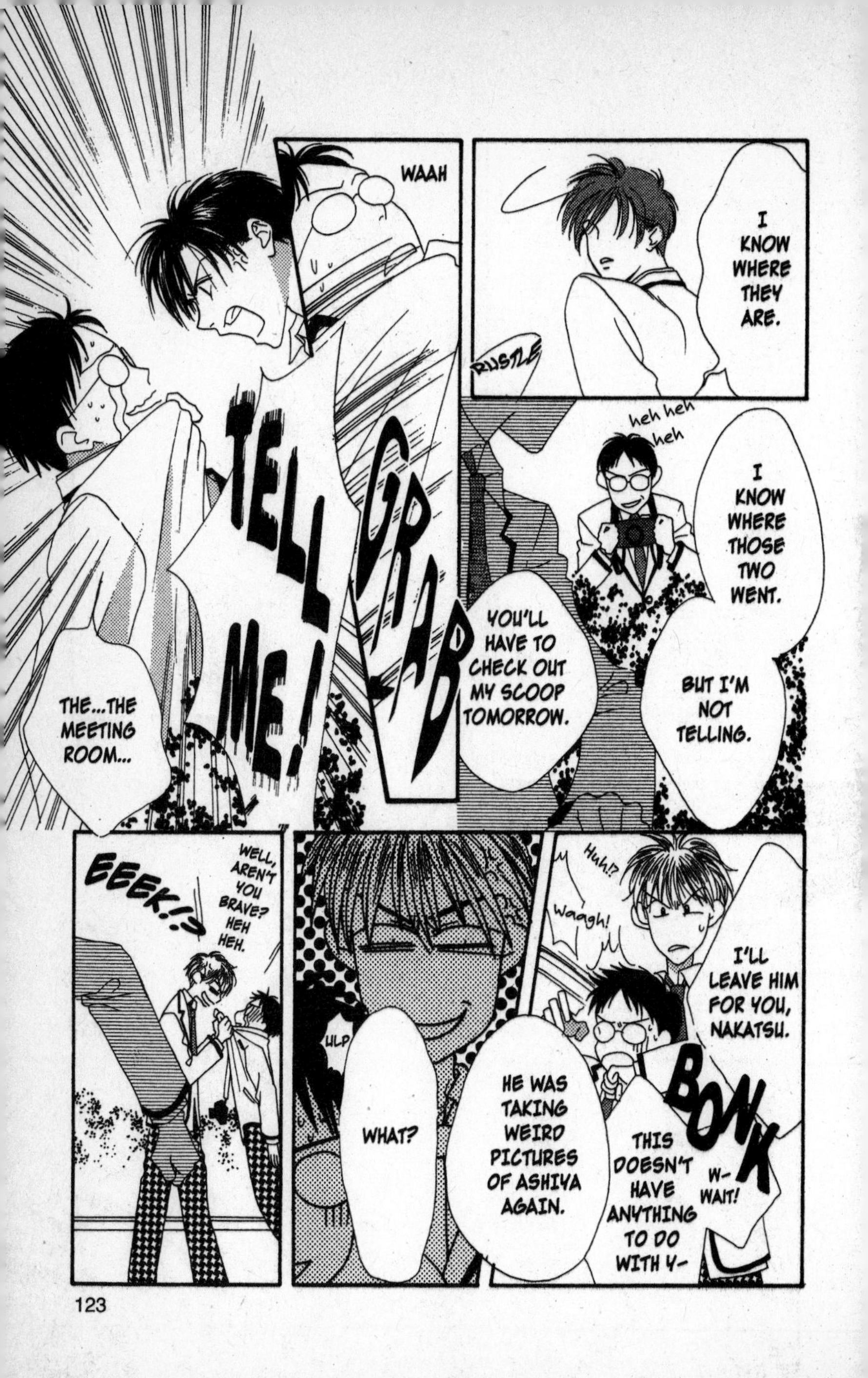
I KNOW WHERE THEY ARE.
RUSTLE
heh heh heh
I KNOW WHERE THOSE TWO WENT.
BUT I'M NOT TELLING.
YOU'LL HAVE TO CHECK OUT MY SCOOP TOMORROW.
WAAH
GRAB
TELL ME!
THE...THE MEETING ROOM...
Huh!?
Waagh!
I'LL LEAVE HIM FOR YOU, NAKATSU.
BONK
W-WAIT!
THIS DOESN'T HAVE ANYTHING TO DO WITH Y-
HE WAS TAKING WEIRD PICTURES OF ASHIYA AGAIN.
WHAT?
HLP
EEEK!?
WELL, AREN'T YOU BRAVE? HEH HEH.

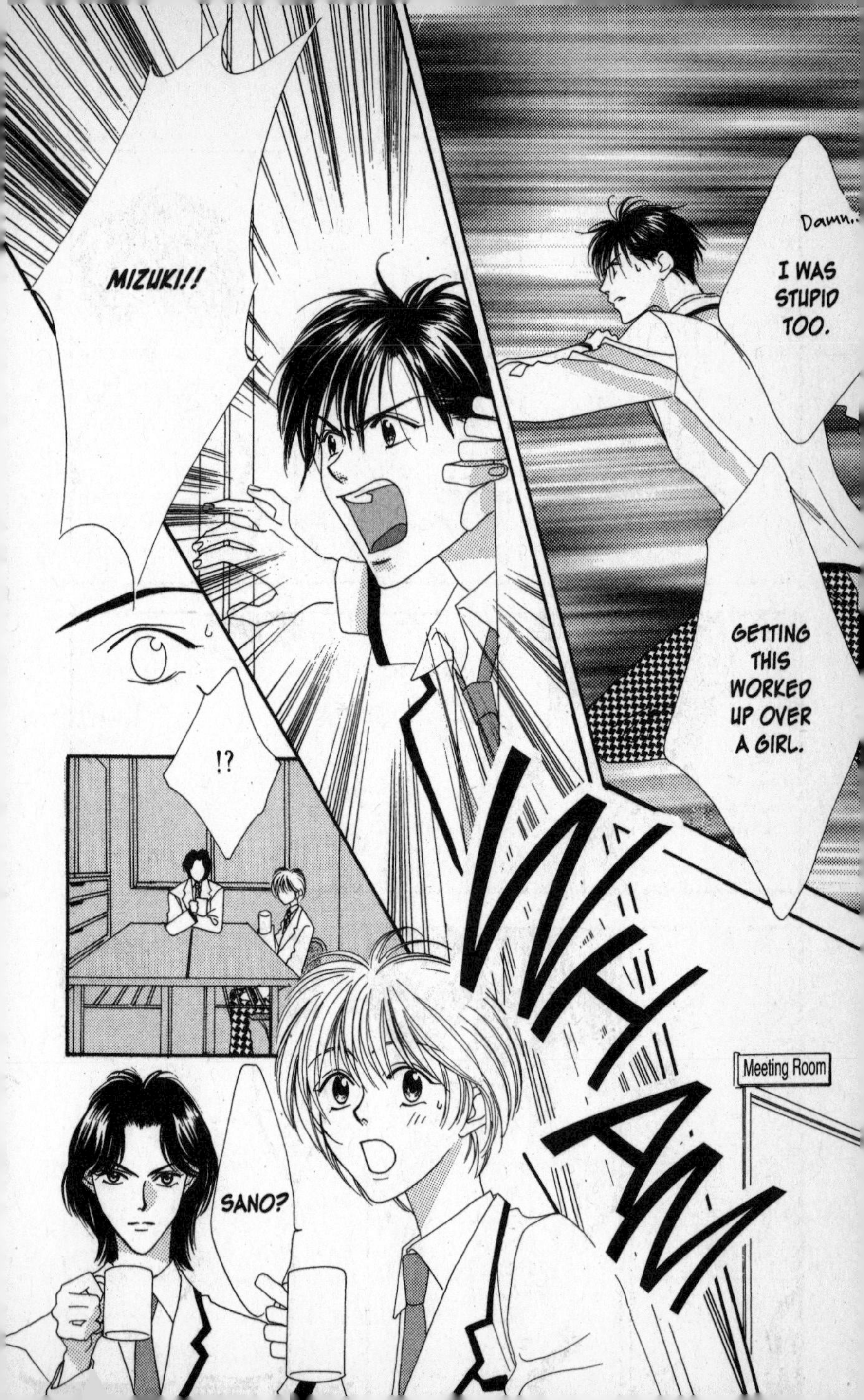
Damn...
I WAS STUPID TOO.
GETTING THIS WORKED UP OVER A GIRL.
WHAM
Meeting Room
MIZUKI!!
!?
SANO?

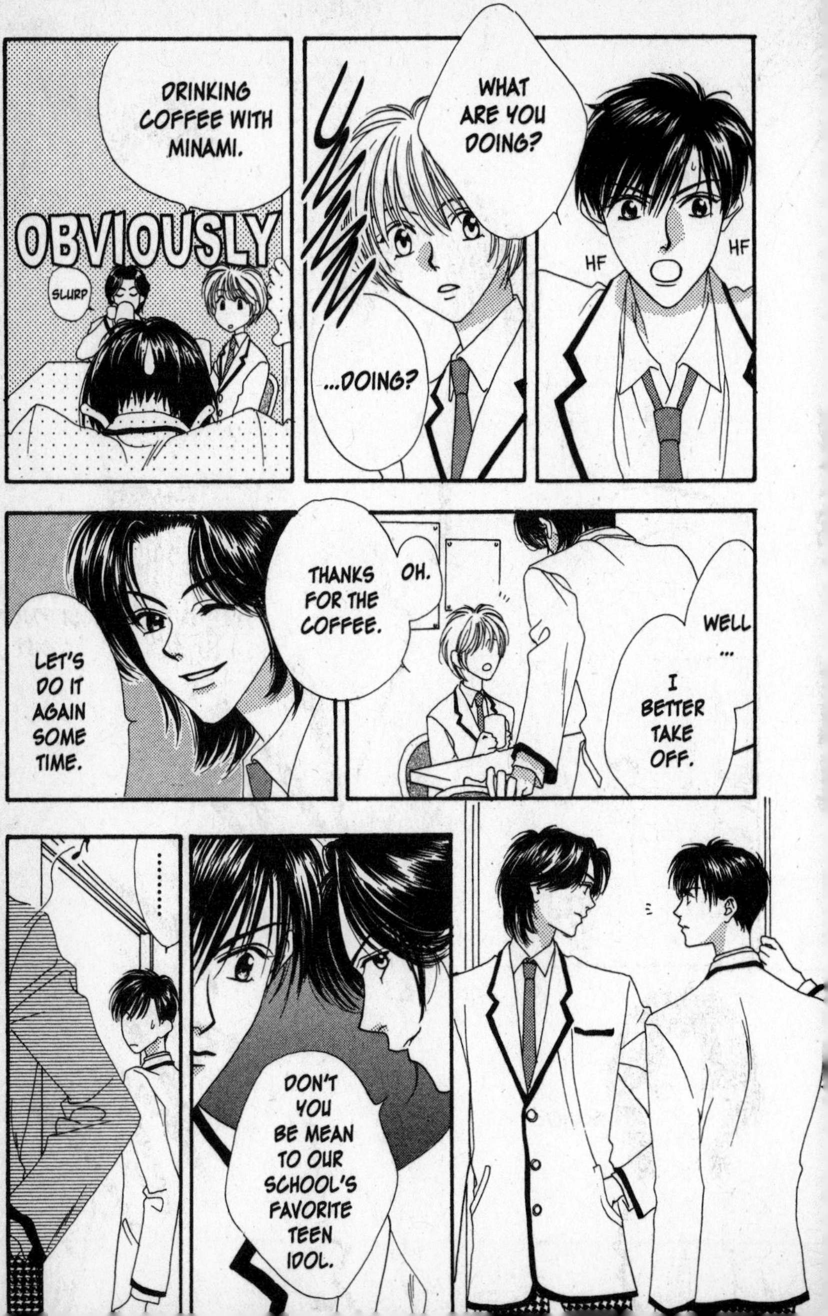

HF
HF
WHAT ARE YOU DOING?
...DOING?
DRINKING COFFEE WITH MINAMI.
OBVIOUSLY
SLURP
WELL ... I BETTER TAKE OFF.
OH.
THANKS FOR THE COFFEE.
LET'S DO IT AGAIN SOME TIME.
DON'T YOU BE MEAN TO OUR SCHOOL'S FAVORITE TEEN IDOL.
......

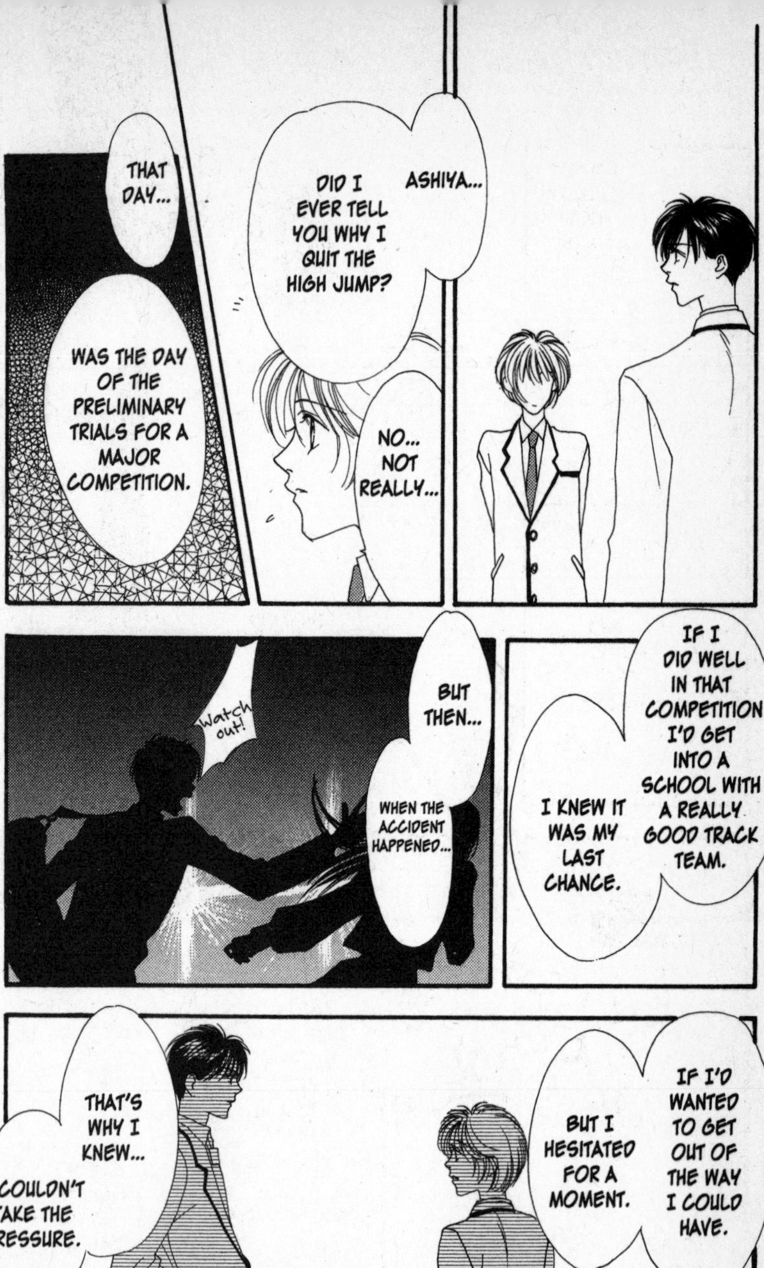
ASHIYA...
DID I EVER TELL YOU WHY I QUIT THE HIGH JUMP?
NO... NOT REALLY...
THAT DAY...
WAS THE DAY OF THE PRELIMINARY TRIALS FOR A MAJOR COMPETITION.
IF I DID WELL IN THAT COMPETITION I'D GET INTO A SCHOOL WITH A REALLY GOOD TRACK TEAM.
I KNEW IT WAS MY LAST CHANCE.
BUT THEN...
WHEN THE ACCIDENT HAPPENED...
Watch out!
IF I'D WANTED TO GET OUT OF THE WAY I COULD HAVE.
BUT I HESITATED FOR A MOMENT.
THAT'S WHY I KNEW...
I COULDN'T TAKE THE PRESSURE.

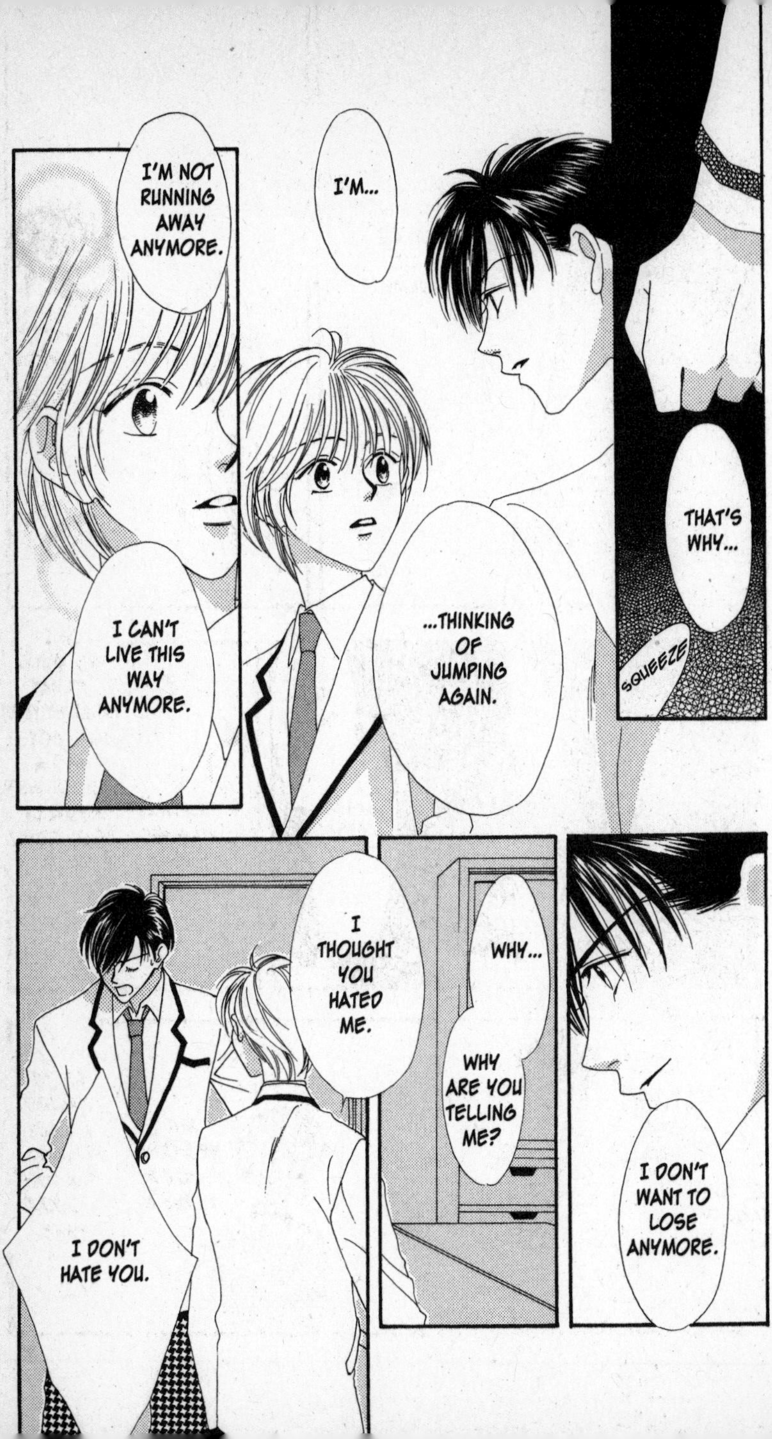
I'M...
...THINKING OF JUMPING AGAIN.
THAT'S WHY...
SQUEEZE
I'M NOT RUNNING AWAY ANYMORE.
I CAN'T LIVE THIS WAY ANYMORE.
I DON'T WANT TO LOSE ANYMORE.
WHY...
WHY ARE YOU TELLING ME?
I THOUGHT YOU HATED ME.
I DON'T HATE YOU.

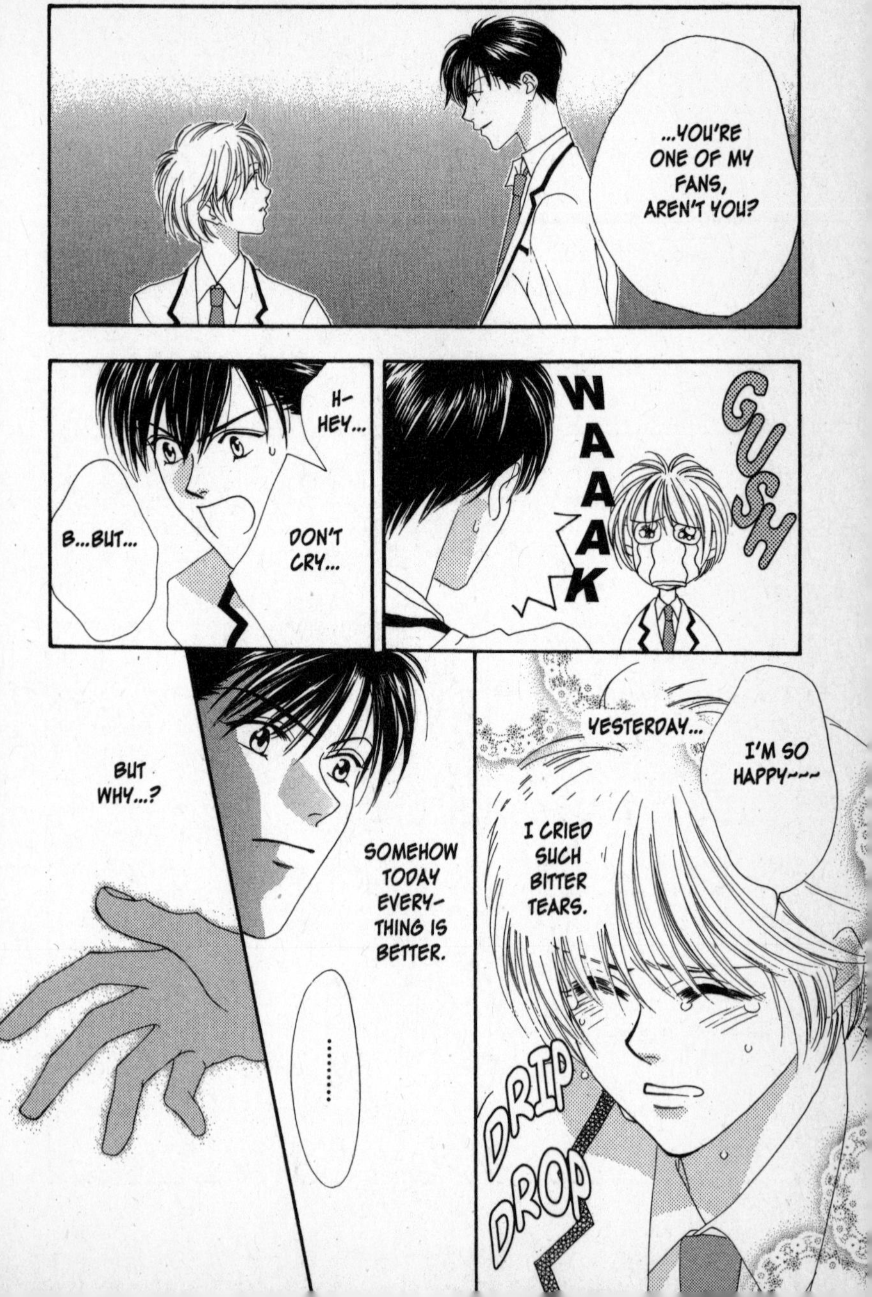
...YOU'RE ONE OF MY FANS, AREN'T YOU?
WAAAK
GUSH
H-HEY...
DON'T CRY...
B...BUT...
I'M SO HAPPY~~~
YESTERDAY...
I CRIED SUCH BITTER TEARS.
DRIP DROP
SOMEHOW TODAY EVERY-THING IS BETTER.
....
BUT WHY...?

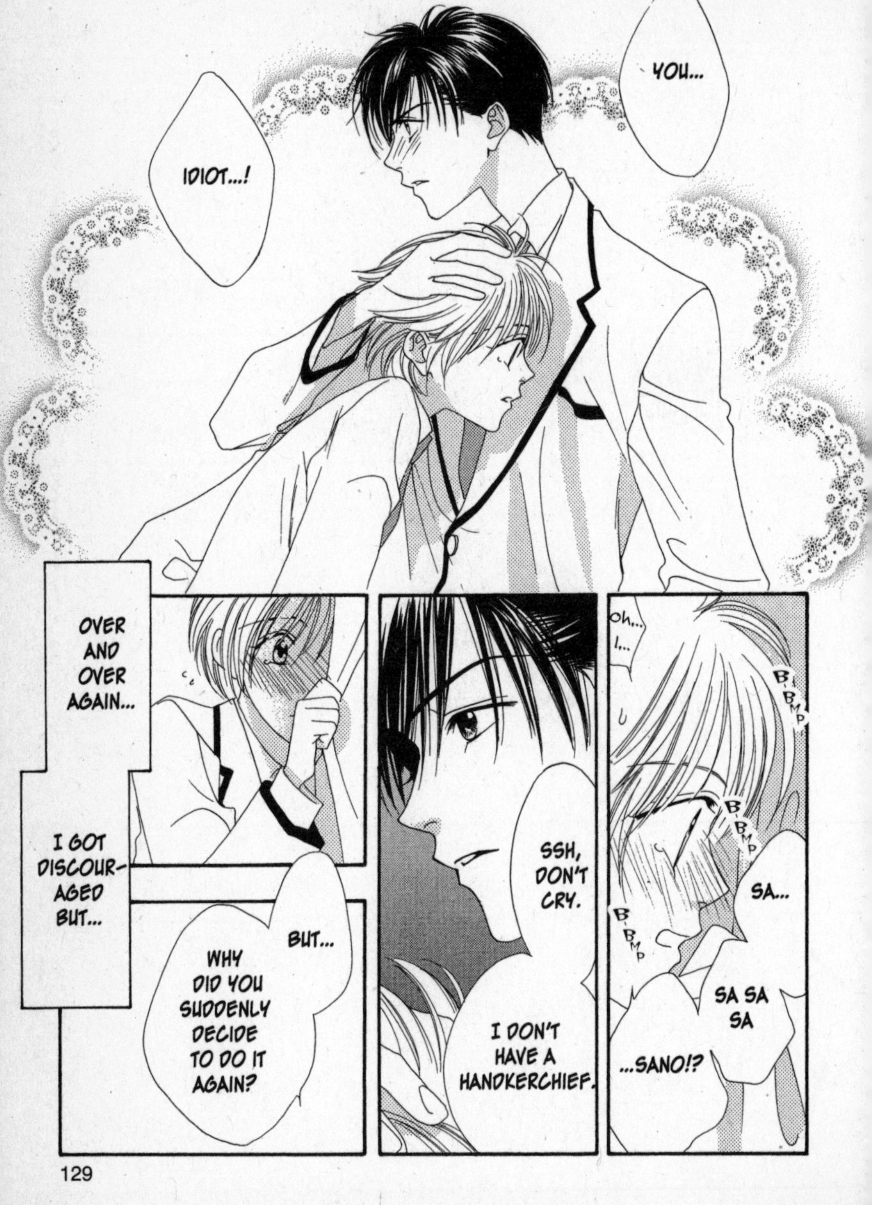
YOU...
IDIOT...!
Oh... I...
B-BMP
B-BMP
SA...
B-BMP
SA SA SA
...SANO!?
SSH, DON'T CRY.
I DON'T HAVE A HANDKERCHIEF.
OVER AND OVER AGAIN...
I GOT DISCOURAGED BUT...
BUT...
WHY DID YOU SUDDENLY DECIDE TO DO IT AGAIN?

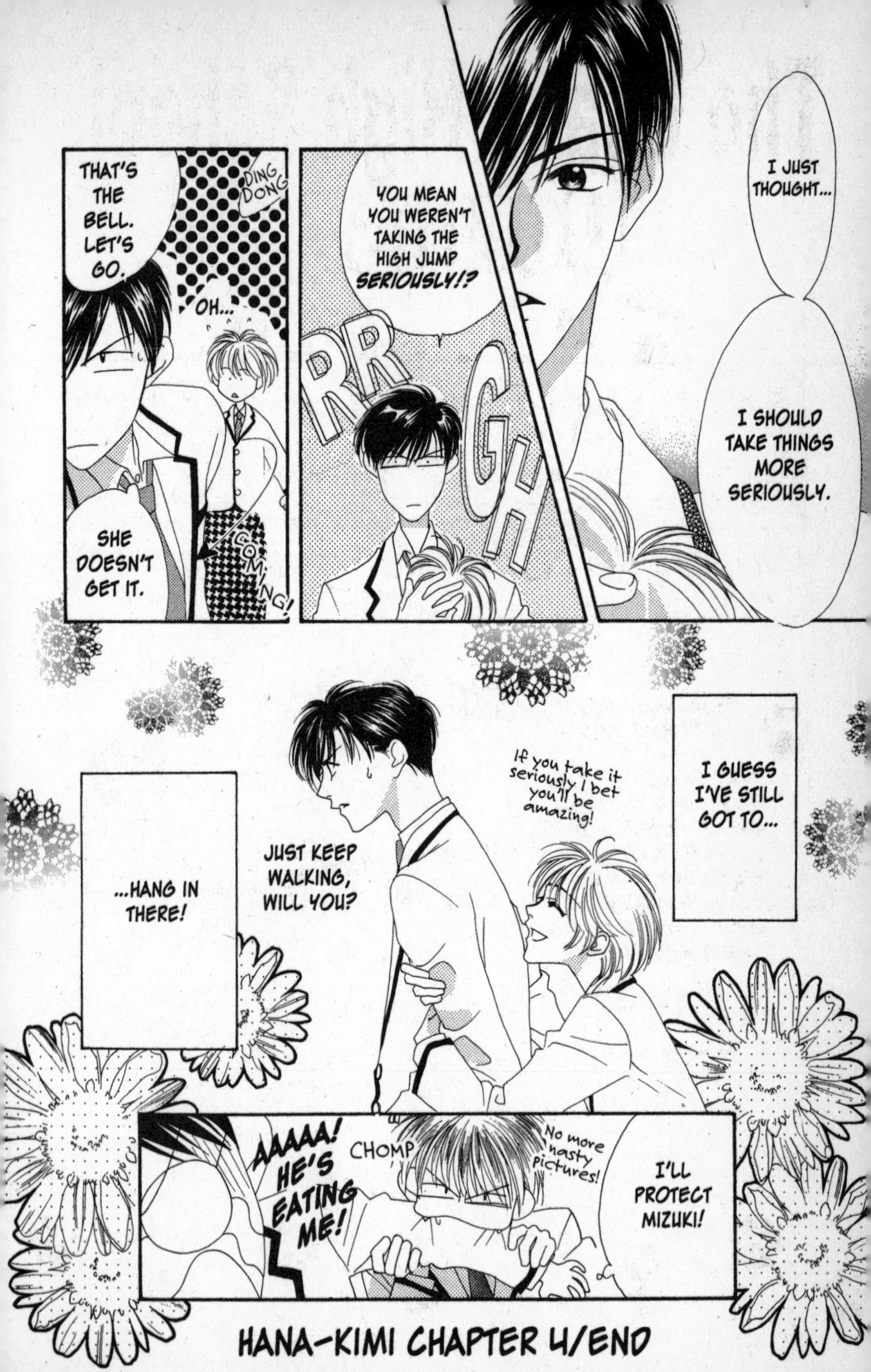
I JUST THOUGHT...
I SHOULD TAKE THINGS MORE SERIOUSLY.
YOU MEAN YOU WEREN'T TAKING THE HIGH JUMP SERIOUSLY!?
RRGH
THAT'S THE BELL. LET'S GO.
DING DONG
OH...
SHE DOESN'T GET IT.
COMING!
I GUESS I'VE STILL GOT TO...
If you take it seriously I bet you'll be amazing!
JUST KEEP WALKING, WILL YOU?
...HANG IN THERE!
I'LL PROTECT MIZUKI!
No more nasty pictures!
CHOMP
AAAAA! HE'S EATING ME!

HANA-KIMI CHAPTER 4/END

The Osaka High School Dorms

EXPLANATION BY YUJIRO

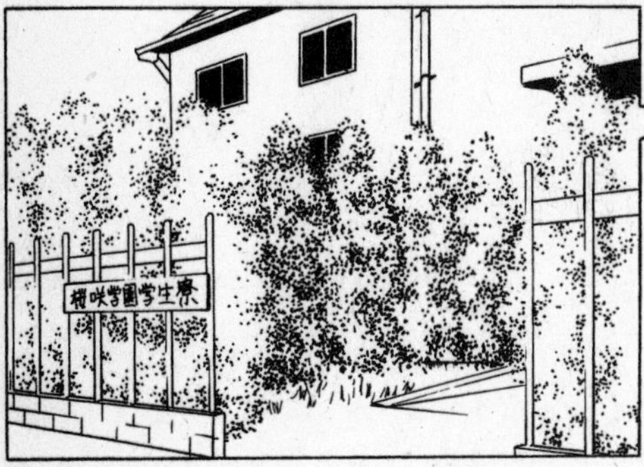
桜咲学園学生寮

OSAKA HIGH DORM BUILDING ONE

THREE STORIES. 18 YEARS OLD. 60 ROOMS (WITH A TOTAL OF 120 OCCUPANTS). TWO-PERSON ROOMS, COMMUNAL BATHROOMS. EQUIPPED WITH HEATER AND AIR CONDITIONER. BREAKFAST AND DINNER PROVIDED.

OSAKA HIGH DORM BUILDING TWO

FOUR STORIES. 8 YEARS OLD. 120 ROOMS (WITH 240 OCCUPANTS). TWO-PERSON ROOMS WITH BATHROOM. EQUIPPED WITH HEATER AND AIR CONDITIONER. BREAKFAST AND DINNER PROVIDED.

*BUILDING 3 IS IDENTICAL TO BUILDING 2.

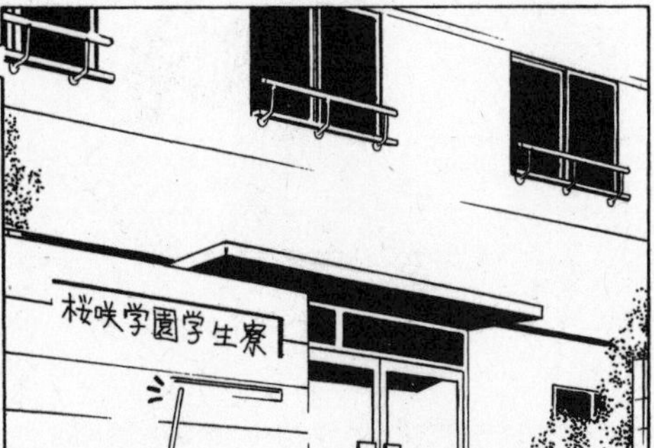
桜咲学園学生寮

AFTER SOME REMODELING

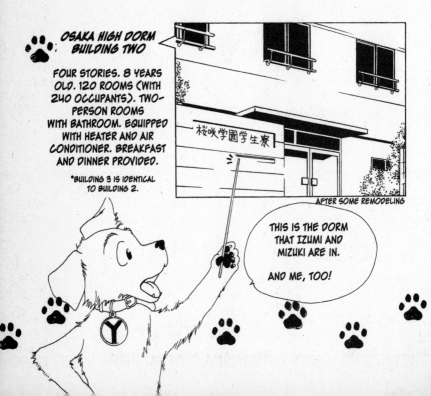

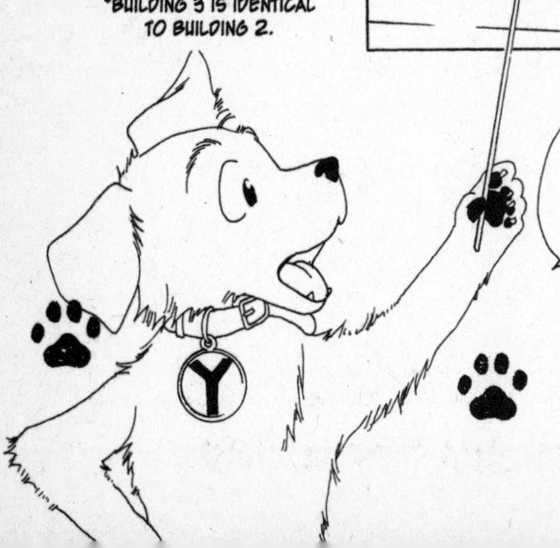
THIS IS THE DORM THAT IZUMI AND MIZUKI ARE IN.
AND ME, TOO!

Room #205

DRAWN FOR YOUR CONVENIENCE!

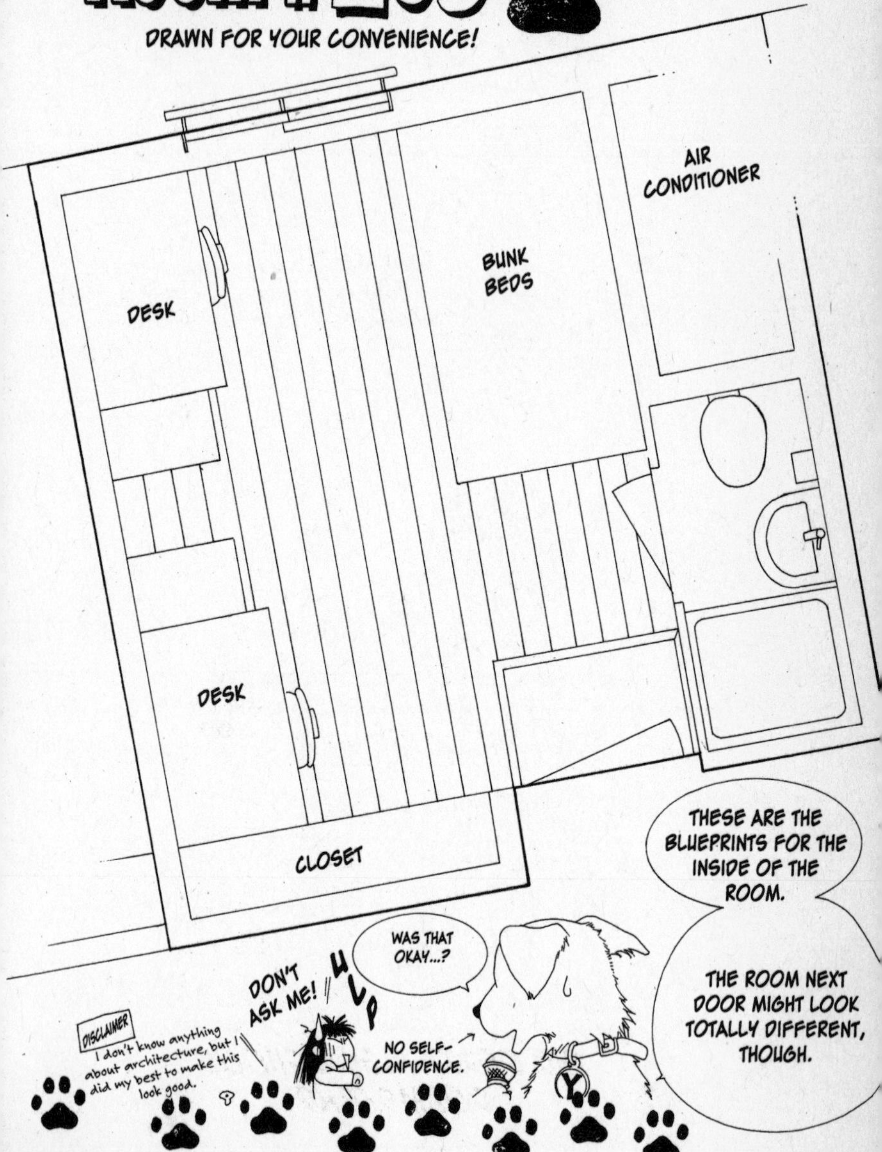
AIR CONDITIONER
BUNK BEDS
DESK
DESK
CLOSET
THESE ARE THE BLUEPRINTS FOR THE INSIDE OF THE ROOM.
THE ROOM NEXT DOOR MIGHT LOOK TOTALLY DIFFERENT, THOUGH.
WAS THAT OKAY...?
NO SELF-CONFIDENCE.
ULP
DON'T ASK ME!
DISCLAIMER
I don't know anything about architecture, but I did my best to make this look good.

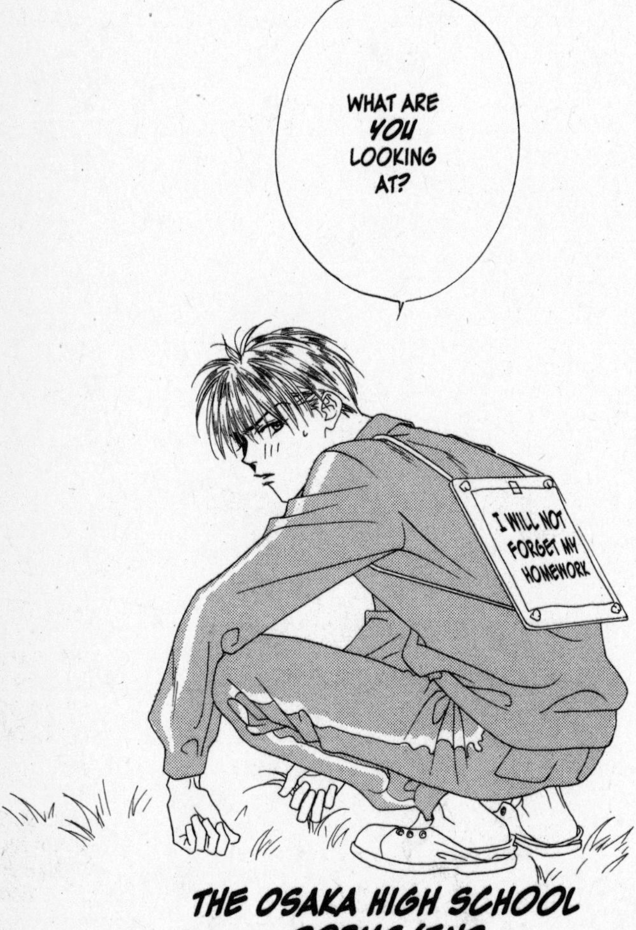
WHAT ARE YOU LOOKING AT?
I WILL NOT FORGET MY HOMEWORK

THE OSAKA HIGH SCHOOL DORMS/END

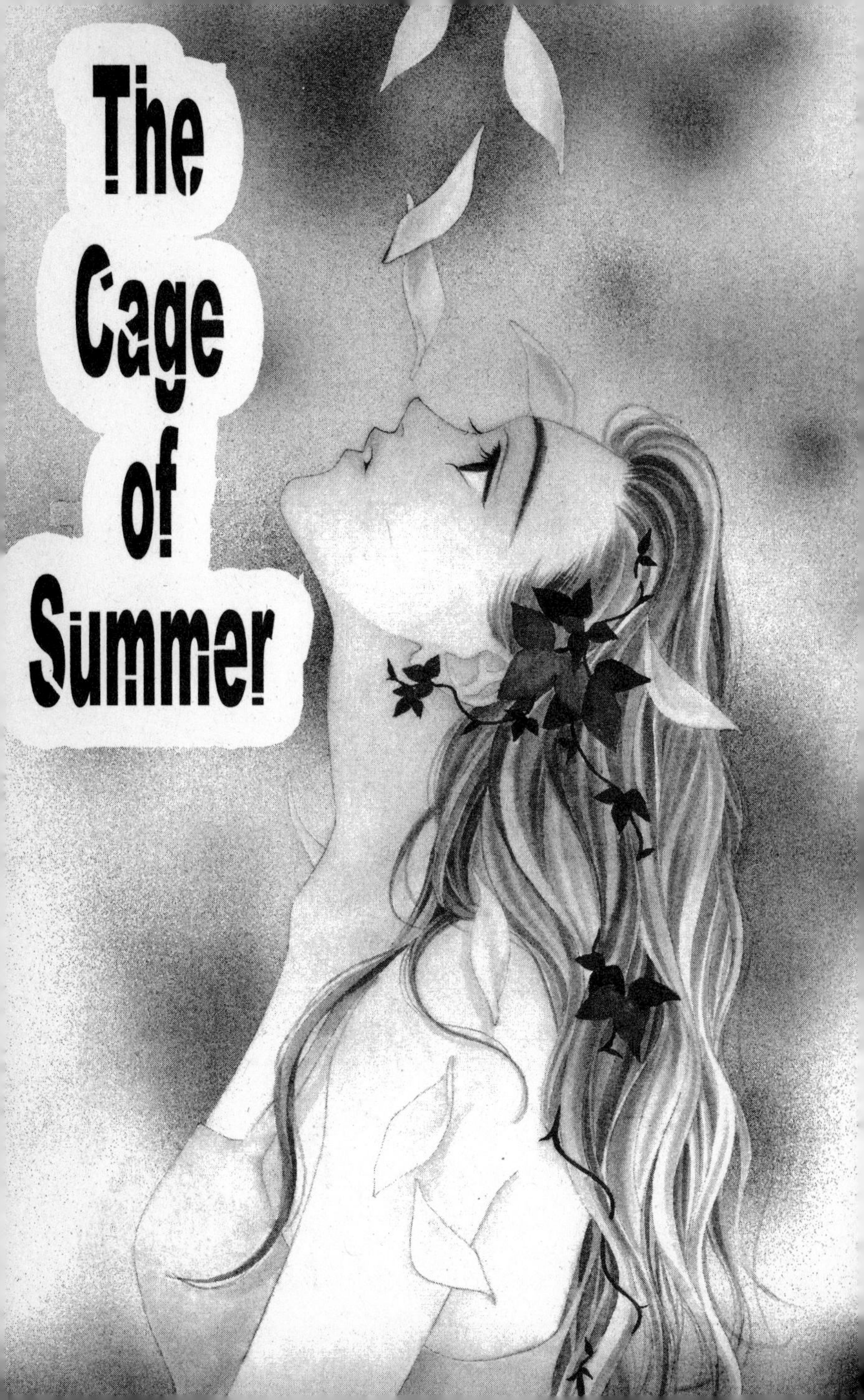
The Cage of Summer

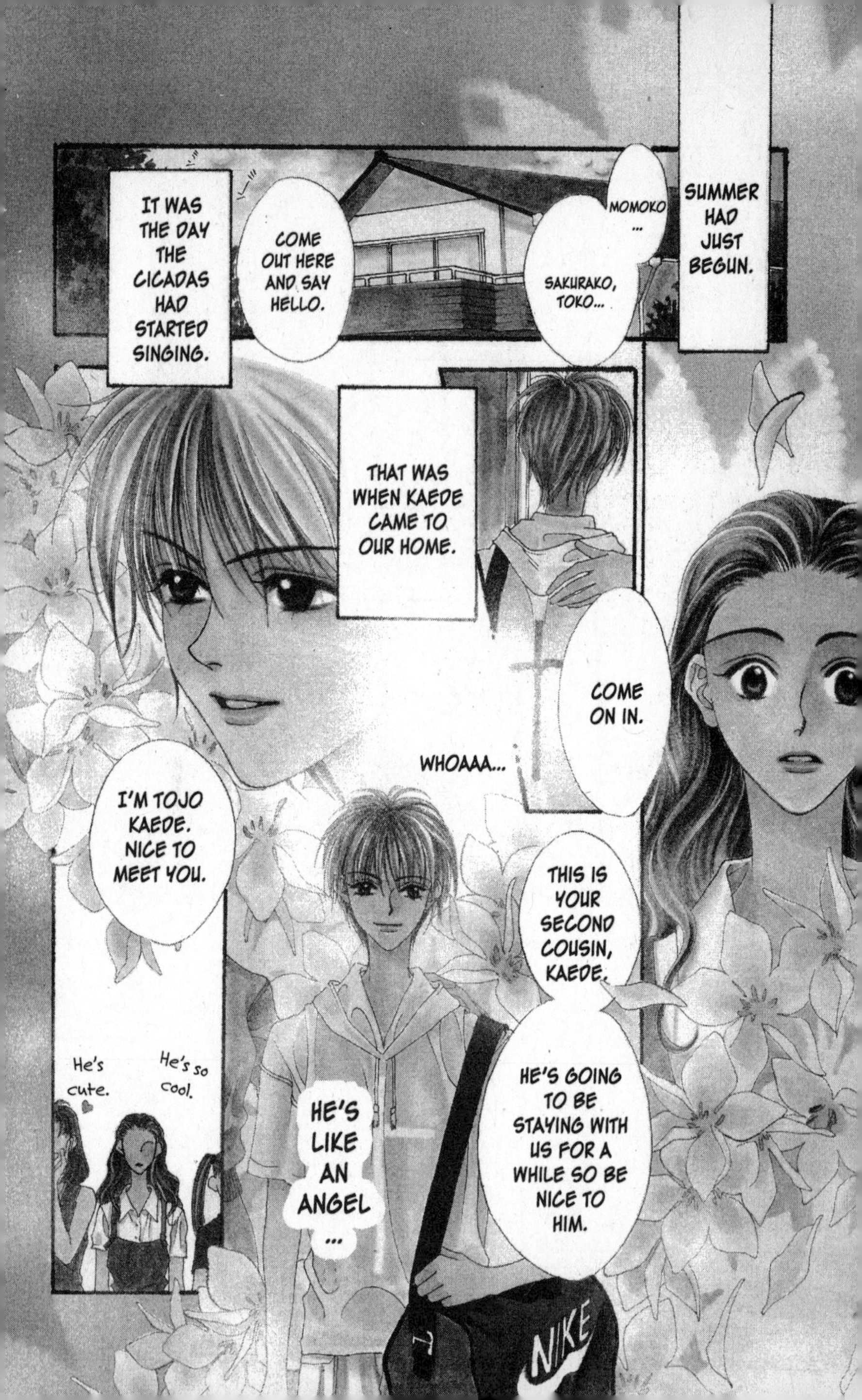
SUMMER HAD JUST BEGUN.
MOMOKO ...
SAKURAKO, TOKO...
COME OUT HERE AND SAY HELLO.
IT WAS THE DAY THE CICADAS HAD STARTED SINGING.
THAT WAS WHEN KAEDE CAME TO OUR HOME.
COME ON IN.
WHOAAA...
THIS IS YOUR SECOND COUSIN, KAEDE.
HE'S GOING TO BE STAYING WITH US FOR A WHILE SO BE NICE TO HIM.
HE'S LIKE AN ANGEL ...
NIKE
I'M TOJO KAEDE. NICE TO MEET YOU.
He's so cool.
He's cute.

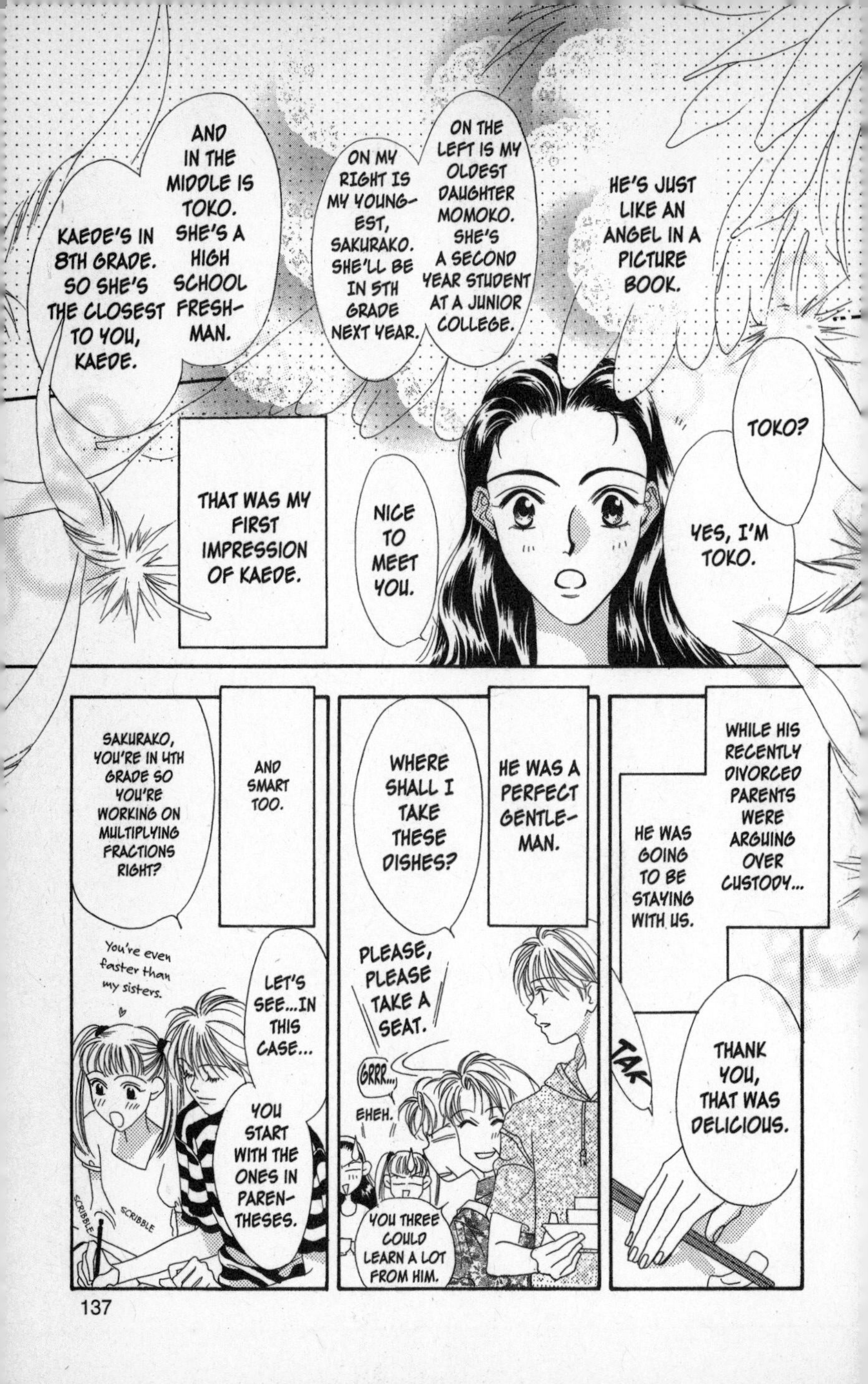
HE'S JUST LIKE AN ANGEL IN A PICTURE BOOK.
ON THE LEFT IS MY OLDEST DAUGHTER MOMOKO. SHE'S A SECOND YEAR STUDENT AT A JUNIOR COLLEGE.
ON MY RIGHT IS MY YOUNGEST, SAKURAKO. SHE'LL BE IN 5TH GRADE NEXT YEAR.
AND IN THE MIDDLE IS TOKO. SHE'S A HIGH SCHOOL FRESHMAN.
KAEDE'S IN 8TH GRADE. SO SHE'S THE CLOSEST TO YOU, KAEDE.
TOKO?
YES, I'M TOKO.
NICE TO MEET YOU.
THAT WAS MY FIRST IMPRESSION OF KAEDE.
WHILE HIS RECENTLY DIVORCED PARENTS WERE ARGUING OVER CUSTODY...
HE WAS GOING TO BE STAYING WITH US.
TAK
THANK YOU, THAT WAS DELICIOUS.
HE WAS A PERFECT GENTLEMAN.
WHERE SHALL I TAKE THESE DISHES?
PLEASE, PLEASE TAKE A SEAT.
GRRR...
EHEH.
YOU THREE COULD LEARN A LOT FROM HIM.
AND SMART TOO.
SAKURAKO, YOU'RE IN 4TH GRADE SO YOU'RE WORKING ON MULTIPLYING FRACTIONS RIGHT?
LET'S SEE...IN THIS CASE...
YOU START WITH THE ONES IN PARENTHESES.
You're even faster than my sisters.
SCRIBBLE
SCRIBBLE

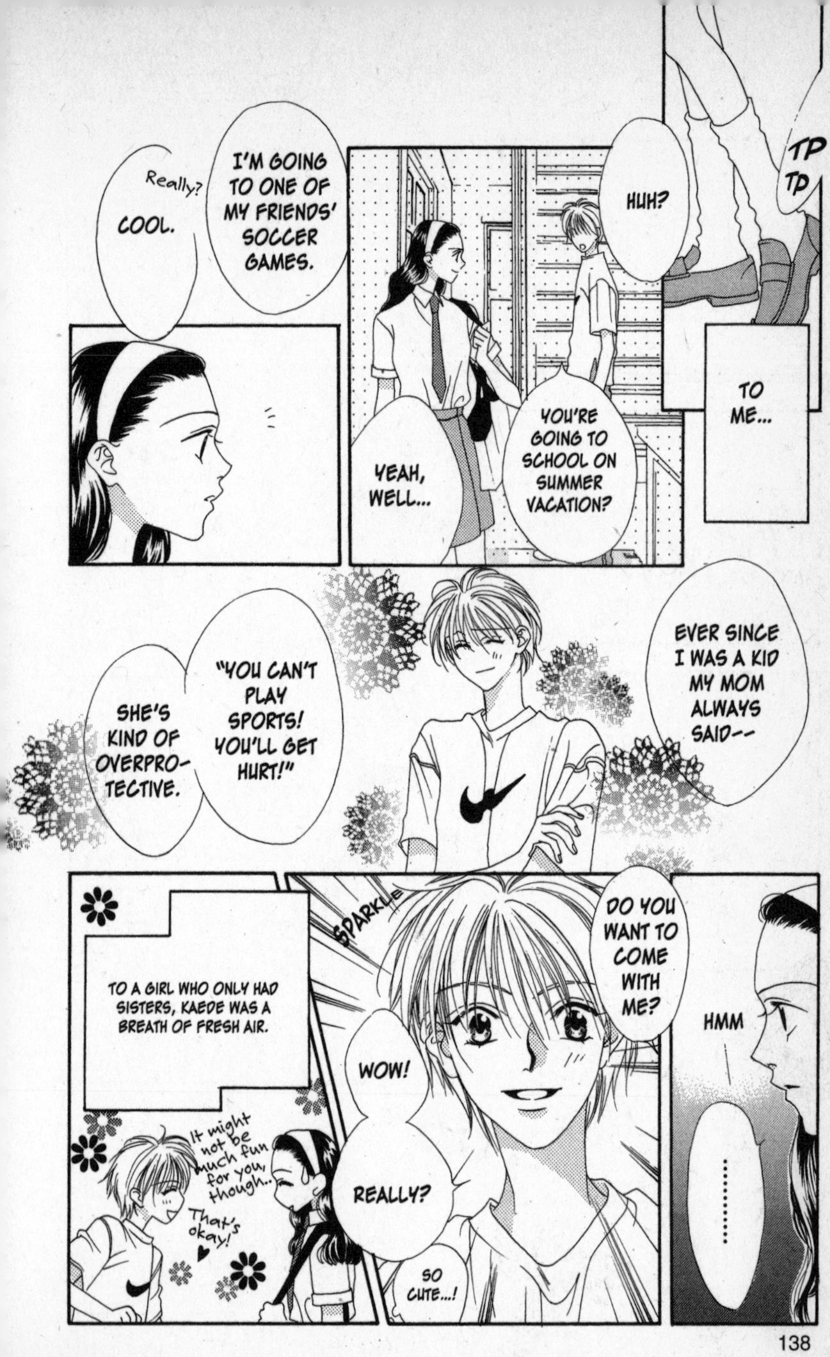
TP TP
TO ME...
HUH?
YOU'RE GOING TO SCHOOL ON SUMMER VACATION?
YEAH, WELL...
I'M GOING TO ONE OF MY FRIENDS' SOCCER GAMES.
Really?
COOL.
EVER SINCE I WAS A KID MY MOM ALWAYS SAID--
"YOU CAN'T PLAY SPORTS! YOU'LL GET HURT!"
SHE'S KIND OF OVERPROTECTIVE.
HMM
......
DO YOU WANT TO COME WITH ME?
SPARKLE
WOW!
REALLY?
SO CUTE...!
TO A GIRL WHO ONLY HAD SISTERS, KAEDE WAS A BREATH OF FRESH AIR.
It might not be much fun for you, though..
That's okay!

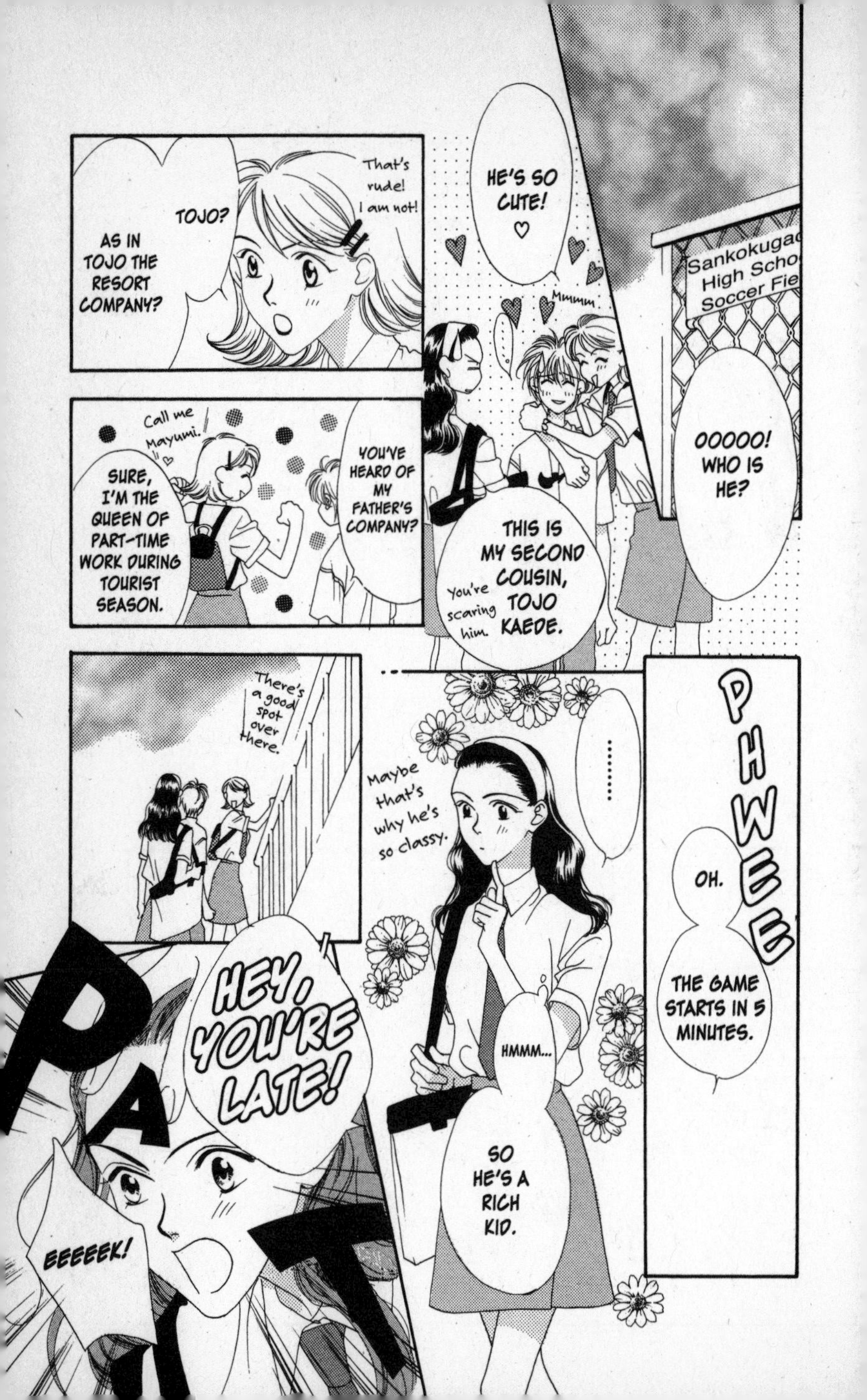
Sankokugac
High Scho
Soccer Fie
OOOOO! WHO IS HE?
HE'S SO CUTE! ♡
Mmmm
THIS IS MY SECOND COUSIN, TOJO KAEDE.
You're scaring him.
That's rude! I am not!
TOJO?
AS IN TOJO THE RESORT COMPANY?
YOU'VE HEARD OF MY FATHER'S COMPANY?
Call me Mayumi. ♡
SURE, I'M THE QUEEN OF PART-TIME WORK DURING TOURIST SEASON.
PHWEE
OH.
THE GAME STARTS IN 5 MINUTES.
......
Maybe that's why he's so classy.
HMMM...
SO HE'S A RICH KID.
There's a good spot over there.
HEY, YOU'RE LATE!
PAT
EEEEEK!

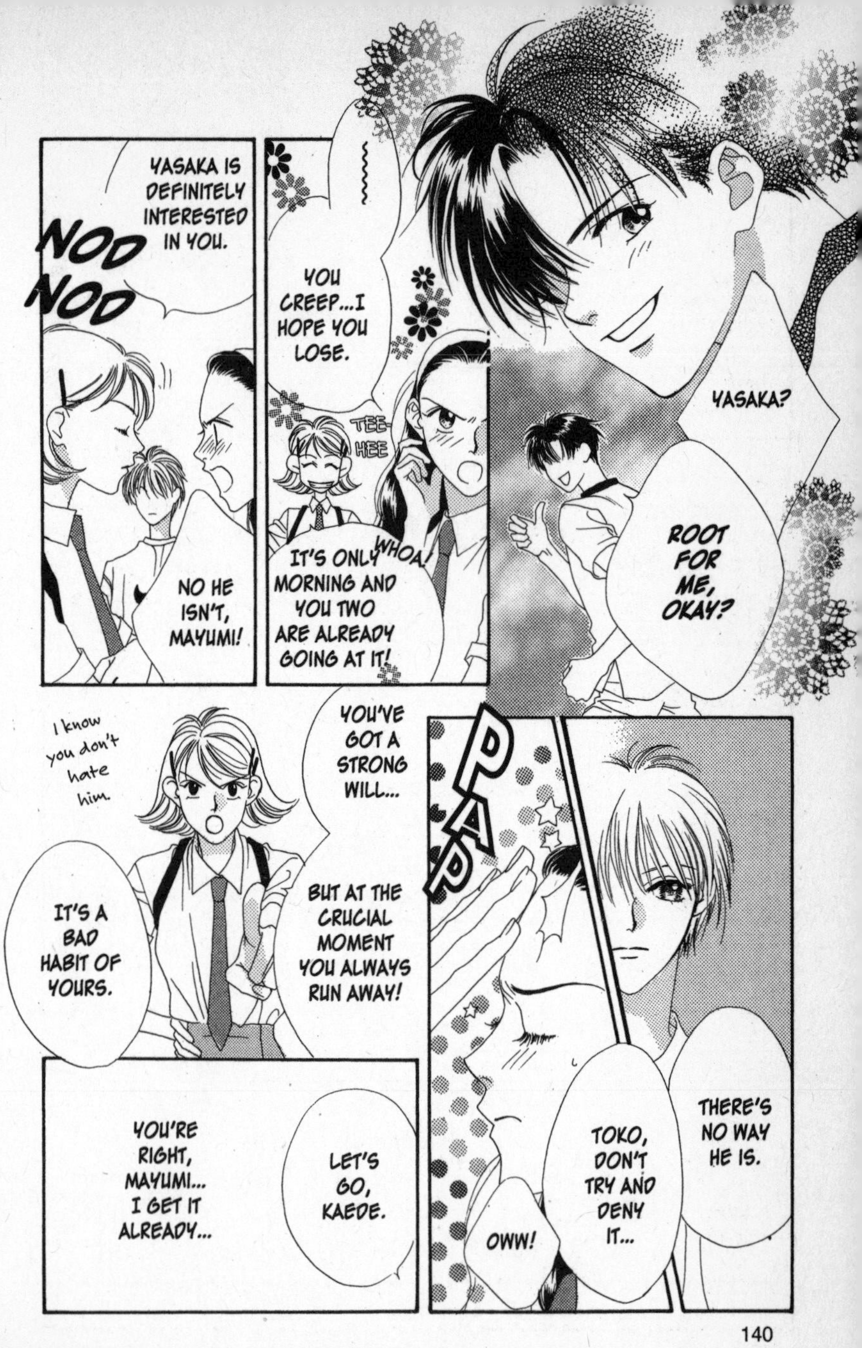
YASAKA?
ROOT FOR ME, OKAY?
~~~
YOU CREEP...I HOPE YOU LOSE.
TEE-HEE
WHOA!
IT'S ONLY MORNING AND YOU TWO ARE ALREADY GOING AT IT!
YASAKA IS DEFINITELY INTERESTED IN YOU.
NOD NOD
NO HE ISN'T, MAYUMI!
PAP
THERE'S NO WAY HE IS.
TOKO, DON'T TRY AND DENY IT...
OWW!
YOU'VE GOT A STRONG WILL...
BUT AT THE CRUCIAL MOMENT YOU ALWAYS RUN AWAY!
IT'S A BAD HABIT OF YOURS.
I know you don't hate him.
LET'S GO, KAEDE.
YOU'RE RIGHT, MAYUMI... I GET IT ALREADY...
~~~

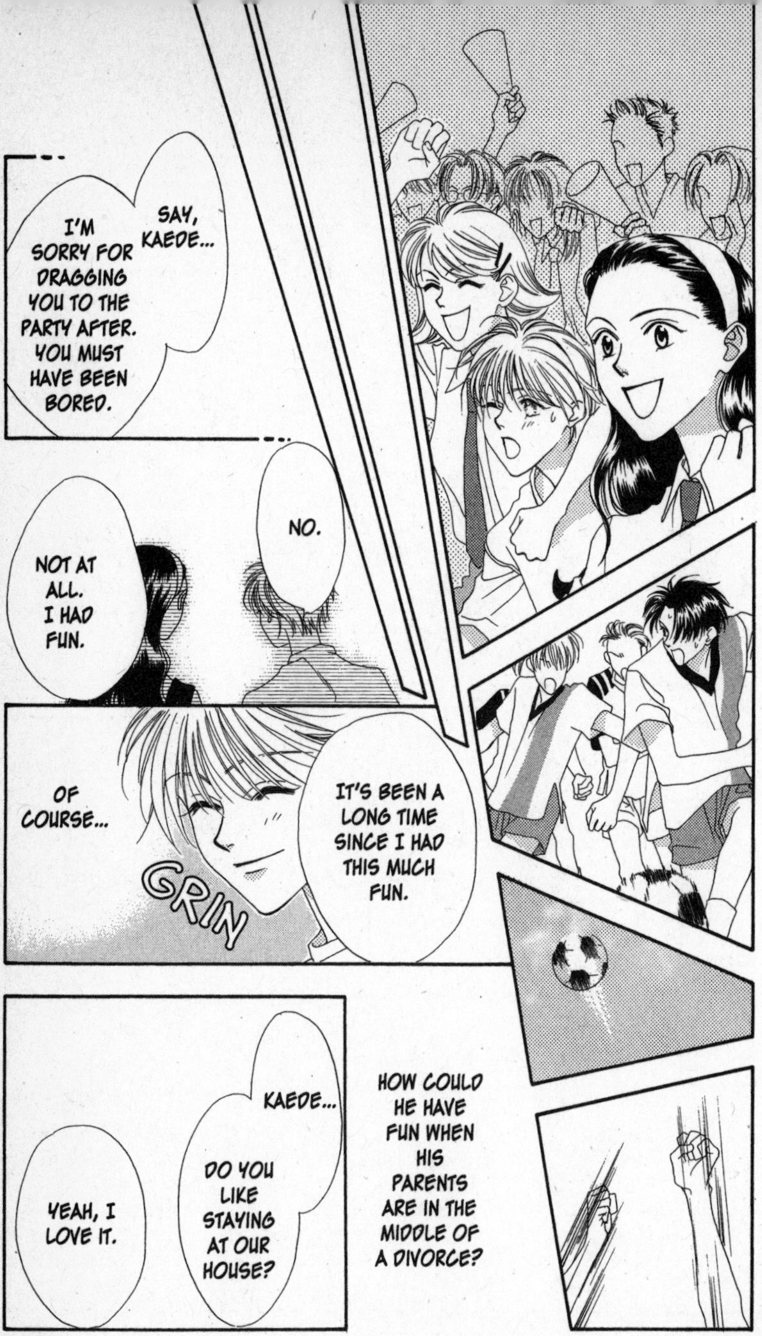
SAY, KAEDE...
I'M SORRY FOR DRAGGING YOU TO THE PARTY AFTER. YOU MUST HAVE BEEN BORED.
NO.
NOT AT ALL. I HAD FUN.
IT'S BEEN A LONG TIME SINCE I HAD THIS MUCH FUN.
OF COURSE...
GRIN
HOW COULD HE HAVE FUN WHEN HIS PARENTS ARE IN THE MIDDLE OF A DIVORCE?
KAEDE...
DO YOU LIKE STAYING AT OUR HOUSE?
YEAH, I LOVE IT.

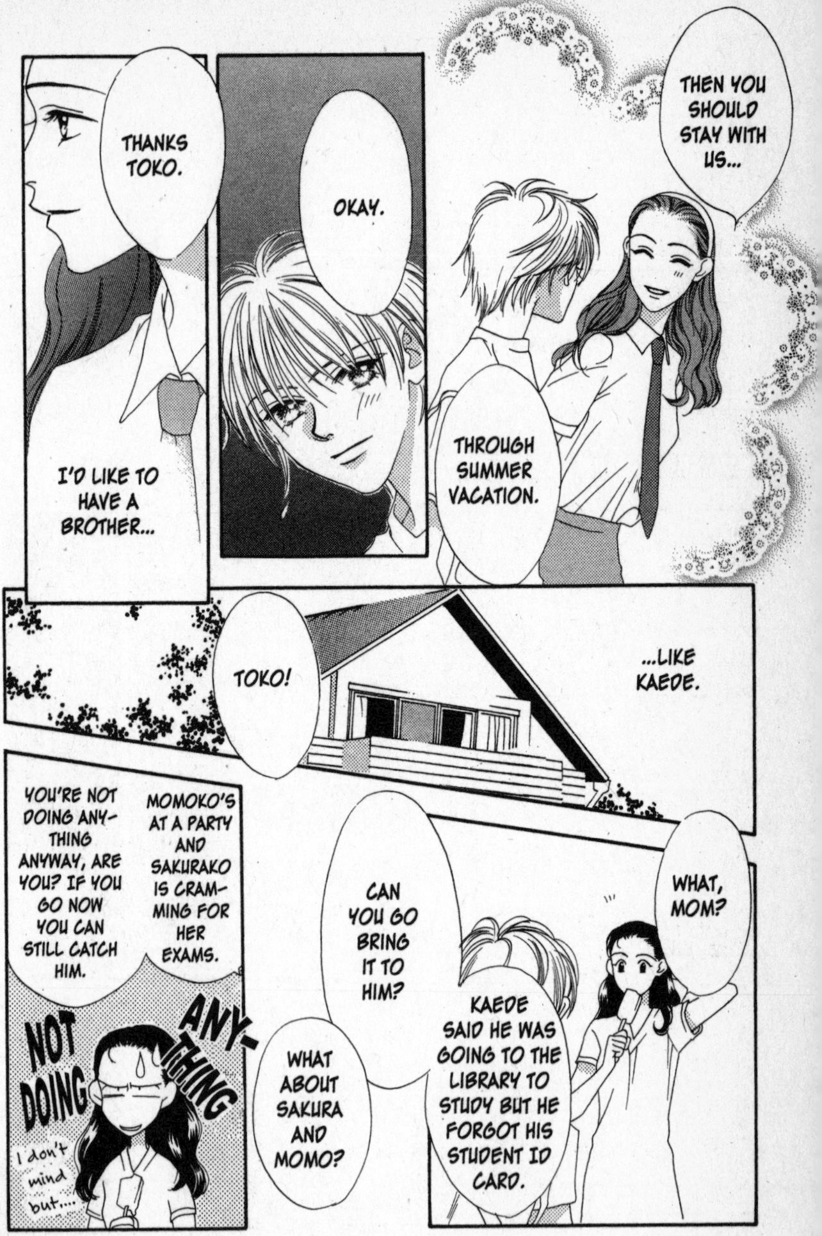
THEN YOU SHOULD STAY WITH US...
THROUGH SUMMER VACATION.
OKAY.
THANKS TOKO.
I'D LIKE TO HAVE A BROTHER...
...LIKE KAEDE.
TOKO!
WHAT, MOM?
KAEDE SAID HE WAS GOING TO THE LIBRARY TO STUDY BUT HE FORGOT HIS STUDENT ID CARD.
CAN YOU GO BRING IT TO HIM?
WHAT ABOUT SAKURA AND MOMO?
MOMOKO'S AT A PARTY AND SAKURAKO IS CRAM-MING FOR HER EXAMS.
YOU'RE NOT DOING ANY-THING ANYWAY, ARE YOU? IF YOU GO NOW YOU CAN STILL CATCH HIM.
NOT DOING ANY-THING
I don't mind but....

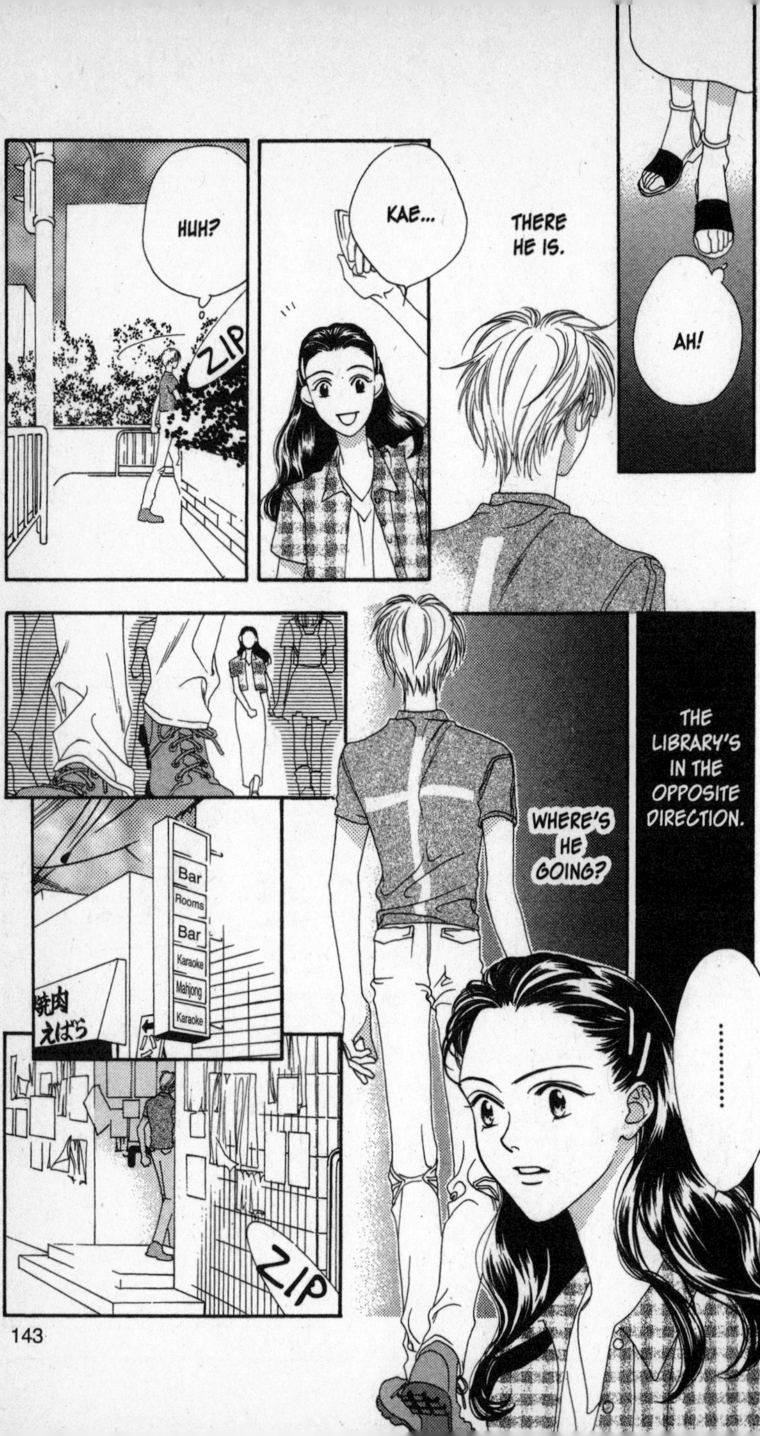
AH!
THERE HE IS.
KAE...
HUH?
ZIP
THE LIBRARY'S IN THE OPPOSITE DIRECTION.
WHERE'S HE GOING?
......
Bar
Rooms
Bar
Karaoke
Mahjong
Karaoke
焼肉
えばら
ZIP

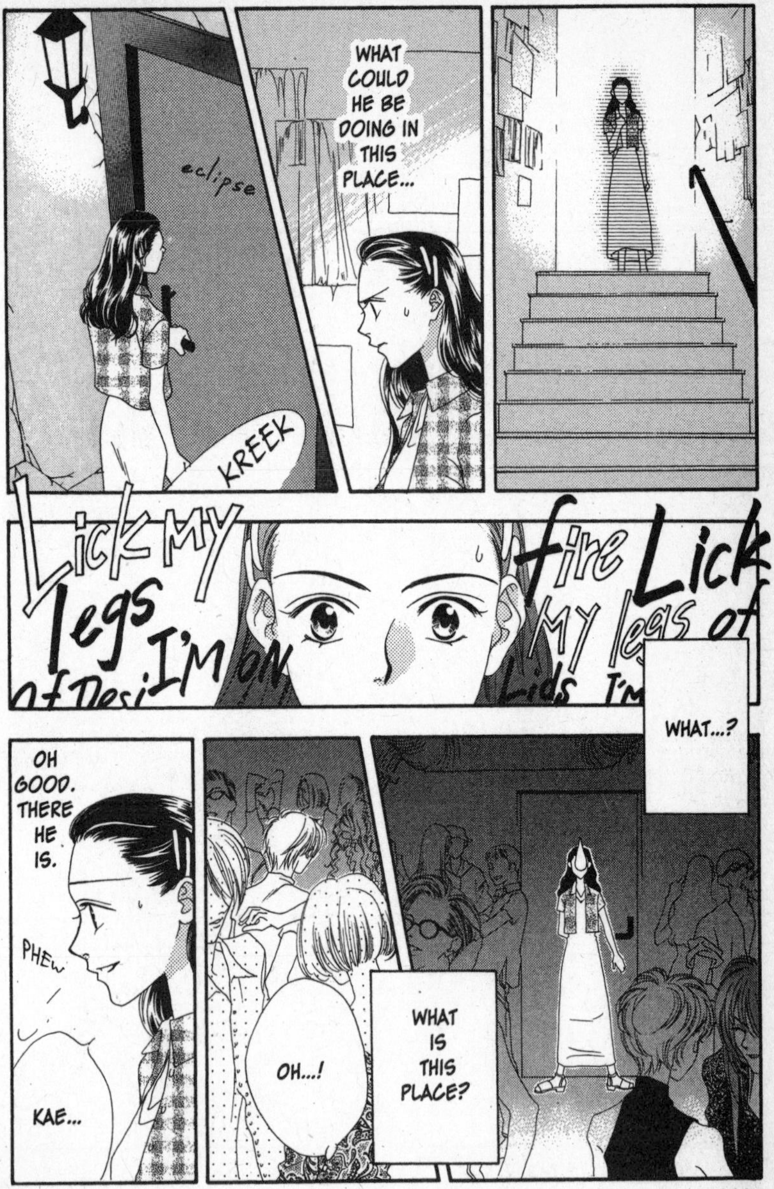
WHAT COULD HE BE DOING IN THIS PLACE...
eclipse
KREEK
Lick my legs I'M ON fire
Lick My legs of
WHAT...?
WHAT IS THIS PLACE?
OH...!
OH GOOD. THERE HE IS.
PHEW
KAE...

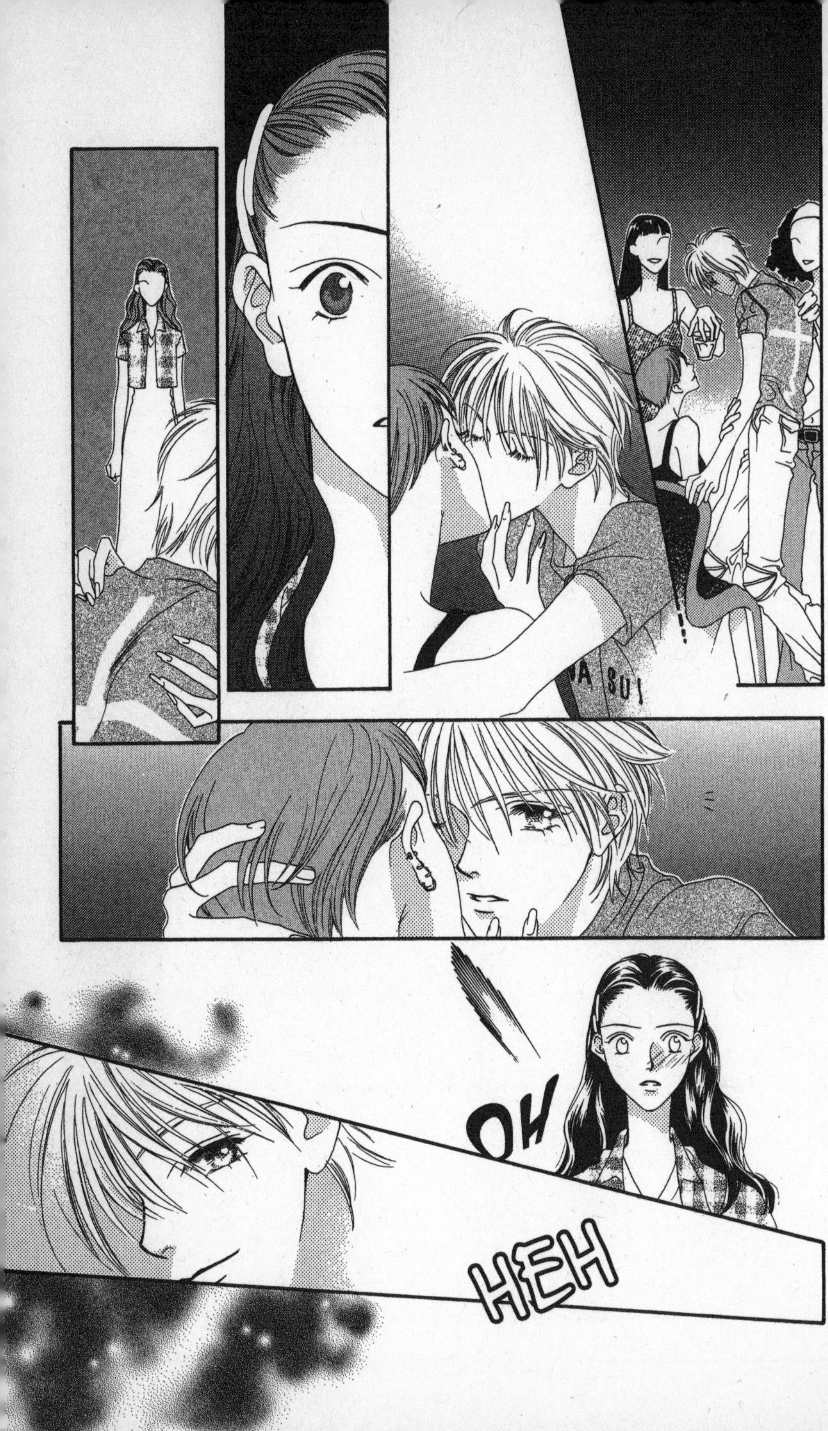
OH
HEH

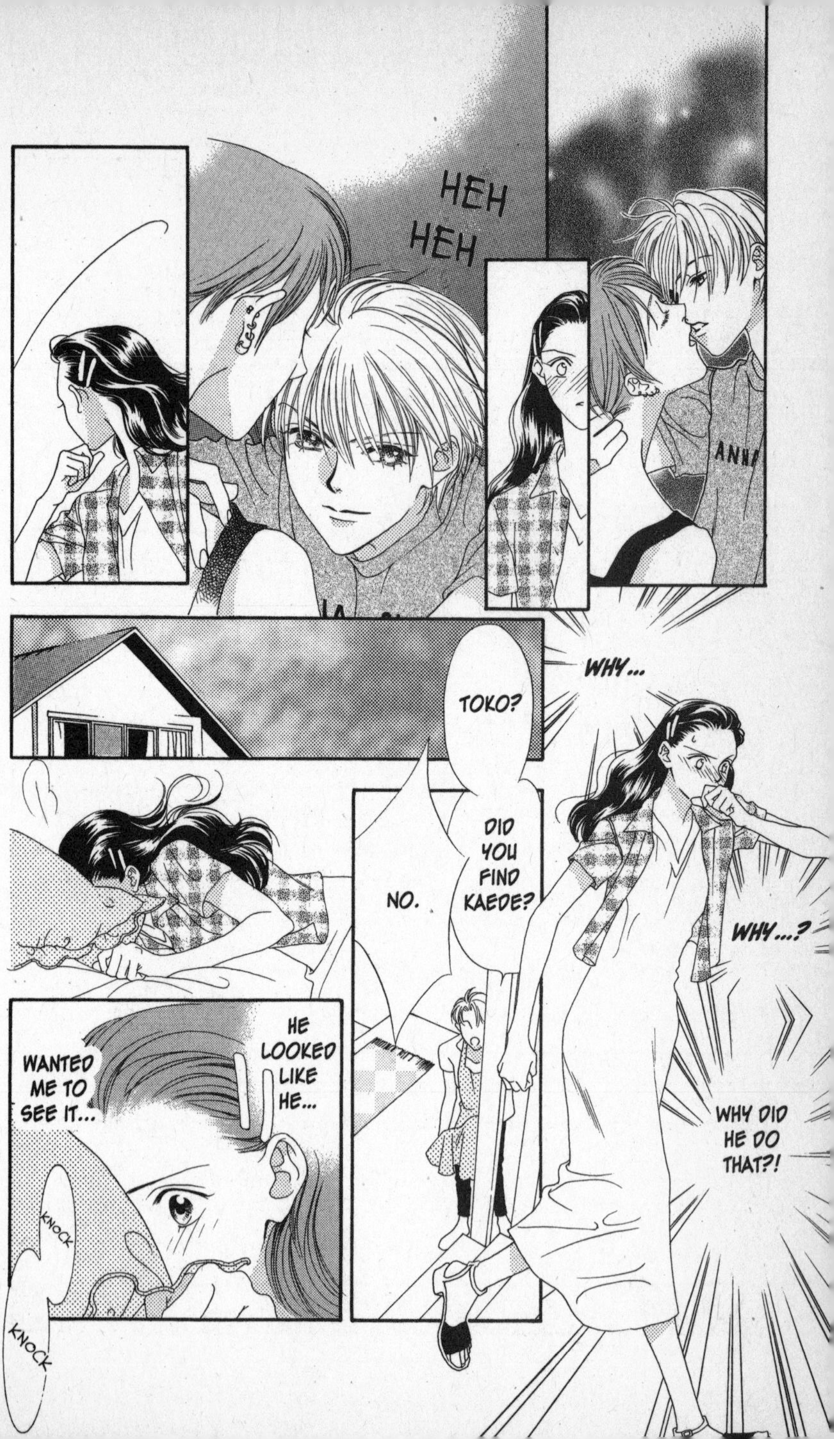
HEH HEH
WHY...
WHY...?
WHY DID HE DO THAT?!
TOKO?
DID YOU FIND KAEDE?
NO.
HE LOOKED LIKE HE...
WANTED ME TO SEE IT...
KNOCK
KNOCK

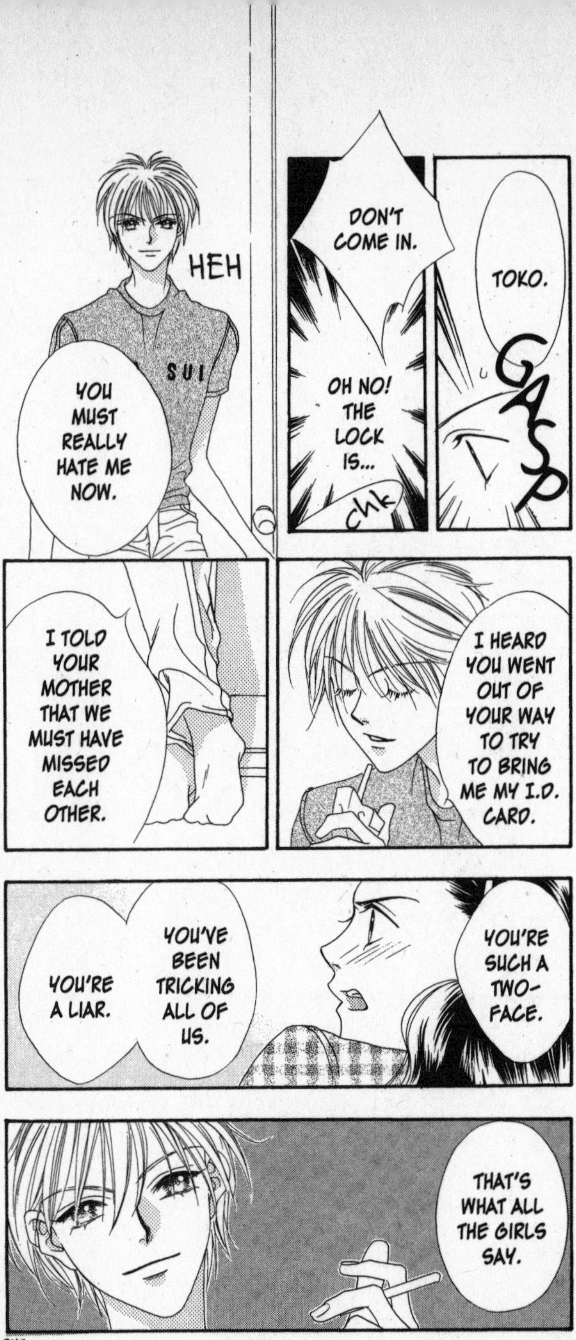
TOKO.
GASP
DON'T COME IN.
OH NO! THE LOCK IS...
chk
HEH
YOU MUST REALLY HATE ME NOW.
SUI
I HEARD YOU WENT OUT OF YOUR WAY TO TRY TO BRING ME MY I.D. CARD.
I TOLD YOUR MOTHER THAT WE MUST HAVE MISSED EACH OTHER.
YOU'RE SUCH A TWO-FACE.
YOU'VE BEEN TRICKING ALL OF US.
YOU'RE A LIAR.
THAT'S WHAT ALL THE GIRLS SAY.

Whispered Secrets

MY FIRST TIME

UGH, I WAS SO EMBARRASSED THE FIRST TIME I SENT IN THE ROUGH DRAFT OF THIS COMIC TO THE EDITOR. I WORKED REALLY HARD ON MY ROUGH DRAFT SO I WAS NERVOUS ABOUT HAVING OTHER PEOPLE SEE IT. BUT EVERYBODY REALLY LIKED TOKO AND KAEDE. IN FACT KAEDE WAS ODDLY POPULAR (HEH). THANK YOU EVERYBODY FOR LIKING KAEDE SO MUCH. SOME PEOPLE THOUGHT THE CHARACTERS WERE BASED ON ANOTHER POPULAR MANGA/ANIME SERIES, BUT THEY AREN'T. THIS OTHER SERIES WAS SO POPULAR THAT PEOPLE WERE GOING CRAZY FOR IT.

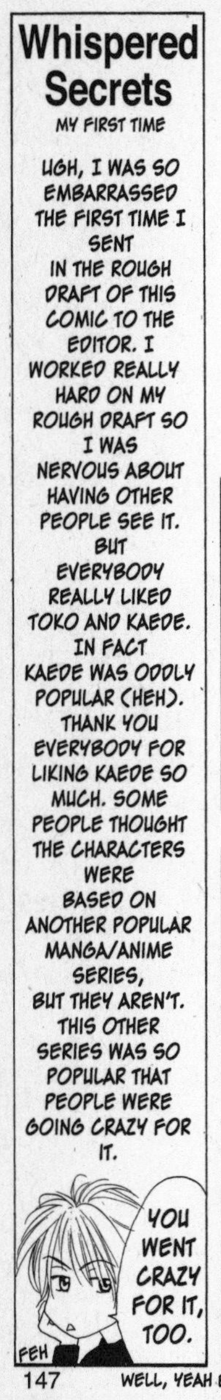
YOU WENT CRAZY FOR IT, TOO.
FEH

WELL, YEAH BUT...

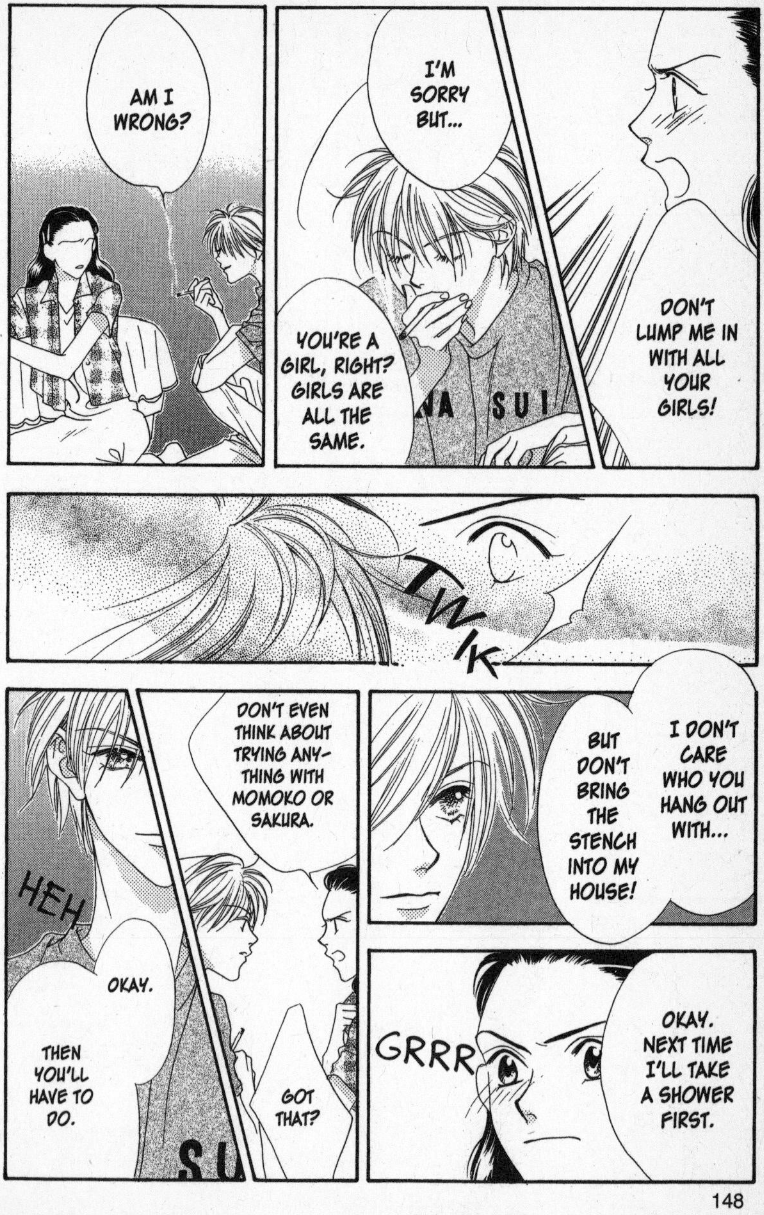
DON'T LUMP ME IN WITH ALL YOUR GIRLS!
I'M SORRY BUT...
YOU'RE A GIRL, RIGHT? GIRLS ARE ALL THE SAME.
AM I WRONG?
TWIK
I DON'T CARE WHO YOU HANG OUT WITH...
BUT DON'T BRING THE STENCH INTO MY HOUSE!
GRRR
OKAY. NEXT TIME I'LL TAKE A SHOWER FIRST.
DON'T EVEN THINK ABOUT TRYING ANY-THING WITH MOMOKO OR SAKURA.
GOT THAT?
HEH
OKAY.
THEN YOU'LL HAVE TO DO.

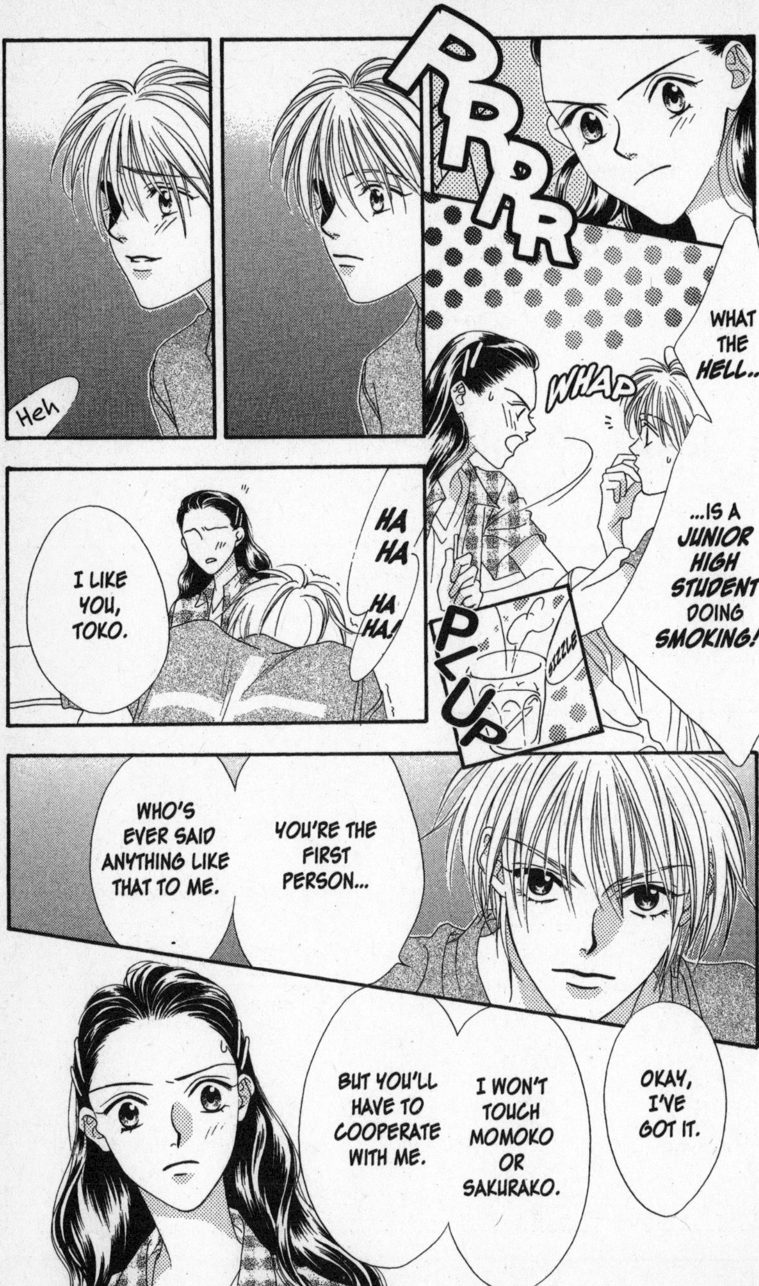
RRRR
WHAP
WHAT THE HELL...
...IS A JUNIOR HIGH STUDENT DOING SMOKING!?
PLUP
SIZZLE
Heh
HA HA HA HA!
I LIKE YOU, TOKO.
YOU'RE THE FIRST PERSON...
WHO'S EVER SAID ANYTHING LIKE THAT TO ME.
OKAY, I'VE GOT IT.
I WON'T TOUCH MOMOKO OR SAKURAKO.
BUT YOU'LL HAVE TO COOPERATE WITH ME.

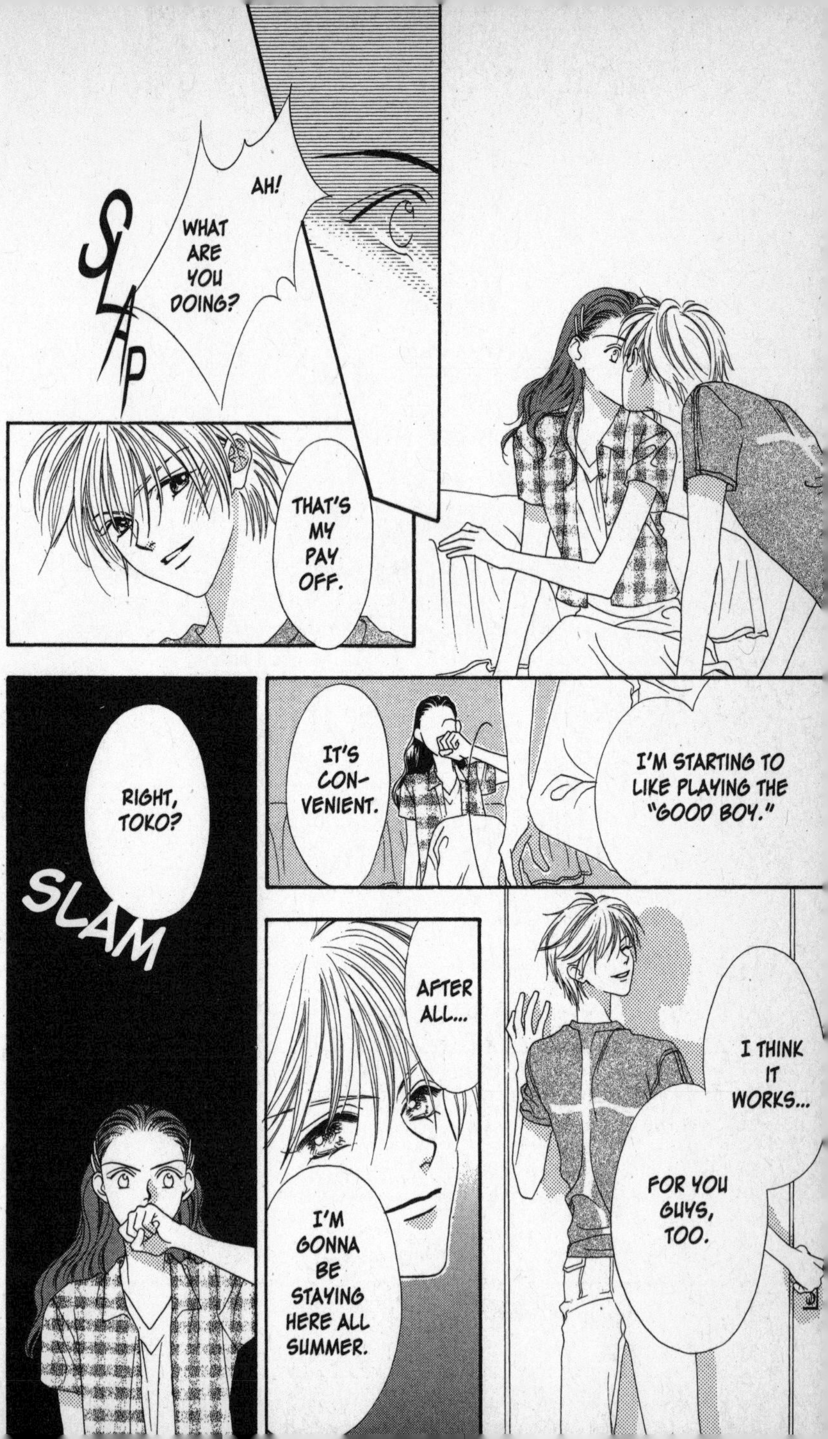
AH!
WHAT ARE YOU DOING?
SLAP
THAT'S MY PAY OFF.
I'M STARTING TO LIKE PLAYING THE "GOOD BOY."
IT'S CON-VENIENT.
I THINK IT WORKS...
FOR YOU GUYS, TOO.
AFTER ALL...
I'M GONNA BE STAYING HERE ALL SUMMER.
RIGHT, TOKO?
SLAM

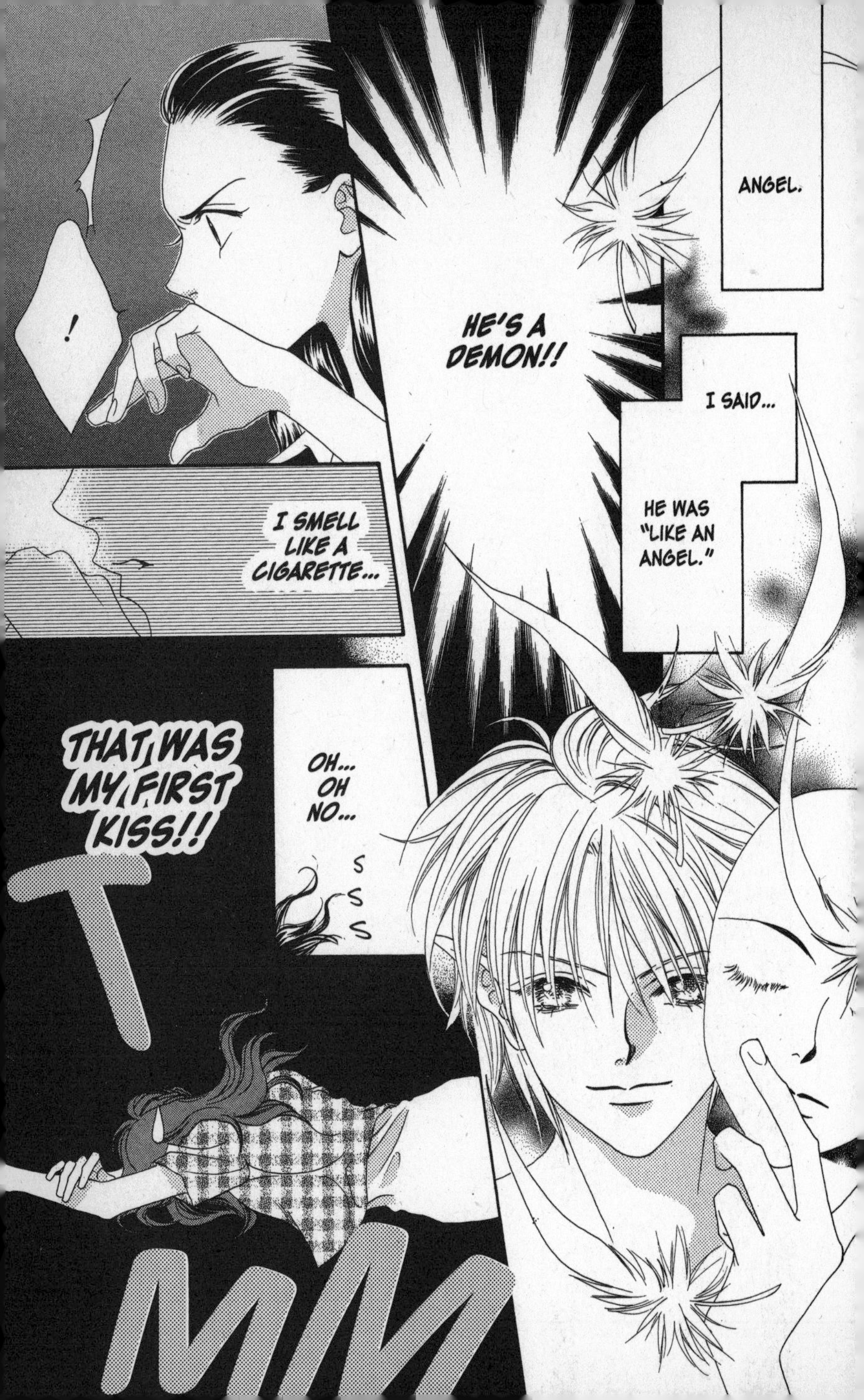
ANGEL.
I SAID...
HE WAS "LIKE AN ANGEL."
HE'S A DEMON!!
!
I SMELL LIKE A CIGARETTE...
OH... OH NO...
SSS
THAT WAS MY FIRST KISS!!
T
MM

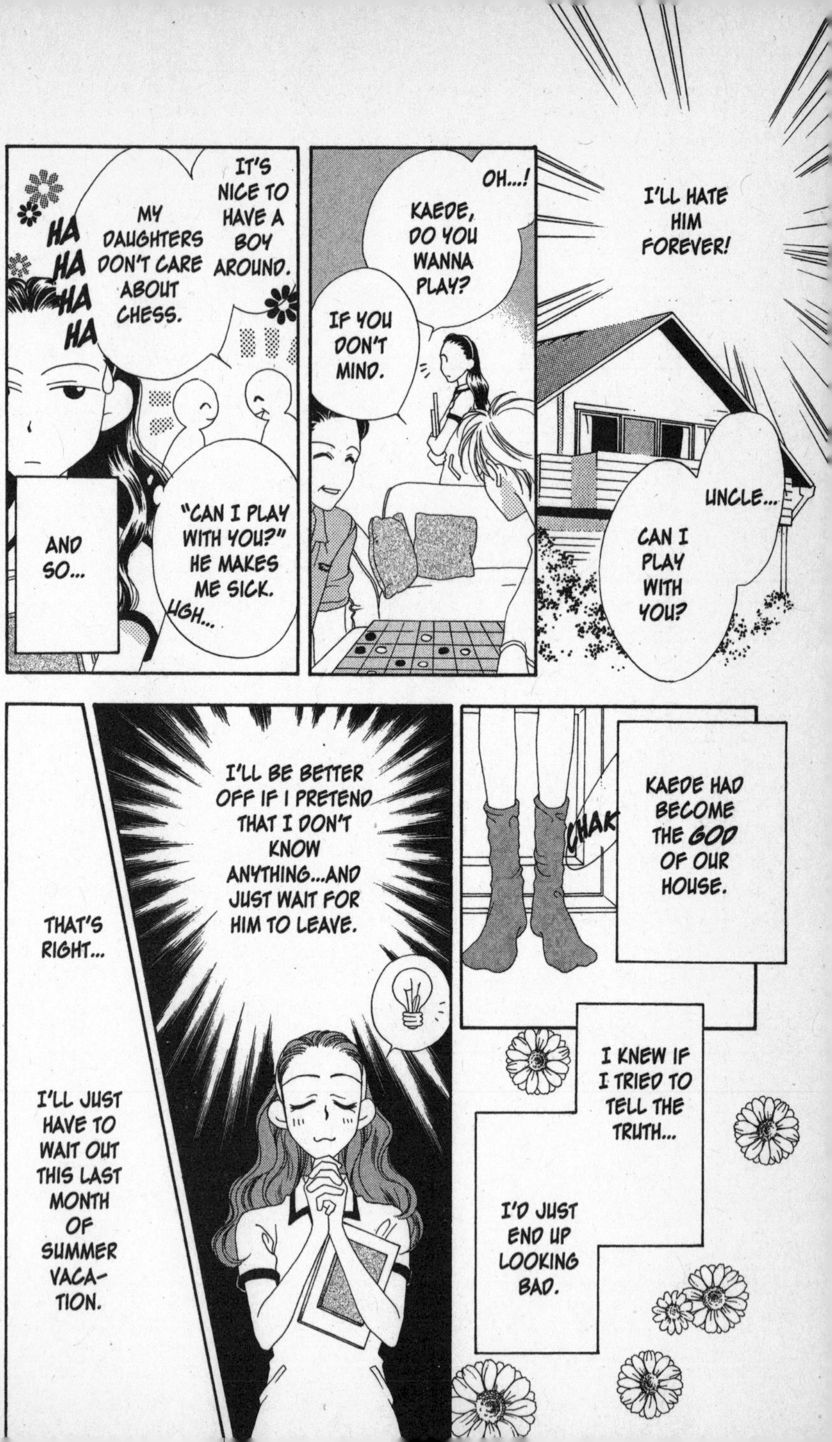
I'LL HATE HIM FOREVER!
UNCLE...
CAN I PLAY WITH YOU?
OH...!
KAEDE, DO YOU WANNA PLAY?
IF YOU DON'T MIND.
IT'S NICE TO HAVE A BOY AROUND.
MY DAUGHTERS DON'T CARE ABOUT CHESS.
HA HA HA HA
"CAN I PLAY WITH YOU?" HE MAKES ME SICK.
UGH...
AND SO...
KAEDE HAD BECOME THE GOD OF OUR HOUSE.
CHAK
I KNEW IF I TRIED TO TELL THE TRUTH...
I'D JUST END UP LOOKING BAD.
I'LL BE BETTER OFF IF I PRETEND THAT I DON'T KNOW ANYTHING...AND JUST WAIT FOR HIM TO LEAVE.
THAT'S RIGHT...
I'LL JUST HAVE TO WAIT OUT THIS LAST MONTH OF SUMMER VACA-TION.

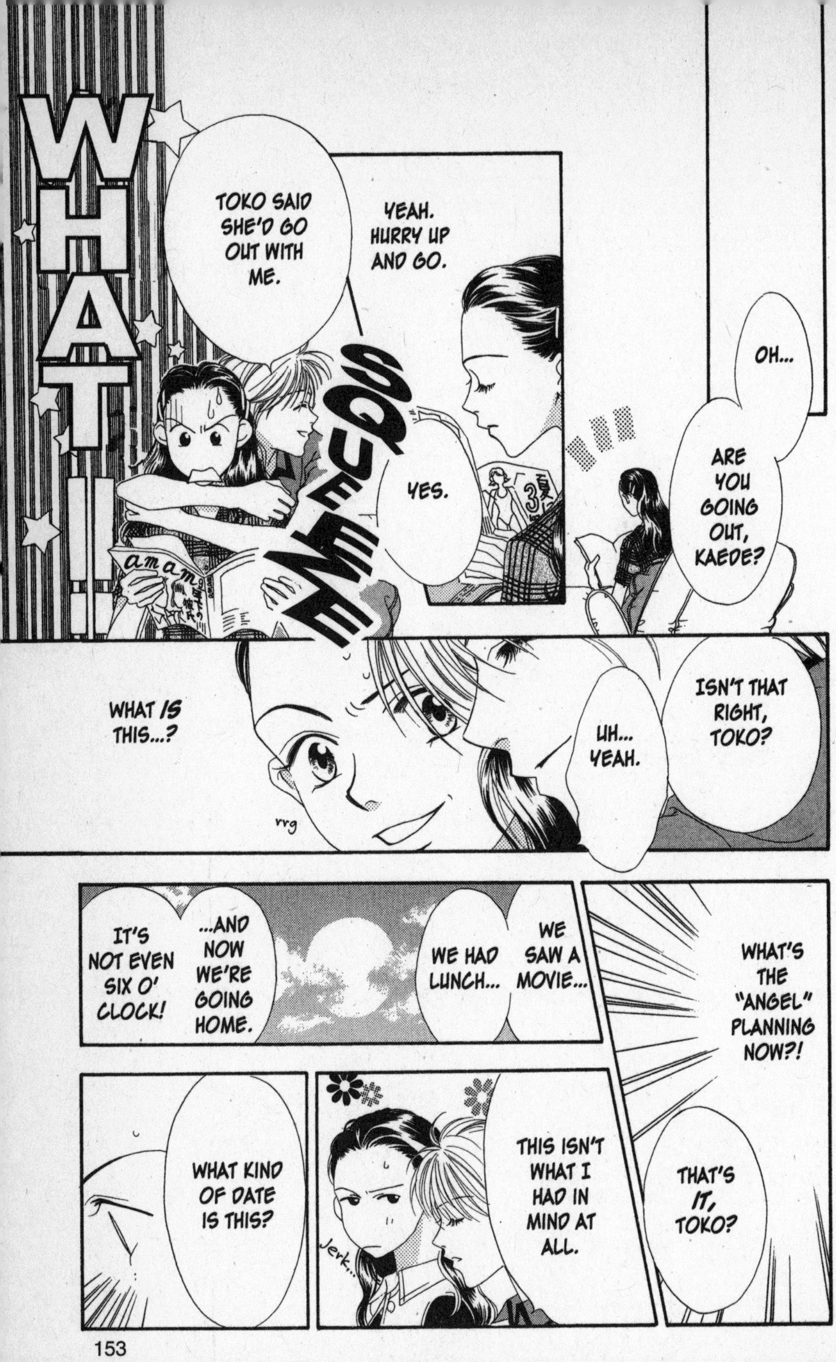
OH...
ARE YOU GOING OUT, KAEDE?
YES.
YEAH. HURRY UP AND GO.
TOKO SAID SHE'D GO OUT WITH ME.
SQUEEEEE
WHAT!!
ISN'T THAT RIGHT, TOKO?
UH... YEAH.
vrg
WHAT *IS* THIS...?
WHAT'S THE "ANGEL" PLANNING NOW?!
THAT'S *IT*, TOKO?
WE SAW A MOVIE...
WE HAD LUNCH...
...AND NOW WE'RE GOING HOME.
IT'S NOT EVEN SIX O' CLOCK!
THIS ISN'T WHAT I HAD IN MIND AT ALL.
Jerk...
WHAT KIND OF DATE IS THIS?

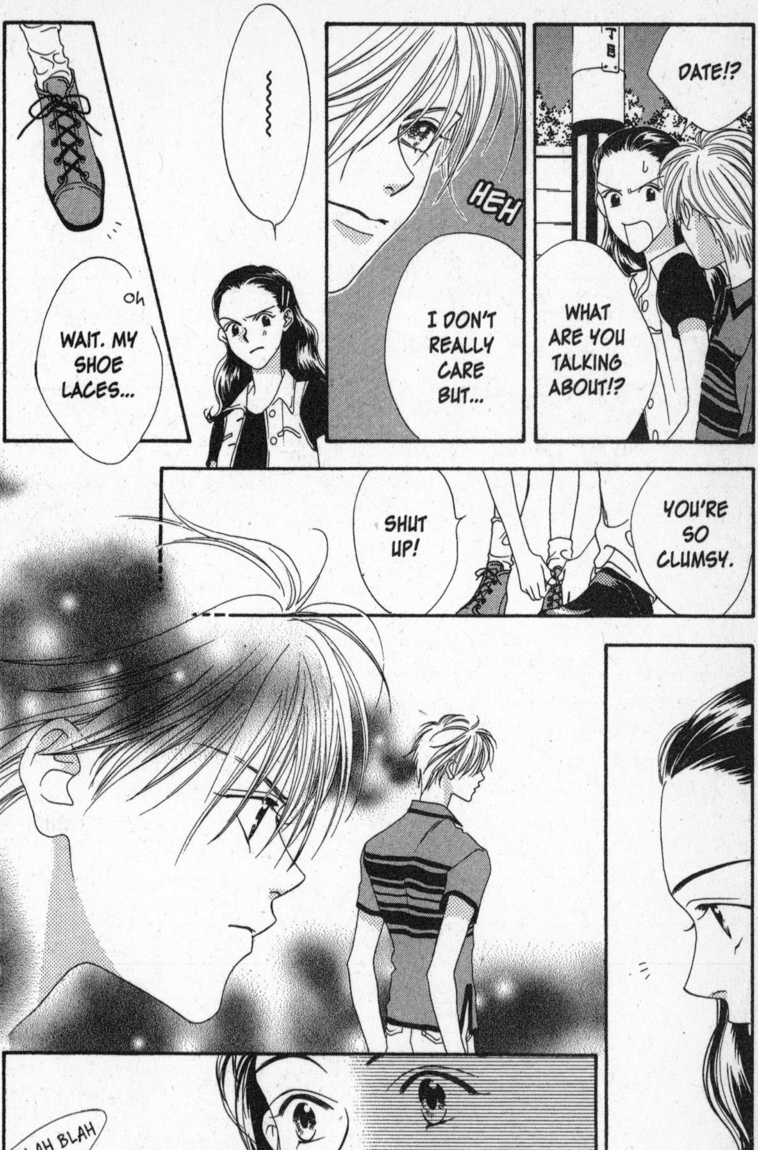
DATE!?
WHAT ARE YOU TALKING ABOUT!?
HEH
I DON'T REALLY CARE BUT...
......
oh
WAIT. MY SHOE LACES...
YOU'RE SO CLUMSY.
SHUT UP!
BLAH BLAH

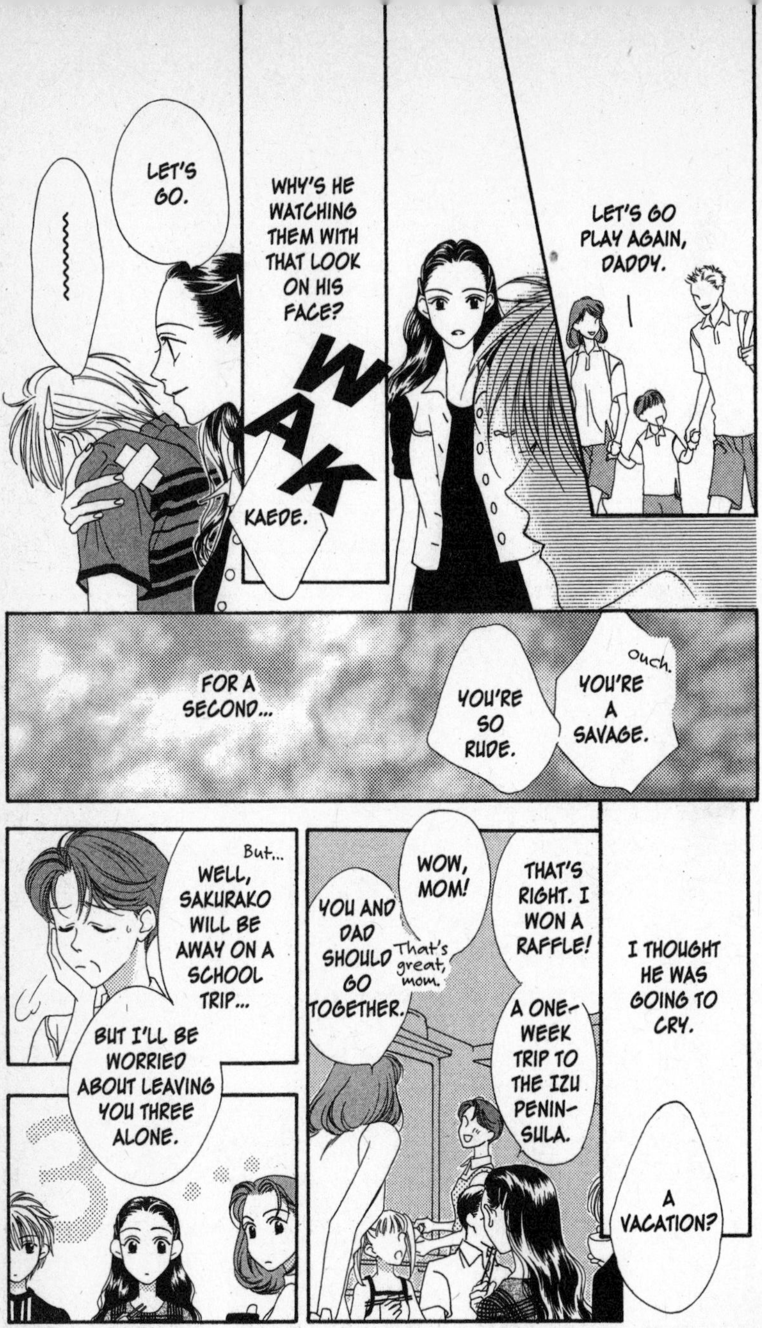
LET'S GO PLAY AGAIN, DADDY.
WHY'S HE WATCHING THEM WITH THAT LOOK ON HIS FACE?
WAK
KAEDE.
LET'S GO.
......
Ouch.
YOU'RE A SAVAGE.
YOU'RE SO RUDE.
FOR A SECOND...
I THOUGHT HE WAS GOING TO CRY.
A VACATION?
THAT'S RIGHT. I WON A RAFFLE!
A ONE-WEEK TRIP TO THE IZU PENINSULA.
WOW, MOM!
That's great, mom.
YOU AND DAD SHOULD GO TOGETHER.
But...
WELL, SAKURAKO WILL BE AWAY ON A SCHOOL TRIP...
BUT I'LL BE WORRIED ABOUT LEAVING YOU THREE ALONE.

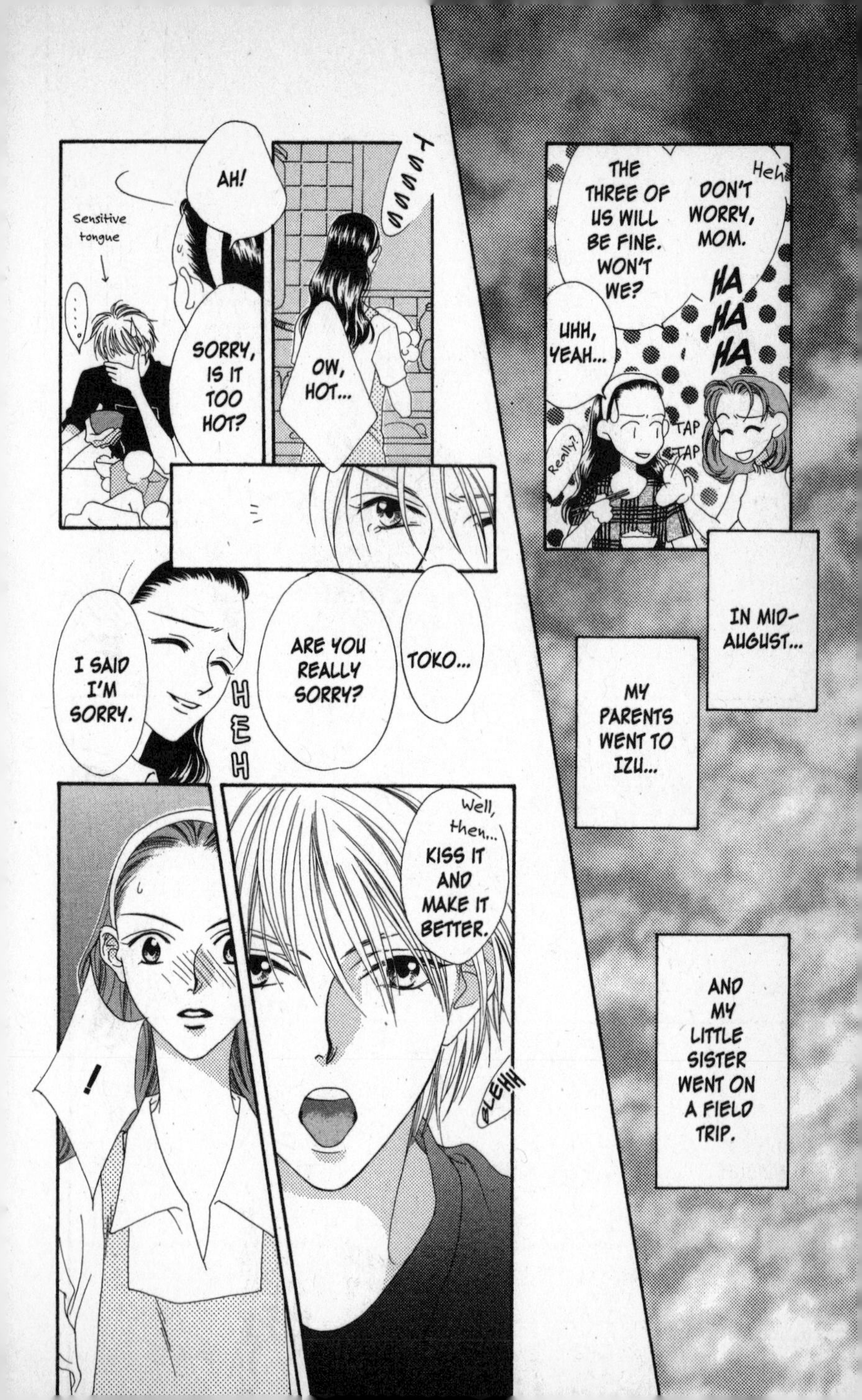

Heh
DON'T WORRY, MOM.
THE THREE OF US WILL BE FINE. WON'T WE?
HA HA HA
UHH, YEAH...
Really?
TAP TAP
IN MID-AUGUST...
MY PARENTS WENT TO IZU...
AND MY LITTLE SISTER WENT ON A FIELD TRIP.
TSSSSS
OW, HOT...
AH!
Sensitive tongue
.....
SORRY, IS IT TOO HOT?
TOKO...
ARE YOU REALLY SORRY?
I SAID I'M SORRY.
HEH HEH
Well, then...
KISS IT AND MAKE IT BETTER.
BLEHH
!

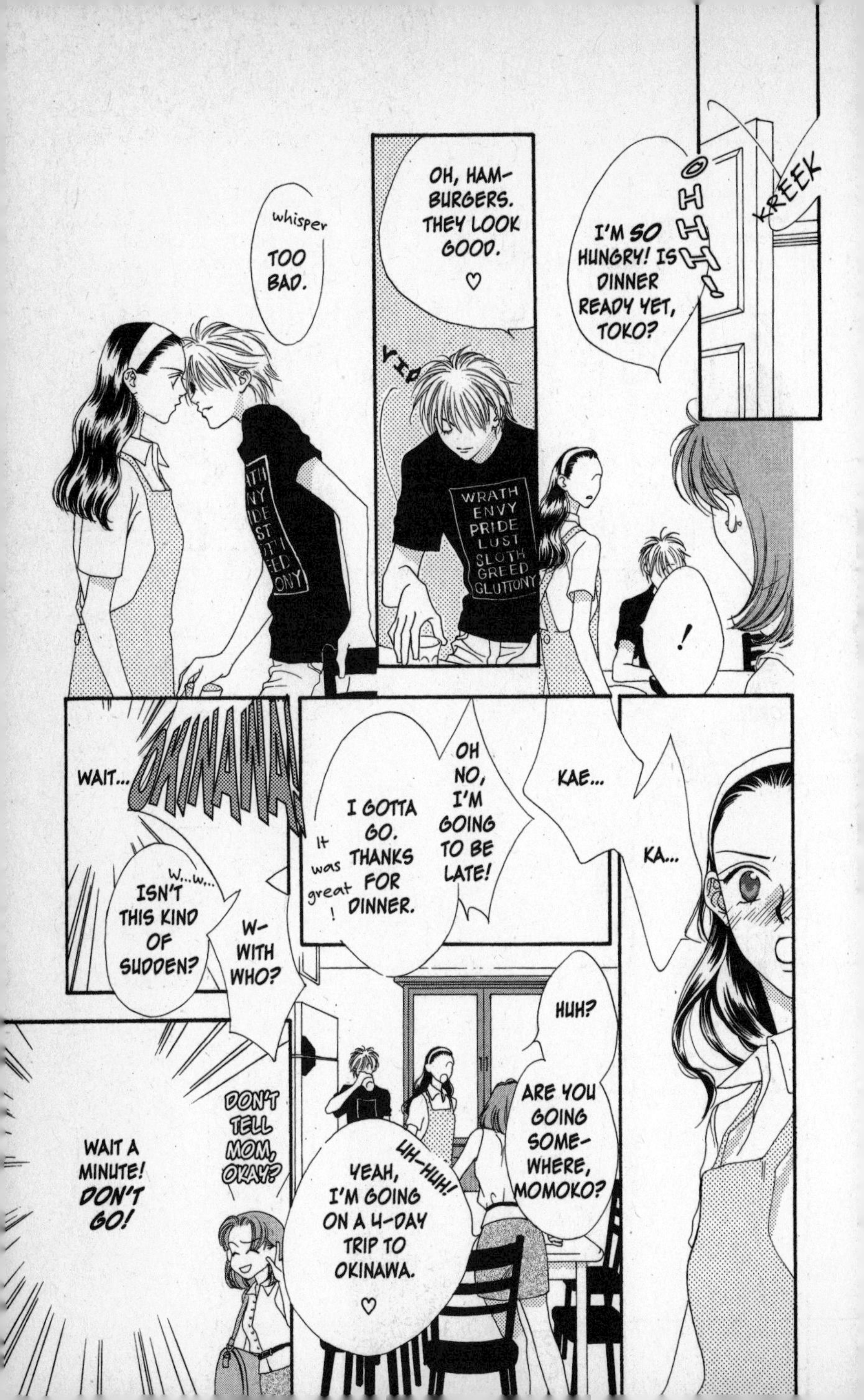
KREEK
OHHH!
I'M SO HUNGRY! IS DINNER READY YET, TOKO?
!
OH, HAM-BURGERS. THEY LOOK GOOD. ♡
whisper
TOO BAD.
KAE...
KA...
HUH?
ARE YOU GOING SOME-WHERE, MOMOKO?
OH NO, I'M GOING TO BE LATE!
I GOTTA GO. THANKS FOR DINNER.
It was great!
WAIT...
OKINAWA!
W...W...
ISN'T THIS KIND OF SUDDEN?
W-WITH WHO?
UH-HUH!
YEAH, I'M GOING ON A 4-DAY TRIP TO OKINAWA. ♡
DON'T TELL MOM, OKAY?
WAIT A MINUTE! DON'T GO!

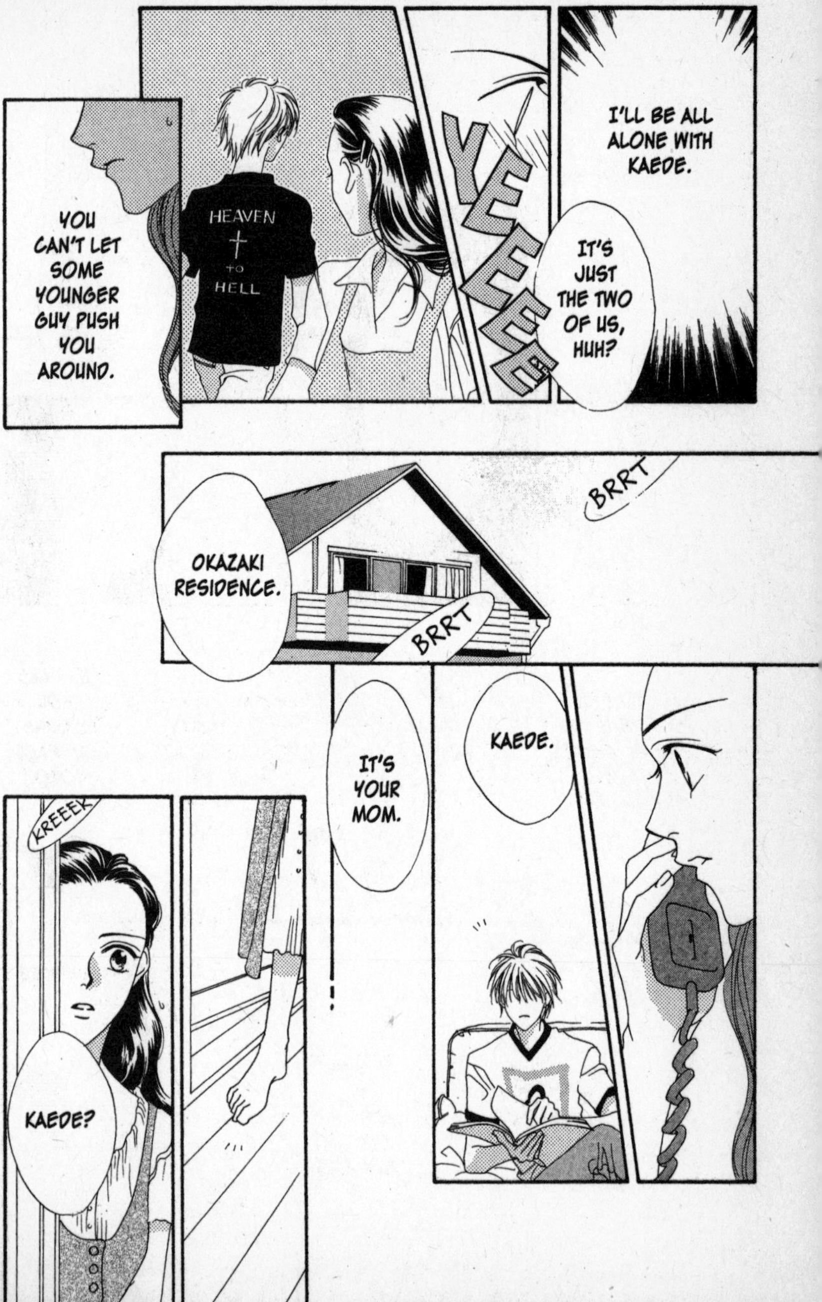
I'LL BE ALL ALONE WITH KAEDE.
IT'S JUST THE TWO OF US, HUH?
YEEEEE
YOU CAN'T LET SOME YOUNGER GUY PUSH YOU AROUND.
BRRT
BRRT
OKAZAKI RESIDENCE.
KAEDE.
IT'S YOUR MOM.
!
KREEEK
KAEDE?

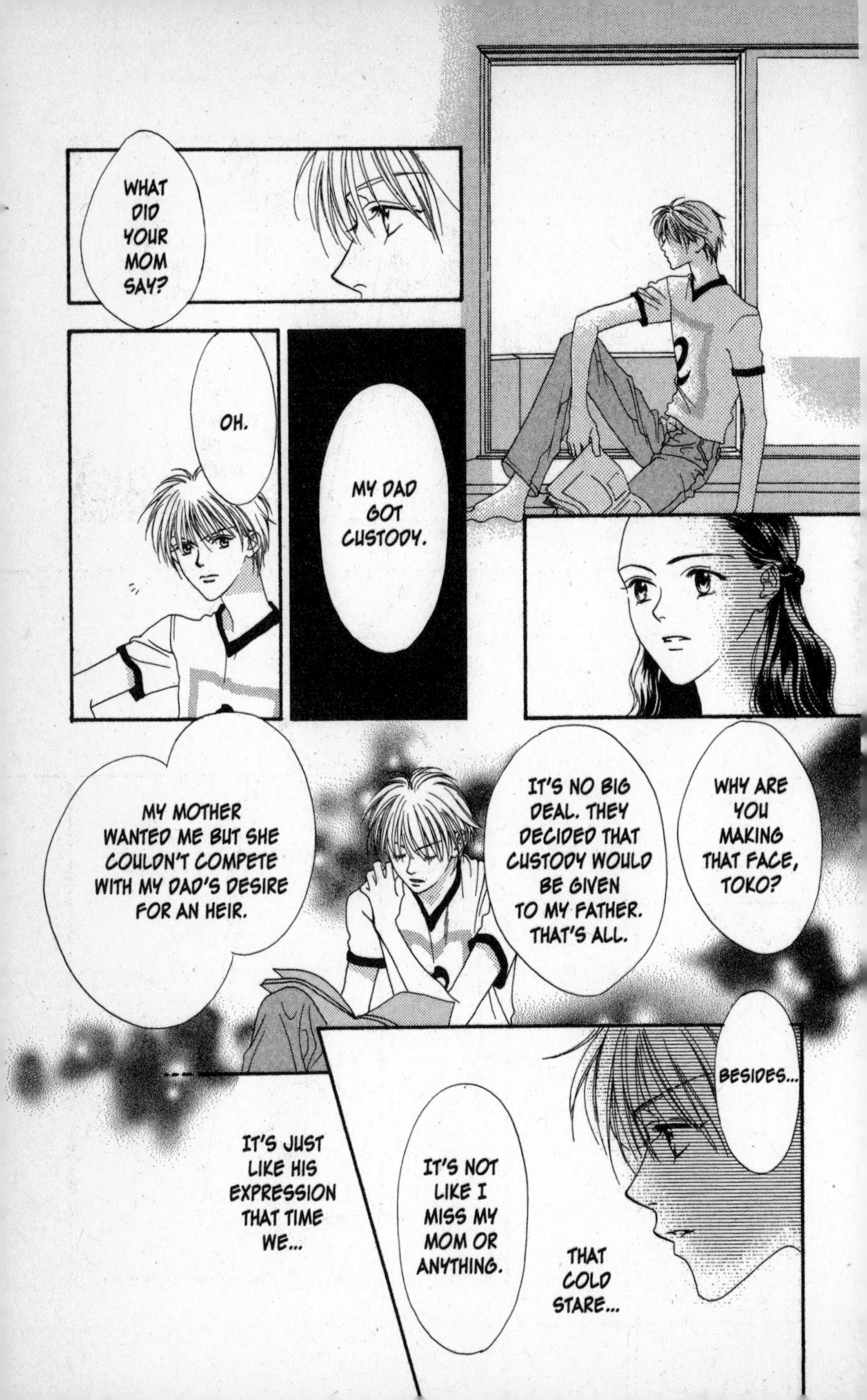
WHAT DID YOUR MOM SAY?
MY DAD GOT CUSTODY.
OH.
WHY ARE YOU MAKING THAT FACE, TOKO?
IT'S NO BIG DEAL. THEY DECIDED THAT CUSTODY WOULD BE GIVEN TO MY FATHER. THAT'S ALL.
MY MOTHER WANTED ME BUT SHE COULDN'T COMPETE WITH MY DAD'S DESIRE FOR AN HEIR.
BESIDES...
IT'S NOT LIKE I MISS MY MOM OR ANYTHING.
THAT COLD STARE...
IT'S JUST LIKE HIS EXPRESSION THAT TIME WE...

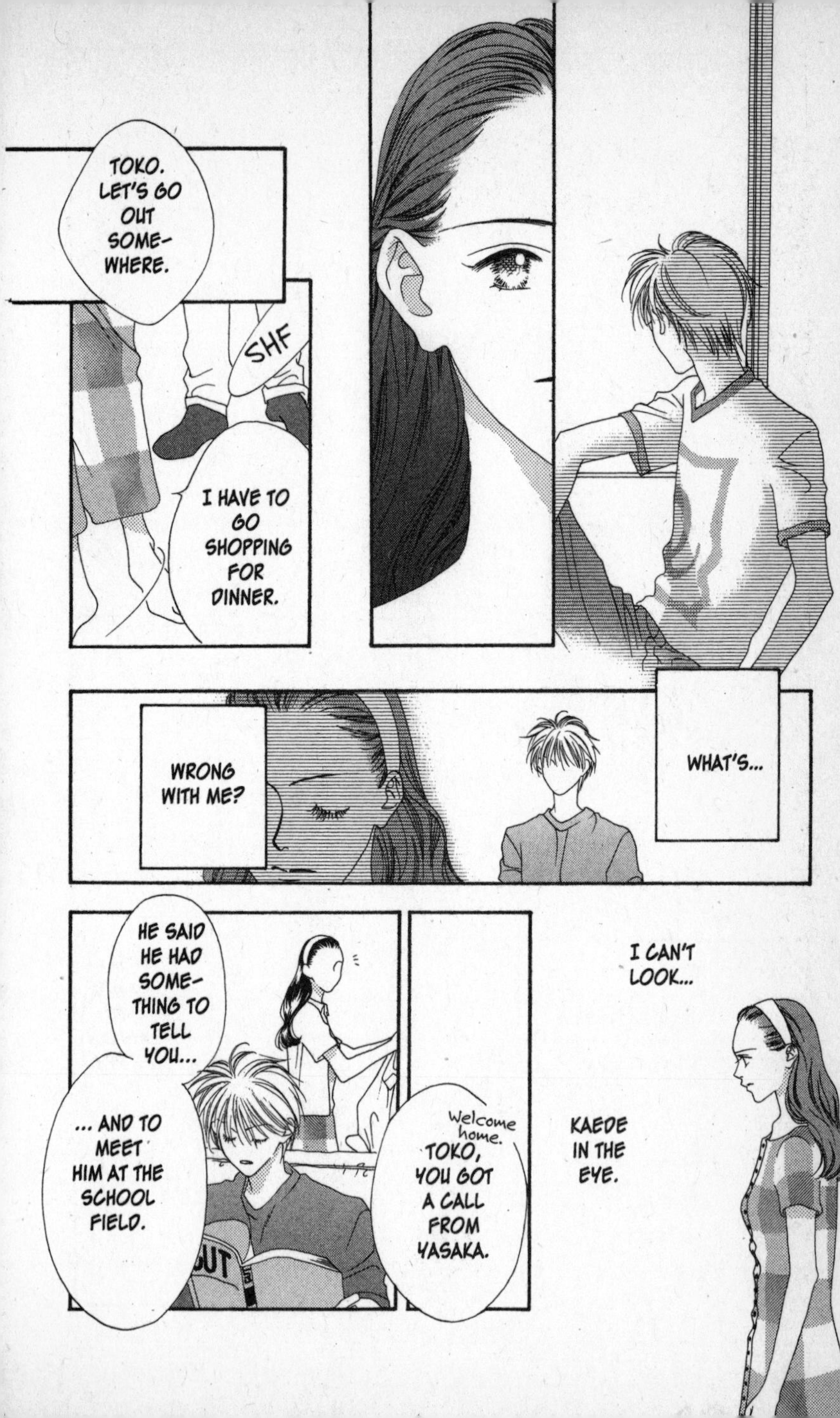
TOKO. LET'S GO OUT SOMEWHERE.
SHF
I HAVE TO GO SHOPPING FOR DINNER.
WHAT'S...
WRONG WITH ME?
I CAN'T LOOK...
KAEDE IN THE EYE.
Welcome home.
TOKO, YOU GOT A CALL FROM YASAKA.
HE SAID HE HAD SOMETHING TO TELL YOU...
... AND TO MEET HIM AT THE SCHOOL FIELD.

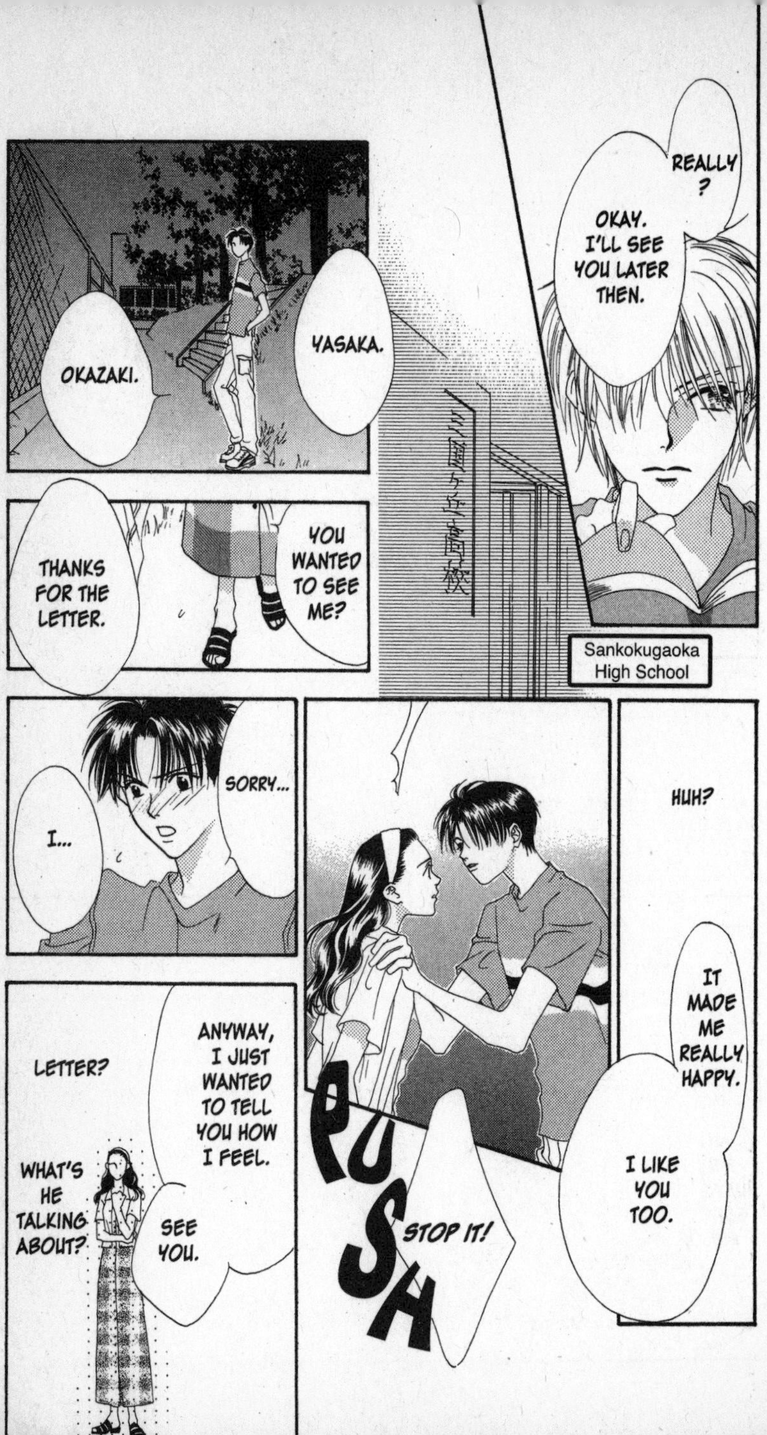
REALLY?
OKAY. I'LL SEE YOU LATER THEN.
三国ヶ丘高校
Sankokugaoka High School
YASAKA.
OKAZAKI.
YOU WANTED TO SEE ME?
THANKS FOR THE LETTER.
HUH?
IT MADE ME REALLY HAPPY.
I LIKE YOU TOO.
STOP IT!
PUSH
SORRY...
I...
ANYWAY, I JUST WANTED TO TELL YOU HOW I FEEL.
SEE YOU.
LETTER?
WHAT'S HE TALKING ABOUT?

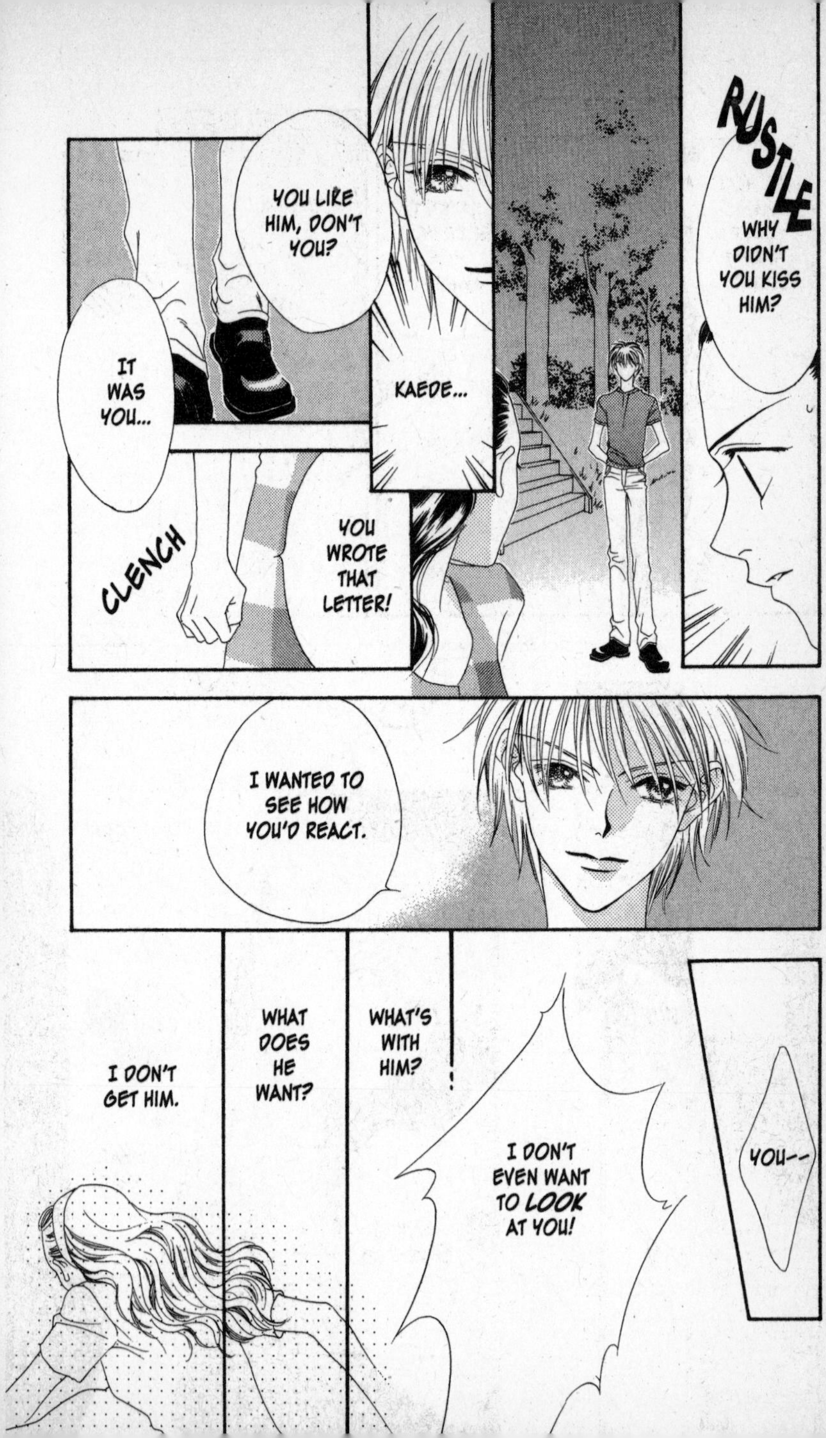
RUSTLE
WHY DIDN'T YOU KISS HIM?
KAEDE...
YOU LIKE HIM, DON'T YOU?
IT WAS YOU...
CLENCH
YOU WROTE THAT LETTER!
I WANTED TO SEE HOW YOU'D REACT.
YOU--
I DON'T EVEN WANT TO *LOOK* AT YOU!
WHAT'S WITH HIM?
WHAT DOES HE WANT?
I DON'T GET HIM.

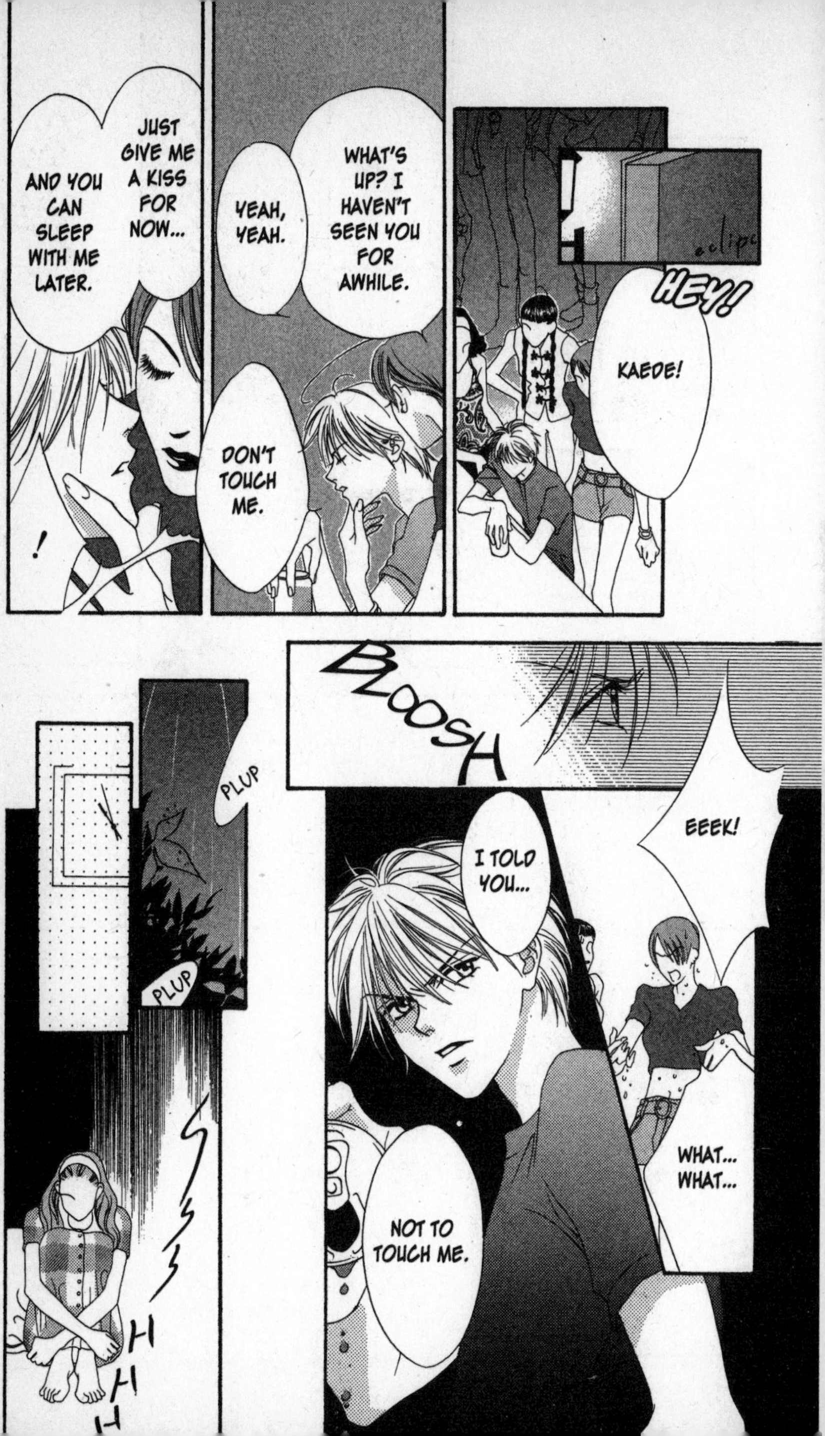
HEY!
KAEDE!
WHAT'S UP? I HAVEN'T SEEN YOU FOR AWHILE.
YEAH, YEAH.
DON'T TOUCH ME.
JUST GIVE ME A KISS FOR NOW...
AND YOU CAN SLEEP WITH ME LATER.
!
BLOOSH
EEEK!
I TOLD YOU...
WHAT... WHAT...
NOT TO TOUCH ME.
PLUP
PLUP
SSSHHH

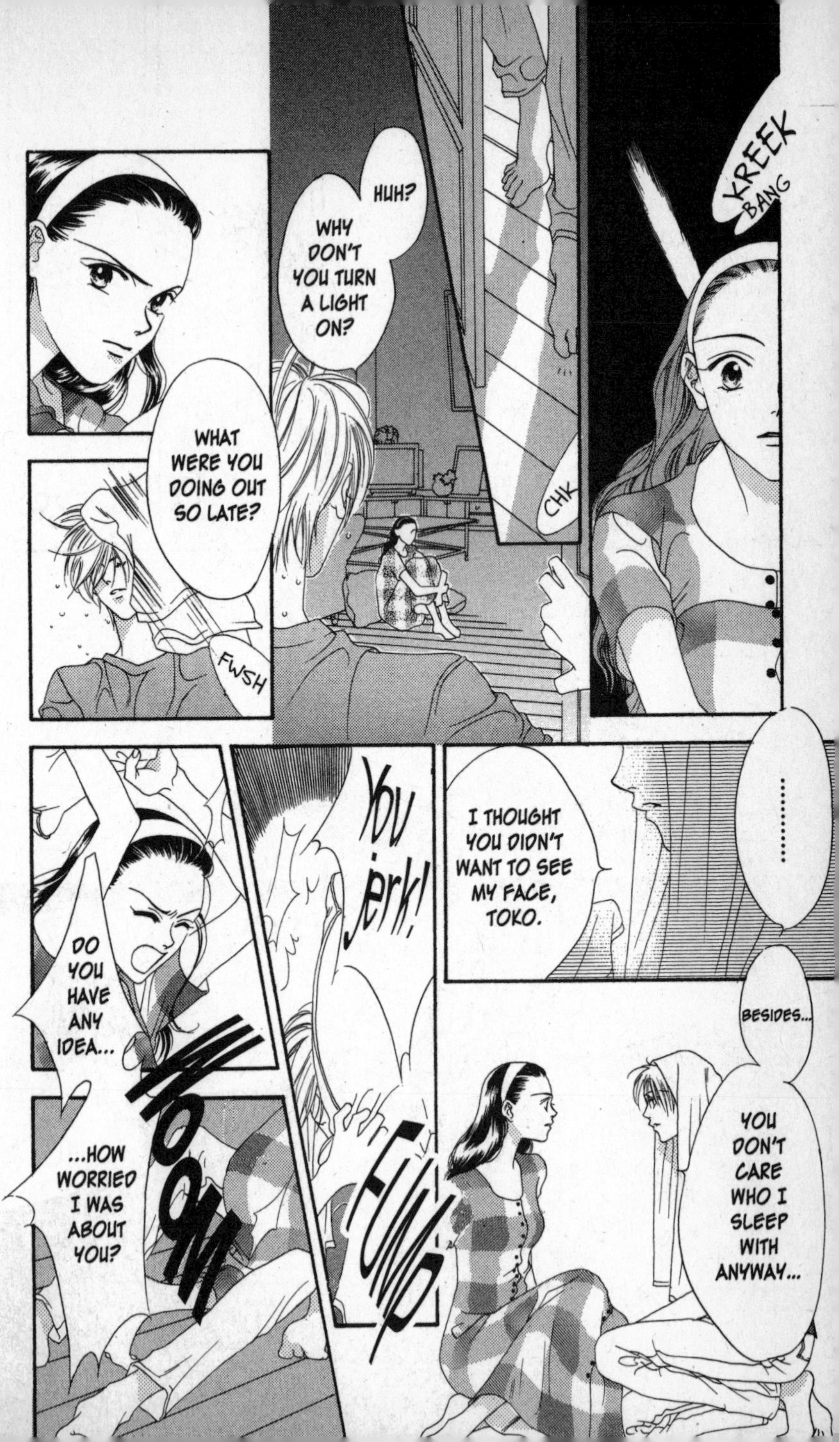
KREEK
BANG
CHK
HUH?
WHY DON'T YOU TURN A LIGHT ON?
WHAT WERE YOU DOING OUT SO LATE?
FWSH
......
I THOUGHT YOU DIDN'T WANT TO SEE MY FACE, TOKO.
BESIDES...
YOU DON'T CARE WHO I SLEEP WITH ANYWAY...
You jerk!
FUMP
DO YOU HAVE ANY IDEA...
...HOW WORRIED I WAS ABOUT YOU?
WHOOM

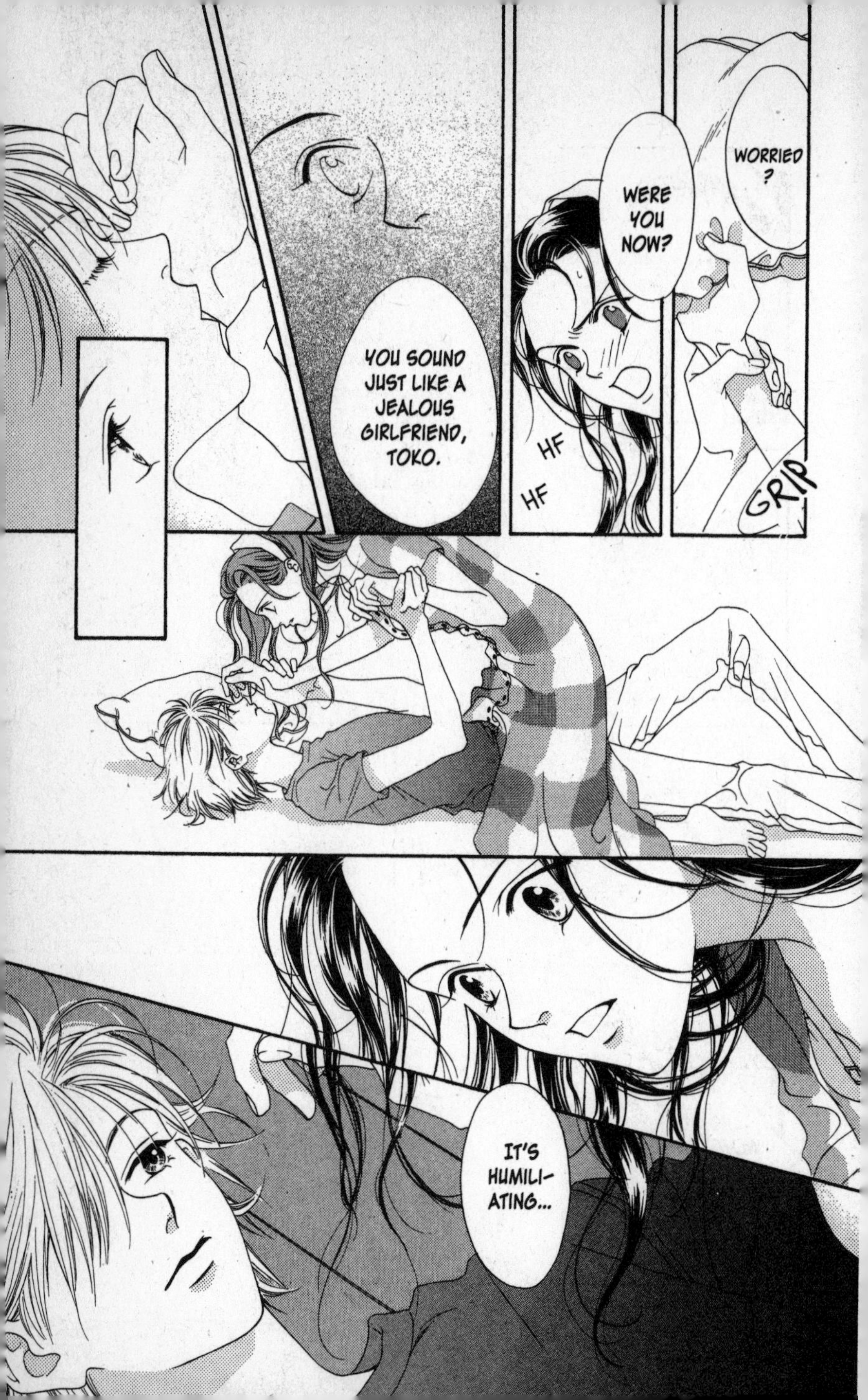
WORRIED?
GRIP
WERE YOU NOW?
HF
HF
YOU SOUND JUST LIKE A JEALOUS GIRLFRIEND, TOKO.
IT'S HUMILI-ATING...

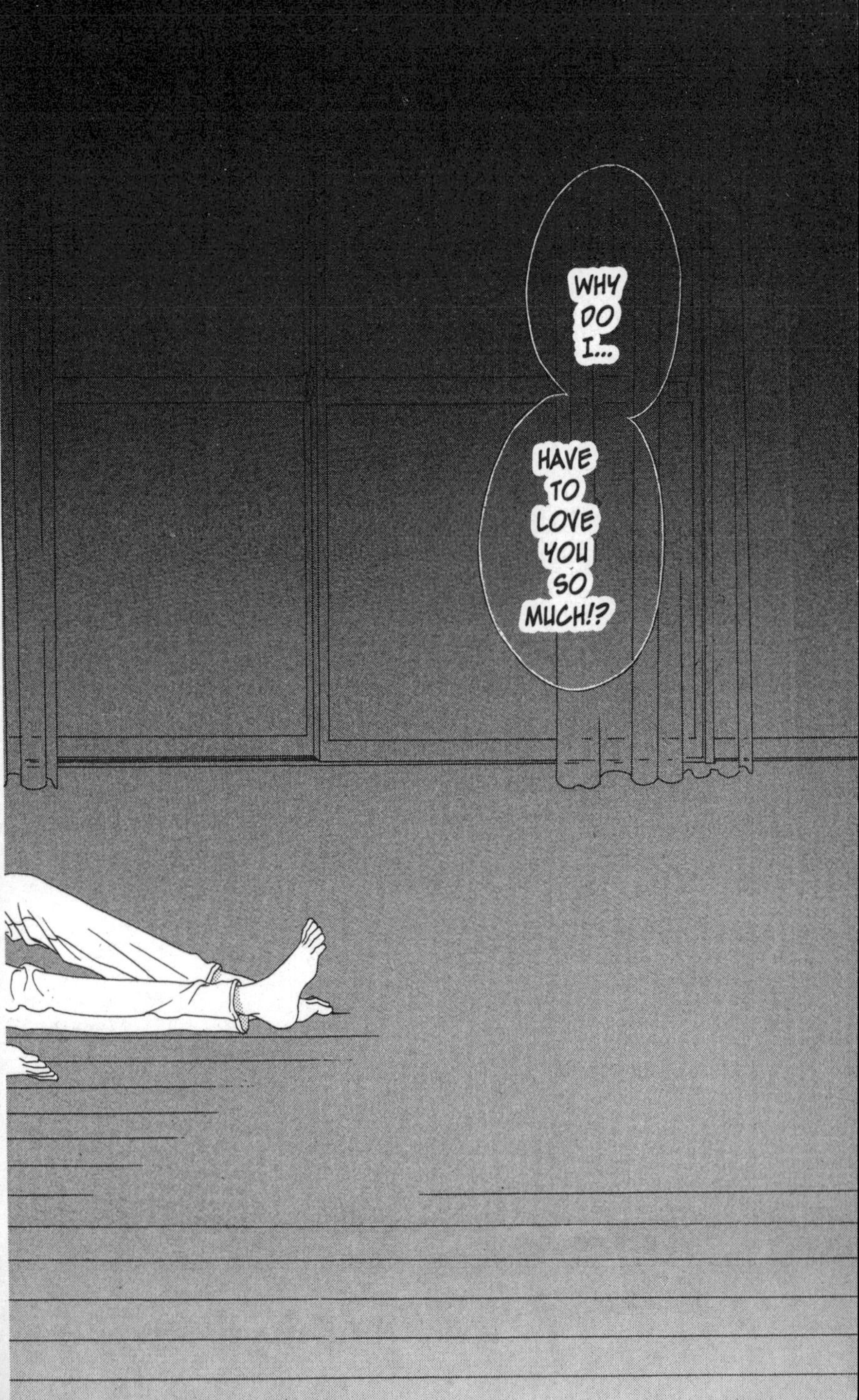
WHY DO I...
HAVE TO LOVE YOU SO MUCH!?

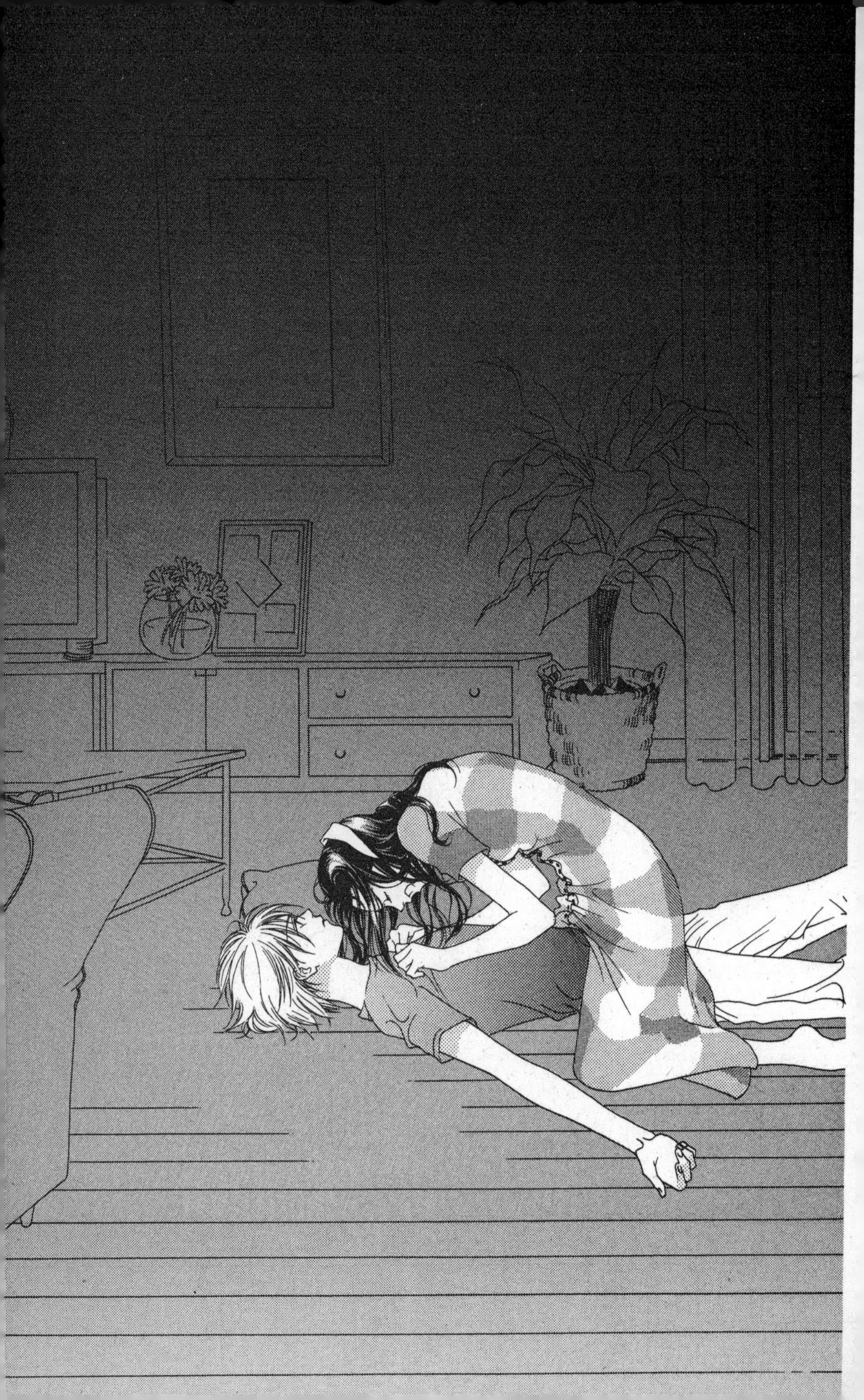

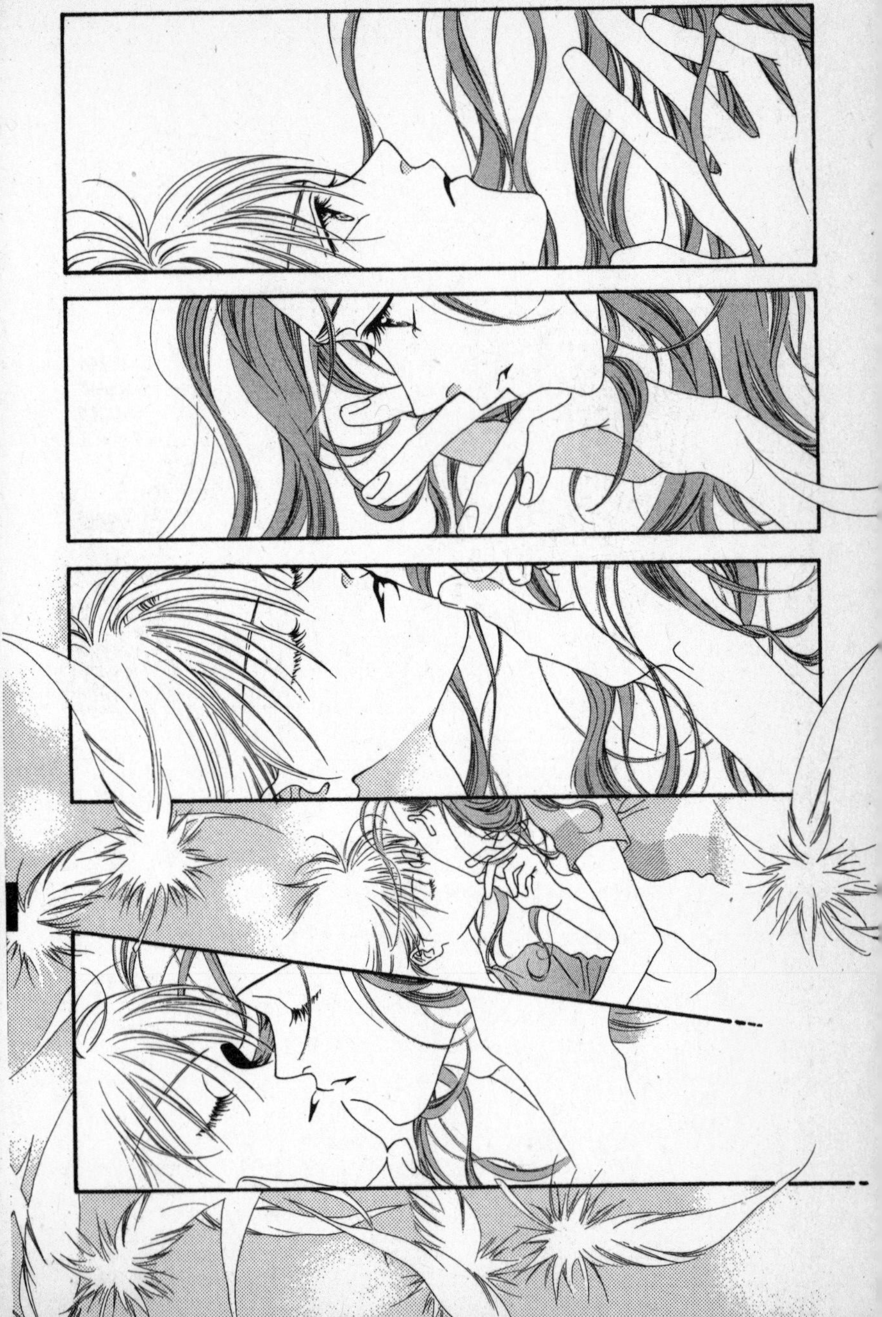

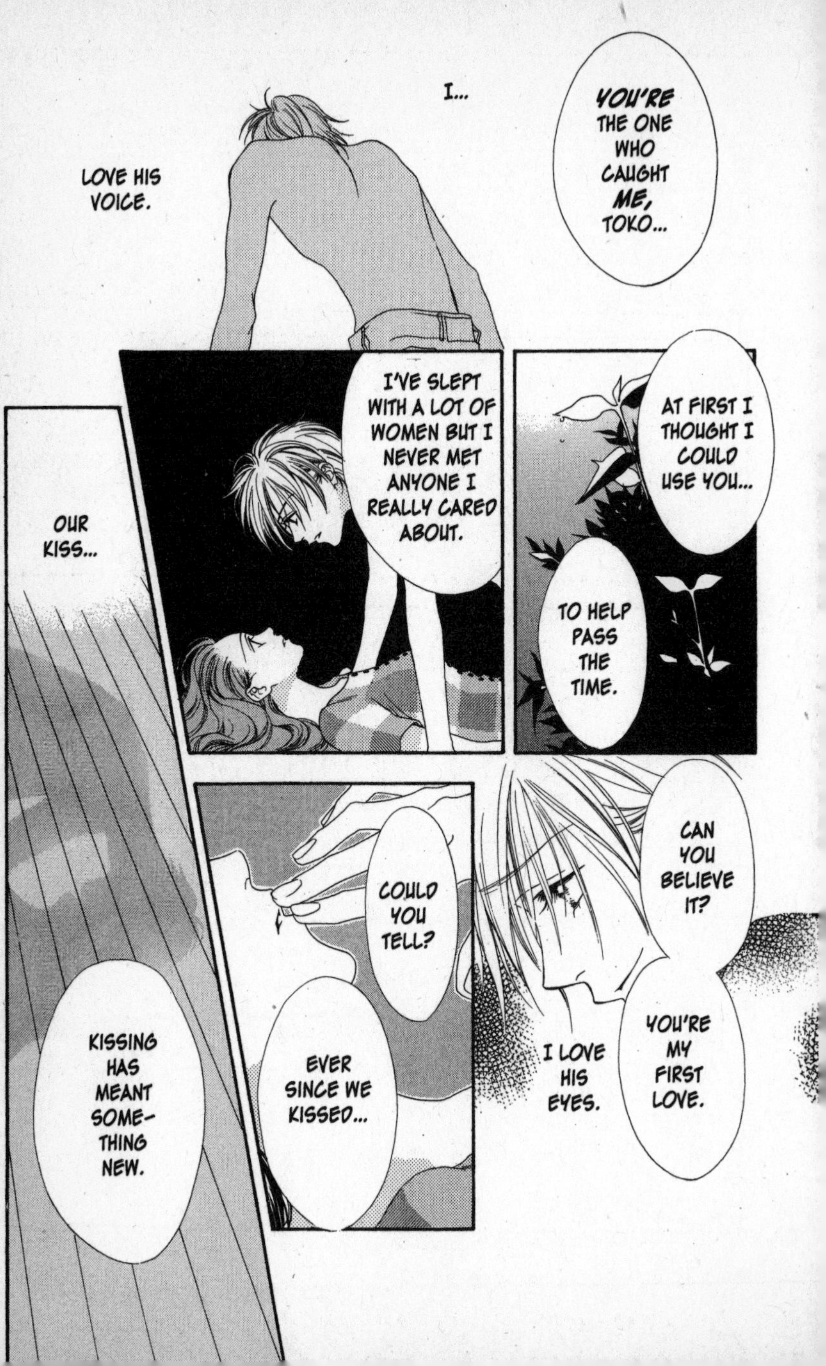
YOU'RE THE ONE WHO CAUGHT ME, TOKO...
I...
LOVE HIS VOICE.
AT FIRST I THOUGHT I COULD USE YOU...
TO HELP PASS THE TIME.
I'VE SLEPT WITH A LOT OF WOMEN BUT I NEVER MET ANYONE I REALLY CARED ABOUT.
CAN YOU BELIEVE IT?
YOU'RE MY FIRST LOVE.
I LOVE HIS EYES.
COULD YOU TELL?
EVER SINCE WE KISSED...
OUR KISS...
KISSING HAS MEANT SOME-THING NEW.

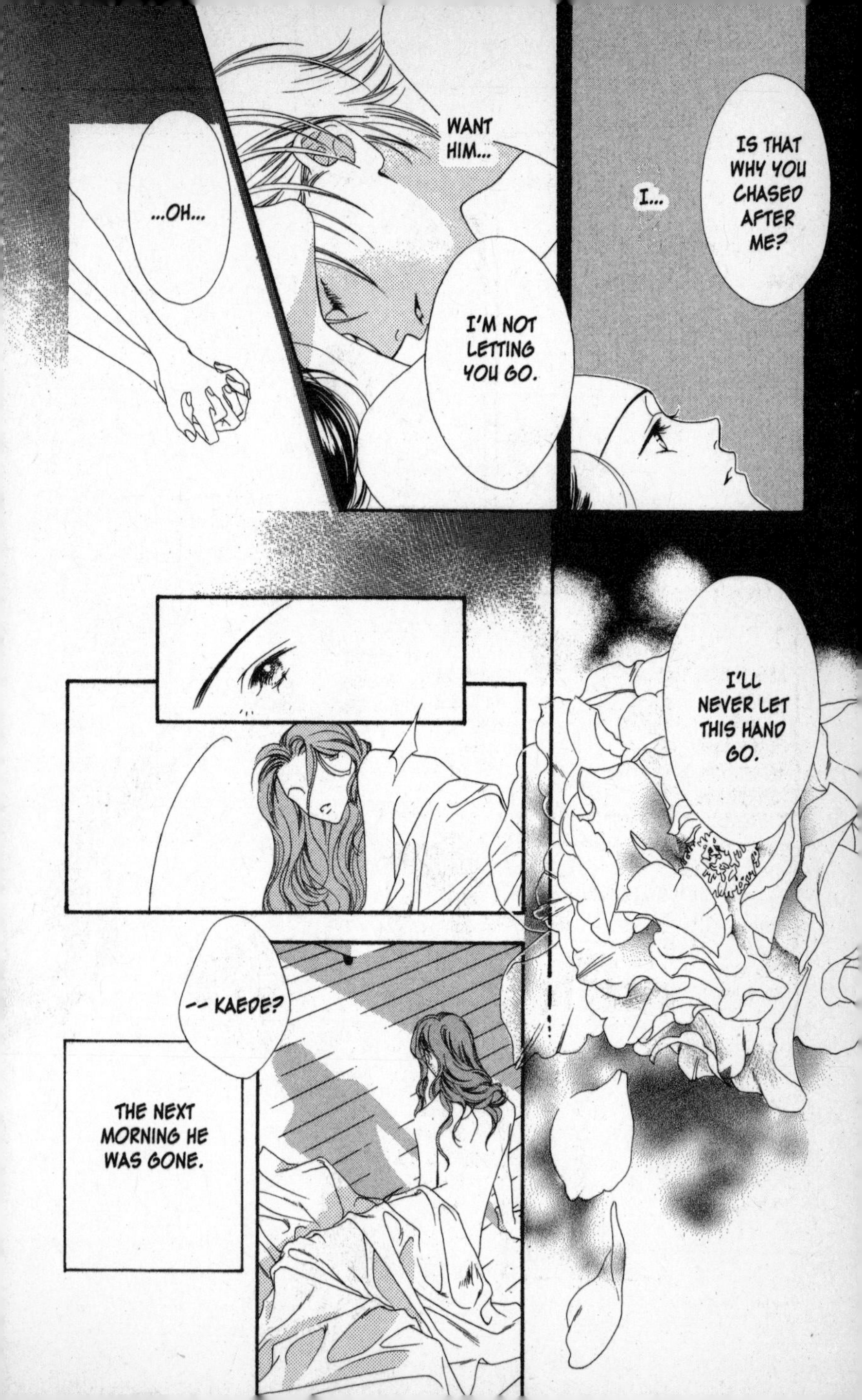
IS THAT WHY YOU CHASED AFTER ME?
I...
WANT HIM...
I'M NOT LETTING YOU GO.
...OH...
I'LL NEVER LET THIS HAND GO.
-- KAEDE?
THE NEXT MORNING HE WAS GONE.

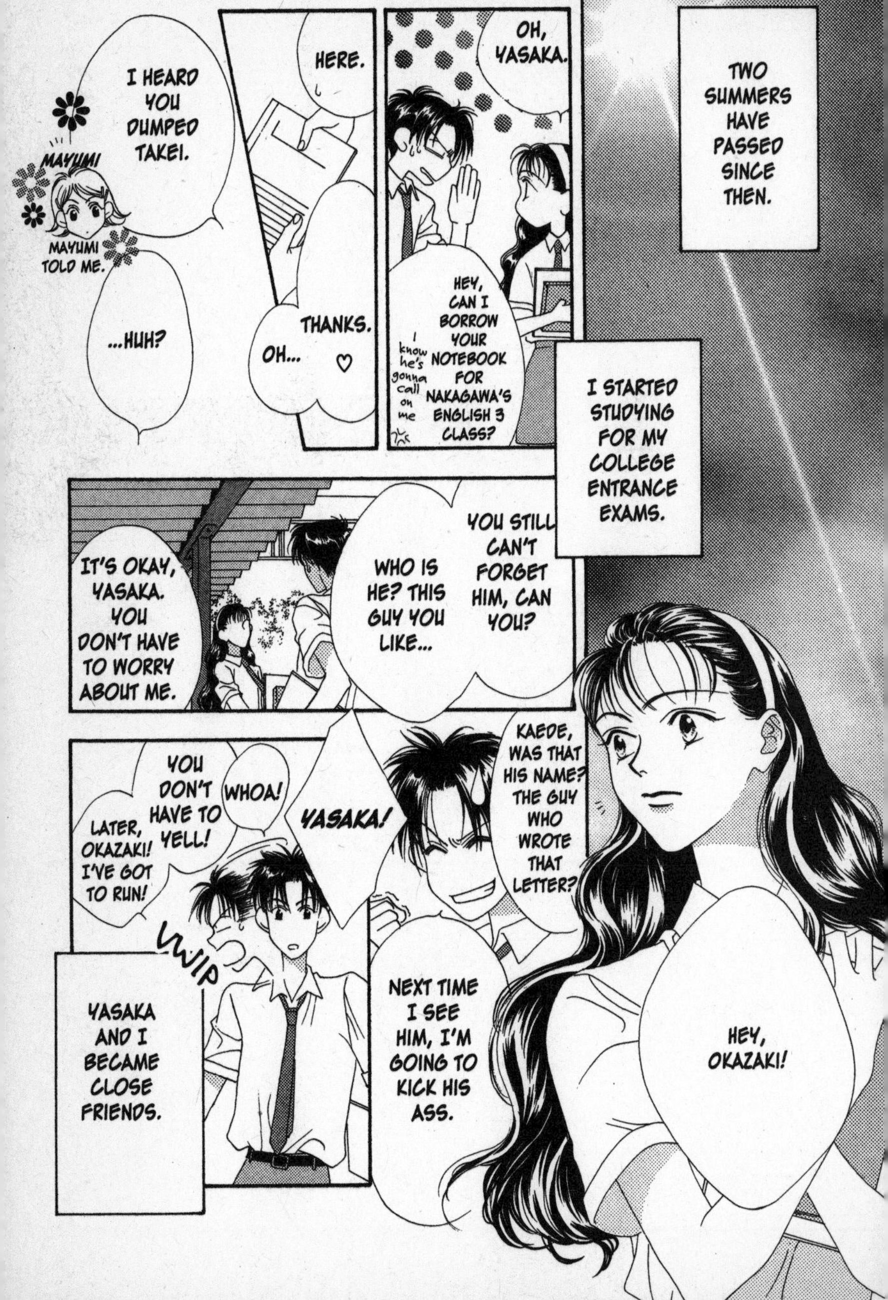
TWO SUMMERS HAVE PASSED SINCE THEN.
I STARTED STUDYING FOR MY COLLEGE ENTRANCE EXAMS.
HEY, OKAZAKI!
OH, YASAKA.
HEY, CAN I BORROW YOUR NOTEBOOK FOR NAKAGAWA'S ENGLISH 3 CLASS?
I know he's gonna call on me
HERE.
THANKS.
OH... ♡
I HEARD YOU DUMPED TAKEI.
MAYUMI
MAYUMI TOLD ME.
...HUH?
YOU STILL CAN'T FORGET HIM, CAN YOU?
WHO IS HE? THIS GUY YOU LIKE...
IT'S OKAY, YASAKA. YOU DON'T HAVE TO WORRY ABOUT ME.
KAEDE, WAS THAT HIS NAME? THE GUY WHO WROTE THAT LETTER?
NEXT TIME I SEE HIM, I'M GOING TO KICK HIS ASS.
YASAKA!
WHOA!
YOU DON'T HAVE TO YELL!
LATER, OKAZAKI! I'VE GOT TO RUN!
WWIP
YASAKA AND I BECAME CLOSE FRIENDS.

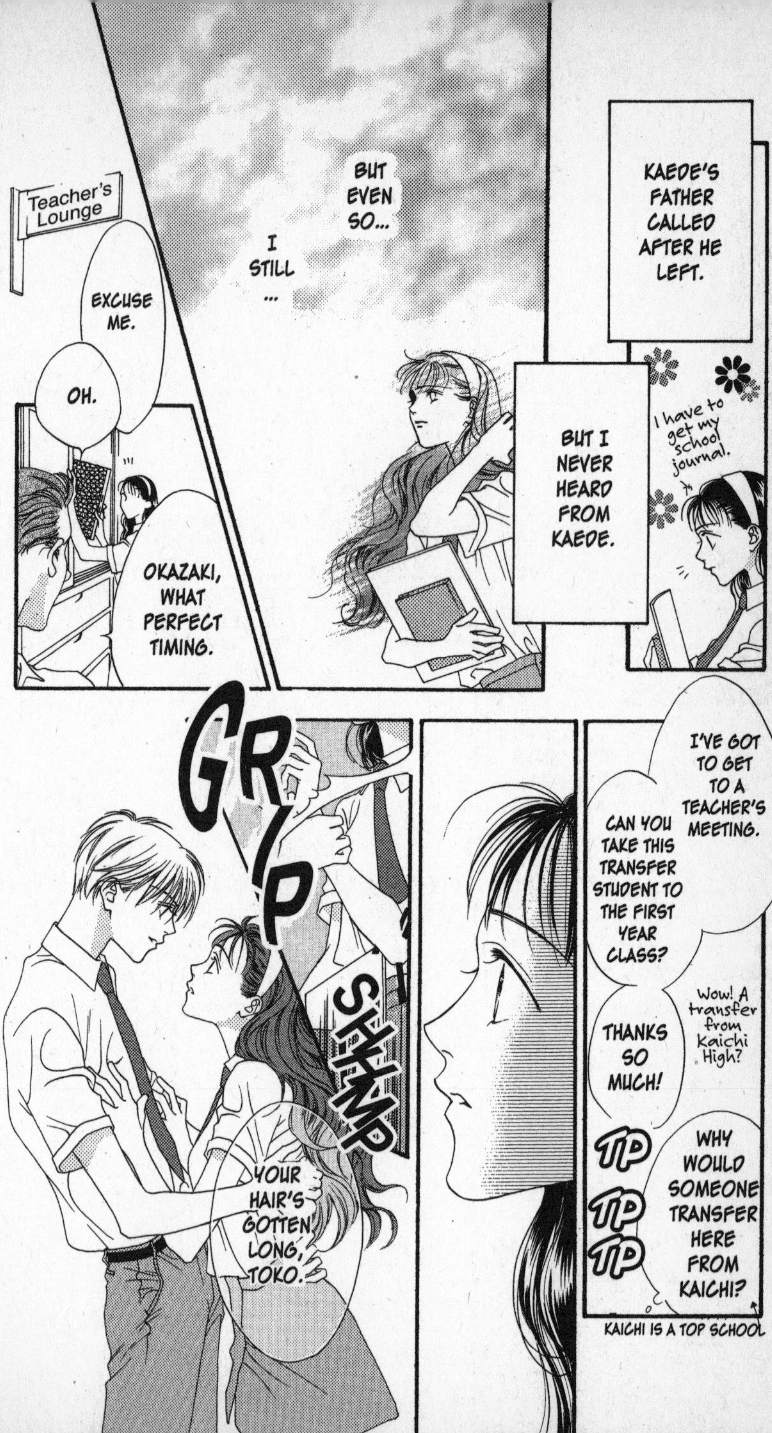
KAEDE'S FATHER CALLED AFTER HE LEFT.
I have to get my school journal.
BUT I NEVER HEARD FROM KAEDE.
BUT EVEN SO...
I STILL ...
Teacher's Lounge
EXCUSE ME.
OH.
OKAZAKI, WHAT PERFECT TIMING.
I'VE GOT TO GET TO A TEACHER'S MEETING.
CAN YOU TAKE THIS TRANSFER STUDENT TO THE FIRST YEAR CLASS?
Wow! A transfer from Kaichi High?
THANKS SO MUCH!
WHY WOULD SOMEONE TRANSFER HERE FROM KAICHI?
KAICHI IS A TOP SCHOOL
TP TP TP
GRIP
SHHMP
YOUR HAIR'S GOTTEN LONG, TOKO.

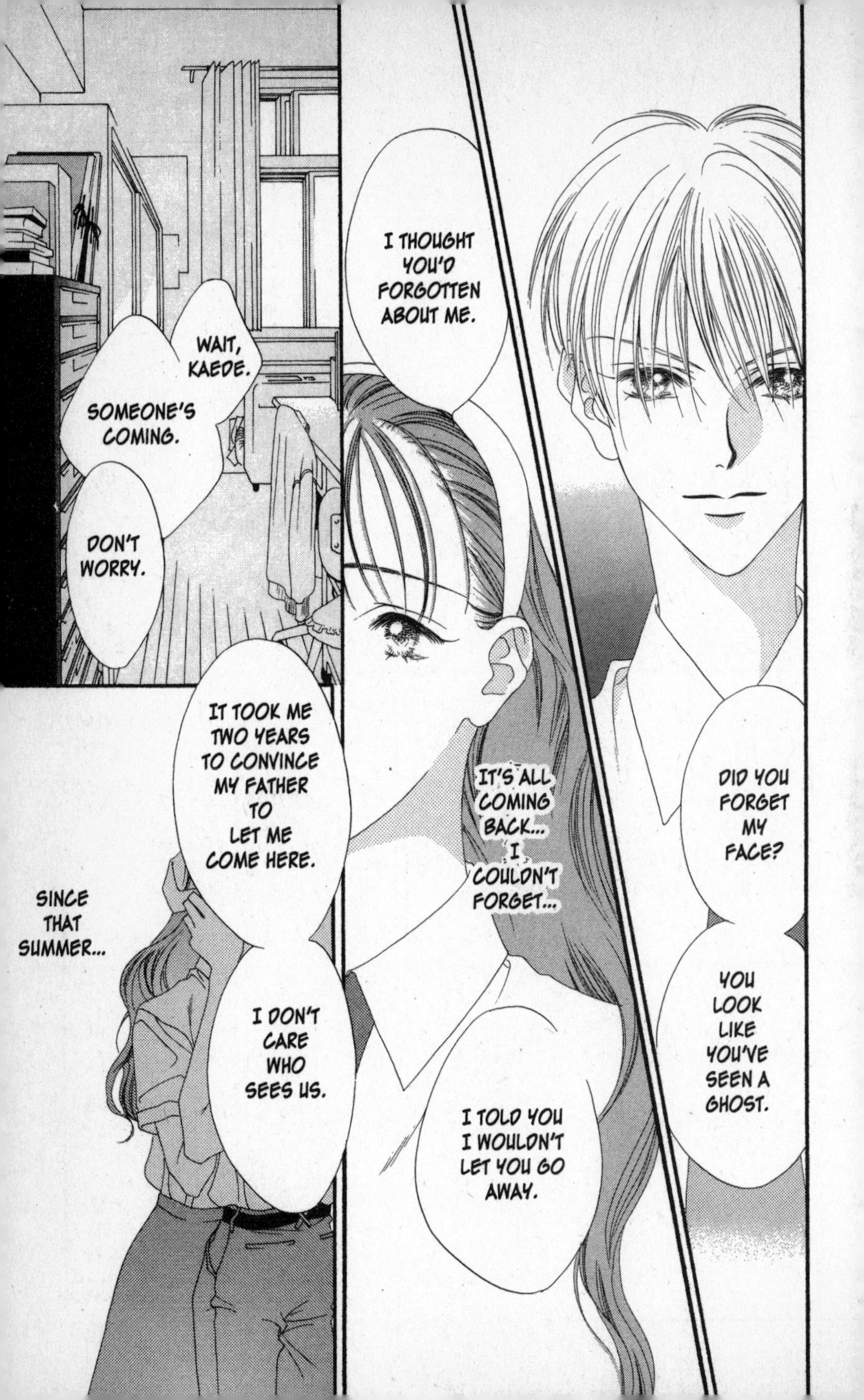
DID YOU FORGET MY FACE?
YOU LOOK LIKE YOU'VE SEEN A GHOST.
I THOUGHT YOU'D FORGOTTEN ABOUT ME.
IT'S ALL COMING BACK... I COULDN'T FORGET...
I TOLD YOU I WOULDN'T LET YOU GO AWAY.
WAIT, KAEDE.
SOMEONE'S COMING.
DON'T WORRY.
IT TOOK ME TWO YEARS TO CONVINCE MY FATHER TO LET ME COME HERE.
SINCE THAT SUMMER...
I DON'T CARE WHO SEES US.

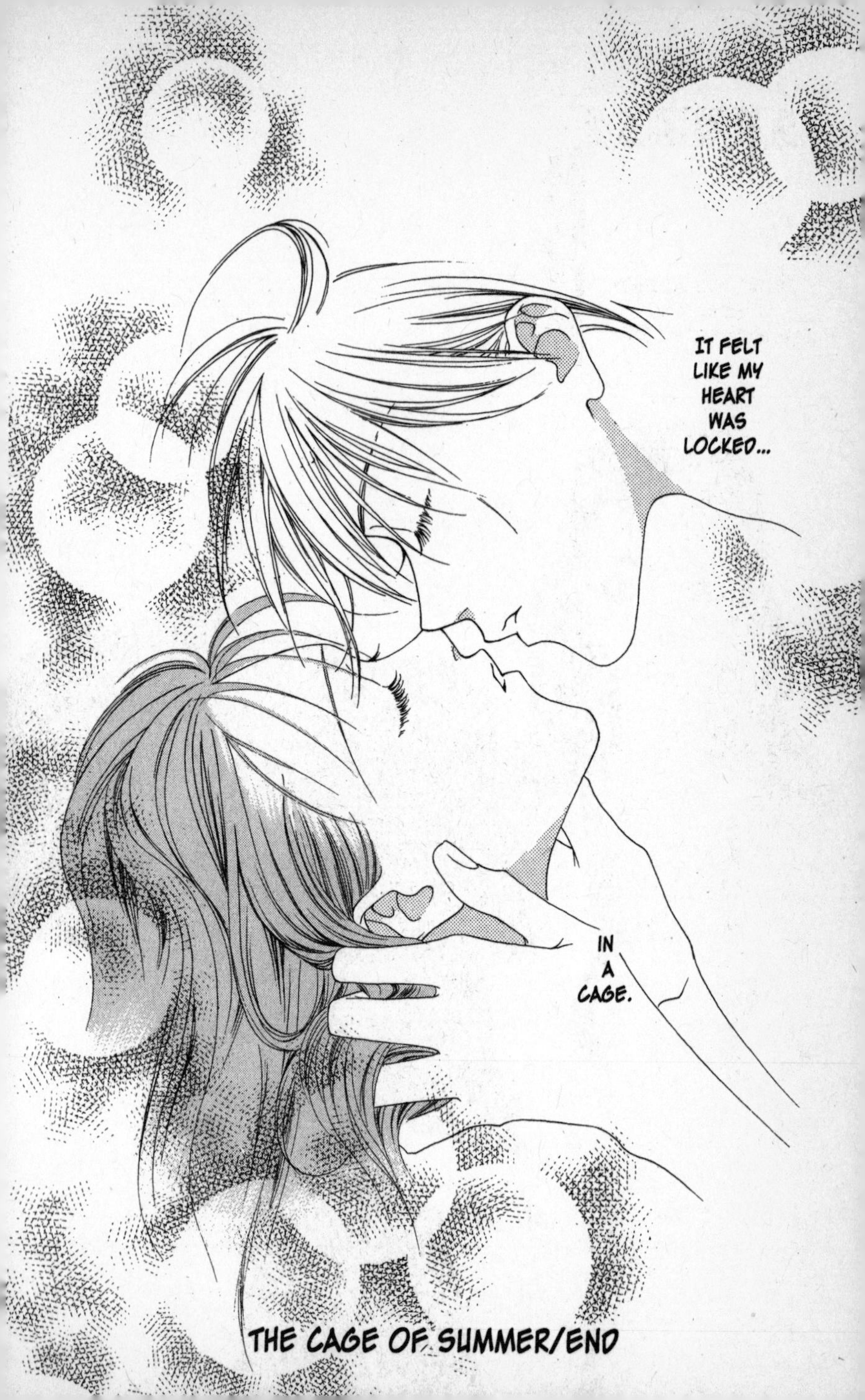
IT FELT LIKE MY HEART WAS LOCKED...
IN A CAGE.
THE CAGE OF SUMMER/END

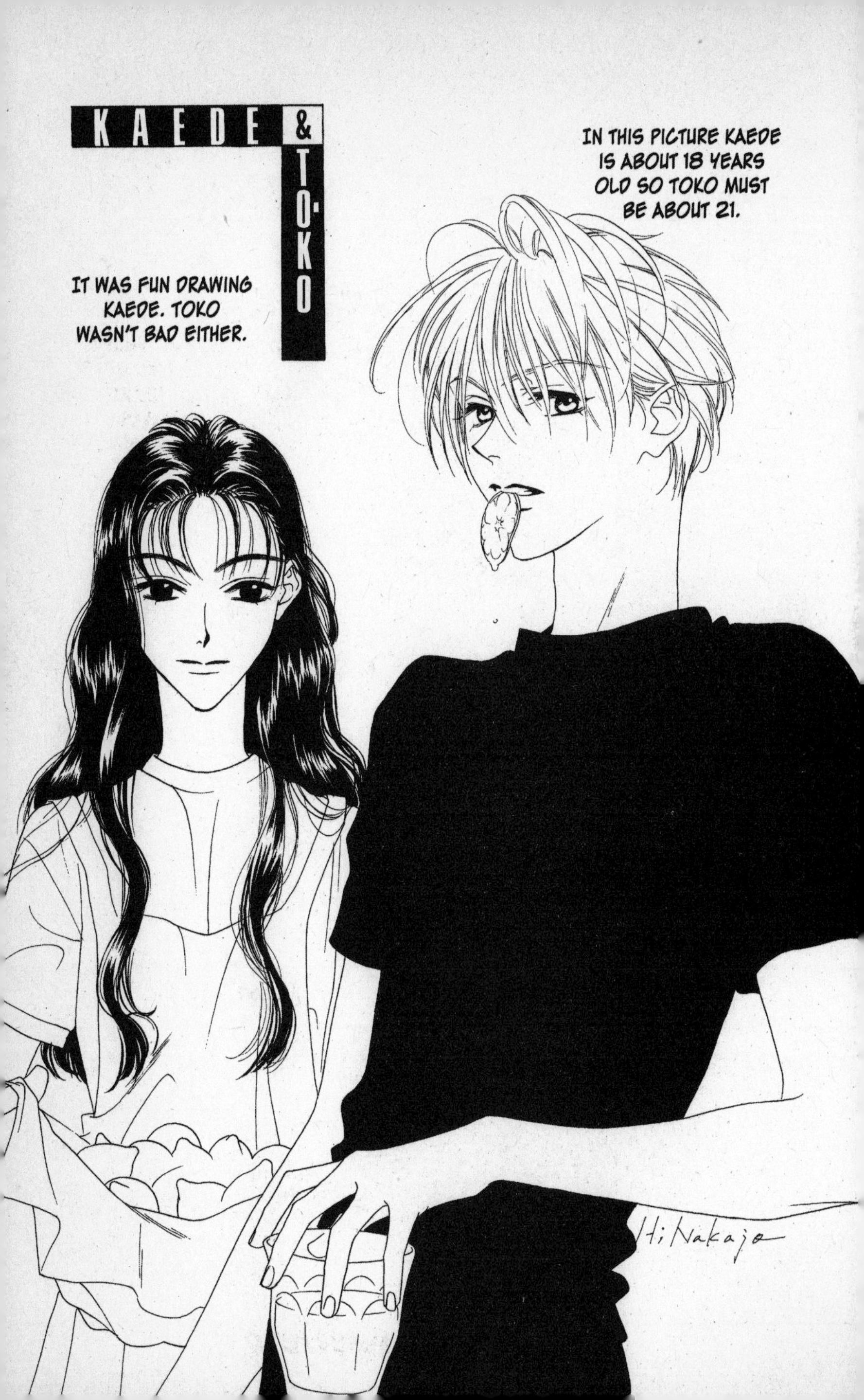
KAEDE & TOKO
IN THIS PICTURE KAEDE IS ABOUT 18 YEARS OLD SO TOKO MUST BE ABOUT 21.
IT WAS FUN DRAWING KAEDE. TOKO WASN'T BAD EITHER.
Hi Nakajo

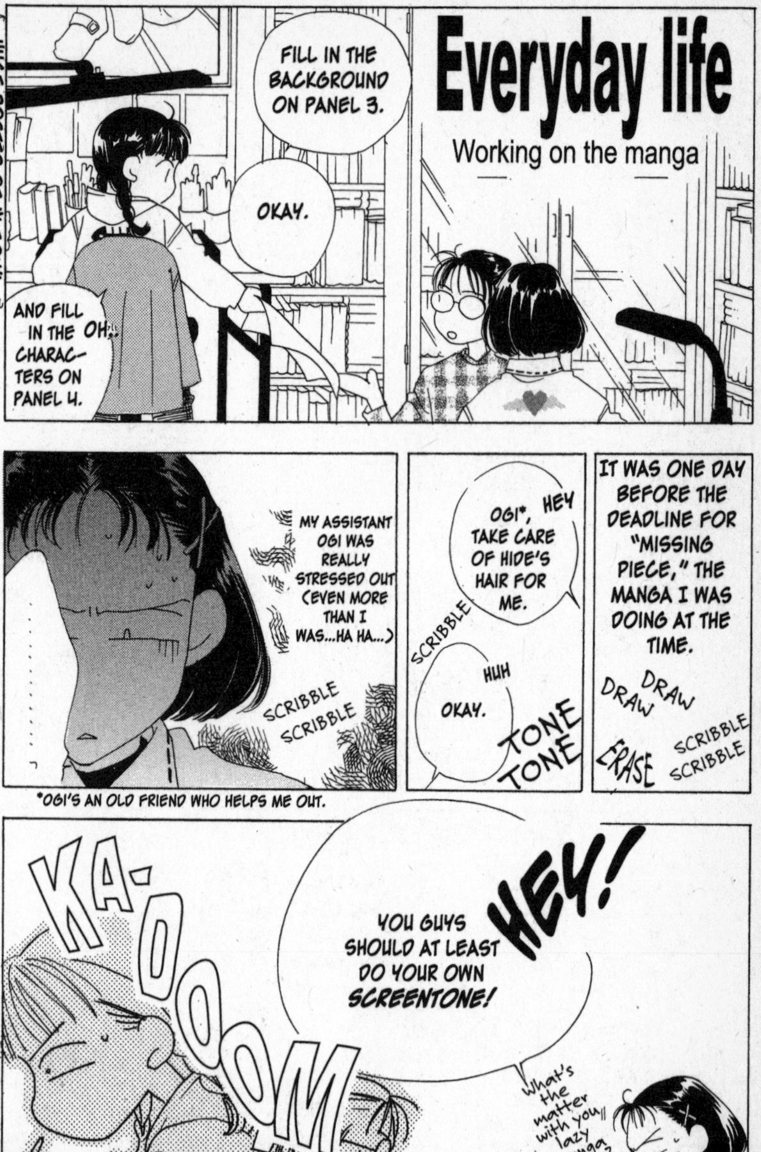
Everyday life
Working on the manga
FILL IN THE BACKGROUND ON PANEL 3.
OKAY.
AND FILL IN THE CHARACTERS ON PANEL 4.
OH...
HUGE POSTER OF "LEON"
IT WAS ONE DAY BEFORE THE DEADLINE FOR "MISSING PIECE," THE MANGA I WAS DOING AT THE TIME.
DRAW DRAW
ERASE
SCRIBBLE SCRIBBLE
OGI*, HEY TAKE CARE OF HIDE'S HAIR FOR ME.
HUH OKAY.
SCRIBBLE
TONE TONE
MY ASSISTANT OGI WAS REALLY STRESSED OUT (EVEN MORE THAN I WAS...HA HA...)
SCRIBBLE SCRIBBLE
*OGI'S AN OLD FRIEND WHO HELPS ME OUT.
HEY!
YOU GUYS SHOULD AT LEAST DO YOUR OWN SCREENTONE!
KA-DOOOM
What's the matter with you lazy manga artists?

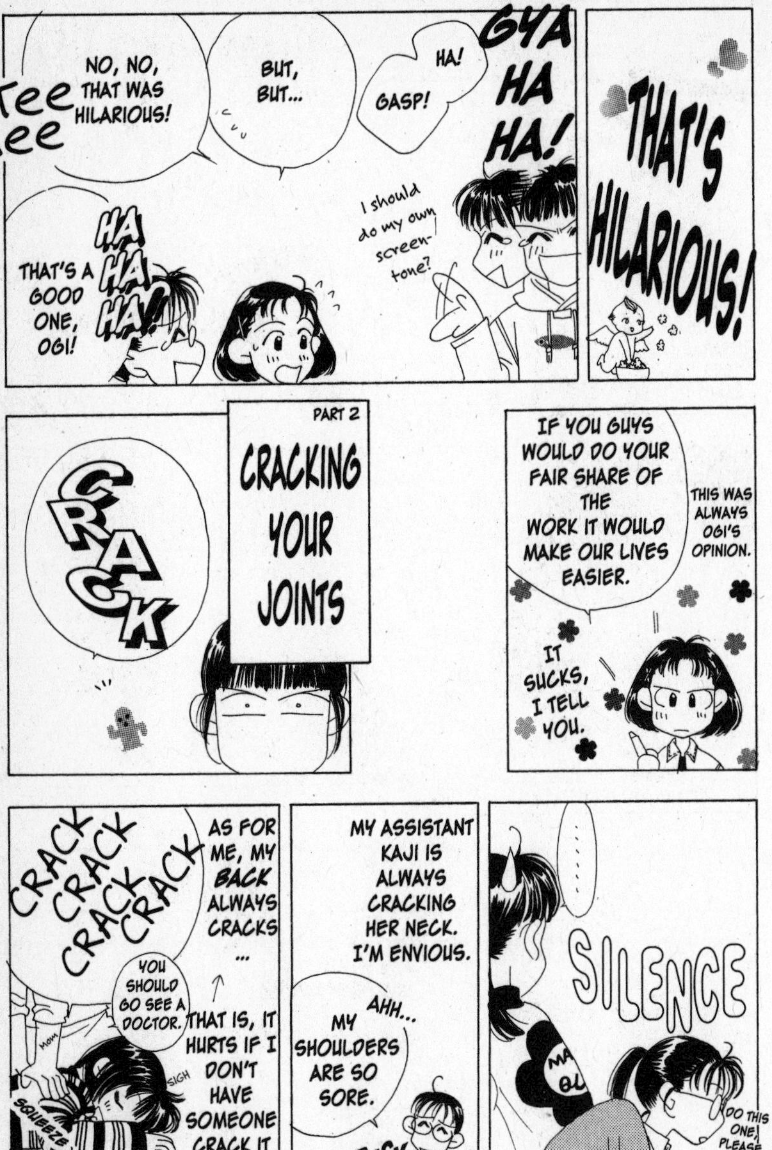
THAT'S HILARIOUS!
GYA HA HA HA!
HA! GASP!
I should do my own screen-tone?
BUT, BUT...
NO, NO, THAT WAS HILARIOUS!
Tee hee
THAT'S A GOOD ONE, OGI!
HA HA HA!
IF YOU GUYS WOULD DO YOUR FAIR SHARE OF THE WORK IT WOULD MAKE OUR LIVES EASIER.
THIS WAS ALWAYS OGI'S OPINION.
IT SUCKS, I TELL YOU.
PART 2
CRACKING YOUR JOINTS
CRACK
......
SILENCE
DO THIS ONE, PLEASE.
MY ASSISTANT KAJI IS ALWAYS CRACKING HER NECK. I'M ENVIOUS.
AHH... MY SHOULDERS ARE SO SORE.
CRACK
AS FOR ME, MY BACK ALWAYS CRACKS ...
CRACK CRACK CRACK CRACK
YOU SHOULD GO SEE A DOCTOR.
THAT IS, IT HURTS IF I DON'T HAVE SOMEONE CRACK IT FOR ME.
MOM
SIGH
SQUEEZE
END
SEE YOU NEXT TIME!

EVERYDAY LIFE/END

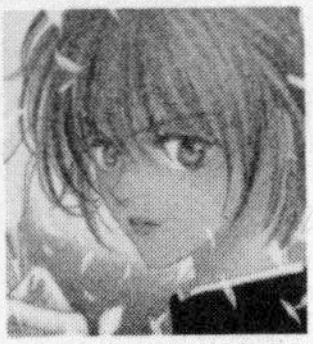

ABOUT THE AUTHOR

Hisaya Nakajo's manga series **Hanazakari no Kimitachi he** ("For You in Full Blossom", casually known as **Hana-Kimi**) has been a hit since it first appeared in 1996 in the shojo manga magazine **Hana to Yume** ("Flowers and Dreams"). In Japan, a **Hana-Kimi** art book and several "drama CDs" have been released. Her other manga series include **Missing Piece** (2 volumes) and **Yumemiru Happa** ("The Dreaming Leaf", 1 volume).

Hisaya Nakajo's website: **www.wild-vanilla.com**

EDITOR'S RECOMMENDATIONS

Editor's Note:

I normally edit shonen (boys') manga, but it's fun to edit a shôjo manga for a change. (Hopefully I can get out of the shonen manga mode...if all the characters in **Hana-Kimi** start saying things like "Now I'll show you my true power!" and "Im-impossible! His battle strength is too high!" then please send a letter to VIZ for a full refund.) In addition to being a great romantic comedy manga with lots of interesting characters, **Hana-Kimi** is a good example of one of the themes manga does best: gender-bending. In shonen manga like **Ranma 1/2** or **Cheeky Angel**, cross-dressing and sex changes are usually played for laughs, but in a shojo manga like **Hana-Kimi** (or **Fushigi Yûgi**, or **Basara**) the romantic and psychological possibilities are handled a little more seriously. Is cross-dressing easier in manga than in real life, because in manga, everyone looks pretty? Is Mizuki's attraction to Sano more on the level of "wants to be like him" admiration or "wants to get with him" love? Maybe it's better not to ask such questions directly. Maybe we won't find out 'till another volume. And there are many more volumes of **Hana-Kimi**, many more twists and turns and characters—male, female, straight, gay—to be introduced ...

If you enjoyed this volume of

Hana-Kimi

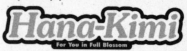

For You in Full Blossom

then here's some more manga you might be interested in.

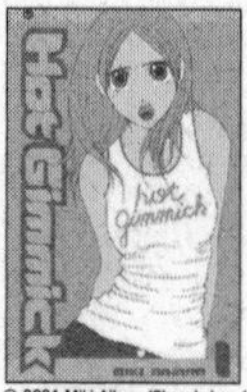

Hot Gimmick

© 2001 Miki Aihara/Shogakukan, Inc.

HOT GIMMICK

Words cannot describe this awesomely angst-filled manga by Miki Aihara! If you are, were, or ever wanted to be a sexually repressed, neurotic adolescent girl, you'll love (or hate) this series about an awkward heroine who gets involved with abusive and manipulative guys.

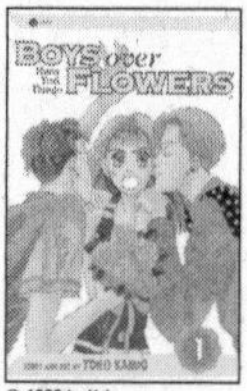

BOYS over FLOWERS

© 1992 by Yoko Kamio/SHUEISHA INC.

BOYS OVER FLOWERS

How about a slightly less demented high-school romantic dramedy? Consider checking out Yoko Kamio's **Boys over Flowers** (aka **Hana Yori Dango**), about a girl from a lower-middle-class family who goes to a school for snobby rich kids.

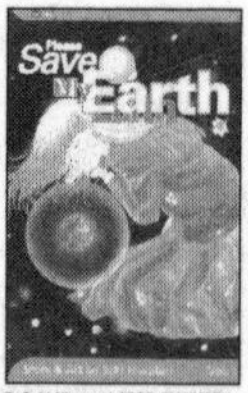

Save My Earth

© Saki Hiwatari 1986/HAKUSENSHA, INC

PLEASE SAVE MY EARTH

On first glance, Saki Hiwatari's classic 1980s reincarnation-and-psychic-powers manga would seem to have little in common with **Hana-Kimi**. But in fact, they were both printed in **Hana to Yume** ("Flowers and Dreams") magazine! If you'd prefer something more Goth-y with a more modern art style, there's also Kaori Yuki's **Angel Sanctuary**, a reincarnation-and-devils-and-angels manga.